VISUAL MERCHANDISING AND DISPLAY

VISUAL MERCH
and DISPLAY

aNDISING

FiFTH EDiTiON

Martin M. Pegler
Educator and Design Consultant

FAIRCHILD PUBLICATIONS, INC.
NEW YORK

Executive Editor: Olga T. Kontzias
Senior Development Editor: Jennifer Crane
Art Director: Adam B. Bohannon
Production Manager: Ginger Hillman
Production Editor: Elizabeth Marotta
Copy Editor: Chernow Editorial Services, Inc.
Cover and Interior Design: Adam B. Bohannon

Fifth Edition, Copyright © 2006
Fairchild Publications, Inc.

Fourth Edition, Copyright © 1998
Fairchild Publications, Inc.

Third Edition, Copyright © 1995
Fairchild Publications, Inc.

Second Edition, Copyright © 1991
Fairchild Publications, Inc.

First Edition, Copyright © 1983
Fairchild Publications, Inc.

Library of Congress Catalog Card Number: 2006921192

ISBN-13: 978-156367-445-7

ISBN-10: 1-56367-445-9

GST R 133004424

Printed in China

CH01, TP11

CONTENTS

PREFACE

Retailing has moved out of the fashion supplements and the advertising layouts of our newspapers onto the front pages and financial pages—and mostly the news is not good! We read of mergers and department store closings—of famous fashion stores with illustrious names being bought out, reduced in size, or reorganized out of existence. These sorry stories do not mean that retailing is dead; they just mean that the field is getting tougher and more competitive. The market isn't getting larger; it's getting smarter, more sophisticated, more aware of what's new, what's desirable, and what things should cost.

Old loyalties to stores and shops are almost nonexistent because customers can no longer be depended upon. They want to be wooed, courted, stroked, and serviced; they want to be entertained and each sale is a first sale. If ever something was needed to distinguish one store from another, to make one specialty shop seem more special, more unique, more tuned in to what the market wants— that "something" is needed *now*. That "something" is ef-fective *Visual Merchandising and Display*. Visual merchandising is the presentation of merchandise at its best; color coordinated, accessorized, and self-explanatory. Display is the pizzazz—the theater, the sparkle and shine that surrounds a presentation of merchandise and makes the shopper stop, look, and buy what has been assembled with care and offered with flair.

During a recession, depression, or in a financial crunch, store owners may take money out of the display budget and put more money into media advertising. However, television, radio, and print ads are worthless unless there is some follow-through at the store. Here at the point of purchase is where display or merchandise presentation becomes absolutely necessary. With changes in retail shopping patterns, such as the growth of malls and giant shopping centers, and the subsequent decline of much of "Main Street" and "in-town" shopping, the display windows that face out to the street are stepping back in favor of display on the selling floor.

ACKNOWLEDGMENTS

In this display world of tinsel, glitter, sparkle, and larger-than-life presentations, I wish to thank all those visual merchandisers, display persons, merchandise presenters, store planners, and display manufacturers and suppliers whose work and imagination made such a deep impression. My thanks to all the above for making the merchandise scene more exciting and fun, and for putting more entertainment into this "show-ing business."

Credits

I would like to acknowledge only a few of the myriad talents whose work I have used to illustrate the text in this edition. I cannot name them all but here are some: Karina Barhumi, Anthony Battaglia, Tom Beebe, Christine Belleck, Lucy Ann Bouman, Stefano Corradi, Mary Costantini, Simon Doonan, Linda Fargo, Timothy Fortuna, Diana Gatterdam, Kelly Gray, David Griffin, James Griffin, Mark Hoch, David Hoey, Jack Hruska, Sam C. Joseph, James Knight, Anne Kong, John Krenek, Kristin Lauer, Sal Lenso, Charles Luckenbill, Keith Madieros, Robert Mahoney, Marc Manigault, Amy Meadows, Paul Muller, Barbara Putnam, Manoel Renha, Robert Rufino, Danuta Tyder, Michael A. Salinas, Todd Schearer, Ken Smart, Michael Steward, Jan Topercer, Gilbert Vanderweide, Eric Werner, and Tim Wisegerhof.

There are many others whose work is shown here but then the list would be endless.

If some of you think the dresses look a bit outdated or "old-fashioned"—if you wait a few seasons they will be back as "retro." The real reason is that I have selected "classics" and "golden oldies" where necessary to make my point. They are still—as concepts, ideas or treatments—as fresh and as vital as they were when they first appeared. I do not apologize for using these "old-timers"—I am only offering an explanation.

A very special thanks to Laurence Fuersich and John Burr of *Retail Reporting* and *Views and Reviews* for the many photographs they allowed us to reproduce in this book, and to the photographers who braved the New York nights to get many of the photos.

My love to those people who are real and make my life real and fulfilled . . . to Suzan, my wife . . . to my children: Karen and Jess, Lysa and Joh, and Risa and Adam . . . and to the next generation: Brian, Amanda, Jake, Sam, Ben, Marley, and Valeria.

Martin M. Pegler

VISUAL MERCHANDISING AND DISPLAY

PART ONE

GETTING STARTED—VISUAL MERCHANDISING AND DISPLAY BASICS

VISUAL MERCHANDISING is no longer just a matter of making merchandise look attractive for the customer. It is the actual selling of merchandise through a visual medium. Visual merchandising is a way for stores to say, "This is who we are and what we stand for." An understanding of basic visual merchandising concepts and theory is essential to the effective presentation of a store and its merchandise to the customer. Part One of this text is devoted to those merchandising "basics."

Chapter 1 introduces visual merchandising and display and, for the first of many times throughout the text, discusses the important concept of store image. The use of color and texture to add excitement to visual presentations is explored in Chapter 2.

Both inside and outside the store, proper lighting is vital to selling. Light directs customers' eyes to the merchandise and invites them to buy. Chapter 3 discusses the various types of light sources available and how they are used in store merchandising and display. Artistic principles such as line, balance, contrast, and rhythm are applied to visual merchandising and display in Chapter 4.

From a one-item display to a variety or assortment display, Chapter 5 covers the gamut of possible display types and settings.

CHAPTER ONE

Why Do We Display?

AFTER YOU HAVE READ THIS CHAPTER,
YOU WILL BE ABLE TO DISCUSS:

- The definition of visual merchandising.
- The concept of store image and its relationship to visual
  merchandising and display.
- The purposes of visual merchandising.

WHY DO WE DISPLAY?: TRADE TALK

   store image
   visual merchandising

We show in order to sell. Display or **visual merchandising** is "showing" merchandise and concepts at their very best, with the end purpose of making a sale. We may not actually sell the object displayed or the idea promoted, but we do attempt to convince the viewer of the value of the object, the store promoting the object, or the organization behind the concept. Though a cash register may not ring because of a particular display, that display should make an impression on the viewer that will affect future sales.

The display person used to be the purveyor of dreams and fantasies, presenting merchandise in settings that stirred the imagination and promoted fantastic flights to unattainable heights. Today's display person, however, sells a "reality." Today's shopper can be whatever he or she wants to be by simply wearing garments with certain labels having a built-in status. The display person dresses a mannequin (possessing a perfect figure) in skin-fitting jeans, flashes the lights, adds the adoring males or females, and reinforces the image of sexuality and devastating attractiveness that is part of the prominent name on the label. Wearing Brand-X jeans, whether size 8 or 18, makes the wearer feel special. She imagines herself to be that slim, sensuous femme fatale she has seen on television, surrounded by gaping admirers. She feels as special when she is wearing her television-advertised slim-fitting jeans.

Today's mannequin often resembles the shopper on the other side of the glass; it may have a flawless figure, but far from perfect features. This prompts the customer to think, "If that mannequin can look so great, why not me?" That's reality! That's selling! The visual merchandiser, therefore, presents more than the merchandise. He or she presents the image of who or what the shopper can be when using the merchandise displayed.

It has been said by presidents and vice-presidents of large retail operations; it has been uttered by experienced shoppers and consumers: "There is very little difference between the merchandise sold in one store and that sold in another." Many department and specialty stores carry the same name brands—the same nationally advertised lines seen on television and in *Vogue* maga-zine. Often the real difference is in the price of the merchandise being offered for sale.

Why, then, does an individual shop in Store A and pay more for the same item selling for less in Store B? Why does a shopper tote the shopping bag from Store C rather than an equally attractive bag from Store D? Why do shoppers cover themselves with garments branded with a store's name on pockets, patches, shoulders, and hips? It has to do with the **store's image!** If everyone believes that people who shop in Store A are young, smart, sophisticated, amusing, clever, trendy, and fun to be with, then a shopper who buys clothes at that store can also be young, smart, sophisticated, and so on. The display per-

Figure 1.1 Displays should entertain as well as attract attention. They should bring shoppers closer to the window so that they can really see the merchandise. Humor, surprise and the unexpected all work to get the shopper's attention. *H-Bendel, Fifth Avenue, New York.*

son reinforces that belief with merchandise displays, the types of mannequins shown, and the manner in which the mannequins are dressed, positioned, and lit. In this way, the display person promotes the store's image and fashion trendiness. Often the visual merchandiser is not selling any one piece of merchandise, but rather the idea that any purchase from that store will guarantee social success and the stamp of the "right" taste level. However, visual merchandising is still *selling*. We shall return often in later chapters to the concept of image and image projection in merchandise presentation.

In addition to selling actual merchandise, displays can be used to introduce a new product, a fashion trend, and a new "look" or idea. The display may be the first three-dimensional representation of something the consumer has thus far only seen in sketches or photos. Displays can be used to educate the consumer concerning what the new item is, how it can be worn or used, and how it can be accessorized. Displays may also supply pertinent information, the price, and other special features.

The visual merchandiser may create a display that stimulates, tantalizes, or arouses the shopper's curiosity to such a degree that he or she is "challenged" to enter the store and wander through it, even though the shopper is not motivated by the displayed product itself. This is still a victory. It gives the display person and the merchant many more opportunities to sell that shopper once he or she is inside the store. To make a shopper a *stopper* and a "walk-in" rather than a "walk-by" is a commercial achievement. And always, as mentioned earlier,

the purpose of visual merchandising is to promote the store image; to let people know what the store is, where it stands on fashion trends, what one can expect inside the store, to whom it appeals, its price range, and the caliber of its merchandise and merchandising.

The visual merchandiser always puts the store's best "face" forward. His or her duty is to bring shoppers into the store, while at the same time ensuring that the interior presentation is in keeping with what has been promised on the outside.

It is important to remember that visual merchandising and display has always been a "hands on" career. Where some jobs may be desk- or table-bound, visual merchandising and display has always been out on the floor, in the window, up a ladder, or down in the shop getting ready for the aforementioned activities. It has always been creative, interactive and involved the person's hands, body and brains to create something special or memorable. What did the display persons of decades ago do before staple guns, Velcro, and Elmer's Glue? Pins, tacks, tape, and small nails worked—maybe not as well—but the display person managed. Well, we have had lots of advances made in the tools we use today.

We are totally and completely immersed in the computer age and digitalization of every form today. To hear some display persons speak, there was no visual merchandising/display before the computer. They wonder how the "old-timers" ever managed before all the wonderful new programs became available that they now use to "draw," "conceptualize," make schematics, floor plans, and three-dimensional visualizations of a space. They managed! Of course, once one masters the computer and the available programs, things are much simpler and the opportunities and results that can be wrought are much more spectacular. Now it is possible to plan a window, "draw" that window and even create the graphics that will fill the back wall of the window with the use of the computer and special programs, attachments, accessories, and such that have become vital tools for visual merchandisers, display persons, and store planners. But, they are still "tools"! They are the "means" and not the "end." It must still all begin with the human mind—the brain—with the creative talent of the individual who can now, working with these great innovations, bring even more exciting and novel effects into the displays in the windows and on the sales floor.

For one thing, and it is a very important thing, access to the Internet means that designers now can surf the

Figure 1.2 Bright lights and strong colors in a display, and something as ordinary as paper lanterns—made extraordinary—will combine to impress shoppers as well as set the look for the garments on display. *Bloomingdales, Lexington Avenue, New York.*

world wide web for ideas, inspirations, and information. Going "retro"? Check under "retro" and actually "see" what "retro" is all about. The Internet has "answers," but the designer must know the right questions to ask and then have the creative spark to take that "answer" and turn it into the basis for a brand image-making display. The computer and the Internet cannot do that for you. They can provide a starting point and provide the basic information but it is always the human element—the display person—that must finish it off.

Aside from the creative end of the display person's job, computers and the Internet serve as a means of communication between the people in the store, display persons and vendors, designers in San Francisco with display installers in New York City, New Orleans, Dallas, and places in between. It can serve up directives, help display persons to "see" the new merchandise before they actually arrive, and coordinate store promotions by accessing all the concerned areas in the store. E-mail has replaced phone messaging and faxing. In the display department, or for the freelancer, the computer can keep records, handle budgets, keep one aware of expenditures, inventory, stock, etc. With computer programs, sign-making and graphics have been revolutionized. Whether it is for directional signage, point of sale information, posters and promotional materials, or banners and headers—there are graphics programs that can handle all of that. It is now possible—with digitalized printing and the new printing machines that have evolved—to create graphic panels that can fill a background, or to make a printed design on vinyl or paper that can be applied to glass, the walls, or even the floors. Custom decoratives and props can also be produced.

Some of the programs that are now available to the display person and store planner include Adobe Photoshop, Adobe Illustrator, Quark Xpress, InDesign (which is rapidly replacing Illustrator), 3D Studio Max, and Vectorworks for rendering and model-making. However, new programs are being introduced all the time that either replace or make existing programs obsolete or inadequate by the day's standards.

In this book much of what is written is still about the "old-fashioned "way, which is still the essential way: it is about thinking, planning, or creating new concepts or revitalizing existing ones. It is about the "human element" in visual merchandising and display. The execution of an idea, in many cases, can be effectively materialized with the use of computers, computer programs, and the vast improvements and availability of digital camera software. So, in the text, we may refer to a hand-operated tool or some electrified gizmo as the means for accomplishing a task, but if the display person is comfortable with the new technologies—by all means let that be the method used to obtain the desired end result. We hope readers will realize that none of these modern electronic wonders takes the place of the human mind, the thinking process, the internal search, and the hand drawn scribbles, squiggles, and doodles that will eventually morph into ideas that can be realized with an assist from the computer.

Why Do We Display?: A Recap

- Sell by showing and promoting.
- Encourage the shopper to enter the store.
- Get the customer to pause and "shop" the selling floor.
- Establish, promote, and enhance the store's visual image.
- Entertain customers and enhance their shopping experience.
- Introduce and explain new products.
- Educate customers by answering questions on the use and accessorizing of a product or fashion trend.

Questions for Review and Discussion

1. Describe the role of visual merchandising in retailing today.

2. Compare and contrast the store images of Kmart and J. C. Penney. How does each store promote the individual image through visual merchandising and display? Relate specific examples.

3. List five purposes of visual merchandising and describe a display that would fulfill each of these purposes.

CHAPTER TWO

Color and Texture

AFTER YOU HAVE READ THIS CHAPTER,
YOU WILL BE ABLE TO DISCUSS:

- The relationship between color and visual merchandising and display.
- The common associations with, and reactions to, various colors.
- Colors in the warm and cool families.
- The concepts of color mixing and of value as it relates to color.
- Primary, secondary, intermediate, and tertiary colors.
- The differences between a tint and a shade.
- The relationship of colors to each other on the color wheel.
- How neutral colors are best used in store design.
- The relationship between texture and color.

COLOR AND TEXTURE: TRADE TALK

analogous color scheme	neutral colors
color	pastels
color psychology	primary colors
color wheel	secondary colors
complementary colors	shade
contrast	tertiary colors
cool colors	texture
intensity	tint
intermediate colors	value
monochromatic colors	warm colors

Color is the biggest motivation for shopping. People buy **color** before they buy size, fit, or price. People also react to the colors around the garment being considered. Some stores, like Gap, will introduce a whole new palette each season. Though the styling may be similar or the same, it is the new color presentation that brings the shoppers into the carefully color-schemed and color-coordinated sales floor. Malls, shopping centers, big box stores, and small specialty stores are all reconsidering the colors they use to attract shoppers and the colors used to keep shoppers in the store once they have been lured inside. The color of a store's signage sometimes says more than the words on the sign: Is it subtle? Is it sophisticated? Is it daring or demanding? Intrusive? Inviting? Ingratiating?

Color says something about the kind of store, the kind of merchandise, and the kind of market the retailer hopes to appeal to. Taste and colors, like everything else in fashion, change and though some basic conclusions can be drawn about color and how people respond to the various hues, tints, and shades, there is still the "in-fashion" or "trend" that determines when a color is "in" and when it is "out."

The Color Marketing Group (CMG) consists of color specialists from most industries for which color is a major factor in what is manufactured. The Group serves as a guide, forecasts direction, and indicates color trends well enough in advance so that the information can be integrated into design and production schedules. Their most recent forecast is that America's color taste is softening up and also warming up and that we are returning

Figure 2.1 Color attracts! Panels of bright color, fashion croquis sketches, and lights of assorted colors create a brilliant, high-fashion setting for the red and green evening gowns. This is all about color. *Barneys, Madison Avenue, New York.*

to the "earth" tones. According to James Martin, an architectural color consultant with The Color People of Denver, Colorado, "People have been stressed out, assaulted by the media and hyped out to the point of exhaustion. They are looking for some shelter from all this. They are returning to classic values, classic homes, and classic clothes. We want comfort, timeless value, and solidity. In addition, people's concern for the environment is affecting what they like in color." Earth tones are now being referred to as "environmental colors." According to Mr. Martin, "the hard edge that emerged in the 1980s has been muted and softened. Sharp, hip and cool has been replaced by convivial, value-oriented, and comfortable." Thus, our color taste—as a nation—is changing.

Many books have been written about color and the psychology of color: which colors expand or go forward, which contract or withdraw, which will "raise the roof" (or the ceiling at least), and which will seem to bring the ceiling down. Some colors make the viewer feel warm, expansive, generous, full of good feelings, all aglow, and responsive enough to buy anything. Some colors will make the viewer feel cold, aloof, unresponsive, moody, and impossible to reach.

To add to the color confusion, everyone does not react in the same way to the same color. A happy childhood, for example, surrounded by a loving family, and associated with a pink and pretty bedroom, pink and frilly dresses, just pink and pampered all the way, can make "pink" a joyful, loving color. But, if the pink room were forced on the person, the pink but not-so-pretty dresses were hand-me-downs, and pink evoked the memory of medicine, hospitals, and sickness, then "pink" will certainly not be a "turn-on" color. The display person/store planner will not be able to provide the ideal setting for each and every customer, but it is possible to satisfy the vast majority while alienating only a few.

Physical and Psychological Reactions to Color

Color psychology is very important in visual merchandising. Many theories have been espoused concerning the effects of color on people and their moods while shopping. Color can immediately create a mood. Most of us have colors that tend to cheer us up when we're feeling down and colors that calm us. Each of us also has colors that can make us physically feel hotter or cooler. The problem for the visual merchandiser lies in the fact that each person may have a distinct reaction to the same color. In our vast and global marketplace, there are cultural and regional differences in color preference. Also, public taste in color changes, sometimes dramatically, over time. However, in trying to predict the effects of color on the public in general, many visual merchandisers rely on these widely researched color responses.

Yellow

It is sunshine and gold; happy, bright, cheerful, vital, fun-filled, and alive; daisies, marigolds, and lemons. It is optimism, expectancy, relaxation, and a wide-open-armed acceptance of the world, suggestive of change, challenge, and innovation. It is spring, summer, Easter, and when it "turns to gold," it is autumn.

Orange

A friendly, sociable color; agreeable, overt, glowing, and incandescent. It is exciting, vibrant, and filled with anticipation. It is fire and flame, a rising sun in the tropics or a setting sun in the desert; Halloween and autumn leaves.

Red

Exciting, stimulating, loving, powerful, and sexy—these are some of the words used to describe red. It can be assertive, demanding, and obvious, possibly even cheap or vulgar. Generally, it comes across as warm, stirring, and passionate. Red is Valentine's Day and Christmas. It is carnations for Father's Day and patriotism—one part of the flag and firecrackers. It conveys "sale," "clearance," a warning, a fire, and a fright. It is a popular color.

Pink

It may be regarded as sweet, lovely, pretty—little girl's complexion, rosebuds, and ribbons and lace. Or it may connote something fleshy, raw, undercooked, and underdeveloped. Pink is also flowers for Mother's Day, for Easter eggs and bunny ears; nightgowns and lingerie; and an elegant approach to Christmas.

Green

An alive, cool, and "growing" color. It is springtime and summer—lawns, bushes, vegetables, trees, and forests—

the perfect accent to almost any setting, especially if it is alive and growing. It is St. Patrick's Day and the other half of a Christmas color scheme. Some shades of green can also be bilious and stomach-turning—or reminiscent of khaki and war.

Blue

Always a popular color choice and the favorite of most. Cool, calm, comfortable, and collected, it speaks of soft, soaring skies, serene lakes, gentle horizons, and the security of hearth, home, and flag. It is quiet, but can become cold, moody, or even depressing. It is always right for spring and summer skies, shadows on snow, and patriotic celebrations.

Blue-Green

The happy "marriage" of blue and green. It is a cool, tasteful color—sensitive and restful, but alive; vital though quiet. It is water, sky, and grass, peaceful and growing, a great summer color to complement white and glowing tan complexions.

Peach

Suggests the warmth and happy excitement of orange (toned down) with none of its grating qualities. A smiling, glowing color, it is easy to be with and delightful to be in. A new "neutral," a pastel earth tone, a friendly color that will go with almost anything.

Rust

The other end of the orange scale, it is deep, rich, earthy without being earthbound. Rust is a full-bodied color with the warmth of orange, but with none of its obvious, blatant, or irritating qualities. It is the earth color that goes with other colors, but is neither invisible nor intruding. It is the personification of autumn.

Violet/Purple

This traditionally regal color has, in recent years, become a favorite with children. In some shades it is a happy, youthful color, while, in its deepest and richest form, it is a color of taste, distinction, and discretion. It is a high-fashion color that has to be sold. Purple can sometimes come off as overbearing and pompous. Lavender may convey "old-fashioned charm," Victorian and Easter trim.

Gray

The neutral barrier that makes separations, but no statements. Gray exists—and exists well—with other colors that have more to say. Gray may be either a depressing, "down-in-the-dumps" color or a super-elegant and sophisticated color that suggests fine jewelry, silver, furs, and designer salons.

Brown

The earth, hearth, and home; the family and the farm; the simple things, wood, clay and other natural materials. It steps back to let other colors go forward but, unlike gray, it does not disappear. Brown is warm and can sometimes cast a glow. From the lightest off-white beige to the deepest charcoal brown, it is relaxed, unexciting, and in no way unnerving. It is the deep color for autumn.

White

The blankest of the blank, but a strong and able supporting player that makes every other color, by comparison, turn in bigger, bolder, and brighter performances. It is innocence and hope, angels and religious celebrations, a wedding gown, and the blinding brilliance of clear light. Cotton-puff white can be a sparkling accent, a sharp highlight, a crisp delineator, or an unpleasant comparison by which other "whites" may come off as dingy or unhappily yellowed. White can also be sterile, antiseptic, bleak, and harsh.

Black

Connotes night, a vacuum, and an absence of light. It is mystery, sex, and death, as well as the color of intrigue and sophistication. Ultra-chic or ultra-depressing, it also can be ominous and threatening or downright dull. It can be as sensuous as satin or as deep as velvet. Black is a neutral, but a neutral that requires careful handling.

Color Families

In the descriptions of reactions to the colors listed above, certain adjectives appeared over and over again. Some colors were described as "warm and glowing," while others were "cool, calm, aloof." Still another group of colors could be categorized as "neutrals." Thus, most colors are grouped into ambiguous but convenient "families."

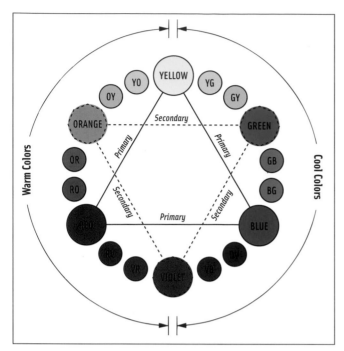

Figure 2.2 Mixing color pigments.

Red, orange, yellow, pink, rust, brown, and peach can all be classified as **warm,** aggressive, spirited, advancing colors. Blue, green, violet, and blue-green are regarded as a group of **cool** and receding colors. That leaves white, gray, black, and brown to band together as the **neutral** color family. Neutrals can be either warm or cool. Black, white, and all the shades of gray are considered cool, while anything from warm off-white through all the shades of beige to the deepest brown is called a warm neutral.

By personal preference, people of certain age and social groups will respond more readily to one family over another. Young children and nonsophisticates, however, commonly delight in and respond to bright, sharp colors: yellow, red, green, brilliant blue, shocking pink, and clear turquoise. Casual, outgoing, fun-loving, high-spirited people who want fashions and settings to match are drawn to the warm colors. Sophisticated people are supposed to appreciate subtlety: the slightly off-colors, toned down and neutralized without being neutered. Elegant and big-ticket merchandise seems to make a better showing and get a better customer response in a "cool" environment. "Serenity" sells silver, furs, and other choice merchandise.

Color Mixing

In working with color, it is wise to have a basic idea about what color is, how it works, and what it can do. If we accept the long-established theory that there are three basic pigment colors from which all other colors can be mixed, we are well on the way to understanding color.

Red, yellow, and blue are called **primary colors.** By mixing red and yellow, we get orange. Blue and yellow combined will produce green. Equal parts of red and blue make violet, or purple. These resulting colors—orange, green, and violet—are **secondary colors.** Furthermore, mixing yellow (a primary color) with green (a secondary)—depending on the quantity of each color used—results in a yellow-green or a green-yellow. This is an **intermediate color.** Mixing two secondary colors (orange plus green or green plus purple) results in a **tertiary color.** All those romantic, exotic names with which fashion and decorating abound, such as shrimp, mango, avocado, chartreuse, peach, pumpkin, plum, and so on, are actually selling names of these tertiary colors.

Value refers to the amount of light or dark in a color. Add white to any of the full-value colors (primary, secondary, or intermediate) and, depending on the amount of white added, the result will be a **tint,** or **pastel,** of that color—a lighter, more gentle variation of the original

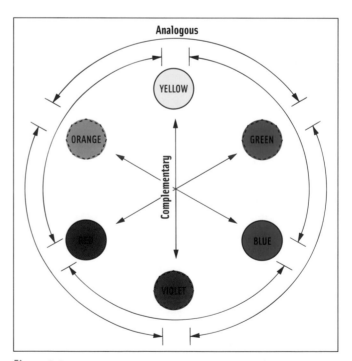

Figure 2.3 Complementary and analogous color schemes.

color. The addition of black to a color will produce **shades,** or deeper, richer, more full-bodied versions of the color. Thus, the addition of white to red could result in a pretty, soft, baby-sweet pink, while the addition of black to red could produce a masculine, heady garnet, dubonnet, or maroon.

Color Schemes

The **color wheel** graphically shows the relationship of colors to each other. The location of colors on the wheel is relevant to the following discussion.

Analogous or Adjacent Colors

Colors that exist harmoniously next to each other on the wheel, because of shared characteristics (and pigments), work together in a display area to create specific effects. Yellow, yellow-green, green, and green-blue are examples of "neighboring," adjacent, or analogous colors, as are yellow, yellow-orange, orange, and orange-red. Adjacent colors reinforce each other; they are compatible and usually can be counted on to create a close harmony. Thus, when used in close groups or clusters, they create an **analogous color scheme;** for example, blue sky and green grass to make a turquoise outfit appear cooler and crisper.

Complementary Colors

Complementary colors are found opposite each other on the color wheel. Red is the complement of green (and vice versa); blue and orange are complements, as are yellow and violet. These "opposites" do not make for close harmony or gentle combinations. Complements bring out the intensity and brilliance of each other. Thus, complementary color schemes are usually strong, demanding, and vibrant. Complementary colors will vibrate against each other (creating kinetic patterns) when placed very close together. They will make "motion" where there actually is none.

Complementary schemes are fine in bright, youth-oriented areas, where the creation of a shocking or attention-getting palette is desired. They can be fun, dynamic, exciting, and sometimes irritating. However, it is possible to minimize or even eliminate some of the dynamic or irritating qualities of the complementary scheme.

This can be accomplished by reducing the **intensity** of the colors being used. Intensity refers to the purity and strength of the color. The addition of white or black will reduce the intensity, as will the addition of some of the complementary color (e.g., adding a little red to green). A pink and apple-green color combination may be basically complementary, but it is easier to live with than a pure, full-strength red and a fully saturated green!

Contrasting Colors

Colors are often selected for the amount of **contrast** they provide. For example: two light colors adjacent to each other provide little contrast; a light color next to a medium one provides some contrast; whereas, a light color next to a dark one creates a bold contrast. That is why one rarely, if ever, finds a garment, fabric, or other product designed with black and navy blue. This is an extreme example of minimal contrast.

Monochromatic Colors

If you start with one color and develop the full range of that color, from the palest off-white tint to the deepest, darkest shade, you will have a **monochromatic** (one color) **color scheme.** Baby-blue and sky-blue, through the intermediate blues, up to a navy or midnight blue, is a monochromatic scheme. This can be restful, easy to accept, and provide a controlled setting for merchandise. It generally "sits back" and takes it easy.

Neutral Colors

Black, white, gray, beige, and brown make up the neutral color family. Neutrals make good backgrounds for stores because they allow the merchandise itself to have full impact. Neutrals evoke less image and tend to disturb customers less. They do not compete with the merchandise on display, but rather provide a complimentary background for the goods.

An all-white scheme can be young, exciting, sparkling, and ultra-chic, or a perfect foil for brightly colored merchandise. However, all white may also come off as absolutely sterile and bland, draining the color right out of the merchandise.

Beige tones have been used a great deal by store designers in the past few years and they remain popular, people-pleasing, and merchandise-complementing. The blending of the casual, but warm, off-whites and beiges with wood tones (from bleached oak to deepest ebony) have a strong following. Generally, this kind of color scheme is easy to live with; it enhances the merchandise, but hardly ever overwhelms. It probably appeals to the rural instincts hidden inside each urban dweller.

From the past, and continuing strongly into the future, comes the gray color scheme. When elegance, the chic, and ultra-new is desired, it can be found with gray—gray by its aloof cool self or made even icier with accents of Lucite and chrome. Gray is a foil for bright colors; it tones them down. It is a relief for the whites; it makes white appear whiter. Gray is a buffer for black, relieving the gloom of this non-color. Neutral gray has long been popular as a setting for silver, furs, and expensive giftware, but it is now reaching into designer areas and even bridal displays.

Black and white may be neutral individually, and most colors will coexist with them, but when used together, they demand and get attention.

Using Color to Promote Color

The display person can usually control the color against which merchandise is shown. The background color is important because it can either add to or detract from the color of the merchandise presented. A white dress shown against a white background can be very effective—or a total disaster! Against a stark white background, a dress that is not a pure white, but a soft, lovely ivory color, can look dingy and yellow. If, however, the background were a deep gray or very dark green, the sharp contrast would make the ivory dress appear whiter.

White against white is usually smart, sophisticated, and subtle. White against black is dramatic, sharp, and striking. The price and type of merchandise, the store's image, and the department or area in a store will determine which background is best for the white dress.

The white against white will be more dramatic and striking if a red light floods the white background and leaves the dress "white," but softly outlined in pink, from the light reflected off the background. The white dress against the black background will seem more elegant if the background is softened with a blue or violet light to ease the sharp contrast between foreground and background. With colored panels or draperies to use behind

Figure 2.4 Nothing says "contrast" like black and white, and in this presentation the strong "op art" pattern in black and white on the background screen serves to draw the classically dressed and positioned mannequin into the "eye of the storm." *St. John Boutique, Fifth Avenue, New York.*

and around merchandise, and assorted colored lights to "paint" those panels, the display person can create the best of all possible settings for the merchandise. The use and effect of colored light is discussed in Chapter 4.

In many ways, the accessories shown with the merchandise can also affect the color. Imagine the white dress with a navy-blue belt, shoes, and handbag, and a red and blue scarf. The white will appear crisp and sparkling by contrast to the navy. Now, suppose that same dress were completely accessorized in toast-beige. The white is softened and warmed by its proximity to the beige. Popularly priced merchandise, however, will often rely on sharper and more contrasting accessories and displays. They help make the garment stand out and look like more for the money.

Visualize a bright red dress with emerald-green trimmings. The red appears redder and more intense because the complementary green intensifies the red. The same red with shocking-pink accessories will seem more red-orange because the "hot pink" of the accessories is bluer by comparison.

Understanding the effect of color on color will enable the display person to select the proper settings and accessories for the merchandise and the store's fashion image.

Texture

Another very important aspect of color is **texture.** The texture—surface treatment or "feel"—can affect the color of the merchandise. Smooth and shiny surfaces reflect light and, therefore, always appear lighter. Satin, chrome, highly lacquered or enameled surfaces, waxed woods, and so on, will all pick up and reflect more light than objects that are flat and lusterless. Rough, nubby, and deep-piled surfaces will absorb and hold light and, therefore, appear darker. Velvet, sandpaper, deep carpets, untreated and natural woods or tree barks—these will all appear darker. Smooth or shiny reflective finishes around merchandise will add more light to the presentation. The background will reflect more light back onto the product being shown.

Textures are also suggestive. They can suggest familiar symbols by which the display person attempts to explain the merchandise in terms of surrounding materials. Soft silks and satins suggest femininity and sensuousness. Velvet is deep and rich, dark and mysterious, subtle, elegant, and expensive. Rough textures, such as burlap, coarse linens, nubby wools, and tweeds, are masculine, "outdoorsy," rugged, natural, earthy, and wholesome. Gravel, sand, stones, brick, and ground-up cork suggest the great open spaces: sportswear, beachwear, camping, and the country.

In creating a setting for a bridal gown, for example, the textures utilized should suggest and, at the same time, enhance the softness and loveliness of the gown. A complementary texture to a satin and lace gown might even be rough wood planking. The gown would seem even more delicate, fragile, and feminine by comparison to the rough, burly quality of the wood. But what would this do to the bride-to-be and her illusions of romance?

Figure 2.5 The background of the window is rich in red textures: rough, worn and weathered ends of logs. Recessed into this field of texture are three slick shadow boxes painted a contrasting green color. The smooth, soft, and subtle garments and accessories are displayed within these openings. *Hermes, East 57th Street, New York.*

In this case, the background should be more of the same: The gown could be enveloped with other soft fabrics and gentle textures—wisps of tulle and net, ribbons and lace. Anything that suggests a fairy-tale setting and a "happily-ever-after" ending should be used with the bridal gown.

The use of opposite textures, however, can work very effectively in promoting other types of merchandise, especially when humor, scale, or shock are the attention-getting devices to bring the shopper over to the display. Imagine a pair of natural leather, outdoor hiking boots, nail-studded and roughly sewn, sitting on a lace-edged, red satin pillow with a sheer, silky fabric draped behind. The copy might read: "It will be love at first sight." The contrast may be silly and out of place, but it is intriguing, unexpected, and attention-getting. Or visualize a woman's nightgown—all pink and lace, soft and sheer—hanging from a peg on a wall of rough, split logs. The juxtaposing of two very different textures, the very feminine against the very masculine, makes the feminine seem more feminine and the masculine even more so. With a copy line like "Why rough it when you can go in style?"—the display person could explain the combination and possibly bring a smile to the viewer's face.

In an ensemble, there should be a relationship of textures, a flow and continuity rather than startling change, unless the merchandise is meant to startle and call for attention. A fine, wool challis tie, rather than a shiny silk one, is the choice for a tweed jacket, just as an oxford cloth shirt is more appropriate to the texture of nubby wools than a fine broadcloth. Similarly, coarsely textured suits are more compatible with grained leather rather than patent leather shoes.

Textures have to be balanced in a display arrangement. Rough textures usually seem heavier or suggest more "weight" in a composition or display. A roughly textured cube, for example, appears to take up more space and volume in the display area than a smoothly lacquered cube of the same size and color. Therefore, a display person may balance a small, coarsely textured element with a larger smooth or shiny one. A textured floor "sits" better than a smooth or shiny one, while a smooth ceiling "floats" better than a roughly textured one.

Some materials are especially popular for use in displays because they are texturally neutral (neither very smooth nor very rough) and because they are available in a wide range of colors. Felt, jersey, and suede cloth have neutral textures and can be used with soft or rugged merchandise. Seamless paper is another favorite with display persons because it, too, lacks texture. These materials will be discussed more fully in Chapter 23, Setting Up a Display Shop.

Color: A Recap

- Color is the biggest motivation for shopping.
- America's color taste is changing—softening up, warming up, returning to "earth" tones.
- The warm colors are red, yellow, orange, rust, and peach.
- The cool colors are blue, green, violet, and blue-green.
- The neutral colors are white, black, and all the grays in-between, as well as warm off-white, brown, and all the beiges in-between.
- The primary or basic colors are red, yellow, and blue.
- The secondary colors are orange, green, and violet. They are obtained by mixing two of the primaries.
- An intermediate color is obtained by mixing a primary and a secondary color.

- A tertiary color is an "in-between" color obtained by mixing two secondary colors.
- Intensity is the purity, strength, and brilliance of a color.
- A tint, or pastel, is a color with white added.
- A shade is a color with black added.
- A monochromatic color scheme is one that includes a range of tints and shades of a single color.
- An analogous color scheme consists of colors that are adjacent to each other on the color wheel.
- A complementary color scheme consists of colors that are opposite each other on the color wheel.
- A neutral color scheme is a "no-color" color scheme of white, blacks, grays, or browns.

Texture: A Recap

- Texture is the surface treatment or "feel" of the merchandise.
- Smooth surfaces reflect light and appear brighter.
- Rough surfaces hold light and appear darker.

- Rough textures seem heavier and suggest more "weight," while smooth textures seem to take up less size and volume.

Questions for Review and Discussion

1. Provide an example of a current fashion trend that supports the Color Marketing Group's forecast of a return to "earth" colors.

2. Why might two people react differently to the same color? Give an example of two diverse reactions to the same color.

3. For each of the following colors, list some common associations and reactions:
   a. blue
   b. red
   c. yellow
   d. black

4. List some cool colors. What types of customers are most attracted to cool colors?

5. Provide examples of the following:
   a. monochromatic color scheme
   b. contrasting colors
   c. intermediate colors
   d. complementary colors

6. Explain the relationship of the terms value, tint, and shade.

7. What are neutral colors? How are neutrals often used in store design?

8. What is texture? How can textures be suggestive of merchandise and settings?

9. Explain the proper relationship of textures in a display setting. How should textures be "balanced" in a display?

CHAPTER THREE

Line and Composition

AFTER YOU HAVE READ THIS CHAPTER,
YOU WILL BE ABLE TO DISCUSS:

- The three major types of lines used in display.
- "Composition" and explain its relationship to visual merchandising.
- The differences between symmetrical and asymmetrical balance.
- How dominance can be achieved in a visual presentation.
- The use of contrasting elements in a display.
- The relationship between proportion and contrast.
- The concept of rhythm as it relates to visual presentations.
- The relationship between repetition and dominance.

LINE AND COMPOSITION: TRADE TALK

 asymmetrical balance
 balance
 composition
 contrast
 curved lines
 diagonal lines
 dominance
 horizontal lines
 line
 proportion
 repetition
 rhythm
 symmetrical or formal balance
 vertical lines

Line

Line is a direction. It is a major part of composition, and second only to color in creating a response to the merchandise in a display. Lines can be vertical, horizontal, curved, or diagonal. The way in which these lines are utilized and combined determines the effectiveness of the merchandise presentation. Each line suggests something else and, like letters combined to form words, lines are arranged to make selling "pictures."

Vertical Lines

What is more inspiring than the soaring spires of a Gothic cathedral? Is there anything more classic or elegant than a tall, fluted Ionic column? How about the power and majesty of a stand of cypress trees? Proud people stand tall and erect. What do the spire, the column, the cypress, and the proud person have in common? They are all straight and vertical. They emphasize and exemplify the **vertical line.** When a display is mainly a vertical one, filled with straight elements that seem to join floor and ceiling, the viewer will get the message: strength, height, pride, majesty, and dignity.

When the vertical elements are not only tall but also thin, an impression of elegance and refinement is conveyed. For example, a mannequin standing erect with arms at her sides, head uplifted, and shoulders back will look elegant. She will add stature and "class" to the garment she is modeling. Fur coats, evening gowns, bridal wear, and well-tailored suits are shown to advantage on a vertical figure. The long, straight, falling line of a garment can be enhanced by the "dignified" mannequin which, in turn, will add a vertical quality to the entire display. A straight line can also be direct and forceful, or rigid and precise.

Horizontal Lines

Long, low, wide, spreading lines—the bands that run across a window or around perimeter walls—suggest an easygoing, restful quality. All is peaceful and calm in a horizontal presentation. A reclining mannequin, relaxed or at ease, is perfectly compatible with robes, loungewear. or nightwear. The horizon sets the world to rest; lazy ripples and gentle waves are horizontal. As the line stretches out and makes objects look wider, it also tends to make them look shorter. A pattern of **horizontal lines** will cut the vertical effect and reduce the "uptight" or dignified feel of a design or setting. A balancing of the

Figure 3.1 The vertical line denotes elegance and refinement. This classically simple window features a realistic mannequin in a long red gown and the vertical line of the figure is restated—over and over again—by the silk cords with tassel endings that drop from the ceiling to enliven the all-white space. *Pilar Rossi, Madison Avenue, New York.*

Figure 3.2 The verticality of the mannequin's pose and the white panel plus the build-up of hat boxes on the left all reinforce the sense of dignity and refinement. The tall, thin, ribbon-tied box, angled into the composition on the right, adds a casual touch to the display. *Bloomingdales, Lexington Avenue, New York.*

Figure 3.3 The soft, flowing lines of the warped timber provide a textural note to the display as well as a sense of femininity and grace to the casual outfits worn by the headless forms. *Gucci, Fifth Avenue, New York.*

Figure 3.4 The horizontal composition is cleverly executed with the line of upholstered chairs across the window space. Note the imaginative use of oranges and the can of soda to emphasize the analogous color palette and the "Citrus Coolers" theme. *Jos Horne, Pittsburgh.*

horizontal with the vertical can create an easy, restful, but elegant setting.

Curved Lines

The **curved line** personifies grace, charm, and femininity. It is soft and enveloping. The curved line or arc can ease the tension that might be produced by too many vertical lines. It is the circle and the sphere, the sun and the moon, the heart, billowing waves, rolling hills, fluffy clouds, the swirl of a seashell, a spiral, an opening rose. Curved lines can also be used for a spotlight or target against which an object is shown, or a spiral that leads the eye from object to object.

Diagonal Lines

The **diagonal line** is a line of action; it is forceful, strong, and dynamic. The diagonal is a bolt of lightning, a firecracker going off, a thrown javelin, rain streaming down, a shove or a push, a seesaw or a sliding pond, an arrow, or a pointing finger leading the eye right down to where the action is. The active sportswear mannequin, for example, is often all angles: arms akimbo, knees bent, head thrust back, and shoulders shrugging. That man-

Figure 3.5 The diagonal line is the line of action, movement, fun, and excitement. It implies "now!" and "new!" Though most of the mannequins are vertical in pose, except for the seated ones, the easel, step-ladder, and other decorative elements create the strong angular emphasis in this composition. *Burberry, East 57th Street, New York.*

nequin is a study in diagonals. It is possible to suggest movement and excitement in a static and predominantly vertical or horizontal presentation by adding some forceful diagonals.

Composition

Composition may be defined as the organization or grouping of different parts or elements in order to achieve a unified whole. In display and visual merchandising, composition is the arrangement of lines, forms, shapes, and colors into a pleasing whole that directs the viewer's eye to the various bits and pieces of the setting and relays a particular message. The quality of the composition will depend on the elements used and where and how they are used.

Balance

A well-designed display should be **balanced.** This involves the creation of an easy-to-accept relationship between the parts of the composition. If a design were cut in half by an imaginary line drawn through its center, and one side were an exact replica or mirror image of the other side, that would be a classic example of **symmetrical** or **formal balance.** In reality, however, the objects on each side of the imaginary line are usually of similar weight and prominence, not an actual mirror image. For example: If on one side of a display, a mannequin is sitting on a chair, while on the other side, a similar mannequin is sitting on a comparable chair, both halves of the composition would be considered the same, equal in weight and importance. This is formal balance and, although staid and traditional, can be very effective where expensive or quality merchandise is being presented.

Asymmetrical balance is more informal and often more interesting. Although the two sides appear to be of equal weight, they are not replicas of each other. The individual units comprising the display may differ, but they achieve a dynamic balance of weight and size at each side of the imaginary central line. For example: There might be two mannequins on one side balanced by a mannequin standing next to a draped table. If, on the table, there is a vase filled with flowers and foliage extending to about the same height as the mannequin's head, then visually, the table with the vase and flowers will be equal in weight and shape to the second mannequin on the other side.

Sometimes, the creative and experienced designer can do marvelous things by balancing color with form. A strong or hot color may appear heavier than a pastel or cool color, so a mannequin in a vivid red dress might be balanced with an armoire painted antique white. This asymmetrical or informal balance is more casual, more interesting, and certainly more exciting.

At times, a display presentation can be completely lacking in any sense of balance and still be very good. This is done for a reason. To create an effect, a lack of balance may be used as an element of surprise: to catch the viewer looking into an "empty" window and wondering where the display went. Or the display person may be catering to a particular traffic flow. He or she may find that most shoppers travel north to south on the store's side of the street. It can make for a better presentation if the merchandise is shown in the southern half of the window—angled to face and attract the shopper walking from north to south. The empty or near empty, less weighty, northern part of the window gets less attention and, therefore, little, if any, merchandising.

Dominance

In every composition, it is advisable that some element be **dominant.** There should be some unit or object that by its color, its size, or its position in the composition, attracts the eye first and possibly directs the viewer to other parts of the composition.

In most displays, the dominant element is the merchandise, often with a big assist from a mannequin that is wearing it. In the "one-item" display, the single unit should dominate—should be the eye-catcher and the eye-filler—and the rest of the design or composition should exist in order to make this one item seem more beautiful and more special. However, some stores with very special images will play games with their viewers. Knowing how very "special" they and their merchandise are, the store designer will casually drop an exquisite single item into a beautifully conceived composition, leaving it up to the shopper to find it. But this can be successfully done only where the store and the display person know what they are selling—and to whom—and can afford the luxury of these little "games."

A mannequin can be dominant in a display by virtue of its size or the color it is wearing. A small object, like a diamond brooch, can be made dominant in a composition by sharply contrasting it with its background, without any distracting props nearby, and with a strong light on the piece. An object may also be made dominant by the arrangement of lines and shapes, the weights of the various elements of the composition, and gradations of color and light. By using these various techniques, the viewer's eye is directed to the main object or the featured item of the display.

Contrast

Contrast is the composition of elements in order to show a sharp difference between them. It consists of a juxtaposition of different forms, lines, or colors in a composition in order to intensify each element's properties—for example, a white gown displayed against a midnight background; a diamond bracelet on a black velvet pad; a pair of red shoes on a green grass mat.

A difference in texture or an incongruity in the objects themselves can also heighten the contrast: a power saw nestling on a fluffy angel-hair cloud. The outrageous difference in the feel and texture between the item or merchandise and its environment will attract attention and maybe even promote the softness, ruggedness, or smoothness of that item. The effective use of contrast makes it possible for the "feel" or "touch" of an item to be more apparent to the eye without actually touching or stroking the object.

Proportion

Contrast can also consist of a difference in **proportion**—the relationship of the size, scale, or "weight" of elements

Figure 3.6 Dominance means taking over, and by its size, color, and texture there is no doubt that the red heart is the major element in this shadow box display. However, the puddle of light on the window floor highlights the piece of jewelry that is the reason for the display. The heart may get the viewer's attention but it is the jewelry that keeps her interest. *Tiffany, Fifth Avenue, New York.*

and between each element and the entire composition. A pair of baby shoes, for example, will appear more delicate and cherishable when placed next to a gigantic teddy bear. A 4-foot tennis racket will bring attention to mere human-sized tennis shoes. The display person must be careful to consider not only the size of the merchandise and props, but the size of the display area as well.

Experience has taught us to take the size of certain objects for granted. We know, for example, that a mannequin is life-size. Yet, the mannequin, in proportion to a greatly oversized table and chair, would appear to shrink from its actual size. Our mind knows the mannequin is still life-size, but our eyes are not so convinced.

Certain proportions or relationships in a composition or display are easily accepted by the viewer's eye: A ring will fit a mannequin's hand; a hat will sit on a mannequin's head. Put the same feathered hat into a straw "nest" that is 3 feet in diameter with "eggs" the size of footballs—the hat now appears to be small and fragile. The "nest" is out of proportion; it is overscaled.

Proportion and contrast are important elements of good composition. Drastically changing the proportions between items and dramatic contrasts of color and texture can work wonders in attracting attention to a display and in helping to promote an idea or a look. These attention-getting techniques will be discussed in greater detail in Chapter 16.

Rhythm

A good display composition should have a **rhythm,** a self-contained movement from element to element, from background to foreground, from side to side. The rhythm should lead the viewer's eye from the dominant object to the subordinate object (or objects), from the major presentation of an ensemble down to the arrangement of accessories or alternate parts of the outfit.

This flow, for example, can be created by the manner in which a mannequin is posed. Her hand may be resting on a chair back which happens to have a coat draped from it; a scarf, which is casually tossed over the coat, is trailing onto the floor over to an arrangement of shoes, bags, another scarf, a flower, some toiletries. The eye is led first to the mannequin (dominant in size, color and "weight"), down to the chair, and then to the cluster on

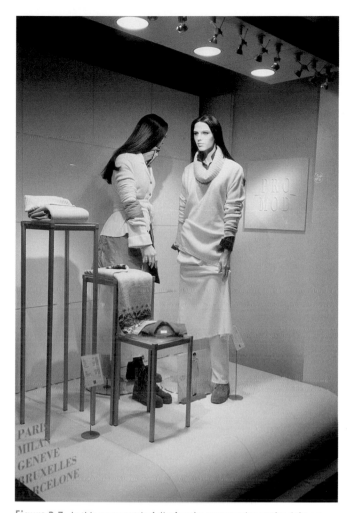

Figure 3.7 In this asymmetrical display the mannequins on the right are balanced by the stepped risers on the left that carry an assortment of coordinates and accessories. *ProMod, Brussels, Belgium.*

the ground. That downward sweep may be subtly reinforced by a background design of lines or shapes and by the use of color and lighting, which also lead the eye in the same direction.

The eye will naturally go around in a circular route if the objects are arranged to lead the way—like a snail's shell swirling inward to a central point. The eye will follow a triangular trail or a pyramidal pattern that leads from a flat, weighted base to an apex, or point. A successful rhythm or flow is a gentle one, one that guides the viewer in easy movements from one stop to another along the way. In some cases, like "sales" or "hard-sell" promotions—where dynamics are demanded—a jumpy and jarring presentation will be more effective.

Figure 3.8 The sharpest contrast is the combination of black and white. In this window the black and white photo blowup shows another variation on the black and white outfit worn by the headless mannequin. The lamp, left, balances the figure in its verticality while the pose of the model in the photograph accentuates the angular line. The simple horizontal "sale" sign completes this well-designed composition. *Banana Republic, Fifth Avenue, New York.*

Repetition

Repetition of a color, a line, a shape, or a form can add to the success of a display composition. By repeating or reiterating an idea or motif, that concept becomes more emphatic, more important, and thus, more dominant. In this way, even a small object can be made to stand out

in a large display area—because the eye has been "trained" to look for it. Try to visualize a dark floor with an appliqué of red footprints "walking" across it. At the very end—in a pool of light—is a pair of red shoes. The pattern or repetition of the red footprints will carry the viewer's eye forward to the single pair of shoes, which now dominates the composition and the viewer's eye—and mind.

Figure 3.9 The contrast in scale draws the viewer's attention to this display. The recognizable Chanel chain is recreated in giant scale up front and leads to the stylized graphic that serves as a background for the dress on the headless mannequin. Note how the light picks out the chain belt and the chain necklace on the graphic. *Chanel, Fifth Avenue, New York.*

Line and Composition: A Recap

- Line is a direction, and a major part of composition.
- There are vertical, horizontal, curved, and diagonal lines.
- Composition is the organization of different elements to create unity.
- Balance is the creation of an easy-to-accept relationship between the parts of the composition.
- Balance can be symmetrical or asymmetrical.
- Dominance refers to the element in the composition that first attracts the eye.
- Contrast is meant to show differences.
- Proportion is the relationship of the size, weight, height, or scale of the elements.
- Rhythm is a self-contained movement that leads the viewer's eye from one element to another.
- Repetition of an element within a display can make a concept more emphatic.

Questions for Review and Discussion

1. Describe a display using vertical lines. What feelings do vertical lines suggest to the viewers?

2. How can curved lines be introduced into a visual presentation? What type of response do curved lines tend to evoke?

3. Differentiate between symmetrical and asymmetrical balance and explain how each can be achieved in a visual display.

4. Provide a quick sketch illustrating first symmetrical and then asymmetrical balance in a display.

5. What should be most dominant in visual presentation? Why?

6. How can contrast be achieved in a display using texture? Color? Line?

7. Describe the concept of proportion and explain why it is important to any visual presentation.

8. How can you tell if a display has rhythm?

9. How does repetition assist in achieving rhythm in a display?

CHAPTER FOUR

Light and Lighting

AFTER YOU HAVE READ THIS CHAPTER,
YOU WILL BE ABLE TO DISCUSS:

- The relationship between color and light.
- The term "visible light."
- Techniques for lighting open-backed windows and closed-back windows.
- Ways in which lighting can be used to draw shoppers to particular areas within a store.
- Primary and secondary store lighting.
- Advantages and disadvantages of fluorescent light and incandescent light.
- Locations where fluorescent lights are frequently used within a store.
- Uses and functions of HID lighting and MR16 and MR11 lamps.
- The effective use of light in visual merchandising.

LIGHT AND LIGHTING: TRADE TALK

baffle	MR16 and MR11
colored lights	PAR bulbs
color of an object	primary colors of light
filters	R or reflector bulb
floodlights	secondary or accent lighting
fluorescent light	secondary colors of light
general or primary lighting	shadows
HID	spotlights
highlights	store's lighting plan
incandescent light	visible light
light	

The Color of Light

Color—as color—means little unless it is considered in relation to the type of light in which the color is seen. It is light that makes things visible. All colors depend on light. There is natural daylight and artificial light, which can be incandescent, fluorescent, or high-intensity discharge (HID) lighting.

It is not quite that simple, however. These three broad classifications of artificial light are further subdivided. There are many different types of fluorescent lamp tubes available, ranging from a warm white deluxe that attempts to create an "incandescent" effect, to the cool, bluish "daylight" quality usually associated with fluorescent lighting. HID lamps are being improved daily and now even approach the warm end of the colored light scale. Incandescent lamps (i.e., bulbs) are warm and glowing, but filters or gels over them can change the color and quality of the light. Let us, therefore, consider the color of light, the effect of light on pigment color, and how light can affect the merchandise and the area that surrounds the merchandise.

Visible light is actually composed of the whole spectrum of colors from violet to red. Imagine a beam of light passing through a glass prism or reflecting in a pool of water or oil, and you will see that spectrum broken up into a rainbow of colors: from violet, through the blues and greens, to the yellows, oranges, and finally red. All light is caused by waves of radiant energy that vary in length. The shortest wavelength of the visible spectrum is violet light; then comes blue light, green light, and so on; and at the other end of the spectrum, with the longest wavelength, is red light. All these wavelengths—the entire spectrum—combine to form visible, or white light, the light we see.

Ultraviolet light, X-rays, and gamma rays have shorter wavelengths than we can see. Infrared and radio waves are too long for us to perceive. Therefore, for the purpose of understanding light and color in display and store planning, this discussion will be limited to the colors that appear in the visible spectrum. We will find that some light sources reflect the shorter wavelengths and emit cooler or bluer light, while others have a warmer light and favor the longer wavelengths.

To comprehend the relationship between color and light and why an object is perceived by an observer as a particular color, it is important to understand that light is capable of being reflected and absorbed. The **color of**

Figure 4.1 A lighting plan in a store combines many elements and types of lamps (bulbs). Hidden fluorescent tubes can illuminate a raised ceiling, wash over perimeter walls, or create an illuminated path along the aisle. Incandescent spotlights can highlight and accentuate merchandise presentations while the low-voltage, MR16 halogen lamps can add sparkle and enrich the colors of the products. Colored filters over the lamps may add a sense of drama and excitement to the space. *Michael K., Broadway, New York. Design: Tobin & Parnes.*

Figure 4.2 Hidden fluorescent tubes accentuate the sweeping curves in the tiered ceiling of the department store. Incandescent lamps are set into the ceiling for the ambient or general light, but they add a sparkle to the scheme as they shine in the suspended chandelier. *Lotte Department Store, Seoul, Korea.*

an object is seen as a result of the object's selective absorption of light rays. Thus, if an object is blue, for example, this means that it absorbs all the wavelengths of light except those of **blue light,** which are reflected back to the observer. The same occurs with other colors, but with a different wavelength being reflected.

If the object is pure white, the full visible spectrum of light is being reflected back in approximately equal quantities. If it is pure black, then all colors in the spectrum are being absorbed by the object.

Light bounces from one surface to another, and in this movement it is capable of throwing off new colors. For example: A wall or panel is painted pink. A wedgewood-blue carpet is installed. If warm, incandescent lights are used, the carpet may turn slightly lavender from the warm pink reflection cast off by the walls. The incan-

descent light may also play up any reds that are in the warm blue carpet. (A warm blue has some purple in it, i.e., red and blue. Incandescent light reflects most in the red end of the spectrum.) If a daylight fluorescent light were switched on instead, the blue of the carpet might seem more sparkling and cool, and the walls would take on the lavender tone. The overall light will affect the color of the walls, the floor, and the ceiling, and bouncing around as it does, most of all it can affect the color of the merchandise.

Planning Window Lighting

You walk by a store. It is daylight. You catch a glimpse of the window and all you see is yourself reflected in the

Figure 4.3 The open-back window allows shoppers to glimpse into the retail store and the merchandise presentation within. To define the window display space and separate it visually from the store beyond, a decorative graphic panel and focused lighting on the up-front merchandise makes it all work. *Duka, Stockholm, Sweden.*

window of a store that may or may not be open for business. In that glimpse you can check out what you are wearing, but you haven't a single clue as to what lies beyond the glass. What kind of store is it? What sort of merchandise is sold there? When a store's windows are not illuminated or are illuminated improperly, they become a giant one-way mirror facing the street or the mall.

Retailers think of their stock; they think of all the money they have invested; but unfortunately, they don't always think about how to show and stock the merchandise they have to sell. They don't seem to realize how sig-

nificantly the shopper's perception of who they are and what they are reflects on that shopper's attitude toward the merchandise. Retailers think hard and long about their location: They want a good address; they want to be where the right traffic is; they want to be where their targeted shoppers are. When it comes to stopping the shopper with an initial razzle-dazzle impression, however, the thinking and spending often stops. Just being where the action is does not make a retailer part of that action. The retailer still has to get the shopper's attention.

The cheapest and most effective starting place in getting attention and recognition is with good lighting. Good lighting does not have to drain the store's operating budget. Lighting can be played like a musical instrument; the "tune" that results makes the difference in the shopper's perception. Without light there is no color! If there is no color, then there are no sales in fashion merchandise. The first and foremost requisite for a sale is the color and how appealingly that color has been rendered. How the shopper perceives color is very important, and lighting can make red sizzle and shock, make blue appear ethereal or chilly, allow orange to scream or turn into a rich, earthy shade. Lighting also makes the first impression. It is the retailer's sign and identification.

Lighting the Open-Back Window

If the store has an open-back window, then the lighting in the display area, up front, must be strong enough and bright enough to attract and keep the shopper's eye from going past the featured merchandise in the display directly into the store on view beyond. The window is not the place for strings of fluorescent tubes casting a deadly dull chill over already lifeless mannequins. Fluorescent lighting also casts a flat, dull, and lifeless pall over the colors of the garments. Use only a few sharp spots—incandescent or MR16 miniature low-voltage tungsten halogen (to be discussed later in this chapter)—and focus the light away from the glass—not into the store, but directly down onto the merchandise.

At all times avoid lighting up the mannequin's face. Chest lighting is the preferred technique; it shows off the color of the garment as well as the detailing of the design while softly illuminating the mannequin's face. If the painted face is viewed in the full glare of the light, it will only point up that it is a lifeless, painted face. The reflected light enhances the mannequin's mystique and makes it seem more "human." Place the merchandise as far back into the space as possible so the spotlights can be most effective and not have to battle the natural glare associated with daylight—and traffic lights at night—on the plate glass windows. Just as a single match lit in total darkness can become a beacon, a spotlight in a relatively low-lit area becomes a sharp, brilliant point of light. The effect created will all depend upon the contrast.

A simple length of fabric of the right color, texture, and/or pattern; a screen; a panel of textured wood; or even a cluster of tall plants can serve as a partial background in the open-back window. The color of the divider can either complement the color of the garments or enhance some value of the color. The divider also effectively separates the display area from the selling floor and the lighting on that sales floor. By cutting out or minimizing the store's light, the window light seems stronger. If a shopper passing by sees the light in the window, he or she will also see the display of merchandise and be aware of the retail space viewed to either side of the partial background. The shopper knows that the store is open; the shopper knows what kind of merchandise is available. If the retailer is enlightened enough, he or she will also add some interesting or exciting props—or furniture—to the display, adding to the image of the merchandise and the store.

Lighting the Closed-Back Window

If the store has an enclosed display window—three walls, a floor, and a ceiling—the display person has greater opportunities for magical lighting effects. Not only can the display person highlight the featured merchandise and bring to it the attention it warrants, he or she can also use light to "paint" the background a complementary or accenting color or dramatize the setting by creating a particular ambience, for example, blue and green lighting to simulate an underwater look, or yellows and oranges mixed with reds to create the atmosphere of a setting sun or a rich day in autumn. Colored lights or colored filters or theatrical gels all work wonderfully well to achieve these effects.

Many theatrical lighting supply stores also carry a variety of cut-out, patterned light filters that create images in light on walls, floors, and even on the merchandise. With these pierced filters one can have rain, snow, lightening, or sunshine; light streaming through a Gothic window for a bridal setting; palm trees in the tropics for swimwear; a starlit night for ball gowns; or fireworks for a red, white, and blue promotion—or a spectacular sale event. More expensive but also more effective are the filters that rotate around the light causing movement and animation in the window.

Using these techniques requires great control over the daylight that might, at certain times of the day, overpower the window lighting and the special effects. Awnings drawn down during the sunlight hours can help somewhat, but even better is setting the merchandise and the mannequins as far back as possible in the closed-back window to take full advantage of the lighting effects and to overcome the effects of glare and reflection.

Incandescent lighting and MR16s, to be discussed later in this chapter, are the most effective sources for window display lighting.

Planning Store Interior Lighting

Now that we know that the store is open, let us step inside and see what is to be seen. **Light** means "seeing." Light serves to lead the shopper into and through the store. It directs the shopper's attention from one featured presentation or classification with stops along the way to appreciate the highlighted focal points and/or displays. It can separate one area from the next; one boutique or vendor's shop from another. The light level and the "color" (the warmth or coldness) of the light in the store create the ambience. Is it warm, welcoming, and inviting? Is it residential, intimate and comfortable? Is it cool and aloof or just cold and depressing? Is it flat and boring or does it sparkle with the contrasts of highlights and shadows? A store's lighting is composed of many different light sources and lamps. It is a "palette" of lamps, of different color variations, intensities, and wattage, and it can also be affected by natural light that comes in through sky-lights or windows.

The **store's lighting plan** includes the general, overall illumination of the retail space and also the accents; the highlighters that point out what is new, unique, or special. It can include atmospheric touches like chandelier, wall, or column sconces or wall and ceiling washers. Though they may not all show off the merchandise, they do show off the attitude of the store. There are also appraisal lights where the shopper can examine things like jewelry, fashion accessories, or cosmetics.

People, like insects, are attracted to light. It is human nature to walk toward the area where the light is brightest. Thus, a store designer can reconfigure a given floor plan using light. If the plan is long and narrow, a strong light on the far wall makes that wall seem closer and encourages shoppers to head toward the rear of the space. If the long perimeter walls are illuminated, the shopper is better able to see the mass display of the wall stock. Bright lights can be added on the displays or displayers set along the aisle while the aisle itself is kept in low light. Between the well-lit back wall and the highlighted aisle displays, the middle area of the shop or department can function in medium or general lighting.

There are definite "moments of truth" that must be considered in the store's lighting plan. One of these "moments" is when the shopper tries on the garment and stands before the mirror. The light that complements the garment should flatter the shopper. The cash/wrap desk presents another such "moment." As the shopper sees the selected garment being boxed or bagged and being paid for, the garment must reach out in the fullness and richness of color to reassure the shopper that he or she has made the right decision.

Let us now consider the different types of lights and the lamps that can be used to create an effective and attractive store lighting plan.

Figure 4.4 Fluorescent tubes are usually recessed in ceiling fixtures and covered with diffusing baffles or filtering shades so that the tubes are not visible. In this shop the fluorescent fixtures are recessed into the ceiling and combined with electrified tracks that are lined up across the retail space. These tracks are equipped with incandescent spotlights. *Paws 'n' Claws, New Jersey. Design by JGA.*

General or Primary Lighting

General, or primary, lighting is the allover level of illumination in an area. It is usually the light that fills the selling floor from overhead light fixtures, but does not include accent lights, wall washers, and display highlighting lamps. (These are forms of secondary lighting.) Also, it does not include "glamour" or decorative lighting: the sconces, counter or table lamps, indirect lighting, and so on.

Fluorescent Lighting

Some retail operations are illuminated by rows of **fluorescent** fixtures that span the length or width of the store. The fluorescent fixture is usually the least expensive and most efficient fixture to use from the point of initial cost, cost of energy, and length of lamp life. Although it is often the popular choice for the contractor to install and the retailer to maintain, it is not always the best choice for many categories of merchandise. Fluorescent lamps can produce a flat, even, and stultifying blanket of light that offers few shadows and provides little depth or textural interest. There are degrees of "warmth" and "coolness" available in fluorescent lamps, from the rosy quality of "warm white deluxe" to the blue of "cool white deluxe"—with many gradations in between.

The merchandise—or the general type of merchandise to be presented under the lighting—should be tested under the various types of light bulbs. No one type or color will enhance everything, but the one that is generally most flattering should be chosen. Some merchandise, like diamonds, silver, kitchen supplies, and maybe even furs, may look scintillating in the cool, brittle light of "cool" fluorescent, but customers and salespeople may appear drained, haggard, and generally washed out in that same lighting. A sparkling white diamond on black velvet may seem all fire and ice, but it would be hard to sell if the finger onto which a ring is slipped, or the neck that a necklace caresses, looks waxy or marred by blemishes. Therefore, a soft, glowing incandescent lamp,

placed near a mirror, will enhance the customer's skin tones as she looks at herself bejeweled. Even if the diamond itself, at that moment, is not super-blue-white gorgeous, the customer's appearance while wearing the jewelry is at its best. That's salesmanship! That's display!

Fluorescent fixtures and lighting can be shielded, filtered, or softened with grids, baffles, or diffusing panels—all to the good. A **baffle** is any device used to direct, divert, or disseminate light. It can be a louver over a light, an eggcrate grid, or even an angled panel that redirects the stream of light. Fluorescent lamps can also be used in showcases or hidden beneath shelves to add the required warmth or coolness that the particular merchandise warrants.

In any area, a ceiling may be regarded as another wall, or the sixth side of a cube, with the walls comprising four

Figure 4.5 Incandescent bulbs are recessed into the metal plates of the ceiling as well as inserted into the moveable lamp holders on the electric tracks applied to the ceiling. While the recessed lamps provide the general illumination for the shop, it is the focusable lamp that picks out and accentuates the individual cosmetics or areas of interest. *Dickson Cyber Express, Singapore. Design: JGA.*

sides, and the floor the fifth. As much as it might be desirable to use different colors of fluorescent in different areas, to do so would break the ceiling pattern and call attention to the changes of color overhead. It is advisable to test and then select a proper mix of perhaps two different color tubes that can be used in the same fixture and provide the best overall colored light for the store. A grid or diffuser will hide the fact that in a single fixture, daylight and warm white tubes are being used in tandem.

Incandescent Lighting

More and more stores are combining **incandescent** lights with fluorescent lights to create their primary lighting. The incandescent are used for warmth, for emphasis, for highlighting, as well as on the merchandise that thrives under them. The fluorescent may light up an aisle, wash a wall, or indicate a change of merchandise or department, but the incandescent do the selling.

In small stores and in special areas or closed-off departments, incandescent light bulbs can be used as the only kind of lighting in the general, overall scheme. However, incandescent bulbs are more expensive to install and use. They do not burn as efficiently or as long as fluorescent tubes. They also give off more heat, which can increase the air-conditioning load, and thus use more energy. Some stores feel the increased costs are worth it because of the effect incandescent light produces.

Incandescent **spotlights** are high voltage lights and are called **PAR bulbs.** They can be used as a primary light source, but are usually used as secondary lighting. Although these lamps cost more to purchase, they do have a longer lamp life. A PAR bulb can burn for 3,000 hours or longer.

An alternative to the PAR bulb is the **R** or **reflector bulb,** which is lower in wattage (about 150 watts) and made of clear glass with a metallic reflector surface mounted behind the bulb. Although it costs less to purchase than the PAR bulb, the reflector bulb does not burn as long.

Floodlights are also incandescent bulbs, but they usually have frosted glass envelopes, or enclosures, and are less concentrated, having a wider beam spread than spotlights.

Figure 4.6 The central, focal counter is not only highlighted by the colors, encircling "ribbons," over-scaled bouquet of fruit, and TV monitors above and on it, it is also illuminated by a ring of adjustable lamp fixtures that surround it. *Harrah's Carnival Corner, Las Vegas.*

Incandescent bulbs can be set into recessed high-hat fixtures in the ceiling, clustered in chandeliers, or hung as droplights. They can be mounted into housings that ride back and forth on ceiling tracks, and can be directed or focused on merchandise or displays. Bare bulbs, silver-bottomed bulbs, 5-inch globe-like bulbs, or tiny, round complexion bulbs can be decoratively lined up, clustered, or "polka dotted" on the ceiling to please the eye, add charm to the design scheme, and "stroke" the merchandise.

High-Intensity Discharge (HID) Lighting

The **HID** lamp, which is very energy efficient, is becoming a strong contender in the field of general, overall

Figure 4.7   The ceiling is blocked with a pattern of 2′ by 2′ fluorescent fixtures that provide the ambient light. Adjustable incandescent spotlights move along the decorative ceiling track to bring accent light where desired. *Hecht's Short Pump, Virginia. Design: Pavlik Design Group.*

store lighting, in some cases replacing the fluorescent with its long and readily apparent fixtures. HIDs are relatively small in size (compared to fluorescent lamps) and will, like incandescents, provide shadows and highlights.

The mercury-type HID may be too green, the metal halide type may appear too blue, and the sodium type is quite yellow, but new developments are producing warmer and more flattering types of light. General Electric's Multi-Vapor IT is an improved metal halidetype lamp that produces a light similar to a standard cool-white fluorescent, which is satisfactory in some areas. It is still cooler and bluer than an incandescent lamp, however. Westinghouse has a high-pressure sodium lamp (HPS), Ceramalux 4, which works well at the warm end of the color wheel, but it is still yellower than an incandescent lamp.

Incandescent spotlighting can be used to accent and highlight with HID overall lighting, but may require col-ored filters (like a pale, "daylite" filter) to go with a MultiVapor II arrangement so that the different types of light do not jar each other. The Ceramalux 4 provides a warm ambience and mixes well with warm white deluxe fluorescent or with regular incandescent. However, since HID lamps do provide so much light, they are best used in areas where the ceiling is at least 15 feet high; otherwise, they will create an excessively bright and sharply lit selling floor.

Secondary or Accent Lighting

Flat, shadowless, overall lighting can create a lethargic and boring selling floor. Glare or overly bright, strong light can be irritating and a detriment to selling. **Shadows** and **highlights** are necessary; they can delight, intrigue, and pique the imagination. Sparkle and shimmer

Figure 4.8 An HID lamp provides illumination with reduced energy consumption by means of an electric current passing through any of several assorted gases. The most common types include mercury vapor lamp, metal halide lamp, sodium vapor lamp.

can stimulate and titillate. A selling floor and especially a display need changes from light to dark, from highlights to shadows. They need flash and sparkle and should make the viewer's eye travel over the area. **Secondary or accent lighting** should accomplish all of this.

Secondary lighting devices can be "candle-lit" chandeliers, wall sconces that suggest warmth and elegance with only a minimum of actual light, lights on a track that serve to supply extra light where it is needed, and hidden lights that wash a wall with light or color and beckon the customer into the department for a closer look. Secondary lighting can also diffuse a ledge area with a glow or an aura of light. It can be a spotlight on a display or the light in a case or under a counter.

Figure 4.9 Dropped ceilings mark off particular areas in a department or specialty store and the shapes and forms on the floor may echo the geometric designs. Exposed and hidden fluorescents are used here as well as recessed incandescents in the dropped shapes. Adjustable incandescent spotlights appear on the tracks attached to the overhead forms. *Marshall Field, Chicago.*

Incandescent bulbs—from tiny bee and twinkle lights, to small candle-like or complexion bulbs, and on up to full-sized globe, pear, or reflector-type bulbs—are most frequently used for secondary lighting. The long showcase or "sausage" lamp is an incandescent that somewhat resembles a small fluorescent tube in shape, but it gives off a warm light and fits, almost invisibly, into display cases or under shelves.

When lamps are hidden behind valances or recessed under grids or baffles, and warmer colors are not needed, fluorescent lights may work effectively to provide secondary lighting. However, incandescent secondary lights will add highlights, provide shadows, mold and dimensionalize the merchandise, and flatter the customer's complexion.

Accent or focal lighting not only highlights the product or the group of merchandise, but also makes it stand out from its surroundings. Under the accent light, the color of the merchandise appears sharper, and more brilliant, the textures are defined, and the details are brought into prominence. The strong, focused light of the accent lamp can make a product stand out in a highly illuminated selling floor or in a sunlit window. It works most effectively when the surrounding area is low-keyed and rather dim so that the accent light seems even more brilliant by contrast. Incandescent spotlights are used as accent or highlighting lamps in the showing and selling areas, in display windows, on platform and ledge displays, and on island set-ups.

MR16 and MR11

The **MR16** and the **MR11** (miniature reflector) are two of the newest and most popular accent/focal lamps currently in use. They are miniature, low-voltage tungsten-halogen lamps that emit sharp bright light and produce a color balance that comes close to sunlight. The 75-watt MR16 lamp will provide a more brilliant light than a traditional 150-watt incandescent spotlight, and will illuminate merchandise at four or five times the ambient level of other lamps. Colors appear truer under the MR16 and MR11 and, once the low-voltage lamps have been installed, they are efficient, relatively inexpensive to operate, compact, and clean. Also, because they are low voltage, they produce much less heat than the incandescent lamps; they burn cooler and do not harm the merchandise.

The popularity of the MR16 is based, in part, on its compactness, its 2-inch diameter, and the efficient low-voltage tungsten-halogen light source. When first introduced they did require a rather bulky transformer, but with advancing technology and the development of lighter and smaller "solid-state" transformers, the MR lamps are indeed smaller, lighter, and more compact. The MR11 is only $1^3/8$ inches in diameter and requires a much smaller lamp housing than the MR16, which is still very small when compared to the standard PAR incandescent lamp.

The MR16 and MR11 are available in a variety of beamspread widths: from very narrow spots at 7 to "floods" at 30. The MR16 is available in 20-, 42-, 50- and 75-watt versions, while the MR11 is currently limited to 12 watts for the narrow spot and 20 watts for the wider beamspread. There are optional attachments for the front of the unit, such as projector lenses to "frame" an object, steel-cut pattern templates to create decorative shadows on walls or objects, and attachments to "wash" the wall with light. There are also special diffusion lenses to feather the light beyond the edges of the beamspread and lenses in gentle colors to balance the tungsten-halogen light with incandescent lights that may be used in the same area.

Purchasing and installing the lamps and the housings for them are expensive, but the results are worth the investment because they do burn cool, have a long life, and are very energy efficient.

Colored Lights and Filters

Just as pigments can be mixed to produce new colors, **colored lights** can be mixed to create new and different color effects. The **primary colors of light** are red, green (not yellow as with pigments), and blue.

White light can be produced by mixing the three primary colors of light. Red and blue light together will produce a magenta or a purplish red. Blue and green will combine to form cyan or cyan-blue, which is actually a bright blue-green. Red and green create a yellowish or amber light. Thus, the **secondary colors of light** are magenta, cyan, and amber.

The display person should be especially concerned with the mixing of colored light on solid, pigmented surfaces. This is usually accomplished with colored **filters** and gels. A red filter placed over a white light on a white or light neutral surface will turn that surface red. The red filter absorbs all the blue and green light waves present in the white light that is going through the red filter; only the red wavelengths will pass through to the painted surface. A blue filter will absorb the red and green wavelengths, producing a blue light on the white painted area.

Tables 4.1 and 4.2 show the effects of different colors of light on various pigment colors. There are, however, many colored glass filters and plastic gelatins on the market, as well as shades and tints of these colors, that subtly can add to the intensity of a color or gently neutralize some of its intensity.

There are all sorts of pinks and "blush" tones available to warm up skin tones or suggest a sunset. There are ambers that go down to pale straw and strained sunlight. A "daylite" filter is a clear, light blue that will fill in an area with the suggestion of a spring day or will chill shredded styrofoam with icy blue shadows. The green gels go from the pastel yellow-greens to the deep atmospheric blue-greens, or cyans.

In most cases, lighter tints are usually used on displays to enrich the color presentation without appreciably changing the actual color. Strong, deep colors are used to create atmosphere—the dramatic side or back lighting, the mood lighting of a window or ledge display, for example. Deeper-colored lights are mainly reserved for modeling and shaping the merchandise by adding color to the shadows and folds as well as by reflecting color from one surface to another.

A word of advice for the display person on the use of light on skin tones—both of mannequins and customers: Green light should be avoided. It plays havoc with the color of cheeks and lips and with blond and red hair, as well as enhancing every skin blemish. Cyan is even worse, although it may work for Halloween or an "out-of-this-world" presentation. Pinks and rose tints are usually most becoming to most skin tones, from the palest white to the darkest browns, and they enhance the warm colors in merchandise.

Planning Store Lighting

Shoppers respond to light, to the quality of light and the color of light, to the brightness and intensity of light. Light makes the colors of a shop come alive and creates the overall ambience. It leads and directs the shoppers around the selling space and makes them stop to see the highlighted displays or merchandise. Light also forms the shadows that add depth and texture to the retail setting and to the merchandise. With the great variations in state and city codes, the ever-increasing desire for an upscale image, and the specialization of areas on the selling floor, a trained lighting specialist is required to perform the lighting magic needed to bring the store to life.

Table 4.1   This chart shows the effects of colored lights on primary and secondary colored pigments. For example, a green colored light on a red fabric or on a red painted surface will turn the red into a "muddy" brown, while a red light on a green surface will make the green appear dark gray.

| | | Primary Colored Pigments | | | Secondary Colored Pigments | | |
		Red	Blue	Yellow	Green	Orange	Violet
Primary Colored Lights	**RED**	Brilliant Red	Brown–Purple	Almost White	Dark Gray	Pale Orange	Rich Wine
	BLUE	Violet	Bright Blue	Green	Turquoise	Gray–Brown	Blue–Violet
	GREEN	Brown	Turquoise	Yellow–Green	Bright Green	Old Gold	Dark Gray–Green
Secondary Colored Lights	**AMBER**	Orange–Red	Dark Gray	Pale Yellow	Gray–Green	Bright Orange	Brown
	CYAN	Gray–Brown	Blue–Green	Light Green	Blue–Green	Brown	Deep Cold Blue
	MAGENTA	Lake or Cerise	Ultramarine Blue	Orange	Blue–Violet	Bright Red–Orange	Red–Violet

Table 4.2   This chart shows the effects of different lamps on painted surfaces of various colors. A similar change takes place on similarly colored merchandise displayed under these various lamps.

Paint Color	Approximate Reflectance Factor	Incandescent Filament	Warm White Fluorescent	White Fluorescent	Standard Cool White Fluorescent	Daylight Fluorescent	Warm White Deluxe Fluorescent	Cool White Deluxe Fluorescent
Cherry-Red	.13	Brilliant Orange-Red	Pale Orange-Red	Pale Orange-Red	Yellowish Red	Light Red	Orange-Red	Good Match
Orchid	.44	Light Pink	Pale Purplish Pink	Gray-Pink	Light Pink	Good Match (Grayer)	Pale Pink	Light Pink
Plum	.04	Deep Orange-Red	Dull Reddish Brown	Dark Brown	Light Reddish Brown	Deep Bluish Purple	Reddish Purple	Darker Brown
Chestnut-Brown	.19	Medium Yellowish Brown	Light Yellow-Brown	Gray-Brown	Light Brownish Gray	Light Gray	Dark Brown	Good Match
Peach	.58	Pinkish Yellow	Light Yellowish Pink	Light Yellowish Pink	Very Light Pink	Fair Match (Lighter)	Light Orange	Good Match (Yellower)
Orange	.44	Bright Orange	Light Orange-Yellow	Pale Yellow	Light Yellow	Gray-Yellow	Yellowish Orange	Good Match
Canary-Yellow	.44	Orange-Yellow	Fair Match (Sharper)	Greenish Yellow	Light Yellow	Fair Match	Good Match (Brighter)	Good Match
Light Yellow	.58	Vivid Orange-Yellow	Medium Yellow	Medium Yellow	Light Bright Yellow	Light Greenish Yellow	Deep Yellow	Bright Yellow
Light Blue	.46	Light Yellowish Green	Pale Grayish Blue	Weak Greenish Blue	Blue-Gray	Fair Match (Lighter)	Grayish Blue	Grayish Blue
Medium Blue	.23	Blue-Green	Light Gray-Blue	Purplish Blue	Light Gray-Blue	Fair Match (Lighter)	Purple-Blue	Reddish Blue
Silver-Gray	.97	Light Yellow-Gray	Light Yellowish Gray	Light Brownish Gray	Very Light Gray	Bluish Gray	Yellowish Gray	Light Gray

David A. Mintz of David A. Mintz, Inc., has lighted over 40 million square feet of retail space for many of this country's largest department and specialty stores. According to Mintz, "Perception is what the lighting actually enhances. It is the customer's perceived attitude towards lighting and merchandise." Lower levels of illumination usually suggest to the upscale customer better or more expensive merchandise. "Retailers too, feel that incandescent light means that softer, finer merchandise is being offered. However, a light level that is too low may not necessarily make a shop look elegant and exclusive;

it might just look dull and gloomy. Mintz personally opts for an "upbeat, brighter rather than duller luminosity in the retail ambience." In low light, people tend to whisper in hushed tones and move as though they were in a museum. The merchandise becomes untouchable and remote. The shopper can be inhibited and that's not good for selling.

Properly lighting a store requires a palette of lamps and light sources to create the total effect. It requires incandescent plus fluorescent lights, tungsten-halogen lamps, and even novelties like neon stripes. According to

Mintz there is no single "ideal" or "best" lighting design for a store. There are too many variables: the changing feeling, texture, and look of the merchandise, the location of a department and what type of merchandise it carries, how the adjacent areas or shops relate to one another. The lighting design is also affected by neighboring establishments (especially in malls), the nature of the clientele and their perceptions, the colors and textures that comprise the decorative scheme, the height and type of ceiling.

With respect to which light source and types of fixtures are best for a store, Mintz feels that the choice of light source is determined by many considerations, including the merchandise for which there are certain guidelines. Cosmetic areas are almost always lighted with incandescents; warm, glowing, and flattering light. Better dresses, gowns, and designer shops usually use incandescents, but not always. Men's wear areas are often filled with fluorescents for the general light but supplemented with incandescents or low-voltage tungsten-halogen lamps for accents or focal light. The standards, codes, and energy restrictions are all integral elements in the lighting design. The lights and types of lamps can be changed to accommodate these codes and standards.

Figure 4.10 Floating ceiling disks bring down the ceiling height in this two story area of a junior department. The focusable incandescent lamps are integrated into these disks as well as used on the tracks that radiate out from this superstructure. The merchandise areas beneath the mezzanine are illuminated by track lighting. *Litio, El Palacio de Herrera, Mexico City, Mexico. Design: Pavlik Design Group.*

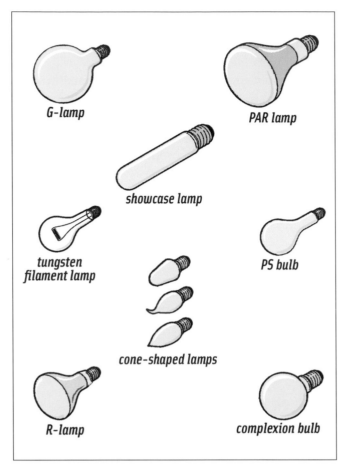

G-lamp

PAR lamp

showcase lamp

tungsten
filament lamp

PS bulb

cone-shaped lamps

R-lamp

complexion bulb

Figure 4.11   Here are some examples of the variety of shapes and sizes of incandescent bulbs (not drawn to scale).

Mintz suggests that visual merchandisers use lamps that will be similar to the light ambience that the objects will ultimately be used in; for example, furs are used out-of-doors, refrigerators are in kitchens, gowns in incandescent lighted rooms. "It's very important to have different lights from different sources for different looks. The selling space needs variety and interest, but try to minimize the number of lamp types used so that the store will maintain the established light design by replacing burnt-out lamps with the same original lamp for color, light and wattage."

Joseph A. DiBernardo, IAID, of J. D. A. Lighting Design, Inc., has been extensively involved in lighting hotels, restaurants, and public spaces and brings a new perspective to the lighting of retail spaces. DiBernardo sees lighting as a vital part of the store's image. "The department store visit is usually of short duration. It isn't like

you live there or spend many hours there. The lighting has to get the customers immediately, grab their interest, hold their attention, and show them what they should see."

"We use accent lights to define selling spaces, or the aisles, and in some cases we may use the accent lights to light up the entire store." Some shops today are almost completely illuminated by the MR16 low-voltage tungsten-halogen lamps. DiBernardo also feels the fluorescents are a part of retail lighting. How much they are used and how they are used depends on the fashion level or attitude of the store and the type and class of the merchandise. He will use them to light surfaces, to wash walls or ceilings, or for cove lighting. He also likes to keep them recessed and inconspicuous, and he uses them for indirect lighting.

Store lighting should be flashier and more exciting and stimulating than home lighting. The lighting designer's job is to create an interesting space rather than simply light up the floor, walls, and fixtures. When lighting a selling floor, there should be variations of light intensity from shop to shop, from area to area, from a low-keyed "living room" ambience to a brilliant, hightech attitude. The shopper seeks warmth and security, and the smart retailer knows that a customer who looks good in the store mirror will buy the garment. In those areas where the shopper and the garment come together, in front of mirrors, in fitting rooms, in places where the real selling takes place, the lighting is vital and must be carefully balanced between animate and inanimate objects.

Lighting is what shows, directs, points out, and makes selling possible. It is part of the store's image; it shapes the customer's perception of the store's fashion attitude and the value of the merchandise being offered. Lighting must be planned and lighting experts and consultants help with the planning.

Suggestions for Using Light Effectively

1. Avoid bright, white lights directly on a mannequin's face, elbows, or shoes. Save the brightest lights for the merchandise, and avoid anything that will detract from the merchandise.
2. Use colored light to create the right setting for the merchandise. Save it for props and backgrounds. If

Figure 4.12 Neon can be a bright and colorful accent in a store's lighting plan—especially in junior and casual areas. Here neon tubes are used to outline the dropped ceiling over the main aisle of the shop. The neon design replays the floor pattern of the aisle below.

colored light is used on a garment to intensify the color, stay with the pastel filters: pale pinks for the reds and red-violets, pale straw for the yellows and oranges, daylight blue for the cool colors, and nile green for the greens.

3. It is more effective to light across a display rather than directly down on it. Direct downlighting can create unpleasant and unattractive shadows. The upper left light can be directed over to the lower right side of the display; the upper right light is then directed over to the lower left. This creates a crossover of light, a more even, more diffused light, and nullifies areas in the display space that are too bright or too dark.

4. The lighting in a window display should be checked at night. Many imperfections, such as wrinkles, are more apparent under the artificial light when the softening influence of daylight does not enter the window. Colored lights will also look different when there is no other source of light with which to contend. What may have seemed perfect during the daylight hours, at night may appear harsh or garish. It is also advisable to check that the lights are not "flooding over" into the street—into the eyes of passersby and the road traffic.

5. There is nothing particularly attractive about electric wires unless they are meant to be part of the decorative scheme. Find ways to "lose" them—hide and disguise them.

6. Display lights are expensive to use. They use up energy. It is wise to set up a timer device that will automatically turn off all lights sometime during the night

Figure 4.13 Droplights over the cash/wrap counter bring attention to the location of this service area in the multi-level shop. They add pattern and interest as well. *Diesel, San Francisco. Design: Checkland-Kindleysides.*

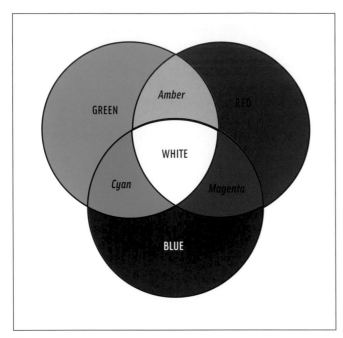

Figure 4.14 Mixing colored light.

how to blend and mix the new technology with existing units.

There are new compact fluorescent lamps available today that emit a warm and glowing light much like an incandescent. These new lamps are relatively inexpensive to use and some stores are replacing the more expensive to burn incandescents with the compact fluorescents and freeing up "energy to burn" money for more spotlights, low-voltage tungsten halogens, and HID lamps. Also economical and efficient are the Phillips Master Color Metal Halide lamps PAR 20, PAR 30, and PAR 38. The crisp white light also has a warm temperature (3,000 K) and an excellent color rendition (CRI 80 to 85). These lamps can be very effective in retail areas. They have a high efficiency (90 to 95 LPW) and low wattages (35 to 100), which result in reduced energy consumption, economical operation, and a long life (up to 9,000 hours), which in turn reduces maintenance costs.

Just as you would seek help from a professional health care provider if you had an ailment, so should you consult with a professional lighting designer/planner when it comes to lighting a retail space. The retailer needs help in planning not only the most effective use of energy required by law, but also the best way to use the energy to enhance the merchandise presentation and displays and create the desired image for the store.

Let there be light: the best light you can afford. This is not the place to economize.

after the street traffic has diminished and the store lighting no longer serves any purpose of display or image.

Each month seems to bring new lighting products and techniques into the marketplace. It takes a lighting specialist to keep up with the new products and understand

---

Light and Lighting: A Recap

- In an open-back window, the lighting up front must be strong enough to keep the shopper's eye from going past the display into the interior of the store.

- In a closed-back window, the display person can use a range of lighting effects, including colored lights and light filters, to create a more theatrical display.

- The most effective sources for window display lighting are incandescent lighting and MR16s.

- When planning a store's interior lighting, a variety of light sources and lamps can be used to create a particular interior lighting "palette," and to draw shoppers to various areas within the store.

- General or primary lighting is the overall ceiling light of a selling area. It does not include the accent or decorative lighting.

- Secondary lighting is the accent and decorative lighting: chandeliers, sconces, wall washers, indirect lighting, spotlights, and lights under shelves, in cases, and in counters.

- Fluorescent lighting is efficient and relatively inexpensive to install and maintain. The tubes are available in a wide range of "white" light, from cool bluish to warm white deluxe, which has more of a peach tone. Smaller tubes can be used in showcases, under shelves, and behind baffles as wall washers.

- Incandescent bulbs produce warmer and more flattering light than the fluorescent, but emit more heat. The lamps do not burn as long or as efficiently as the fluorescents. They are available in a wide range of sizes, shapes, and wattages. The lamps can be decorative as well as useful. The incandescent spotlight is a display "must."

- The HID lamp is an efficient and relatively inexpensive light source that is being color improved for use inside the store.

- Different light sources can be used on the same selling floor. It is possible to highlight and accent a fluorescent primary lighting scheme with incandescent secondary lighting.

- White light is composed of a rainbow of colors of different wavelengths, from violet to red.

- The primary colors of light are red, blue, and green.

- The secondary colors of light are magenta, cyan, and amber.

- A colored filter produces a particular color of light by filtering out or absorbing all the other colors in the white light except the color of the filter or gel.

Questions for Review and Discussion

1. What is the relationship between color and light? Explain your answer by detailing the reason why when looking at a red dress, we see red, rather than some other color.

2. Why can wavelengths of light be seen by humans while we cannot see ultraviolet light, X-rays, gamma rays, infrared light, and radio waves?

3. Explain how you might plan lighting for a men's wear store that is shallow and wide, and where a great deal of natural light floods the space.

4. Define general or primary lighting and provide examples of this category of lighting.

5. Provide examples of the differing effects that various types of lighting have on merchandise and skin tones.

6. Highlight the advantages and disadvantages of incandescent lighting.

7. Why has it been said that incandescent lights do the "selling" in the store?

8. What are the special qualities of HID lighting?

9. What types of light sources would you select for a lingerie department or shop? Why?

10. Why have MR16 and MR11 lamps gained favor in visual merchandising and display?

11. What advice would you give to someone regarding the use of colored lights in display?

12. In selecting the types of lighting and light fixtures for a store, what factors should be taken into consideration?

13. Where should the brightest light be focused within a display?

14. What adjustments, if any, should be made to the lighting within a display window for day and night?

CHAPTER FIVE

Types of Display and Display Settings

AFTER YOU HAVE READ THIS CHAPTER,
YOU WILL BE ABLE TO DISCUSS:

- The four major types of display.
- Promotional and institutional displays.
- Five categories of display settings.
- The purpose of buildup presentations in display.

TYPES OF DISPLAYS AND DISPLAY SETTINGS: TRADE TALK

abstract setting
buildup display
environmental setting
fantasy setting
institutional display
line-of-goods display
one-item display
promotional display
realistic setting
related merchandise display
semirealistic or "vignette" setting
variety or assortment display

Fashions change and so do the ways in which fashion is presented. During the "Golden Age" of display—back in the 1950s and 1960s—window displays were events or happenings and shoppers were treated to spectacular trims that are now only seen at Christmas. Shoppers couldn't wait to walk down Main Street to see the newest extravaganza in the department store and specialty store windows. Mannequins were stately, glamourous, and beautiful beyond belief. They were models of perfection: none of your "girl-next-door" looks or "Cinderella-before-the-ball" types.

In the 1970s and early 1980s, such spectaculars gave way to "street theater": shock 'em, sock-it-to-'em displays meant to disturb or agitate the viewer. Mannequins developed "warts"—bumpy noses, eyes too close together, squints—and they took on spastic poses to compliment the "way out" fashions of the moment.

In the 1980s and 1990s, displays became a matter of "hang 'em," "drape 'em," or "lay 'em on the ground." While today's mannequins may make a rare guest appearance, more often we see hangers, drapers, forms, and torsos and a sameness of presentation as we walk down Main Streets or cover the aisles inside malls and shopping centers. Closed-back windows have given way to open-back windows and "propping" is sometimes limited to a plant.

But—display is not dead nor is it dying. It is simply changing and display persons and/or visual merchandisers are learning to accept and even triumph over budget cuts and staff cuts and even over the loss of display windows, the production facilities, and the magical lighting systems that once turned a display space into a theater. What has not changed is the fact that shoppers, now more than ever, are looking for entertainment in the retail store and that the entertainment is often to be found in the displays. The displays have, in some stores, disappeared from the windows only to revive and thrive inside the store on platforms, on ledges, on T-walls, or around the fascias over the stocked merchandise. Though it is only one of the techniques used to bring attention to the new and featured merchandise, "humor" is more and more frequently being used to deliver the store's fashion image statement. It has become a significant and important element in visual language.

A humorous or amusing display says something up front about the store and about its customers. The humor can be broad and obvious or subtle and clever. It can be a "belly laugh," a giggle, a titter, or even a knowing smirk. With humor, we reach out to our particular customer and say—"You'll get this one!" Americans have a long history of appreciating humor—we are a fun-loving nation that would rather smile than sigh, laugh than cry—and it is a great approach to effective displays, especially since improvisation is what display is all about.

Types of Displays

The primary purposes of displays are to present and to promote. A display is at its best when it simply shows a color, an item, a collection, or just an idea. Types of displays include the following:

- One-item display
- Line-of-goods display
- Related merchandise display
- Variety or assortment display

One-Item Display

A **one-item display** is just that—the showing and advancement of a single garment or any single item. It might be a gown designed by a top designer, a one-of-a-kind piece of ceramic or jewelry, or a new automobile.

Line-of-Goods Display

A **line-of-goods display** is one that shows only one type of merchandise (all blouses, all skirts, or all pots and pans), although they may be in a variety of designs or colors. A window display showing three or four mannequins wearing daytime dresses of assorted colors, styles, and prints would be an example of a line-of-goods display. However, for a more effective presentation, and

Figure 5.1 In a one-of-a-kind display a single garment or product is featured. It becomes special, unique, and thus, more desirable. In this elegant vignette setting, the large mirror and chair suggest a rich and luxurious room, and the mirror also provides the shopper on the street with a look at the front of the gown worn by the mannequin. *Ralph Lauren, Michigan Avenue, Chicago.*

for better comprehension and acceptance by the shopper, there should be some connection or relevance indicated as to why these three or four articles are being shown together. They could all be designed by the same designer, or created with the same fabric or print, or they could all feature a common theme.

Related Merchandise Display

In a **related merchandise display,** separates, accessories, or other items that "go together" are displayed because they are meant to be used together, because they are the same color, or because they share an idea or theme. It could be an "Import Window" where all the items are from the same country (from clothes to handicrafts, to kitchen utensils to furniture, and so on). It might be a color promotion where all the clothing in one window is red, and the next display setup may consist of all-red household supplies and hardgoods. That presentation may be followed by a room setting in which red is the dominant color. Or, it could be a display of lizard shoes, bags, and belts—all related because they are made of lizard skin. Red, white, and blue-striped hats, sweaters, scarves, and stockings would be a related merchandise display. The items go together and reinforce each other.

Variety or Assortment Display

A **variety or assortment display** is a potpourri of anything and everything. It is a collection of unrelated items that happen to be sold in the same store. It can be work shoes, silk stockings, tea kettles, Hawaiian print shirts, wicker chairs, red flannel nightgowns, and cowboy boots. It is a melange of odds and ends, a sampling of the merchandise contained within.

Figure 5.2 A line of denims is shown in this amusing display where a pair of headless mannequins support a half form dressed in denim jeans. Pairs of shoes "walk" about on the white floor and the blue mylar panel visually cuts the window in half. The viewer becomes focused on the frieze of jeans that go around the white walls of the window. *Barneys Co-Op, New York.*

Figure 5.3 This is a fun "mix and match" display and Valentine's Day is the theme. Assorted heart-splattered garments are shown in a variety of combinations along with red accents to show how the related pieces can be worn. Blowups of personal want ads appear on the back wall and gift ideas are shown in the built out shadow boxes. *Saks Fifth Avenue, New York.*

Figure 5.5 China, glassware, and decorative tableware are beautifully arranged by color into a harmonious display that includes a variety of products to be found within the store. The aqua/green theme is carried through to the linens as well. The budding branches break the dynamic symmetry of the composition and add a flush of complementary pink to the cool palette. *Crate & Barrel, Michigan Avenue, Chicago.*

Figure 5.4 Chanel's tops, jackets, and skirts, in a unique black and white patterned fabric, are shown as two different outfits on the headless mannequins. The black and white motif is further fortified with decorative cutouts of Chanel inspired logos and signature pieces. These are applied to the folding screen with clear Lucite panels for a most unusual effect. *Chanel, Fifth Avenue, New York.*

Promotional vs. Institutional Displays

A **promotional display** can be a one-item, a line-of-goods, a related merchandise, and even, for storewide sales, a variety type of display. The display advances or emphasizes a particular concept, trend, or item. It promotes! As an example: Father's Day is coming up and is to be promoted by the store. A theme has been developed for advertising the event. That theme will be carried out in newspapers, on radio and television, and the displays (windows and interiors) will tie in with and advance that

theme. If the store's promotion is "Dad—Our Kind of Man," then the displays would be related. In one window there could be a display for "Dad, the Athlete," with everything from active sportswear to sporting equipment, sports magazines, and even spectator sports items. Another window could have gifts for "Dad, the Connoisseur," consisting of a collection of dress-up clothes, classical records, wine, gourmet foods, and exotic cooking equipment. Each different "Dad" would be gifted with a variety of merchandise based on a particular type of man.

A sale can also be the basis for a promotional display. It might be a storewide sale, an anniversary sale, a pre- or post-holiday sale, or an end-of-season sale. As another example, if blue is the "in" spring color and the store is investing heavily in blue merchandise, then blue should be promoted inside and outside the store.

Often, a one-item type of display is used to promote the store's fashion image. The presentation is designed to tell the shopper where the store stands on fashion trends, what it thinks its customers want to look like, and to whom it is trying to appeal. So, even though a particular outfit is not being promoted as an outfit, the display is promotional in that it is advancing the store as something special.

An **institutional display,** on the other hand, promotes an idea rather than an item or a product. The display presents the store as a worthwhile and interested member of the community. If a national hero dies, a window may be set aside to honor his or her memory, and no saleable merchandise will be included in that display. If the Community Chest has a drive, or any other worthwhile charity is in need of support, and the store promotes the organization and all the good it does, without including store merchandise, that would be considered an institutional display.

The local opera company or symphony orchestra may be starting its new season and need more subscribers. The store might promote this cause in a small window or shadow box. Remember, this is not the same as using posters and paraphernalia of a visiting ballet company to provide a background for a window filled with ruffled petticoats or ballerina-like dance dresses. That is a good example of the use of a current event or what is new in town to set the scene for store merchandise, but it is not purely an institutional display.

An institutional display helps further the store's image. It is a sign of goodwill toward its neighbors and the neighborhood. It shows the store as a concerned party interested in the welfare of the community. The big Christmas extravaganza, full of animation, fantasy, and the delight of children eight to eighty, may not sell any special merchandise, but it certainly sells the store. People may travel from all over to see a store's institutional Christmas windows and, often, the "tourists" end up inside after having seen the "free show" outside.

Types of Display Settings

In presenting any display, there are some basic approaches the visual merchandiser can take to set the scene for the merchandise or the concept to be sold. These approaches include the following:

- Realistic setting
- Environmental setting
- Semirealistic setting
- Fantasy setting
- Abstract setting

Realistic Setting

A **realistic setting** is essentially the depiction of a room, area, or otherwise recognizable locale, reinterpreted in the allotted display area, either in the windows or inside the store. The realistic setting is best controlled and most effective in a fully enclosed display window. Here, the display person can do a miniature stage setting. He or she can simulate depth and dimension and use color and light with great effect—all viewed, as planned, from the front, through a large plate-glass window. The scene can be a restaurant with wallpapered walls, carpeted floors, matching tables and chairs, flowers, ferns and potted palms, china and crystal, candles and chandeliers. It seems so real, so complete, so recognizable that the viewer can relate to it. Showing formal or semiformal clothing, for example, in this setting would be very appropriate.

Sometimes the cleverness and fastidiousness given to the details of the setting can work against the presentation of the merchandise. The viewer might get so involved in the settings and the background that the merchandise, the "star," is upstaged by the "set."

At certain times and in certain stores, however, a realistic setting can be most effective. Some holidays are just right for a true-to-life presentation. On Christmas morning, for example, mannequins wearing assorted robes and loungewear might be busily engaged in unwrapping more of the same merchandise. On New Year's Eve, a gala party is the perfect setting for gala clothes. Thanksgiving is a time to show tableware, while the family is "dressed" for dinner. Import promotions can be attention-getting displays when the settings are realistic, though foreign. People do want to see how other people live.

When realism is the thing, scale is of the utmost importance. The display area should not be weighted down with props or elements so large that the scale of the setting shrinks by comparison. A realistic setting requires the careful blending of color, textures, shapes, and the proper lighting to keep the background at a proper distance. It must still be attractive enough to be the "come on" for the merchandise presentation.

Environmental Setting

This is a merchandise presentation that shows an assortment of various related items in a setting depicting

Figure 5.6 It's a man's world and this display underscores the statement. The furniture and furnishings provide an idealized setting for successful men who know how to dress. There is also a bit of a challenging mystery here for the viewer to solve. *Bergdorf Goodman, Men's Shop, Fifth Avenue, New York.*

how and where they may eventually be used. In this form of realistic setting, the "background" is actually the "foreground" because the details that make up the realistic set are actually the merchandise being promoted in the display.

An example of an **environmental setting** is a display depicting a corner of a room with a bed, made up with matching sheets, pillow cases, and comforter; a window with coordinated curtains and drapes; and an area rug of the appropriate color and design. A chair near the bed has a robe casually tossed over it, and there is a pair of slippers on the floor. The setting also includes a bedside table, on which is an arrangement of frames, boxes, a lamp, and a clock. Everything on display in this setting is for sale in the store.

Semirealistic Setting

When space and budget do not allow the time or effort for a fully realistic presentation, the display person may opt for the very popular, **semirealistic or "vignette" setting.** The visual merchandiser presents the essence, the tip of the iceberg, and leaves the rest to the active imagination of the shopper. In many ways, this is a more effective but simpler approach to merchandise settings. The merchandise and mannequins do not have to compete with the "look-at-me" cleverness of the down-to-the-last-detail setting.

As examples of displays in a semirealistic setting: In a predominantly black or dark gray window (walls, floors, and side walls), imagine a small table covered with a red and white checkered cloth, two bentwood chairs with cane seats, a candle stuck into a straw-encased Chianti bottle already heavy with rivulets of melted wax, some breadsticks in a water tumbler, a brass hat stand, a potted palm. Couldn't this be any romantic, old-fashioned, neighborhood, Italian restaurant? Or, simply, a palm tree dripping heavy with green leaves, a mound of sand, an open, boldly striped beach umbrella—anybody would know it was some faraway island in the sun. Who needs to look beyond this into the nebulous, no-color, no-detail background?

On ledges, in island displays, and in store windows with open backs, a semirealistic setting works most effectively. It is theater-in-the-round, but the viewer does not go beyond the fragment being shown. To the display person, it means getting to the heart of the setting, presenting that "heart," and then fleshing it out only as necessary. A park bench, a tree, some pigeons or a squirrel, the hint of sky, some grass and gravel—it's a park! An awning swagged off the dark back wall, a small metal table for two, two ironwork chairs, a bottle of wine and two glasses, a suggestion of a kiosk, over to the side, bedecked with French posters—it's romance, it's April in Paris!

Fantasy Setting

A **fantasy setting** can be as detailed or as suggestive as the display person, budget, and time permit. It is creative, it does require thought, energy, and lots of planning, but it can be very rewarding.

It may be surrealistic or just a "touch of the poet"; it is a strange "never-never" land, a fairyland, Oz, an enchanted forest, Alice's Wonderland. A fantasy setting can be tables on the ceiling and chairs on the wall. It can be 6-foot toadstools, or a mannequin drifting, in midair, on a magic carpet. It can be a world frozen in ice and icicles, or a trip in a spaceship to visit a family of robots. A fantasy setting can be a stairway going nowhere with a crystal chandelier to light the way, or an underwater spectacular of swimsuited mermaids and giant seashells.

These are just some examples of the touches of whimsy that can be a delightful change of pace after several realistic or semirealistic installations. A good imagination is the most important requirement.

Abstract Setting

An **abstract setting** might seem as if it would be the easiest to do, but it is often the most difficult. The least

Figure 5.7 Fantasyland—where the colors are richer and brighter, things grow bigger and bolder, and everything is picture perfect. Several of the designer's "way out" shoes have been cleverly integrated into this "never-never land." The viewer has to find them! *Stuart Weitzman, Madison Avenue, New York.*

amount of display often makes the biggest statement. In an abstract setting, the merchandise is the dominant feature and the setting supports and reinforces the message, often subliminally. For example, a viewer may look at some white ribbon streamers hanging down from an overhead grill and know that the classic gown in front of the streamers is elegant.

The abstract setting is predominantly an arrangement of lines and shapes, panels, cubes, cylinders, triangles, curves, arcs, and circles. It is like a nonrepresentational painting done in three dimensions, in various planes. The design does not really represent or look like origin. To display different dinnerware place settings, one is dealing with a group of objects that are similar in material, construction, and use, but are decidedly different in appearance. It is the difference in pattern, color, shape, and size that will make one design of dinnerware more attractive to a customer than another.

In doing a display of five, six, or more place settings or groupings of different china patterns (or pots and pans, luggage, toiletries and cosmetics, or other "related" types of merchandise), certain methods of presentation are more effective than others. The overall display must be balanced and easy to look at. There has to be a movement from grouping to grouping or item to item. Each group or item should be able to be viewed as a separate entity, somehow set apart from the others.

If, as in the case of the china, the display person is working with objects of the same general size or weight, he or she might use assorted size cubes or cylinders clustered together to create a **buildup display.** It is easy for the viewer's eye to travel upward, making a stop at each level to absorb what is being shown before moving on to the next level and the next showing. Thus, each group is separate and apart in space. Each group can be dominant as the viewer's eye climbs the setup. The topmost group, by its position, could be assumed to be the best or the most attractive—the most desirable. Therefore, if the display person wants to make all the items equally "best"

Figure 5.8 This abstract composition is made up of simple shapes and forms that support the main theme. The rectangular framed pictures and graphics form an interesting design around the two headless forms center. One is further accentuated by the frame that outlines it. The artwork in this display was from a collection of graphics that was to be auctioned off for a charity, making this display an institutional or good-will display, as well as an effective merchandising one. *Bergdorf Goodman, Fifth Avenue, New York.*

anything in particular, but it does evoke certain responses from the viewer. An abstract setting is like a skeletal stage set in that there is form that functions. It divides the space, and the lines, shapes, and forms give a graphic message.

Buildup Display

There is a vast difference between creating a one-item or line-of-goods display and a mass display of a variety of items "related" only in use, material, color, or place of

Figure 5.9 A vignette setting suggests a time and place without fully filling in all the details or realistically reproducing the desired ambiance. Here a bed and table are more than enough to tell the viewer that this is a bedroom and the assorted linens, hardware, and home accessories are presented with imaginative flair. *Sherle Wagner, East 57th Street, New York.*

or "beautiful," the top step could be reserved for a plant, a vase filled with flowers, or any decorative or related item or prop.

The buildup itself can be a series of forms of different sizes, arranged in a straight line with each cube or cylinder butting up to the next tallest one, but all flush in front. For the sake of interest and effect, there can be a combination of bigger steps and smaller steps. In a formal or traditional arrangement, however, each step would be exactly the same increment of height (e.g., 6 inches, 9 inches) until the next plateau is reached.

Where there is sufficient depth in which to set up the display, the buildups can go from front to back as well as from side to side. It would be like creating a pyramid with risers or cubes building up from either end while, at the same time, building from a low point out in front to the high point in the center.

When displaying merchandise that is related, but of different sizes and shapes (e.g., handcrafted ceramics which includes boxes, plates, bowls, decorative figures, and maybe even urns and vases), the step or pyramid buildup will work, but it requires a very deft feel for balance, especially asymmetrical balance. It is now a matter of building up one riser (or platform) with an object on it while balancing it with another riser that has a different-sized object displayed on it. The overall height and look of the riser plus the merchandise must be visually weighted against the other riser and merchandise. It might, therefore, require a lower platform or elevation to hold a tall vase, for example, if it is to balance with a low, squat bowl on a taller riser. This asymmetrical buildup must be arranged so that the viewer's eye will still move comfortably, through the various levels, to the top.

Types of Displays and Display Settings: A Recap

- The purpose of a display is to present and promote.

- A one-item display shows only a single item.

- A line-of-goods display shows one type of merchandise, though the merchandise might vary in size or color.

- A related merchandise display shows items that are meant to be used together.

- A variety or assortment display is a combination of any items that are not related.

- A promotional display emphasizes a particular theme, for example, Father's Day.

- An institutional display promotes an idea, rather than an item or product. For example, a national hero or a community drive might be promoted in a window display. This presents the store as an interested member of the community.

- Display settings can be realistic, environmental, semirealistic, fantasy, or abstract.

- A realistic setting display is a recognizable display such as a room.

- An environmental display shows how and where various related or coordinated items can be used.

- A semirealistic setting presents the essence of a setting and leaves the rest to the imagination.

- A fantasy setting is usually suggestive, creative, and unusual.

- An abstract setting is an arrangement of lines and shapes, with the merchandise as the dominant feature.

- A buildup carries the viewer's eye from grouping to grouping by means of a combination of steps, such as a series of forms of different sizes arranged in a straight line, but all leading the eye to one point.

Questions for Review and Discussion

1. Classify the following display examples as one-item, line-of-goods, related merchandise, or variety displays.
   a. Three mannequins wearing ensembles from Liz Claiborne's new spring collection.
   b. An evening gown by Armani.
   c. A window filled with leather items including bags, jackets, caps, briefcases, and skirts.
   d. A display of small appliances from Black & Decker.
   e. A pawn shop window filled with samples of their latest wares.

2. Explain the difference between a promotional and an institutional display and provide an example of each.

3. When is it appropriate to display an abundance of a single item in a display?

4. How does a realistic display setting differ from a semirealistic display setting?

5. Describe how a fantasy setting might be achieved. What props would you use to help set the stage?

6. What is usually the most dominant feature in an abstract display? What elements can be used in the creation of abstract displays?

7. What is a buildup presentation and under what circumstances are buildups most effective?

PART TWO
WHERE TO DISPLAY

FOR RETAILERS TO BE SUCCESSFUL, they must first entice customers to enter their stores. Even before stepping through the door, customers receive their first impression regarding the retailer's character and image. The store exterior and windows must be inviting, with the intent of bringing the customer into the store to spend money. Chapters 6 and 7 focus on the store exterior and window display types and treatments found in today's malls, strip shopping centers, and downtown areas.

Counters, islands, columns, fascia—all are likely areas for store display. Locations within the store suitable for merchandise presentation are discussed in Chapter 8.

CHAPTER SIX

The Exterior of the Store

AFTER YOU HAVE READ THIS CHAPTER,
YOU WILL BE ABLE TO DISCUSS:

- Key exterior items that impact store image.
- How banners can be tied in with seasons and store promotional events.
- Advantages and disadvantages of the four major windows used in storefront design.

THE EXTERIOR OF THE STORE: TRADE TALK

    angled front
    arcade front
    awnings
    banners
    corner window
    fenestration
    marquees
    outdoor lighting
    planters
    signs
    straight front

How and where we display depends largely on the architecture and **fenestration** (window placement) of the structure, the physical layout of space, and the fixtures inside the building. First, let us consider the facade of the building and the arrangement of the display windows in the storefront design. We will follow with an in-depth survey of the various types of display windows used in retail operations, as well as the advantages and limitations inherent in each type of window.

Signs

The store's **sign,** on the outside of the building, makes the first impression on the shopper. It sets the look and image of the store. How the sign is lettered, the materials used, the style of the lettering, the color—all are important. Its size and scale, in proportion to the store's facade, the size of the building, and the signs around it, can make points for or against the store's image. Unlit or missing light bulbs are definitely minus points. Flaking paint, cracked and peeling backgrounds, and outrageous, highly luminous colors can also be minuses. The sign should be the store's "signature"—personal, original, and recognizable. It should make a statement.

Marquees

Some older stores as well as some of the very newest have **marquees,** or architectural canopies, extending out over their entrances. The marquee, a permanent awning for protection from the elements, is an integral part of the building facade. It is often cantilevered out over the street, in front of the main entrance to the store. It is similar to the porte cochere (a porch at the door of a building for sheltering persons entering and leaving carriages) of the last century, or the big signboards with running lights that used to identify movie houses and theaters in the 1940s and 1950s.

The marquee can be an exciting place to start the display of a storewide event or promotion. A "change of seasons" can be announced here. The fact that the marquee protrudes from the building line offers the advantage of increased visibility and greater prominence compared to all the other store signs from the surrounding operations. If the marquee is so designed, it could have changeable announcements (like the change of movie titls). A flat-topped marquee is an excellent place for the grouping of seasonal plants and foliage as well as larger-than-life-sized props. It is a perfect location for a giant Santa or even his sleigh and eight clamoring reindeer.

Figure 6.1 The store's name appears on the horizontal band over the display window of this two story shop on a "walking street." The giant photo blowup in the window serves as a background for the actual garments shown in front of it. *Escada, Munich, Germany.*

Outdoor Lighting

There is a whole industry involved in creating and installing **outdoor lighting** displays. The use of hundreds and hundreds of lights on building facades and canopies can be most effective for holidays and store events. The lights can be draped or swagged or wired to frames to form recognizable symbols or letters. However, this type of display does require an extra expenditure of electrical energy, and the effect of the lighting is limited to the twilight and evening hours when the store may not be open for business. In suburban operations, however, with their later operating hours, the use of lights in the evening may be especially worthwhile. Very often, the strings of lights or the framed light units are wrapped or covered with tinselly, shimmering materials that reflect light during the daylight hours. This provides some degree of decoration to the store exterior during those hours when the lights are not on or when they are barely visible.

Banners

Outdoor fabric **banners** are inexpensive and expendable, but they are colorful, eye-catching, and eye-filling devices that flutter and flap in the wind. They can be and should be changed with the seasons or the store events. A few holes, worked into the design, will allow the wind to sweep through without tearing the fabric. The banners can be hung from flagpoles, projected from the building, or hung flat against it. The same banner design, reduced in size and scale, could be hung from the marquee, between the display windows, or projecting from the columns inside the store. To be truly effective, however, the idea should not be overused. If there is always a banner flapping overhead, after a while, the shopper won't even look up. He or she will just assume it is the same "old" banner that was flapping there the week before. When a banner is used, it should be different in color, size, or shape from the one previously flown, and it should be introduced only after a decent interval has passed, for example, another season, a new promotion, a sale event.

Since logos and graphics are so important in today's scheme of image and identification, the designs used for the banners could be based on the special wrap or store bag design that was created for the season or promotion. The store's window displays could, in color and concept, reiterate the same graphic theme—but with a difference. If, for example, at Christmas, a store used an irregular gold star on a cerise and white peppermint-striped background, the same theme could be carried to the display window filled with dozens of cascading gold stars of assorted sizes, invisibly suspended. All through this book, we will constantly refer to the advantages of displays that tie in with and enhance what is going on inside the store, in the newspaper ads, on television and radio, and in the store mailings. In order to work, display should not only attract and excite; it should reinforce an idea and present dimensionally what was, until then, a flat representation.

Planters

Planters, flower boxes, and plants outside a store add to the general ambiance of the store, especially if the store is on a "concrete and glass" Main Street, with neither a leaf nor blade of grass in sight. This is a social amenity, a way the store can show its good neighborliness, its friendliness, its being part of a community.

The planters can become a part of the display scheme, with changes in the varieties and colors of the plants to go with promotions or seasons. Red geraniums could call attention to a "country-casual" display, or add color to a "red" promotion—anything from fashion to housewares—or even a spring-into-summer story. White flowers would certainly enhance any bridal setting, and mums and asters speak colorfully for fall and back to school.

Planters, set below and in front of a display window, actually dramatize the window presentation by adding greater depth to the setting. Artificial flowers and plants will do, but the real thing is so much nicer.

Awnings

Awnings add another gracious touch to the exterior of the store. Not only do they supply shelter for the shopper during inclement weather, but they also make viewing a window display more pleasant during the heat of the day.

Some display persons use the awning as a device to cut down on the glare and reflection that turn show windows into giant mirrors. However, awning users are now relying on them to add color and eye appeal to the storefront. The awning can become part of a seasonal display or announce a storewide promotion. The use of awnings is also discussed under "Closed-Back Windows" in Chapter 7.

Windows in Storefront Design

Straight Front
Straight front windows run parallel to the street. The entrance to the store may be located between a pair or a run of windows, or to one side of a single window. The windows themselves may be closed-back, open-back, or elevated.

Angled Front
With the **angled front** design, the store entrance is recessed from the street and the display windows lead back from the street to the entrance, creating an aisle for the shopper. The windows may go back at an angle to the entrance, thus becoming wider in the back than they are in the front. The back end of the window is actually on the same wall as the entrance; that wall can be completely closed, partially closed, or open-backed. Usually, in an angled front (and the arcade front, which follows), the

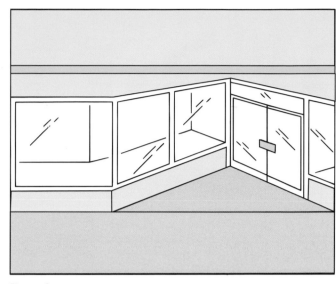

Figure 6.3 An angled storefront.

display windows are under some kind of enclosure, cutting down appreciably on glare. These windows may also be rather shallow to allow an unimpeded entrance into the store and more walk space for shoppers and potential customers.

Arcade Front
The **arcade front** consists of a series of windows with backs and three sides of glass, coming forward from the entrance wall, which is set back from the street. The win-

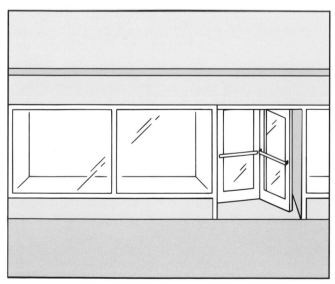

Figure 6.2 This straight storefront consists of the entrance and a bank, or series, of display windows.

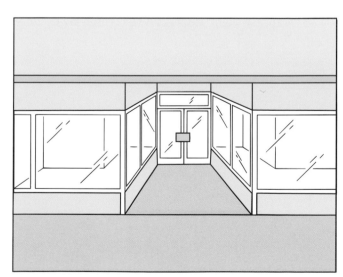

Figure 6.4 An arcaded storefront.

Figure 6.5 The open-back window provides an unhindered view into the shop. Though that openness is often desired and makes the shop seem more spacious, it does take something to make the display in the window to show up. It requires a backing, like the graphic panel, to separate the display area from the shop beyond. *Jil Sanders, Dusseldorf, Germany.*

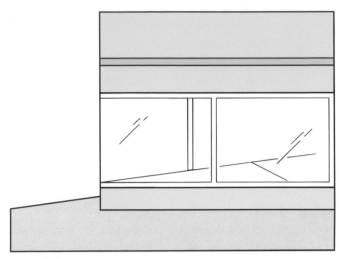

Figure 6.6 A corner window.

dows are "peninsulas" of glass attached to the store and are usually under some kind of overhead cover. The shopper enters between protruding display windows.

Corner Window

The **corner window** faces two streets that are perpendicular to each other. It is a window with a double exposure and double traffic. The corner window may be the sole display showcase for a store with an entrance near the corner of a street, or it may be the end of a run of windows.

Usually, this window will have two adjacent panes of glass meeting at right angles. The back may be open or closed. Most stores convert this type of window into a triangular plan. The two glass fronts are the "legs" of the triangle and the long back wall is the "hypotenuse." The space that is cut off from view becomes valuable storage space. Because the two windows are at right angles to each other, the viewer can almost always see the overhead and side lighting—as well as a view of other stores and signs beyond the display area. Customers can find themselves distracted by viewers looking in from the other side of the window and by mirrored backgrounds that reflect traffic lights and the signs from other stores.

The Exterior of the Store: A Recap

- Display depends largely on the architecture and fenestration (window placement) of the structure.
- The store's sign makes the first impression on the shopper.
- Stores with marquees, or architectural canopies, can use them for announcements. A flat marquee can be used for a prop display.
- Outdoor displays include lighting, banners, planters, and awnings. Strings of lights can be draped or swagged, or wired to frames to form recognizable symbols or letters.
- Banners are inexpensive and expendable, but they are colorful and eye-catching and can be changed with the seasons or store events.

- Planters, flower boxes, or plants add to a store's ambiance. Set below and in front of a display, they dramatize the window setting. If possible, the plants should be part of the display scheme, and the color of the plants can be changed according to the season or the promotion.

- Awnings add a gracious touch to a store's exterior while providing shelter from inclement weather and shade during the heat of the day. They also cut down glare and reflection.

- Straight front windows run parallel to the store.

- An angled front window is recessed from the street, and the display windows may go back from the street to the entrance, creating an "aisle" for the shopper.

- An arcade window consists of a series of windows with backs and three sides of glass, coming forward from the entrance wall, which is set back from the street.

- A corner window faces two streets that are perpendicular to each other. Usually it will have two adjacent panes of glass meeting at right angles.

Questions for Review and Discussion

1. Describe how window display and the store exterior convey a store's character and image.

2. Comment on the concept of the exterior sign being a store's "signature."

3. What is a marquee and how can it be used in visual merchandising?

4. Give an example of a theme and explain how that theme could be promoted in the media and reinforced through elements of the store exterior.

5. Explain the difference between awnings and marquees.

6. List the four major types of exterior store windows and provide an advantage and a disadvantage of each type.

CHAPTER SEVEN

Display Window Construction

AFTER YOU HAVE READ THIS CHAPTER,
YOU WILL BE ABLE TO DISCUSS:

- The benefits of closed-back windows for use in display.
- Methods for reducing glare and reflection in window displays.
- Three types of floors commonly used in display windows.
- The function of ceiling grids in display windows.
- Methods for turning a large display window into a smaller one.
- Advantages and disadvantages of open-back windows.
- The problems inherent in displaying in island windows.
- Merchandise categories best suited to display in shadow box windows.

DISPLAY WINDOW CONSTRUCTION: TRADE TALK

bank of windows	open-back window
ceiling grid	pier
closed-back window	proscenia
deep window	(proscenium, singular)
elevated window	raised floor
elevator-type window	raked floor
enclosed window	run-on window
fins	shadow box
flying	side walls
island or lobby window	tall window
masking	teaser

Closed-Back Windows

A closed-back window is the typical display window with a full back wall, sides, and a large plate-glass window facing the pedestrian or street traffic. It is also known as an **enclosed window.**

A noted visual merchandiser, discussing trends in display, has stated, "For real drama and excitement in display, there is nothing to compare with what you can do in an enclosed display window." In the familiar and traditional giant, plate-glass fronted "fish bowl," which some merchants and store planners feel is extinct, the display person can arrange tableaux and vignettes from life in idealized settings. Here, under perfectly arranged lights, the cast of characters stay where they are placed, remain smiling through sleet, rain, snow, and slush, and wear the garments with nonchalant ease and grace.

The display person is the stage designer, the lighting designer, the prop person, the director, and the producer. The only thing the display person does not have to produce is the merchandise, although he or she may be responsible for the accessorizing. This is the "fun" and "creative" part of the job. The same visual merchandiser who was quoted above predicts that the enclosed window will be brought into the store. These oversized show boxes will become a part of the show and spectacle of interior display.

To understand what can or cannot be accomplished in a display window, it is necessary to understand the physical construction of the window and the limitations imposed by that construction.

A small store may have a single display window, or a pair of windows, often separated by the entrance into the store. Larger stores, some specialty stores, and downtown department stores will often have a "run" or group of windows (called a **bank of windows**)—maybe two, three, or four windows—and then a physical divider between the windows like a doorway, a wide area of masonry **(pier),** or even a small shadow box. The windows in the group or bank may be separate entities, completely framed and delineated from each other by a heavy molding or pier.

The display window may also be one very long, **run-on window** of 20, 30, or more feet. The only visible divider in this run-on window is the thin metal band that retains the plate-glass windows. Often, the visual merchandiser will add dividers inside the window to separate the one long stretch of glass into two, three, or four individual areas. In the case of the single long window, the display person does have greater flexibility and control over the presentations. He or she can, at times, have a mass scene with five or more mannequins arranged in a realistic grouping in a setting that continues through the length of the long window and, at other times, divide the run into small, separate presentations where a single mannequin is "starred" in a solo and very concentrated performance.

This flexibility makes a change of pace possible. Some shoppers are so used to seeing the same physical arrangement of window and mannequin that they no longer "see" the window or the display. A shopper who becomes over-familiar with the same type of display setup week after week will not notice that the merchandise has been changed. But, if one week the mannequin is gone and replaced by a dress form—or the merchandise is draped from a chair—it can be the change itself that will stop the shopper.

Where the architecture of the store is such that the size of each window in a group is predetermined, and the display person cannot move dividers to make the windows wider or narrower, there still are options open to the creative window dresser. We will discuss those options shortly, when we consider proscenia and the masking of windows.

One of the greatest problems the visual merchandiser has with a display window is the glare in the glass that blinds the shopper and cuts down on the visibility of the merchandise presented. Another problem is reflection. Often, shoppers get a better view of what's going on out in the street and in the shop across the road than in the window into which they are looking.

Figure 7.1 The display window can be a see-through space with the selling floor beyond, or it can be, as shown here, a contained "stage" with side walls or "wings," a rear wall, floor, and ceiling. The "audience"—the shoppers—stand outside and look through the glass "wall" at the well-lit presentation. *Bloomingdales, Lexington Avenue, New York.*

In some newer stores, architects have experimented with tinted glass, angled sheets of glass, curved glass, and even deeply recessed windows. Tinted glass affects the color of the merchandise and requires more energy to light the window properly. Curved windows can be even more disastrous than flat glass when it comes to reflec-

Figure 7.2 A floating graphic panel with the store's logo serves to separate the three white, stylized mannequins in red from the store behind. *Ivonne, Mexico City, Mexico.*

tions. Deeply recessed windows leave costly pockets of space that might otherwise be used for storage or selling. In the past, manufacturers have come up with yellow or green transparent vinyl window shades that look like oversized fly-catching strips. Although they do prevent sun fading, they do not cut down much on glare or reflection, and they also distort the color presentation of the merchandise.

Many stores, in conjunction with their visual merchandisers, have used decorative awnings to shield their windows, thus cutting down on the glare. Reflection is still a problem, but some visual merchandisers have found that the use of lighter-colored backgrounds in the window creates better balance with the light coming from outside, as well as minimizing the reflection somewhat. Decorative awnings are changed seasonally, or for holidays, or store promotions. This affords the store an opportunity to enhance its exterior appearance, to promote a special event, and also to provide a degree of comfort to the prospective customer who would like to "do" the window before entering the store.

Display persons have also found that placing the merchandise and the lighting further back in the win-

Figure 7.3 The ornate wire work balustrade that appears on the rear wall of the enclosed window is actually painted on panels of fabric that are applied to the wall. The drawing creates an architectural element that completes the vignette setting. *Frette, Madison Avenue, New York.*

dow, away from the glass, makes it possible to see the merchandise in the proper light and setting. The shopper's eye is drawn past the glare and reflection. The major problem, however, in setting and lighting the merchandise back in the window is that the storefront may appear unlit or dimly lit until the viewer is directly in front of the window. The viewer can only look at the merchandise from 5 or 6 feet away instead of getting a really close-up view. Display manufacturers have been experimenting with optical devices, mirrors, and odd-shaped panels of glass in order to overcome the glare problem.

Floor

Once past the plate glass and into the window proper, the floor must be considered. Most display window floors are raised anywhere from 8 or 9 inches to 24 inches from street level. Rarely is the floor of a standard 8- or 9-foot-high window raised more than 2 feet—that would place the mannequin too high above eye level.

A **raised floor makes** it possible to dramatize an object by forcing the viewer to look up to it. The elevated position adds prestige and also makes it possible for passersby to see over the heads of window shoppers.

Figure 7.4 A floor upon the floor. The raised platform consists of fluorescent tubes covered with translucent plastic, and as a platform/light box, it becomes an eye-catching feature in the display space. Note how the squares on the floor are tinted to match the colored plastic pieces angling into the composition. *Lord & Taylor, Fifth Avenue, New York.*

Even though the entire window will not be seen over the street traffic, it is possible to glimpse some of the presentation. Hopefully, it will be enough to make the viewer want to come in for a closer look.

Some stores have installed **raked floors,** where the back of the floor is several inches higher than the front, creating a ramp effect. When merchandise is displayed on this inclined floor, small objects like shoes, handbags, cosmetics and such, when placed at the back, are more easily seen. Some visual merchandisers rely on platforms and risers to elevate groups of merchandise or mannequins for greater visibility, separation, or dramatic impact.

A few stores, like Lord & Taylor in New York City, have **elevator-type windows.** The floor is actually an elevator platform that can be lowered to the basement level where the "window" is prepared and set, and then raised to the desired level. Sometimes, the floor is below street level, and the shopper is invited to come in really close and look down into the setting. At other times, it might be raised above the usual floor level for a special effect.

Most display-window floors are finished with parquet wood tiles or carpeted in a neutral and subtly textured broadloom carpet. The display person may use floorboards cut out of fiberboard (Homosote and Masonite are two popular trademarks) to cover the existing floor. These floorboards can be painted or covered with fabrics, decorative papers, scattergrass, and so on, to change the look of the floor without damage to the permanent floor. This padded floor also permits the display person to use pins and nails without affecting the finished floor. Where the floor of the window has been left unfinished (concrete or rough wood), the visual merchandiser may have two sets of floorboards: one in use in the window, and a second set in the display department, where it is available, should a different "floor" be required for the next window change. Regular vinyl floor tiles are also frequently used by the display person to create color and style changes. They are simply laid down, perhaps with double-faced masking tape, and easily removed and stored for future use.

Back of the Window

The back of the traditional display window goes from floor to ceiling and is usually fully constructed. Some stores have removable panels closing their windows so they can, when they wish, change from a closed-back window to an open-back window, or convert the display space into selling space. The part of the constructed window back that faces into the store may be part of the main floor interior. It may be shelved, hung with merchandise, or be a backup for a counter area. In some stores, there is a storage area between the back of the display window and the actual selling floor.

In any case, where there is a constructed back, there is usually a door or sliding panel that allows for the passage of merchandise, mannequins, and trimmers. The size of the back opening and the angle of entry can affect the size of the props and what will or will not get into the window. It may necessitate making backgrounds and props in sections that can then be assembled inside the window. The back wall itself, unless it is wood paneled or an especially good quality surface (marble, travertine, brick, etc.), is often painted a neutral color, and special draperies, appliqués, graphic panels, or decorative props are placed in front of it.

A ceiling track that accommodates drapery to cover the back wall may work effectively to promote different looks, seasons, or types of merchandise. All the display person need do is change the fabric to suit the particular need. Where there is ample depth to the window, it may be possible to use photo projection techniques—either from the front or the back. Where the window is very deep, and the merchandise being featured is small and requires close-up viewing, the depth of the window can be cut down with the use of screens or panels that are brought in toward the glass line.

Ceiling

The ceilings in the window areas of older stores and even in some of the newer ones are often quite high and made of concrete or some other impenetrable material. The window lighting equipment is often set into the ceiling. It may be an electrified track on which the lamp housings can be moved back and forth to target the light where it is needed. In some operations, the track may be installed directly above the front glass, and it may be supplemented by lighting poles on either side of the window. If there is a side lighting source, it should be covered or hidden behind a panel or teaser. In that way the shopper on the street or in the mall is shielded from looking into the strong light.

Ceiling Grid

Because it is difficult, if not impossible, to attach things into a dense ceiling, a very good investment is the installation of a **ceiling grid.** The actual grid may be metal wire, pipes, or even wood lattices. Grids are usually available in modules: 2 feet by 4 feet, 2 feet by 6 feet, or 2 feet by 8 feet. Depending on the size of the display area, the

Figure 7.5 Things don't just dangle or drop from the ceiling of the window. Usually the ceiling is an impenetrable piece of concrete. As in this display, the ends are tied to a metal grid that is permanently attached a few inches down from the ceiling. Yarn, yarn-wrapped forms, and strings of colored lights fall and are festooned throughout the window for this great effect. *H-Bendel, Fifth Avenue, New York.*

display person may want to cover only the central part, the rear part, or even most of the ceiling with grids. The grid should, ideally, be dropped to about 9 feet off the floor, and it can be suspended by pipes and flanges bolted into the ceiling or hung by chains—and thus, easily removed. If suspended by chains, the chains are linked into screw-eye bolts fastened into the ceiling. The open distance from the actual ceiling allows the display person to manipulate props, hanging elements, or even lighting equipment.

When the window is open-backed, an attached ceiling grid can be located where the display area ends and the sales floor starts. This location simplifies the hanging or attaching of panels or other decorative devices that will screen off the window area: ribbons and streamer curtains, photo blowups, foliage, balloons, fabric panels, and so on.

To add greater emphasis to the display lighting in a window display, the lighting can be moved closer to the back end of the window space along with the merchandise to be displayed. In this way, it doesn't have to battle the daylight that fills in the front part of the window area. The ceiling grid facilitates moving lighting fixtures to where they will be most effective and permits the wiring to snake through the grid and then be dropped down to the most convenient electrical outlet. Though some stores may use grids such as framed panels of solid wood or pierced wood panels as decorative "dropped ceiling" designs in their windows, most stores prefer to have the grids disappear and be invisible to the window watcher. In that case, it is recommended that the grids and ceiling be painted the same dark color, for example, deep brown, charcoal gray, midnight blue, or black.

A note of warning: Do not hang heavy objects from a grid unless you are sure the grid and the ceiling attachment are strong enough and secure enough to support the weight. Thin metal wire grids, such as those used decoratively to display pots and pans in a kitchen, may be fine for balloons, ribbons, and even some drapery but not for chairs floating, tables upended, or mannequins flying. If you are interested in such theatrical and spectacular effects, invest in a truly sturdy and secure grid installation. The ceiling grid can also be an asset inside the store, especially over designated "focal display areas" like T-walls, platforms, ledges, or island displays. Without heavy and cumbersome props, the grid will allow the display person to add light and fun effects above the mannequins or forms. These above-eye-level display elements will also direct shoppers from across the store to where the merchandise is being featured.

Side Walls

Where the display windows are constructed as "rooms" (with three side walls, a window wall, a floor, and a ceiling), the **side walls** may be painted out or used as part of the display theme. Even with side walls, the display person may opt for panels or **fins** set against the front glass and angled in toward the center of the window. These panels are similar to flats or **teasers** used in stage design. They limit the view of what is on the sides and concentrate the viewer's sight line on stage center.

Side-lighting strips or panels may be masked behind these dividers or teasers, making it possible to bring lights further back in the window, while keeping the source of light hidden. The angled panels also add a feeling of depth to the window by creating an aspect of forced perspective to the merchandise presentation.

These panels also work to divide the run-on or overly long, nondivided window into smaller viewing areas. Self-standing screens, dividers, flats, or hung drapery will separate one display group from the next, yet allow the continuous flow of a theme or promotion.

Proscenia

Some stores take the theatrical quality of their display windows seriously and enhance the theater-like setting by using **proscenia** (the plural of *proscenium*) around the window glass. The proscenium, from the Greek "before the scenery," is the structural arch, usually rather ornate, often seen in a theater surrounding the curtain.

In the display window, the proscenium consists of a top valance, which masks the lighting across the top of the window, and side valances, which separate one window or display grouping from the next and also hide any side-lighting devices. There are display persons who use the valance as a decorative frame for the window and will use different colors, perhaps enhanced with branches, lights, or other decorative motifs for Christmas or spe-

Figure 7.6 The side walls of the window carry through the same motif that decorates the rear wall of the window. The series of assorted colored tie-dyed sun spots complement the different colored gowns in the foreground. *H-Bendel, Fifth Avenue, New York.*

cial storewide events. In some instances, the valance or proscenium is structurally fixed, unchangeable, but definitely a part of the store's architecture and its image.

Masking

As previously mentioned in this chapter, there are options available to the display person with a large plate-glass window and a small merchandise presentation. One option is **masking** the window and turning a large area into a small shadow box (see Chapter 18). The plate glass can be painted out with an opaque paint or partially covered by panels set against the glass inside the window. A small constructed box can then be set into the opening that remains.

Stores that do not want to change large windows too often, or are limited in staff, find it expedient to mask off these windows and do small shadow-box presentations of accessories and separates. This is especially effective on side streets or in windows facing parking lots or low-traffic areas. Even an occasional change on the main traffic street can have special value. It is the surprise, the jolt, the change from the norm or the traditional that can attract attention and bring the shopper closer to the store and, hopefully, into it.

Figure 7.7 The proscenium is the frame around the display window and can be four sided but usually frames only two sides and the top of the window glass. It can also be, as shown here, a pair of wings or side units that contain the display. This type of framing is often used to tie a group of connected windows together to promote a season, holiday, or promotional theme. *Moschino, Madison Avenue, New York.*

The display person may also find it effective, at times, to mask off the window opening of a full-sized window so that, though the window is still dressed and treated as a full window, it can only be viewed through the limited opening in the window mask. It is like the "peephole" in the construction barrier that always draws the curious. There is something about looking through a keyhole or a slit that makes the viewer feel as though he or she is in onto something special. When used with care and with the appropriate merchandise—but not overused—this "knothole in the fence" technique works particularly well. Both proscenia and masking are discussed at greater length in Chapter 18.

Open-Back Windows

An **open-back window** has no back wall, but offers a direct view into the selling area beyond. Much of what has been written about the closed-back window is relevant to the open-back window. The open back creates particular problems for lighting and background presentations, and extra effort is demanded of the display person to maintain a sense of excitement in the window, while at the same time, the in-store merchandise and lighting are competing for the viewer's attention. It need not be a losing battle, and neither area has to suffer or take "second place." The open-back window does, however, require special handling.

Figure 7.8 The front glass has been masked off so that the viewer's field of vision has been reduced—and concentrated. For a Mother's Day promotion all the windows have been blacked out with an adhering gel and only the silhouette of the mother has been cut out so that we can look through it. Through her head we can see the sort of outfits she sees herself in. This same effect can be achieved with seamless paper or foam core panels—cut out—and applied against the front glass. *Saks Fifth Avenue, New York.*

Glare and reflection in the window are still problems. Approaches to lighting the open back must always be balanced with the effect that the window lighting will have inside the store; lighting the back of the window may also mean lighting up the selling floor. Spotlights that are used to light the window merchandise may be irritating to the customer as he or she approaches the open-back window from inside the store. When possible, the display person might use a panel, screen, drap-

ery, or ribbon curtain to partially block the view of the store interior and, at the same time, create a positive background for the merchandise featured in the window. The panel or screen can supply the desired color and texture to complement the merchandise and possibly deliver the seasonal or promotional message as well. The display person must then divert the attention of the viewer to the area in front of the panel, toward the window foreground.

Some display persons will take advantage of the view of the store interior and "dress" the area directly behind the window to enhance the merchandise being presented. This is especially successful in smaller stores

Figure 7.9 Repetition can be an object repeated over and over again or, as illustrated, a series of mannequins looking the same, in the same pose, and wearing same or similar outfits. It is the repetition that makes this simple display so eye-catching. *Mathilde, Stockholm, Sweden.*

and boutiques where the shop owner has greater control over what is being shown and what is being sold. If the color red is being promoted and only red garments and accessories are being displayed in the open-back window, it is an effective display and merchandising technique to bring the red merchandise on the selling floor up to the front of the store. Thus, the interior selling story reinforces the window story and, at the same time, provides a compatible back-up for the window display. The message becomes stronger and more emphatic. (When we discuss store interior display in Chapter 8, we will again refer to the effectiveness of placing the garment displayed next to the on-floor stock of that garment.)

Where a panel, screen, or fabric curtain is used to separate the selling area from the selling space, without completely closing it off, the decorative device should be finished on both sides. While the side facing the street is usually decorative and appliquéd, the side facing the selling floor may or may not be. Using one panel, it is possible to use one kind of fabric on the front to complement the merchandise in the window and a different fabric or treatment on the back of the panel that will blend with the decoration or the merchandise seen inside the store.

Sometimes plants are used as dividers and, depending on the merchandise and the store image, these can be very effective. At other times, semisheer curtains, fine metal mesh, security grids, or beaded chains have been used as dividers. Most of these will allow some daylight into the store, permit a view in as well as a look out, and, in the case of the smaller store, provide a feeling of greater openness.

Island Windows

An **island window,** also called a **lobby window,** is a window that has glass on all four sides, allowing the merchandise presentation to be viewed from any angle and from any direction. Paraphrasing theatrical terminology, it is "displayed in the round."

Since there is no back in an island window, the display techniques required for this type of setup are specialized and very different from those used for the standard three-wall display window.

Presenting the merchandise is a major problem. The display person cannot gather, pin, or tuck away anything in the back because there is no back. Unless the window is equipped with a turntable floor, there should be something interesting and attention-getting from whichever direction the window is approached.

Usually, there is some distinct traffic pattern, and the display person will play up one view and play down some other view or approach. For example, if an island window is located directly in front of a store, it would be more important to emphasize the view from the street. It is safe to assume that the side opposite the main entrance is the one seen by the customer as he or she leaves store, while the face fronting onto the street should entice the shopper to walk around the island window and come into the selling space proper.

The turntable floor, or a turntable set on the floor, is an excellent device that can be used occasionally to get special action or reaction. The turntable supplies motion in the window (almost always an attention-getting device), and makes the entire presentation viewable while the shopper stands in one place.

If a single suit or garment is presented in an island window, it can be accessorized in four different colors or four different attitudes, for example. Each view gets a different accessory story. A three-dimensional, full-round prop (a statue, a plant, a flower-filled vase, and so on), raised up on a platform or riser, can be used to supply a centralized high point or focal point in the window. The merchandise groupings might then be fanned out around that prop so that they blend into each other without losing their individual fashion message.

Lighting is a serious problem in an island window. The overhead lights will be visible from some direction, no matter how they are positioned. Some will strike a passerby full in the eye. Care should also be taken to get the light on the merchandise and off the glass as much as possible. Light on the glass can actually create a "barrier," preventing the merchandise from being seen!

Adding to the problems stated above is the inevitable one of glare and reflection. In the island window, this probability is multiplied by four. Like the open-back window, the conflict and confusion of what is going on around and behind the glass is compounded. If not properly lit and demarcated, the all-glass unit can become a store liability with prospective customers walking into the glass. (This sometimes happens with un-lined or unbanded all-glass doors.)

In older stores, the island display window unit is often located under a marquee or in an enclosed foyer, with closed-back display windows on either side of it and the store entrance behind it. By minimizing the overhead lighting in this area and keeping the walk-around space in semidarkness, the lighting in the island window and the other display windows will be more effective and more dramatic. Glare and reflection will be minimized and the visibility beyond the island window greatly reduced.

Special Windows

Shadow Boxes

A **shadow box** is a small, elevated window used for the close-up presentation of special merchandise or accessories. The size varies, but it is usually about 3 feet by 5 feet, either "portrait" (vertical) or "landscape" (horizontal). Besides having a smaller window surface, the shadow box is often shallower (18 to 24 inches deep) and higher from the street level than the standard display window. All of this tends to bring the merchandise nearer to eye level and the closer scrutiny of the shopper. Since the space is so confined, merchandise is shown sparingly. It can be tacked onto the back wall, which is not very far away, or stepped up with platforms or risers.

Lighting is usually limited to a very few minispots or pinpoint spotlights, and the lights are generally directed right at the merchandise. Some stores, selling only small, precious merchandise (jewelry, shoes, belts and ties, cosmetics, small leather goods), may have more exciting lighting installations, including back and side lighting, atmospheric or wash lighting, and highlighting of the merchandise.

Since the glass surface is smaller and the sight line funnels in, dramatic effects and strong color contrasts are required to attract the shopper's eye. Shadow boxes often appear on side streets (they sometimes are full-size windows that have been masked off to create small feature windows), or on either side of an entrance to a store. Where the store has a foyer or some area of separation between the street doors and the doors into the selling floor, one will often find shadow box display cases to

Figure 7.10 The shadow box is a small display window usually not larger than 30″ by 48″, and it is ideal for showing small fashion accessories, jewelry, and toiletries. Since the opening is smaller the opening is often higher off the ground than a traditional window, and thus places the smaller objects closer to the viewer's eye level. *Tiffany, Munich, Germany.*

brighten up the area and to "sell" the persons waiting to go inside. (Shadow boxes may also be incorporated in the interior design of the selling floor; this is discussed in Chapter 8.)

Elevated Windows

An **elevated window** may have its floor raised up to 3 feet above street level. It may be only 5 feet tall and the display area may be much shallower than is necessary to show certain kinds of merchandise. This higher but shorter and shallower window does present problems, but none are insurmountable. They do require different treatments and nonstandardized solutions.

A regular, full-size mannequin—be it realistic or abstract—will not be able to stand up in this window, but it can sit, kneel, or lie down. There are many fine mannequins designed to be used in just those positions. This is fine when a horizontal or diagonal presentation (see Chapter 3) will work with the merchandise and the store's fashion attitude. If the informal and rather relaxed mannequin will not do justice to the garments, then a dressmaker form or suit form might do the job. A shorter, headless, and possibly legless form may also fit in the low-ceilinged window.

Another technique for showing merchandise in these shallower, elevated windows, without the use of a three-dimensional form is called **flying,** by which the garments seem to be in movement, soaring through a display window controlled by invisible wires, pins, and tissue-paper padding. Many boutiques also make an "art" of shaping, draping, and adding dimension to clothes against walls, on panels, and from furniture. (See Chapter 10.)

In an elevated window, the floor is higher and thus closer to the average viewer's eye level. It is a good window in which to do a lay-down presentation of the merchandise and the accessory groupings with an occasional buildup for special interest. Some stores prefer this type of display setup because it creates a boutique-like atmosphere and gives the store the opportunity to show more merchandise, especially if the merchandise is separates and related fashion accessories. (These techniques will be discussed more fully in Chapter 20.)

Deep Windows

A very **deep window,** even if it is of standard height and width, presents another type of problem. It may require too much merchandise, too many mannequins, and too much electrical energy to light the back of the cavernous window. Also, the back may be so far from the front glass that showing merchandise in the rear may be worthless. The viewer cannot really see that far back and misses the details of the merchandise and nuances of the display.

If the deep window has an open back, a screen or drapery with a finished back can reduce some of the depth of the window as well as providing a setting for another display, this one viewable from the inside of the store. Thus, by cutting the depth, the display person can create two

display areas, tell two different merchandising stories, and provide shopping interest inside and outside the store.

If the deep window has a closed back, the display person may build a new back wall, closer to the glass line, and utilize the space between the existing back wall and the new back wall for the storage of props, fixtures, and/or mannequins.

A self-standing screen or drapery hung from a ceiling track will also work to cut down the depth of the window.

Tall Windows

Where the window glass soars—well above the usual 9 or 10 feet in height—the display person has several

Figure 7.11 The extra tall window lends itself to more dramatic presentations. White balloons—dozens of them—float up to the very top of the tall window while the white abstract mannequin steps out in her white gown in an all-white-on-white setting. The cool lights add to the unique look of the airy and spacious window. *Bergdorf Goodman, Fifth Avenue, New York.*

problems with which to contend. The simplest solution, it would seem, would be to add a valance or top proscenium. Either of these devices will visually cut down the window size, but may be at odds with the architectural look of the building. They may destroy the sweep of the line or the repetition of shape and pattern intended by the store's architect.

In a very **tall window,** the overhead lighting, which is usually attached to the ceiling above the front glass line, is so far away from the merchandise or mannequin on the floor that it is almost worthless as a strong accent light. The display person will either have to rely on side lighting for the emphasis and use the overhead lamps for atmospheric wall and floor washes, or possibly drop the ceiling lights down to a better, more useful level, making the equipment completely visible to the street viewer. This may prove to be distracting, or it might, in fact, add a theatrical quality to the setup. Some stores feel that the display lighting is an honest and integral part of the display; they see nothing wrong in showing the lighting equipment as part of window construction.

In such a window, the display person can elect to take full advantage of the extra height and raise the mannequins onto pedestals, piers, or columns. The merchandise can soar, if the architecture and style permit, to create new and startling effects. Instead of a horizontal lineup of mannequins, they can be staggered on different levels. The assorted heights will tend to separate the mannequins from each other and, though part of the same composition, each will be individualized and highlighted. If it is right for the store's fashions, or if a bit of whimsy is desired, a mannequin can be made to float, fly, or just be suspended in midair à la Mary Poppins—umbrella and all! The magic of suspended forms or gravity-defying feats is certain to gain window attention.

Display Window Construction: A Recap

- A closed-back window is the typical display window. It has a full back wall, sides, and a large plate-glass window facing pedestrians on the street. It is also called an enclosed window.

- Glare and reflection are two of the greatest problems with display windows.

- Decorative awnings help to shield windows and cut down glare.

- Light-colored backgrounds help to minimize reflection.

- Most display window floors are raised anywhere from 8 or 9 inches to 2 feet above street level.

- In a raked floor, the back of the floor is several inches higher than the front, making it easier to see small objects such as shoes and cosmetics.

- An elevator-type window is actually an elevator platform that can be lowered to the basement and prepared.

- Most display-type window floors are finished with parquet wood tiles or a neutral, subtly textured carpet.

- Some stores have removable panels closing the backs of their windows so the window can be used as a closed-back or open-back window, or the display space may be converted into selling space.

- A ceiling grid enables the display person to attach lighting fixtures or other devices when the window ceiling is concrete or another dense, impenetrable material.

- A proscenium is the structural arch, usually rather ornate, often seen in a theater surrounding the curtain. In the display window, the proscenium consists of a top valance and side panels.

- Masking a window is accomplished by painting out part of the window with opaque paint or partially covering the window with panels set inside the glass, thus creating a shadow box. Masking is helpful when working with a large window and a small merchandise presentation.

- An open-back window has no back wall, but offers a direct view into the selling area beyond.

- An island window, also called a lobby window, has glass on all four sides.

- A turntable floor allows an entire presentation to be viewable while the shopper stands in one spot.

- A shadow box is a small, elevated window used for close-up presentation of specific merchandise.

- "Flying" is a technique by which garments seem to be in motion, controlled by invisible wires, pins, and tissue-paper padding.

- A deep window presents problems because it is difficult to light and requires too many mannequins and too much merchandise.

- Tall windows can be difficult to light but offer opportunities for striking, elevated displays.

Questions for Review and Discussion

1. Explain the problems of glare and reflection in window displays and identify possible solutions to these problems.

2. Are there advantages in the use of ramped windows? If so, describe them.

3. Describe the benefits of an elevator window.

4. What are proscenia and masking and what purpose do they serve in display windows?

5. Compare and contrast open-back and closed-back windows. What are the advantages and disadvantage of each type?

6. Explain the problems inherent to displaying in an island window.

7. What advantages are gained by the use of elevated windows?

8. What type of merchandise is best displayed using shadow box windows? Give specific examples.

9. What is the difference between an elevator window and elevated window?

10. Describe a display that could be very effective in an elevated window, in a deep window, and in a tall window.

CHAPTER EIGHT

Store Interiors

AFTER YOU HAVE READ THIS CHAPTER,
YOU WILL BE ABLE TO DISCUSS:

- The term focal point and describe its uses.
- The unique characteristics of island displays.
- The use of counters and display cases for merchandise presentations.
- The differences and similarities between museum cases and demonstration cubes.
- Displays appropriate for ledges within the store.
- How structural columns can be used for interior display.
- The term fascia and list its uses.
- The use of T-walls in the store interior.
- 100-percent traffic areas within the store.

STORE INTERIORS: TRADE TALK

columns	ledges
counter	museum cases
demonstration cubes	100-percent traffic areas
display cases	platforms
enclosed displays	risers
fascia	shadow boxes
focal point	T-walls
island display	

O nce a shopper has passed through the air screen or foyer, he or she is on the selling floor. In older stores, including those built in the 1960s, there were usually massive departmental identification signs hung from overhead, or secured and bolted, immovably, to the perimeter walls. The problem of designating what is being sold, and where, is now part of the display person's job. Rather than using strong, quickly dated signs that cannot be easily changed, the display person combines fashion and color, not only to let the shopper know which department he or she is approaching, but also to make a definite contribution to the ambience of the whole store and the specific area.

The signage used today is coordinated to the look and architecture of the store and is part of the overall "texture" of the selling floor. Signs identify an area, but the actual selling is left to the merchandise presentation. By showing the merchandise, properly accessorized, on the right kind of mannequin, form, or hanger—with the right props and decorations—the display person invites the shopper in to peruse more of the treasures only suggested by the display setups.

Focal Points

In planning traffic patterns and store layout, architects, store planners, and visual merchandisers will often speak of locating focal points. The **focal point** is a generic term that refers to any place in the retail setting where emphasis has been placed to attract the shopper. This can be an area on a rear wall that has been painted a strong color against which a well-lit armoire or fixture or furniture arrangement has been placed and then arranged with featured merchandise. The focal point can be a mannequin or form on a platform with an unusual prop, in a pool of light, or a product display collage, again—targeted with light—set above wall units filled with the merchandise shown above. The focal point is the exclamation point in the design—and it is always well lit!

It is the accented area on the floor where special merchandise is usually featured. Sometimes the focal point can be a large photo blowup, a graphic, a painting, a huge seasonal floral arrangement. Even though merchandise is not featured at the focal point, the focal point serves to reinforce the store's fashion image. It also serves as a beacon that attracts the shopper and then as a directional force that points the shopper toward other displayed products in the space.

Island Displays

In newer mall stores, where the windows are played down and the interior is played up, the shopper will be greeted immediately on entering the store by an **island display,** a featured display space viewable from all sides. This is an important area, well lit and clearly identified by a raised platform, a change of flooring material, or an area rug. An abstract construction may highlight the area.

Figure 8.1 The Armani boutique is one of several designer shops within this Korean department store. Each boutique, entered off the main aisle, has its own distinctive brand look and designer image. It is like walking along an upscale shopping street of designer boutiques. *Lotte Department Store, Pusan, Korea. Design: Pavlik Design Group.*

Figure 8.2 The unique, free-standing wall/partition is a focal element in the store's design. Displays appear way above eye level and the merchandise is presented within reach of shoppers. The size of the wall and the way the garments are displayed on it make it an attention getting device. *Maison Simon, Quebec, Canada. Design: Watt International.*

In an island display, the store presents a special story—be it a color, a style, an event, or a storewide promotion. If a color trend is recommended in the island display, the display person will usually follow through on the rest of the selling floor by playing up the same color in related merchandise (accessories) or even nonrelated merchandise (throw pillows, luggage, china and glass, and so on.). An island display that is on a slightly raised platform can be more effective and get more attention than an on-the-floor display, but whatever the "architecture," it should be changeable or rearrangeable, just as the merchandise and the promotions change.

When an island display is laid out on the store's floor plan, effective lighting for that area should be planned. The display person may still find it necessary to supplement the lighting in this area for more drama and emphasis. As in the window setup, some kind of ceiling grid would be desirable for the suspension of props and/or lights. Though the presentation is thought of as a full round, the view from the entrance is the most important aspect of the "show."

Risers or Platforms

A **riser,** or **platform,** set just off the aisle and spotlighted from above, will also serve to identify an area and pro-

mote a particular piece of merchandise. If a shopper sees a mannequin raised up on a platform for better visibility, over the traffic on the floor, wearing a robe or a nightgown, would it not be logical to assume that robes and nightgowns were being stocked next to or behind that figure? That is merchandising *and* that is display.

In Chapter 12, Fixtures, we will discuss this concept of selling and also go into more detail on the many free-standing floor fixtures that are available not only to hold and sort garments, but to present a display of that merchandise to the prospective customer. We will explain the use of kiosks, easels, drapers and costumers, outposts, and so on.

Figure 8.3 Mannequins, raised up on a low platform at the junction of two major aisles, serve as an island display for featured fashions. The overhead graphics reinforce the position of the group and appeal to the target market for the clothes on display. *Robinsons, Las Vegas.*

The Runway

A fashion show staple has become the new show place in retail settings. The wide, spacious drive or central aisle of a store that may have previously featured a small mannequin arrangement on an island platform may now have given way to a longer platform—a long runway such as one sees used in fashion shows.

Where window display space is either too shallow or too scarce to do a real presentation—or does not exist at all—the runway becomes the focal display element inside the store. The raised platform—often no more than 12″ to 18″ in height and under-lit so that it seems to "float" off the ground—starts near the shop entrance. This up-front location makes it visible through the open entranceway, and also serves to bring the shopper to the rear of the store. Shoppers follow the runway as it goes back into the heart of the retail setting.

A line of mannequins or forms on this platform can show off the newest or most exciting fashions available. The presentation has even more impact if it is accentuated by a line of spots directly over the long platform. The accenting lights turn the lineup into an eye-arresting spectacle.

As in all good visual merchandising, the runway presentation is enhanced if all the garments have a common denominator: a color, pattern, look, or theme. If that single concept is carried through, the effect can be dynamic. Propping can be a nice touch but is not necessary. This is all about merchandising.

The Catwalk

Where a store has an extra high ceiling—anything from 15′ to 20′—the designer may add overhead "walkways" or "catwalks" that cross over the sales floor. These are used to show off mannequins in featured garments. The figures may be positioned in life-like clusters or in line-ups on these metal framed units that have wire mesh or clear lucite floors. That way the shopper always has a clear view of what is on show, and the ceiling lighting can still come down to light up the floor fixtures and the merchandise on them. Adding to the interest and spectacle is the use of seated figures on the floor of the catwalk, which look down onto the shoppers below. The term "catwalk" comes from theater where there is usually a bridge that goes across the stage, way up above the theater-goers' sight line.

Counters and Display Cases

There are many places on the selling floor where the display person can use his or her own special blend of fashion "know-how" to affect the selling environment. **Counters** and **display cases** are two such areas.

A counter is a major area for merchandise presentation. It is truly the "point of purchase"—the place where the merchandise is presented and the sale is concluded; the money or credit card is taken and the bagged or boxed purchase is delivered to the shopper. Some store planners are predicting the demise of the "counter," calling it obsolete, unduly and unnecessarily expensive to purchase and maintain. It must be staffed and it does take up a specific amount of floor space. More often than not, it is fixed in place. For the counter to be truly effective in producing sales, specific fixtures beneath and/or behind it, to hold and show the merchandise being sold, are required. There are many different types of counter fixtures available and many are designed to do specific things. Counter fixtures will also be discussed in Chapter 12.

Figure 8.4 The long aisle of the women's floor serves as the major in-store display area. Raised up on platforms set against T-walls and partitions, the headless mannequins serve as advertisements for the classifications of merchandise available in the shops behind them. The mannequins are sometimes accompanied by decorative props, plants, pieces of furniture, screens, etc. *Lotte, Daejun, Korea. Design: Pavlik Design Group.*

Figure 8.5 The counter is often more than a place where merchandise can be purchased. It is usually designed as a showcase for small accessories or impulse items to catch the shopper's eye while he or she waits to be served. *Harrah's Jackpot Store, Las Vegas.*

more open, and less nailed-down-looking interiors. The bottom, or floor, of the display case, if not part of the interior architectural scheme (made of marble or bronze or fine wood), can be equipped with floorboards of cardboard or fiberboard and covered with various fabrics and decorative papers that can be changed with the seasons or the color of featured merchandise.

Since display cases are often about 2 feet deep, it is advisable to use risers and saddles (see "Counter Fixtures" in Chapter 23) in the case to raise some of the merchandise closer to the shopper's eye level, or to make interesting setups of assorted merchandise at different levels. Small groupings can also be shown as individual collections by varying the viewing levels. For example, for Valentine's Day it is possible to cover the floor of the case with red felt or red satin, and use assorted risers covered in the same red fabric (perhaps edged with paper lace doilies) for a display of cosmetics, costume jewelry, and/or any other small accessories to stimulate a point-of-purchase sale for that particular gift-giving time.

If the all-glass-fronted case/counter is used for stocking merchandise, the stock should be arranged in neat, orderly, color- or pattern-coordinated groupings contained in see-through boxes or trays. A seasonal or promotional touch can still be added: a red ribbon tied about a group of scarves; a cluster of Christmas ornaments and a spray of greenery tucked in with some sweaters; the top shirts (of stacks of shirts) accessorized with bright green ties for St. Patrick's Day; or violets scattered over a case filled with handbags when the store has decreed that violets mean spring.

Museum Cases

The **museum case** is primarily a display case that can, on occasion, serve as a counter or demonstration area. As the name implies, the case is similar to those found in museums and consists of a column or pedestal (usually rectangular) with a five-sided glass case on top. It is often taller than a counter, and the merchandise, precious and special, is raised up closer to the viewer's eye level. Again, the base of the case or floor pad should be coordinated with the merchandise presented and/or the seasonal theme. The museum case is approached and viewed from all sides, and small platforms or risers can

The counter itself may be no more than a tabletop or ledge on which a sampling of the merchandise can be displayed or presented to a potential customer. The counter may be the top surface of a piece of furniture that stocks merchandise on shelves or in drawers below, or it can be an all-glass or partially glass case for a below-eye-level display. Today's most common, basic display case design has a glass or transparent plastic top and at least three sides of glass. This enables the shopper to see the merchandise displayed for sale, while at the same time protecting the setup from "touch, feel, and steal." The unit is usually raised off the ground on a pedestal, and seems to "float," in keeping with the trend for lighter, be used to enhance the presentation and to help delineate the assorted pieces of merchandise in the same case.

Demonstration Cubes

Demonstration cubes are rug-upholstered, laminate-covered, or wood-finished blocks found on and about the selling floor. These cubes are prepared in various sizes (3 feet by 3 feet by 3 feet is a popular size), and they can be grouped and clustered, or used individually. The cube can be used as a mannequin platform, a display surface for a "lay-down" of accessories with a single suit or outfit raised on a costumer or draper (see Chapter 12, Fixtures) or, as the name suggests, for demonstrations. A salesperson for anything, from skin care lotions to toaster ovens, can set up for business on one of these cubes. The raised surface can be used to show, to explain, and to sell an item. These cubes are particularly popular as mid-traffic islands to gain attention for a special product, or used right off the aisle as a "draw-into-the-department" device. Shoe departments will often use them in clusters or in an echelon formation, along an aisle or as a low divider, to show sample shoes. Low cubes—17 or 18 inches tall—also double as seats or benches.

Figure 8.6 The demo cube is usually a 30″ to 36″ high surface upon which a product may be demonstrated or displayed. It can serve as a tabletop upon which parts of an outfit can be assembled by the salesperson for the shopper's approval. As shown here, the wood cube with the glass top not only serves as an assembly point but some accessories are displayed under the glass top as well. *Lois Ferraud, Rotterdam, Belgium. Design: Umdasch.*

Ledges

The traditional **ledge** is raised about 5 feet from the floor and is often an "island," that is, freestanding on the selling floor. The ledge is usually the top surface of a backup storage unit behind a selling counter. In most stores, that would be a two-sided storage unit, about 3 or 4 feet deep by 5 feet tall, with bins, shelves, or cabinets, surrounded by counters. The length of the ledge would depend on how many storage units are lined up together on the floor, the type of merchandise being sold, and the size, design, and nature of the department itself. The ledge can also be the top surface of a storage unit that is set flat against a perimeter wall with a counter set in front of it. This type of ledge would be viewed only from the front.

In the department and large specialty stores built before the mid-1970s, it was not unusual to have 18- to 25-foot ceilings on the main floor. With this great openness above the level of merchandise and customers, the ledge displays were the major focal display areas inside the store. It was here that fantasies grew to unprecedented heights. Each new season or promotion was greeted with fully dressed and accessorized mannequins, often in groupings, in settings complete with budding trees or towering flower and foliage arrangements. In this elevated location, above the traffic of the floor, the ledge display was an eye-filling spectacle.

The lowering of store ceilings and budgets and the rising of energy costs have simplified the type of ledge displays in use today. The newer selling floors and stores that are actively renovating their selling areas are bringing the ceilings—and thus the lights—closer to the merchandise. Some of the mall stores being currently designed use a dropped ceiling for emphasis as well as for economy in heating, air-conditioning, and illuminating the floor. The lower ceiling brings and focuses the shopper's attention onto a particular spot. It also creates a more intimate feeling. Shops within shops, or boutiques, use this technique to separate the special area from the rest of the floor or department. Though some ledges will still accommodate standing mannequins, more stores are using kneeling, sitting, or reclining figures on their ledges; the scale, in relation to the lower ceiling, is better.

Customers cannot and should not be able to handle merchandise displayed on ledges, but since it is space

Figure 8.7 The T-wall in this women's area is actually a mirrored partition with a platform upon which a stylized mannequin stands. The garments are racked up behind the T-wall and separated into bays by vertical panels every four feet. *Harvey Nichols, Edinburgh, UK. Design: Four IV.*

that is very visible, the display person should not lose any opportunity to use the ledge for seasonal or promotional displays that may include merchandise and props.

A ledge that backs up onto a wall may have colored panels or drapery backgrounds behind the merchandise presentation. Headless forms or torsos, as well as drapers or costumers, may work well in these areas to show the garments dimensionally.

By the nature of their location, ledges are usually lit from overhead by wall washes or by fluorescent lights hidden behind fascia boards. The displays will probably need more definition and brightness, and a few well-aimed spots from overhead could achieve that.

Shadow Boxes

As previously discussed in Chapter 7, **shadow boxes** are miniature display windows—or elevated display cases. Very often, however, they are worked into the design of the selling floor. They may appear above and behind counters, when the counters are situated in front of floor-to-ceiling walls or partitions. They are usually at eye level, are shallow, and offer possibilities for limited lighting effects. Small merchandise and fashion accessories are commonly shown in shadow boxes.

Every effort should be made by the display person to keep the shadow-box displays fresh and current, in keep-

Figure 8.9 The runway or catwalk has become a popular way of presenting a new color, look, trend, or season in a windowless store or one with minimal window display space. Mannequins are lined up on long, low platforms with males on one side and the females on the other. These runway platforms start near the store entrance and extend into the depth of the shop encouraging shoppers to move to the rear of the retail space. *Nike D'Porentis, Guadalajara, Mexico. Design: Ares Architects.*

Figure 8.8 Mannequins stand atop ledges and merchandising fixtures to create points of interest and show how various garments can be worn. The effectiveness of the mannequin presentation is highlighted by the giant circular "lampshades" suspended from the cut-outs in the ceiling which accentuate their locations while dramatically lighting them. *Maison Simon, Quebec, Canada. Design: Watts International.*

There are many compact and attractive highlighting fixtures available on the market today; if the lamp is in keeping with the decor, it can be integrated into the shadow-box presentation. Let the lamp show! It might even become an attention-getting device and add to the interest of the presentation. Small, high-intensity lamps also fit into the scale of small shadow boxes and, at the same time, do a big accent lighting job.

Enclosed Displays

Larger than a shadow box, an **enclosed display** is usually a fully glassed-in platform that can hold a mannequin or two. It may be located at the entrance to a department, line an aisle, or be part of a perimeter wall. In size and construction, an enclosed display may be very similar to a closed-back display window found in the front of a store. The purpose is the same: to show the merchandise in a protected area.

With the increasing incidence of in-store theft and the soaring cost of merchandise, merchants not only want to protect their displayed wares from "walking off" the selling floor, but they want to cut down on eventual "as-is"

ing with the store's promotions and seasonal changes. They should be changed frequently. The colors and textures of the floor, background, and riser should be varied. Arrangements should be altered. In keeping with the seasonal theme, props should be used to complement the merchandise and the department. If the interior design of a shop or area dictates a monochromatic color scheme, the clever display person can still work wonders with patterns, textures, and unusual materials within the restrictions set by the store architect or designer.

If the lighting inside the shadow box is limited to a thin-line fluorescent tube or an incandescent "sausage" lamp (a long, pencil-like lamp often used to illuminate display cases or below-counter areas), the display person may attempt to introduce a minispot in the shadow box.

Figure 8.10 A focal point is a beacon in the store. It draws shoppers to a particular area. In Encompass by Shell, a shop devoted to Shell Oil products and souvenirs, this dimensional underwater attraction with live fish shows what goes on beneath the ocean drilling equipment. A miniature oil drilling rig sits above the "ocean." *Encompass by Shell, Dallas. Design: Michael Malone Architects.*

Columns

Columns are an integral part of a store's construction. They hold up ceilings, support the weight of the roof, and are an excellent place to hang decorative props. Columns often delineate a department's beginning and end. They may be lined up on either side of a major aisle, adding vertical highlights on a horizontal floor. That is where the column shines in the display scheme of things: Banners can hang from them, wreaths can adorn them, garlands can entwine them or be swagged from them. Arches can spring from them and cross over aisles and ledges for dramatic effects. Storewide event posters can illuminate them and, if need be, a column can be a directory or signboard for a shop or area. The column can be a background panel for a mannequin on a platform. It can be a four-sided mirror, which adds the illusion of space to a department or supplies the necessary reflective surfaces into which most customers want to look.

Columns not only hold merchandise, they can also be used to show merchandise decoratively. Some ledges are adjacent to columns, and the combination of ledge and column can offer interesting display possibilities. Columns can be covered with panels, painted, or camouflaged, but the wise display person will take advantage of the rhythm and repetition of columns in the floor plan of the store—and their obvious verticality—and of their visibility above the traffic, and use them creatively whenever possible.

Fascia

A **fascia** is a band—a horizontal board or panel. In stores, the fascia is often found $6^1/2$ to 7 feet off the ground, above the bins, shelves, or clothing rods that are attached to a wall or partition. It can be used to conceal lights and as a background for merchandise displays.

Any ceiling lights that are directed down to the merchandise on the selling floor will lose intensity because of the distance. Therefore, it is a common practice and good merchandising to bring a light source closer to merchandise that is to be inspected. These lights are often placed 7 feet above the ground and are extended out from the wall or partition. The fascia covers the light fixture from the shopper's view and also helps to focus the light down onto the merchandise.

sales. Who wants to buy a $300 dress that has served as a "hand towel" for hundreds of people? Who wants a negligee snagged by the ring or bracelet of a passerby? Inside the glass display window, on a mannequin or form, the garment can be shown at its best and can get an assist from some well-chosen and expensive accessories. The merchandise can be properly lit and come out a week or two later as crisp, fresh, and saleable as it was when it went in. And all the accessories will still be there—including the mannequin's hands! This is one way to add drama and excitement inside the store, especially when there are no display windows out front.

Figure 8.11 An "antique" armoire set against the perimeter wall not only sets the period feeling for this men's department but also serves to highlight some of the featured garments. The sitting area, in the foreground, carries out the same gracious "old South" tradition. *The Parisian, Birmingham, Alabama.*

In the past, a broad expanse of fascia (starting at 7 feet off the ground and often reaching up to the ceiling) was the area that carried department identification either in permanently attached letters or supergraphic symbols. Today, with departments in flux, expanding and contracting as merchandise and seasons dictate, big signage and permanent wall decorations are virtually "out" as elements of store design.

The fascia is a panel that is 4 or more feet wide. It is close to the ceiling lights and is usually visible from across the floor and certainly from the aisle. It has become a popular place to pin up merchandise and seasonal decoratives: jeans, shirts, sweaters, accessory groupings, and so on. The display on the fascia is used as both a merchandising and decorating technique. The fascia still functions to identify the merchandise in the department and, at the same time, calls the customer to come over.

As the type of merchandise sold in a specific area changes (i.e., from skiwear to swimwear), the display can change the identity and ambience of the area. Colored panels can be superimposed over the wide, flat face; decorative appliqués, photo blowups, forms, or figures can be used, or garments may be pinned up imaginatively or

Figure 8.12 With more department stores featuring soaring atriums with escalator wells, designers are adding enclosed window display areas facing the open space or the aisles around it. Here the enclosed displays face the shoppers as they go up and down the escalators. *Harvey Nichols, Edinburgh, UK. Design: Four IV.*

arranged in geometric patterns. The seasonal or promotional events that take place in the store can be tied in with the fascia trim. A spotlight should be directed at the above-eye-level display to attract more attention to the display and to the area below.

If properly used, the fascia will tell what is being sold below, suggest the variety, and also specify the time of the year or the "look" that is in vogue.

T-Walls

Often one area or department will be separated from another by bins or double-sided, open-faced "closets" hung with merchandise. These two-sided walls or partitions—called **T-walls**—will extend from the back or perimeter

wall out to the aisle. The flat end of this unit, on the aisle, can be converted into a valuable display space. A panel to cover the end of this unit makes the top stroke of the "T." The merchandising wall is the upright of the "T."

A platform can be placed on the aisle, in front of the panel, to highlight the merchandise stocked behind the display. A fully dressed and accessorized mannequin, a prop, a piece of furniture to hold another garment or complementary outfit, a plant, a colored panel to emphasize the outfit on display, or a seasonal device—all can add to the importance of this wall, which is often only 4 to 6 feet wide and 8 feet tall.

100-Percent Traffic Areas

There are locations throughout the store that get very heavy traffic, and they are referred to as **100-percent traffic areas.** These areas are in front of and around escalators or elevators, at entrances or exits, and near major featured spots like restaurants, atriums, and central meeting areas. Displays in these areas are, and should be,

Figure 8.13 This column in Macy's Sport department serves not only as a support for merchandise display but also to carry some of the colorful graphics that add so much to the sense of excitement. The column is painted gray to "disappear" in the all gray environment, and what remains is the color of the garments and graphics. *Macy's Sport, New York. Design: Chute Gerdeman.*

Figure 8.14 A composite drawing showing some of the architectural, lighting, and fixturing details that might be found in a real operation. The selling floor has been trimmed for an "Americana" promotion. Note the many ways and in the many places that the theme was used for a . "storewide" impact.

A. Fluorescent lighting fixtures
B. Incandescent high hats in the ceiling
C. Track lighting with spotlights for highlighting
D. Ambient or task lighting
E. Task lighting inside the cases
F. Structural column
G. Selling and display counter
H. Ledge
I. Museum case
J. Case display

K. Platform
L. Shadow box
M. Fascia
N. T-wall
O. Draper
P. Rope displayer
Q. Security case
R. Shell form
S. T-stand
T. Mirror
U. Risers or buildups
V. Trunk form

changed frequently, and they are often combined with a salesperson or demonstrator plus a certain amount of stock for quick, "impulse" shopping. Low-priced, easy-to-sell merchandise is promoted in these locations, and the displays serve as flags to catch the attention of and slow down shoppers long enough to get them involved in what is being offered. Color, motion, and even sound can be effective here.

Store Interiors: A Recap

- A focal point refers to any place in the retail setting where emphasis is placed to attract the shopper. It is used to reinforce the store's image and to lead the shopper to particular products in the space.

- An island display, which is viewable from all sides, is usually found immediately upon entering the store.

- The counter is a major area for merchandise presentation because it is the point where the sale is concluded and the merchandise is packaged.

- The display case usually has a transparent glass or plastic top and at least three sides of glass. It enables the shopper to see the merchandise, while protecting it from being touched or stolen.

- A museum case is primarily a display case that can be used as a counter or demonstration area. It consists of a column or pedestal with a five-sided glass case.

- Demonstration cubes are rug-upholstered, laminate-covered, or wood-finished blocks found on or about the selling floor. They vary in size and can be used alone or clustered, or can serve as mannequin platforms or display surfaces for lay-down displays.

- In large department and specialty stores built before the mid-1970s, ledges were major focal display areas. The 18- to 25-foot ceilings in these older stores provide space for dressed mannequins or groupings of mannequins as well as promotional settings.

- In newer stores, the ceilings are lower and focus the shopper's attention on a particular spot, creating a more intimate feeling. The scale of the display, in relation to the lower ceiling, must be considered. Newer stores, therefore, are using kneeling, sitting, or reclining mannequins.

- Structural columns can be used to hold decorative props, delineate a department's beginning and end, or add vertical highlights. They can be used to hold banners, garlands, arches, posters, signboards, directories, or can be used as background panels for a mannequin. A column can also be a four-sided mirror, which adds the illusion of space and necessary reflective surfaces.

- A fascia is a band—a horizontal board or panel 4 or more feet wide, about $6\frac{1}{2}$ to 7 feet off the ground—above the bin, shelves, or clothing rods that are attached to a wall or partition.

- The T-wall is a two-sided wall or partition extending from the back or perimeter wall out to the aisle. A panel to cover the end of this unit makes the top stroke of the T. The merchandising wall is the upright of the T.

- Locations throughout a store that get very heavy traffic are called "100-percent traffic areas." These areas are in front of and around escalators or elevators, at entrances or exits, and near major features such as restaurants, atriums, and central meeting areas.

Questions for Review and Discussion

1. Identify the specific functions of counters and display types.

2. What types of merchandise are best suited for presentation in display cases?

3. What is a ledge? What types of displays are best suited for ledges?

4. What are some of the advantages of enclosed interior display areas?

5. How can structural columns be used creatively as display areas within the store? How might you use a column for display in a children's department? A lingerie department?

6. What is fascia? Explain how fascia is used with lighting; with signage; with merchandise display.

7. How should displays in 100-percent traffic areas be handled?

PART THREE

WHAT TO USE FOR SUCCESSFUL DISPLAYS

AS "SILENT SALESPEOPLE," mannequins speak a clear message to customers regarding the store image. Chapter 9 examines the use of the mannequin and provides detailed instructions for proper assembly and dressing. Aside from mannequins, retailers may select from a variety of forms and other mannequin alternatives in displaying apparel items. Chapters 10 and 11 deal with a myriad of alternatives to the use of mannequins and discuss their proper use.

Chapters 12, 13, and 14 explore fixtures and systems used for merchandise presentation. Instructions for assembling, positioning, dressing, and stocking of fixtures and systems are also discussed.

Since the beginning of theater over 3,000 years ago, props have been used to help set the scene. As in theater, props are being used today in visual merchandising to tell a story about the merchandise. Furniture props such as chairs, tables, and armoires can quickly establish the mood or theme in a visual presentation. Chapter 15 details the creative use of furniture as both props and selling fixtures.

CHAPTER NINE

Mannequins

AFTER YOU HAVE READ THIS CHAPTER,
YOU WILL BE ABLE TO DISCUSS:

- The diverse physical characteristics available in today's mannequins.
- Appropriate measures for proper care of mannequins.
- The different types of mannequins available.
- Situations in which headless mannequins would be appropriate.

MANNEQUINS: TRADE TALK

abstract mannequin
child mannequin
full-figured mannequin
hard and soft wigs
headless mannequin
junior mannequin
junior petite mannequin
male mannequin
mannequin

misses or missy size
   mannequin
petite mannequin
preteen mannequin
realistic mannequin
semiabstract mannequin
semirealistic mannequin
young man mannequin

The selection of a mannequin is probably one of the most important professional decisions a display person is called upon to make. There are so many mannequins available: various sizes and age groupings, racial and ethnic types, makeup and hairstyles, poses and attitudes. In addition to the many "images" to select from, there is also the serious consideration of construction and cost.

A **mannequin** may be a store's most valuable asset: It is a "silent salesperson," speaking the clearest fashion message. A mannequin will stand tirelessly for hours and days, in the same place, in the same position or attitude, always smiling, fresh, and pleasant. A mannequin does not gain or lose pounds or inches; it does not get colds or headaches, it does not ask for time off or for cost-of-living increases. However, it does require "love" and attention. Mannequins should be carefully handled—not manhandled. They are usually constructed to take a certain amount of wear and tear, but they can chip, crack, and be disfigured.

A mannequin should be given "time off"—a rest period out of the customer's view—but this is more for the customer's sake than the mannequin's benefit. Too much familiarity with a particular mannequin's makeup, hairstyle, and pose, can cut down on its efficiency in "selling" a new and different outfit. A change of hairstyle (a different wig) may help, or an alternate pose, accomplished by a change of arms, may do it. When selecting and purchasing a realistic mannequin, it might be economical and good display planning to invest in some "alternate" accessories. It will give the mannequin a longer and more versatile life.

Types of Mannequins

Realistic Mannequins

The **realistic mannequin** of the past looked like a famous model or a classically beautiful movie star. Today's realistic mannequin, more often than not, looks like the face *outside* the display window, the one looking in.

Mannequins are becoming more natural, more true to life, more animated, and more identifiable as the people who shop the stores. The mannequin may be young, wholesome, and homebred, or it can appear worldly, sophisticated, and right out of the champagne-and-caviar circuit. Its nose may have a slight bump, with

Figure 9.1 Realistic mannequins in natural poses not only wear and show off the garments but also create a "fashion attitude" for the clothes and the store. The pose and attitude show the garment off to the best advantage and also suggest where, by whom, and when it can be worn. *Patina V Mannequins.*

making "bigger" mannequins that are attractive and proportioned.

The same realistic female mannequin that appeals to the bright, sparkling young woman on her way up, can be equally appealing to the comfortable, successful woman who has "made it." All it takes is a change of makeup and a different wig style. In some areas of the United States, particularly in the West, the mannequins have a tan and an outdoor-like glow because the customers in these areas revel in a "sunshine" way of life. In other areas, where life primarily is indoors under artificial light, complexions may be softer, paler, and more delicate. If a store's customers want the latest in fashion,

Figure 9.2 Men and women of different skin coloration and ethnicity are now available in realistic mannequins. With internationalization and more ethnic groups shopping malls and boutiques, retailers often find the need to make a more direct approach to these markets; and these "ethnic" mannequins work. *Reeger Mannequins.*

its eyes too close, lower lip too fleshy, teeth a bit bucked, but who is perfect? Whatever the mannequin is, it will be well made up, proportioned to wear a particular size, and well positioned to show off a certain group or style of merchandise.

The realistic female mannequin can be a chubby preteen, a blossoming teenager with freckles and pigtails, a student at college, a junior who is petite, or even a mature petite. It can be a svelte size 4, an exquisite size 6 or a fuller size 14½. Mannequins depicting the fuller woman are being seen more and more frequently. A greater number of manufacturers are sculpturing and

Figure 9.3 Semi-realistic male mannequins are usually preferable to realistic mannequins since they are devoid of "makeup," artificial coloring, and wigs. These beautifully sculpted males are finished in a soft, neutral color and appear strong, virile, and very masculine. *Patina V Mannequins.*

Figure 9.4 These semi-realistic child mannequins avoid being too cute or sugary-sweet, yet they are appealing to mothers as well as doting grand-mothers and aunts. Though they lack a realistic skin color their neutral finish makes them more adaptable to a variety of garments and ethnic markets. *Ralph Lauren Polo, Manhasset, New York.*

a mannequin's makeup, no matter what the skin color, should be in keeping with the current "look" as mandated by such fashion "bibles" as *Vogue* and *Harper's Bazaar.* The subtler, more delicate application of color to the mannequin's cheeks and eyes can provide the right look for a store that caters to customers who buy traditional styles. (Many stores send mannequins to specialists to have the makeup updated or changed.) Thus, makeup and wig styles can target in on a specific type of customer.

The mannequin's pose can also help suggest the type and class of merchandise being presented. The erect mannequin with only a slight bend to an arm or a subtle weight shift to a hip is ideal for showing formal clothes, fur coats, coats and suits, or elegant lingerie. Tailored clothes are best shown on an "unanimated" mannequin. The vertical line promotes the unbroken flow of the garment—the sweep of a gown—and as discussed in Chapter 3, it does suggest elegance and refinement.

When action clothes are shown, they look even sportier when the mannequin is all angles and diagonals: arms akimbo, head thrown back, hip thrust out, legs spread or seemingly in motion. The diagonals suggest the dynamics of movement and add to the excitement of the merchandise presentation. Bent arms and legs, however, are difficult to dress and may cut the line of the gar-

ment, causing creases in the pants and sleeves. If the fabric of the garment is heavy or bulky, the resulting wrinkles at the bent joints may resemble a "washboard" of bunched-up fabric without any regard to the flow or design of the garment.

Using seated mannequins makes for a change of pace. They add variety and interest to an arrangement of two or three mannequins. Where the display areas have ceilings too low to allow the use of a standing mannequin, sitting, kneeling, or bending mannequins can work effectively to show separates, casual wear, lingerie, and active sportswear.

There are also horizontal mannequins available (lying down flat on the back or stretched out on one hip).

Figure 9.5 Teenagers make up a very large part of today's retail market and retailers can appeal to them with realistic mannequins designed and proportioned to wear junior or youth sizes. They are available as males, females, and also some ethnicities. *Windows Mannequins.*

Figure 9.6 For the more "way out" and trendy teenagers there are many amusing, caricature-like mannequins available, like these shown with over-sized heads and exaggerated poses. *Patina V Mannequins.*

leg to suggest an at-ease stance. While it might not be the most effective for every kind of garment, this type of mannequin can still be used to show a full range of merchandise—from the most formal to the very informal.

All mannequins start out as sculpture. Though usually based on standard sizes and proportions, the sculptors of mannequins create different bodies and different shapes, attitudes and positions that will further the image of the garment when the figure is dressed. The measurements and sizes given below are only approximations—guides to suggest rather than finite conclusions. The visual merchandiser or display person may have to try the same garment in three different sizes—from 4 to 8—to get one best suited to the particular mannequin. Mannequin manufacturers are reluctant to give a "dress size" for their mannequins today because many are sculpted "from life"—based on the body proportions of a noted model or celebrity—and thus not a "perfect 6" or an "ideal 8" as mannequins have been in the past. One "Miss" mannequin may have a 34″ bust while another may have a 35″ or even larger bust. Waist measurement will vary from 23″ to 25″. American manufacturers tend to make their mannequins "bigger," more athletic and muscular than European manufacturers do. Also, some mannequins will be less muscular, softer and better suited—physically—for evening wear rather than casual outfits or swimsuits where "stronger" bodies would be

These should be used only for special merchandise: nightwear, lingerie, swimwear, and some sportswear. Though the relaxed and easy horizontal line can enhance the presentation of sleepwear, it does not necessarily show the merchandise to its best advantage.

Since mannequins are rather expensive and usually limited to just two or three years of being "in fashion," smaller retail operations generally limit their purchases to two or three mannequins. It is suggested that where the budget for mannequins is limited, the display person should not select mannequins on which the makeup is too highly stylized or the pose too extreme. The best choice would be figures that are standing in a natural and relaxed attitude with just enough bend to the arm and

Figure 9.7 The abstract mannequin often has a simple, egg-shaped head with little or no sculptural definition. The torso, arms, and legs may be longer and more attenuated, and thus make the figure more graceful and decorative. Abstracts can wear any classification of clothing—from casual to formalwear—and come in any price range since they are basically "dimensional hangers." *Bonaveri/Schlappi Mannequins.*

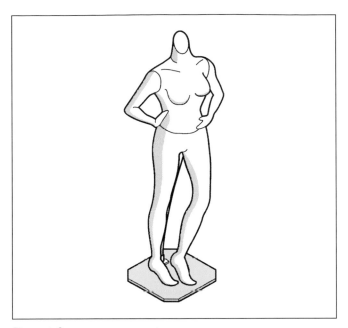

Figure 9.8 A headless mannequin.

preferable. This is true for male mannequins as well. European manufacturers may offer bodies that are slighter, more slender, and less muscular than American mannequins. American made ones tend to be more muscular, "buffer," and "hunkier" when stripped down to outfits that show off the body.

Then there is the problem of the sizing of the garments. European-styled, cut and manufactured garments are often smaller than the same size would be in an American cut dress or suit. Thus a European garment size 4 would be closer to an American size 6. It does become a matter of "trial by trying on" or just knowing the cut of the garments most often used on the mannequins the visual merchandiser or display person has selected to represent the retailer and his merchandise.

When selecting a mannequin—realistic or otherwise—it comes back to considering the following points:

1. Does this form and its proportions represent your target market?
2. Will your customer relate to "her"?
3. Is she shaped and proportioned to wear the type of garments you show? Tall enough? Short enough? Soft or Muscular?
4. Does "she" make the kind of fashion statement your store wants to make?

Many mannequin manufacturers sculpt figures that will relate or interact with other mannequins of the same collection. Two or three mannequins can be used together in a natural and realistic arrangement or grouping. The display person can show related merchandise, alternate colors, and/or different accessory setups in one display area, by showing a cluster of mannequins wearing variations of the same costume or examples of coordinates, pleasantly involved with each other. Some groupings are designed to include both males and females interacting with each other. By using alternate arms that are available for the same mannequin, it is possible to create different positions, and by adding, subtracting, or replacing one of the mannequins in a group, it is possible to form a whole new tableau or scene from life.

Types of Realistic Mannequins

Most female mannequins manufactured today are a **misses** or **missy size mannequin.** They wear size 4 to 8 depending upon the cut and the mannequin's proportions. Depending on the manufacturer and pose, this mannequin can stand anywhere from 5 feet, 8 inches tall to almost 6 feet tall. The measurements are approximately 35″ bust, 24″–25″ waist, and 35″ hips; and the shoe size will vary from $6^{1}/_{2}$ to 7B, on up to 8 and $8^{1}/_{2}$B. (These measurements vary with the manufacturer.)

Figure 9.9 A three-quarter form.

Figure 9.10 Bigger may be better and large or full-size mannequins are available for the larger woman—and man. Shown here are some specially designed size 18 dress forms, and set against the wall is a "pregnant" abstract mannequin. What was once hidden is now shown—up front. *Lifestyle Apogee Mannequins.*

At one time, the display person would spend hours and reams of tissue paper in padding and puffing a dress, or pinning away loads of excess fabric in the back because the mannequin did not really "wear" its clothes. Today's mannequin will usually carry off the costume with style and flourish and little or no "filling out" to emphasize the fullness of a skirt, the roundness of a sleeve, or to encourage a limp fabric to make a crisper statement.

The **junior mannequin** is a size 5, with all the proportions to match (32-22-32). Bust, waist, and hip measurements may vary slightly, depending on the manufacturer. The figure averages about 5 feet, 7 inches to 5 feet,

9 inches in height and is a bit shorter in the waist than the missy mannequin. Many juniors are positioned and made up as young and active figures, but with the proper pose, makeup, and wig, this figure can be representative of a young executive or sophisticate.

A **junior petite mannequin** is the smaller woman's mannequin (about 5 feet, 5 inches tall), short-waisted, and wears size 3–5, with clothes proportioned for the smaller woman. Again, wigs and makeup can make all the difference; this figure can be a cute and perky high-school cheerleader, or mature enough to be the mother of the bride.

Smaller in all proportions, the **petite mannequin** has a 32-inch bust, 21- to 22-inch waist, and 32-inch hips. It is only about 5 feet to 5 feet, 4 inches tall. This figure wears a size 4 or 6. The shoe size is about 6 to $6^1/_2$B.

A store catering to certain ethnic groups, especially Pacific Rim clientele, may need a shorter than "normal" mannequin to show off garments to women who may be smaller in size and proportions. The store may want to select a junior mannequin but avoid any "realism," like makeup, skin color, or wigs that may too closely specify a particular shopper; but be vague enough so that any number of smaller women of any ethnicity or age group can relate to the figure.

The **full-figured** mannequin is the size 14 woman with bigger bust, waist, and hip measurements but still agreeably proportioned. It is fairly tall in proportion as well. This mannequin represents a woman who wears large or plus sizes, presenting her as "Rubenesque" (like the voluptuous women painted by the 17th century Flemish painter Ruben)—rather than fat.

The **preteen mannequin** is designed to wear the young girl's dress, sizes 8 to 10, which is proportioned for the ten- to twelve-year-old. The sculpting suggests the beginnings of a woman's body, but the figure is still relatively flat, uncurved, and childlike.

The **male mannequin** is about 6 feet tall and wears a size 39 or 40 jacket and size 32 trousers (with an inseam measurement of $31^1/_2$ inches). The chest measurement is about 39 to 40 inches, and the shoe size is anywhere from 9 to 10. Without clothing, many male forms seem "skinny" and not virile enough for shorts, swimsuits, and active sportswear. However, active-sports figures are appearing on the market that, in addition to their animated poses, have better muscular definitions.

Figure 9.11 Since not everyone is a perfect "size" and not all bodies can be neatly categorized, some manufacturers are now creating "lifestyle" forms with more human or realistic shapes. *RHO Mannequins.*

Some manufacturers also produce a **young man mannequin** that wears "preppie" sizes; that is, size 16, 18, or 20.

Child mannequins range from tiny tots to the preteens and teens in a variety of ethnic groups, facial expressions, poses, and makeup styles. The various types include "the kid next door"—freckle-faced, eyeglasses barely poised on a snub nose, and maybe even braces capping the teeth—and a porcelain, Victorian-like doll with no sculptured features, but an artfully painted face and hairstyle. Depending on the child's size and the target market (appealing to the young mother, the sports-conscious father, affectionate grandmother), the choices are many.

Accessories for Realistic Mannequins

Most of the realistic mannequins manufactured today come with removable wigs. It is usual to purchase several wigs for a mannequin, especially if the display person or retailer is buying several mannequins from the same group. The different wigs add some variety to the presentation and change the mannequin's appearance.

Fashions change, and what may be "in" one year may become dated the next. A mannequin with perfectly acceptable proportions and anatomical details may become obsolete because the hairstyle is no longer in fashion. The display person or retailer should select hairstyles as well as makeup that are compatible with what their current customers are wearing and with the way they see themselves. A new wig or having an old wig recut or restyled can sometimes "save" a mannequin.

There are two major types of wigs used for mannequins: **hard wigs** and **soft wigs.** A hard wig is highly lacquered or plasticized—never to be restyled. At one time, this type of wig was virtually the only kind used. The hard wig usually features coarser "hair," less subtle colors, more elaborate and decorative styles, and is generally better suited to the semirealistic or highly stylized mannequin.

Soft wigs emulate the softness of natural hair and usually can be combed and brushed. Some synthetic hair fibers can be reset with hot rollers. The texture is more natural; the wig looks and feels more like real hair. Most realistic wigs have a skullcap for a base and hairs are woven into it. Some of the better and more natural wigs have the hairs at the forehead set in by hand in a slightly irregular pattern to simulate a natural hairline. The hairs are then feathered and blended back, giving the hairline an indistinct rather than a sharp, artificial look.

Some manufacturers provide an alternative to eyes subtly painted directly on the mannequin. They produce mannequins that have very natural-looking glass eyes set into open eye sockets. These eyes can be focused so that the figure can be made to "look" in any direction, including up or down. When used in groupings, the mannequins can actually "look" at each other.

Semirealistic Mannequins

Semirealistic mannequins are proportioned and sculpted like realistic mannequins, but with makeup that is neither natural nor realistic, but more decorative or stylized. They may also possess a completely realistic face with sculpted features, but without any makeup at all. The entire figure may be all white or all black, or a color to match a particular department or area. The "hair" may be part of the sculpture—it may not be changed, replaced, or restyled. Although the viewer knows the mannequin simulates a real "type," the lack of makeup definition keeps it from being categorized as a realistic mannequin.

Some display persons find the semirealistic male mannequin preferable to the realistic one. They feel that makeup and removable wig on the realistic male mannequin make him appear unmasculine in comparison to the all-white, bronze or terra-cotta semirealistic, semiabstract, or abstract male mannequin.

Semiabstract Mannequins

The **semiabstract mannequin** is even more stylized and decorative than the semirealistic mannequin. Its features may be painted on or merely suggested, such as a bump for a nose or a hint of pursed lips. The semiabstract mannequin will often have a hairstyle painted onto its otherwise smooth, egg-shaped head. This type of mannequin is doll-like and decorative, and more popular-priced than elegant in appeal.

Abstract Mannequins

The **abstract mannequin** represents the ultimate in style and decoration. The arms and legs may be overly long or slender. It is more concerned with creating an overall effect than with reproducing natural lines and proportions. Rarely is there an attempt made by the sculptor to indicate features or specific details: fingernails, elbows, musculature, and so on. The abstract figure is frequently finished in white or black, or sprayed in a color to match an interior design scheme or a specific color promotion. Some manufacturers will supply abstracts in chrome, copper, gold, metallic, or pearlized finishes.

The abstract mannequin is a quite sophisticated and versatile figure. Depending on the pose, it can wear a wide range of clothing: fur coats, gowns, lingerie, or sportswear. In small retail operations, where the display budget and the number of mannequins available are limited, the abstract mannequin may prove to be especially satisfactory. There are no wigs to style or change; the "shoes" are often sculpted right onto the figure. Because it has no ethnic qualities and is so nebulous and

indefinite, the abstract mannequin can be whatever the visual merchandiser cares to make of it with color, accessories, or the surrounding trim. The abstract mannequin can wear the clothes of the future or of the historic past and look more comfortable in these fashions than a realistic figure will. It crosses color and ethnic lines and knows no age limits.

Headless Mannequins

The **headless mannequin** has a full-size, realistic, or semiabstract body with arms and legs but no head. The pose is often a natural one—a body swing, for example—and it may stand, sit, or recline; but since it is headless, it offers no face, no personality, and no "image."

Figure 9.12 Increasingly popular with retailers and display persons are the headless mannequins. No wigs to go awry, no makeup to fade or date the mannequin, and no skin color to worry about affronting any group of shoppers—the headless form has all the positive qualities of regular mannequins. Plus, there is the ease of dressing them and they are usually less expensive. Here they are shown in a bridal window. *Marshall Field, State Street, Chicago.*

A headless mannequin will work in windows where height is a problem. A regular mannequin may appear overly compressed by a ceiling that is too low. Where the ledge is high and the fascia or ceiling comes down low, the headless mannequin may solve the problem of how to show, on a form, a complete outfit with curves and dimension. Since there is no head, makeup, or wig, this type of form is considerably cheaper than a realistic mannequin.

Mannequins: A Recap

- A mannequin may be a store's most valuable asset and its selection is one of the most important decisions a display person can make.

- Every mannequin should be given a "rest period" so as not to become too familiar to the customer.

- Types of mannequins include realistic, semirealistic, abstract, semiabstract and headless.

- Today's realistic mannequin resembles the everyday person rather than a movie star.

- Formal clothes should be displayed on an "unanimated" mannequin.

- Action clothes should be shown on a mannequin seemingly in motion.

- Seated mannequins add variety and interest to a group of mannequins and can work to show separates, casual wear, lingerie, and active sportswear.

- Horizontal mannequins should only be used for specific merchandise such as nightwear, lingerie, swimwear, and some sportswear.

- Types of realistic mannequins include: misses or missy, junior, junior petite, petite, full-figured, preteen, male, young man, and child.

- There are two major types of wigs used for mannequins: hard wigs and soft wigs.

- A hard wig is highly lacquered or plasticized and cannot be restyled.

- A soft wig emulates the softness of natural hair and can usually be combed and brushed. Some synthetic hair fibers can be reset with hot rollers.

- A semirealistic mannequin is made like a realistic mannequin, but its makeup is more decorative and stylized.

- The semiabstract mannequin is more stylized than the semirealistic mannequin, and its features may be painted or suggested rather than defined.

- The abstract mannequin is concerned with creating an overall effect rather than reproducing natural lines and proportions. Features such as elbows, musculature, or fingernails are rarely indicated.

- A headless mannequin has a full-size or semirealistic body with arms and legs but no head. It offers no personality or image.

Questions for Review and Discussion

1. Detail the criteria used to select a mannequin for a store.

2. What is the average fashion life expectancy of a mannequin?

3. Explain how a mannequin can be a store's "silent salesperson."

4. What is the relationship between mannequins and store image?

5. Make a list of the types of realistic mannequins and indicate measurements and sizes for each type.

6. How should wigs be selected for store mannequins?

7. Briefly describe each of the five major types of mannequins: realistic, semirealistic, semiabstract, abstract, and headless.

Chapter Ten

Alternatives to the Mannequin

AFTER YOU HAVE READ THIS CHAPTER,
YOU WILL BE ABLE TO DISCUSS:

- Alternatives to the traditional mannequin used in design.
- Visual merchandising techniques frequently used in Europe.
- The increased use of mannequin alternatives.

ALTERNATIVES TO THE MANNEQUIN: TRADE TALK

articulated artist's figure	inflatables
body trunk	lay-down techniques
bra form	pants form
bust form	panty form
coat form	pantyhose form
cutout figures	pinup techniques
cutout form	rigged suit form
draper	shell form
dress form	shirt form
European display	soft-sculpted figures
techniques	stocking form
flying	suit forms
form	three-quarter form
hangers	torso form

Attitudes and concepts in merchandise display not only vary from country to country—they can and do vary from city to city and from store to store. There is no one right "answer." Throughout this book, some techniques, some "truths," some tried-and-tested methods and approaches are discussed and illustrated. However, there is no one way that will do all and be all for every store and for every type of merchandise.

Many small stores, especially in France, Italy, Germany, and England, show just their merchandise without any great effort to establish their customer's image. Their own image is established and reiterated in the merchandise they display, how much they display, and how that merchandise is displayed. They usually set out their wares in simple-to-see and easy-to-relate-to arrangements. They present garments, accessories, and alternatives all together. They do not make decisions for the shopper. They do not say, "This is what you should wear!" Rather, they seem to be saying, "These garments can be worn in a variety of ways and in many different combinations. You, with your own good sense of style and what is right for you, will put together the parts that please and suit you."

Figure 10.1 The traditional dress form is shown here with the old-fashioned wire basket "skirt" and cast iron base on wheels. For this line of skirts the tops are left bare and the attention is on the lower half of the form. The shoulder pads can be removed and arms attached. In some forms the neck plates can be removed and fabric covered egg heads attached. *Barneys, Madison Avenue, New York.*

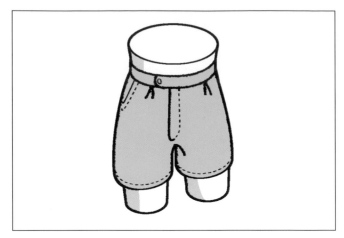

Figure 10.2 A body trunk or trunk form.

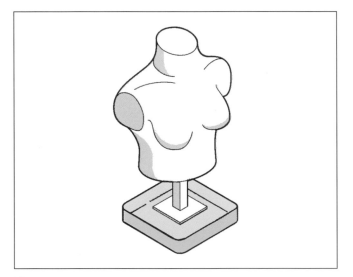

Figure 10.4 A bust, blouse, or sweater form.

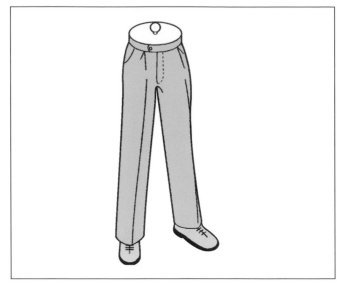

Figure 10.5 A pants or slacks form.

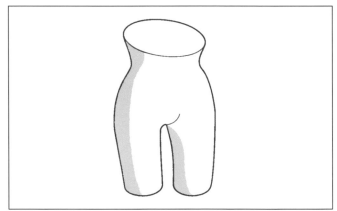

Figure 10.6 A panty form.

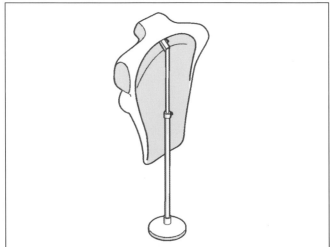

Figure 10.7 A shell form.

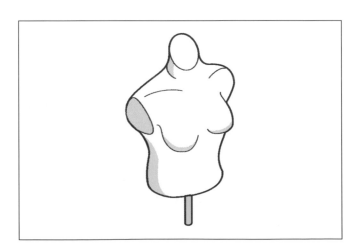

Figure 10.3 A bra form.

Many shoppers in the United States are intimidated by the vast number of choices available to them—the many, many possible ways to go, the quick-changing swings of fads and fashions. On the other hand, Europeans and boutique clientele all over the world seem to make their own decisions. Each purchase appears to be an "investment" and part of an ongoing wardrobe rather than an individual "outfit."

In many cities in Europe, the "promenade" is a way of life—and a way of shopping. Stores will close on Saturday, after lunch, and sometimes remain closed until Monday at noon. The store's windows, however, will remain "open" much of the time. The lights will stay on until midnight; the merchandise, even expensive furs and silver, will remain on view through the long weekend. At night and through the weekend afternoons, it is a thing to do: to "do" the windows on the main boulevard. This activity almost seems choreographed. First, the pedestrian strolls up one side of the street; each window is examined, scrutinized, and digested—and the prices noted. The return stroll is on the other side of the street, following the same procedure. Along the way, there may be a stop for coffee, with time out to watch the other strollers. Since the stores are all closed, no attempt is made at that time to get the strollers inside. Rather, it is a less promotional, more leisurely approach to presenting one's wares—a display truly intended to "show" the merchandise in the best possible presentation.

It is important to understand this type of shopping because there is a trend at present toward creating shopping streets without vehicular traffic in many urban renewal areas. These urban malls are used for sitting, strolling, and shopping. Even in bustling New York, some streets are closed to traffic at certain times of the year just to allow pedestrians to stroll the shopping streets and sidewalks more freely and leisurely. This slowdown of the tempo on Main Street is giving downtown a new look and can affect the type of displays being created.

Many shopping centers and malls, as they are designed today in the United States, do not encourage strolling. When the stores open, they consist of large, gaping openings, ready to swallow in the passerby with little or no window presentation at all. When they are closed for the night, the view is of assorted grids, grills, and metal meshes. Some malls, however, are designed with stores that have windows, storefronts, and actual entrances. In these malls, strolling is encouraged, even after closing. The promenade is enhanced by cafes, restaurants, and theaters that continue operating through the evenings and weekends.

With this brief introduction, it should be easier to understand these small shop or boutique-type display techniques, which are labeled **European display techniques.**

It used to be that only the large and better specialty and department stores would use mannequins and the small mom-and-pop shops would rely on dress forms or partial forms to show off their wares. Mainly it was a matter of cost; a good mannequin is expensive and the cost of a collection of mannequins for various occasions and types of clothing can be overwhelming for the small shopkeeper. In the past few years, we are finding that more and more mannequin houses are creating their own competition; they are designing and producing an infinite variety of alternatives to the mannequin. That does not mean that the mannequin, as we know it, is a thing of the past. As it has been for the past 100 years, it will continue to be reincarnated each year or two with a new body shape or proportion, a new face, a new body attitude, a new lifestyle to emulate—and a new representation of the next wave of shoppers. However, it will probably not become less expensive. To keep a mannequin looking its very best takes time and money. It takes an occasional new coat of paint and a new makeup, or a make-over. New wigs with current styles and colors are not inexpensive if they are going to really enhance (and fit) the look of the realistic mannequin. Dressing the realistic mannequin not only takes time—it also takes talent and a feeling for how the clothes should fit. The mannequin alternative often simplifies the dressing process while it adds a fresh look and attitude to the display space and the merchandise. The traditional mannequin—whether realistic, semirealistic, or even abstract—visually provides a sense of body beneath the garment and is really the most effective way to show off how a dress drapes, falls, and fits. However, seeing the same mannequin or her clone or very close relative standing week after week in the same spot in the same window or the same ledge does rob some of the excitement from the new outfit being shown. It can get visually boring. After a while the shopper no longer "sees" the mannequin; it becomes invisible and what it is wearing just isn't seen. What is needed is a change, a different approach to break the pattern, to take the dullness out of the routine.

Today, the display person has so many options to the mannequin that it is possible to give the mannequin a much-needed rest—a vacation away from the viewing public and out of the sun's fading rays. When it makes a return appearance, it actually means something to the display and to the garment being offered.

Image is of the utmost importance in selecting the alternatives. What is used says something about the garment displayed on it and though it may not and often does not show off as effectively how the dress molds, blends, and enhances the body of the wearer, it can show how various components can be blended into an outfit—how separates can be paired off and be paired differently, how accessories will complement and enrich an outfit—all the while treating the merchandise as part of an elegant still-life arrangement with the emphasis on style and class. Sometimes it can say, "You know how beautifully this will fit—we really don't have to show that to you." This is a kind of snobbery that will sell merchandise to certain shoppers.

As one walks up and down the fine fashion streets in the United States, Sloane Street or South Moulton Street in London, the Faubourg St. Honore in Paris—anywhere haute couture, prêt-à-porter garments, and designer merchandise is sold—one will rarely see a realistic mannequin in the window modeling the clothes. One might come across abstract mannequins or stylized figures all of one color with no makeup or wig, but the prevalent trend seems to be toward dress forms, torsos, drapers with hanger-hung outfits, or merchandise draped and beautifully arranged on pieces of furniture (see Chapter 15, Furniture as Props).

Many of these European-style, nonmannequin displays have been introduced into the United States by the noted designers whose boutiques now appear on the major shopping streets in many cities across the country as well as in top, upscale malls. American designers such as Ralph Lauren favor the use of dress or suit forms over any sort of "human" representation—realistic or stylized. Many of the trendier, youth-oriented, and fun-fashion shops like Gap, Banana Republic, and Express have taken to dressing hangers or using drapers rather

than mannequins. Not only does this add a kind of panache and a "devil-may-care" attitude to the display and the product being displayed, it is also faster and simpler than properly dressing a mannequin. Also, the hanger/draper is significantly less expensive than a fashionable, up-to-the-moment mannequin. What is needed is a style and a flair for dressing the hanger or draper so that the garment doesn't look like something pulled out of a closet: creased, wrinkled, formless, and bodiless.

Types of Alternatives to Mannequins

Let us review some of the ways apparel and accessories can be shown without the use of a mannequin.

Three-Quarter Forms

A **form** is a three-dimensional representation of a part of the human anatomy, such as the torso, the bust, or the area from shoulder to waist or from hips to ankles. The **three-quarter form** has a body extending to the knees or just below the knees, and can have an adjustable rod (located beneath the form or in the butt) and a weighted base. It usually has a head. (A headless three-quarter form that comes just to the knees is commonly called a **torso form.**) The legs are usually parted. It may or may not have arms. (The **dress form** is an armless version of the three-quarter form.) The lack of detailing means that this neutral, three-dimensional body form does not make a "statement."

The three-quarter form can wear a wide variety of clothes. There may be a degree of swing and movement to the torso. The form can be raised or lowered on the rod to accommodate it to the height of the area in which it is being used and to the merchandise it is required to wear. The torso can be lowered almost to the cut-off knees in order to model swimsuits, shorts, a teddy, or a slip, or it can be raised way up to show off a long gown, a robe, a full-length skirt, or even trousers.

These forms are not as expensive as mannequins, but do very little to promote a fashion image. In experiments conducted on the selling floor, it has been found that the partial form or torso is more effective than a hanger or draper, but less effective than a mannequin.

Soft-sculpted Figures

The **soft-sculpted figure** is a European favorite that is making inroads into the United States display scene. This is a life-size doll—male, female, or children of all ages—and is available covered in black, dark brown, or off-white, jersey-like fabric with little or no facial details. The skeleton is a bendable wire armature that can be shaped and positioned. The armature is imbedded in a soft, spongy, foam filler that holds its shape inside the jersey "skin."

The figures are abstract, not realistic and, if well-handled, they completely disappear in the display setting. They hold and give shape to the merchandise, but the dark body becomes invisible when seen against a dark background. The lighting will pick up the merchandise, but will disregard the body wearing it. The floppy figure needs to be positioned properly in order to look real; it has to be propped, pinned, and secured in place, or wired in order to stand. The soft sculpture may require extra padding or primping.

Some manufacturers in the United States produce funny, frolicsome, white canvas "dolls" that add a light-hearted eccentric quality to the display. These figures are not as costly as regular mannequins. They are novelties and can be very effective in displaying active sportswear, sporting goods, maybe swimwear, or in any presentation that aims for a humorous approach. Soft-sculpted children's figures are especially popular and adaptable.

Articulated Artist's Figures

These life-sized figures are based on the small wooden miniatures used by artists and designers to get correct anatomical proportions and poses for figure drawing when a live model is not available. Movable joints can be swiveled or turned into new positions. They are usually made of wood or white plastic.

The abstractness of the full-sized **articulated artist's figure** lends itself to decorative and undressed applications as well as fully dressed and accessorized setups. These figures can be made to stand, and can interact with other abstract, articulated forms. They can wear only accessories (belts, ties, scarves, hats) and still not look underdressed. The figures—male or female—have no age, no personality, no ethnic quality, and can be anything to anybody. In addition, they are fun to work with—in windows, on ledges, or anywhere in the store.

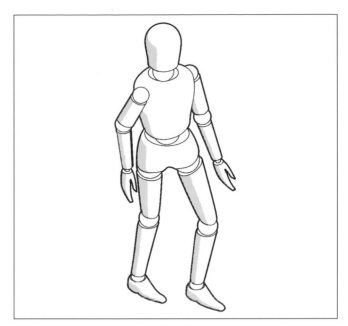

Figure 10.8 An articulated artist's figure.

Dress Forms and Suit Forms

The dress form has had its greatest renaissance in the last few years. It has come out of the atelier, or designer's workshop, and into plain sight on ledges, standing on platforms in front of designer boutiques, and in windows completely dressed and accessorized. The old metal basket and roll-around, cast iron base is often reproduced today to look as it did a century ago—to enhance the "old-fashioned," tailored, crafted, and designer look of the garment. The dress form actually provides an image to the garment. Some stores and designers prefer the classic natural linen upholstered form that has neither arms nor head; a metal neck plate and arm plates are used instead. Some manufacturers are producing egg-shaped heads that can be added onto the neck and even articulated arms made of wood—hinged and movable—that can be added to make the form seem more like a figure. Simple legs are another accessory for the dress form that now turns it into a stylized, fabric-covered figure rather than the traditional form. Of course, the forms are now available in a vast selection of fabric finishes and colors, or they can be reupholstered for special promotions.

The traditional upholstered forms are the dress form for women's wear, which extends down to mid-thigh,

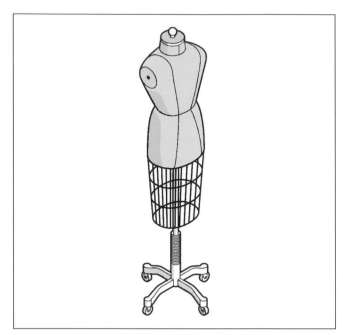

Figure 10.9 A dress form.

and the men's **suit form,** which is usually hip length. Blouse and shirt forms end at the waistline. The form is usually supported by an adjustable rod that is in turn held upright by the base. Since the rod is usually centered on the form, it is simple enough to put a skirt or dress on the dress form, but trousers won't work. The same is true of the men's suit form. What is usually done is to pin the pants or trousers across the front of the dress or suit form and let them hang down in front of the supporting rod. Dressing the dress and suit form is discussed in Chapter 11, Dressing the Three-Dimensional Form.

A recent addition to the dress/suit form design is the off-centered supporting rod. The rod extends up not to the center of the form but to one side of it and makes it possible for the display person to dress the form and even pull up a pair of pants with the rod hidden in one leg while the other hangs free or can be "posed" to suggest some style or animation. It does look somewhat lopsided or cantilevered when the off-centered rod is not hidden by the trouser leg, but it looks great when dressed.

It used to be that suit forms were rigged. As the reader will see in Chapter 11, Dressing the Three-Dimensional Form, **rigged suit forms** were dressed and pinned to perfection so that there were no wrinkles or creases and the

arms usually hung straight down, with the shirtsleeve neatly positioned to peek out. Today's younger male shopper wants his comfort. He wants to be stylish; he wants to have his fashion and enjoy it. Even when business suits or formal wear is being shown, the form is usually dressed rather than rigged; it is relaxed, casual, and easygoing. Often the display person will "humanize" or "animate" the form; the arm (which may not really be there) is bent, the sleeve may end up in a pocket, a tie may be flipped, a sweater may be casually tied over a jacket, the shirt's top button may be left open, the single-breasted suit flapping, and there is a sense of freedom and joie de vivre about the whole presentation. The display person may pouf and pad, add some crushed tissue to fill in a chest that isn't there or reinforce a sagging shoulder. Two sausages of tissue may double for the upper and lower arms so that when the sleeve is pulled back and angled to go into the pocket, there is some "body" in that sleeve.

Some display personnel create "invisible" people with dress forms by floating hats over where the head might be. Scarves unfurl around neck plates, gloves extend down from jacket or coat sleeves with tissue paper "rolls" inserted into each finger of the glove so that the "hand" can assume a shape or make a gesture. Tubes of corrugated paper can be turned into legs to give the trousers a sense of "being," and shoes used to plug up the tubes. If the form itself is suspended, it can be tilted or angled so that the whole "body" seems to be moving. It helps when this illusion is performed in a black, black window with only pinpoints of light to play up what should be seen. The many wires that are used to rig the trick remain invisible.

Cutout Figures

The **cutout figure** is trendy, high style, and avant-garde—young, fun, and sassy. True to human proportions, this figure is a silhouette cut out of wood or heavy board. Clothes are pinned or draped over it for a frontal or elevated view of the merchandise. Since the figures are flat cutouts and virtually two-dimensional, they provide very little form to the merchandise. The garments can be made to sag on the figure, or the display person can stuff and fill the garments with pads and tissue in order to provide greater form and roundness.

Some stores use **cutout forms** that are almost cubist —reminiscent of Picasso—in order to dehumanize the

Figure 10.10 The traditional men's suit form cuts off at the hip or where a jacket would usually end. Here they are shown on traditional wrought iron bases and used to underscore the "made to measure" quality of the garments. Since tailors "create" on suit forms and dress forms, the form has become a recognizable symbol for custom designing or tailoring, and thus up-scales the garment displayed. *Loro Piana, Madison Avenue, New York.*

forms even further. Other stores, however, when using cutout techniques, have attempted to make these forms appear more "real." Photographs of life-sized frontal views of men and women are applied to wooden silhouettes about 3 or 4 inches thick. The arms may be removable to facilitate dressing this type of "mannequin." The end effect is sophisticated and trendy, with a sense of style and a semblance of reality. This is a boutique look rather than a department store approach.

Inflatables

Inflatables are life-sized "balloons" that simulate parts of the human anatomy. The most popular inflatable resembles the lower half of the body (waist, hips, and legs) and is used to show jeans and pants.

These forms will work for some merchandise and for certain types of stores. They show, impersonally, clothes with dimension and form. The inflatables are stiff and rigid; they usually lack grace and beauty of body line, but they are inexpensive and can be used in multiple groupings for garments that do not have to project a high-fashion look.

Drapers

Time was when a **draper** was a simple, uncomplicated, and often underused alternative to the mannequin. In its simplest and purest form a draper is a shaped hanger set atop a vertical rod that is supported by a base. It is often produced with an adjustable rod and, although not versatile enough to display a jacket on a table or ledge, it can be extended to its full height and stand on the selling floor or in the window and show off a complete suit, a dress, or even a gown. Sometimes the basic draper can be designed so that the skirt or trousers can be either clipped on under the jacket or the pants can be folded over the slack rod and be shown alongside the jacket. This is the basic form. However, in the past few years the draper has been recognized by display persons everywhere as a decorative prop as well as a mannequin alternative. You can see drapers in every Gap store, Banana Republic, Limited, Express, Armani A/X, and so many more highly visible operations.

The market is overflowing with wonderful and unique "fixtures" that are often pieces of sculpture. Abstract heads or decorative finials of metal, wood, or plastic are incorporated over the hangers to suggest "heads" and also to add height and stature to the drapers. The shaped wooden hanger or the metal arc that serves as a hanger is sometimes replaced with a dimensionalized semibust form with shoulders and chest, which adds "body" and some shape to the garment draped over it. Drapers today are available in wood, metal, plastic, and assorted combinations of the three. Whether completely dressed or just hung with fashion accessories like scarves, belts, and bags, the drapers are decorative additions to the shop or boutique. They are often selected or especially designed to enhance the look and image of the retail space. Drapers in a single retail establishment may vary in design, material, and finish depending on the area in which they are used and the kind of merchandise they are used to promote. Just as different kinds of mannequins are used with different merchandise classifications, so are the drapers selected to further a look or lifestyle in men's suits, men's active sportswear, women's suits, lingerie, and so on.

Some drapers are equipped with shoe platforms so that the shoes can be shown along with the outfit, though shoes are also shown on the floor next to or on the base of the draper.

Hangers

A simple **hanger** can be an alternative to the mannequin, but without taste or talent it can also look like something

Figure 10.11 There is no mannequin or form hidden in this cleverly conceived and executed example of a stuffed outfit. Stuffed gloves become the hands, the hat is suspended over where the head would be, if there was one, and the shoes are placed below the cuffed trouser legs. This type of dressing takes time—and talent—and expert lighting to keep how it was all done a mystery. *Paul Stuart, Madison Avenue, New York.*

that was just pulled out of stock or off the rack without fuss, bother, or presentation. Ideally, a padded or dimensionalized hanger should be used, or hangers that are variations on bust forms should be used to ensure that the garment drapes better.

As with the draper, in dressing the hanger—if a complete outfit is to be shown—the blouse or shirt goes on first. The pants or skirt is pinned onto the blouse or shirt where the waistline would be. The jacket or coat is then put on top to finish off the presentation. Scarves or ties can be knotted around the neck and/or jewelry such as necklaces, chains, or brooches can be added. A shoulder bag can be secured over the shoulder; it would have to be pinned so that it doesn't slide off. If trousers are shown,

the excess material is folded back inside the leg and a pair of appropriate shoes can be set beneath the trousers. Even a dress can be accessorized with the right shoes, bag, and gloves arranged on the floor beneath the dressed hanger.

The hanger can either be hung by invisible wire from a ceiling grid or it can be hung from a hook that extends from a wall or panel. With some imagination, the display person can create more seasonal or promotional ways of suspending the hanger such as from a bare tree branch pushing through a back wall, or tied from above with festive ribbon streamers or ticker tape or streamers and confetti. It takes some ingenuity, but it can be done. A little judicious padding wouldn't hurt and some "animation" can be achieved by bending a sleeve, crossing a leg,

Figure 10.12 A dressed hanger—layered with vest and jacket over the shirt and the pants that are suspended off the shirt—makes this a unique way of showing a complete outfit without a mannequin or form. The hat is tipped over the top, the coat draped over the shoulders, and an ascot jauntily tied at the neck. Shoes are positioned below. The panel that supports the hanger also serves as a surface to pin parts of the draped garments onto. *Frankovia, Dusseldorf, Germany.*

object in a smooth and harmonious manner. **Lay-down techniques** can be used in windows, on ledges, in cases, pinned onto boards, and against walls or columns.

For a window lay-down presentation, the merchandise is arranged on the floor of the window. Often, a step or two, a platform, or a riser is added for interest or to separate groupings.

The following is an example of a typical lay-down presentation. A jacket, with a blouse or shirt folded inside, may be artfully stretched out on the top of a platform with one sleeve akimbo and the cuff tucked into the jacket pocket. The skirt (or pants) could then start from under the lower end of the jacket and flow down off the platform onto the floor of the window, where the skirt could swirl out to its fullest, or could be rippled, or be finely pleated. The skirt (or pants) might then be crossed or banded with a selection of belts, which could lead the shopper's eye over to a pair of shoes backed up with a handbag or two and several pairs of well-arranged gloves. To the other side of the skirt (or pants) there could be an assortment, fanned out in echelon, of other tops and scarves or neckties that would also complement the outfit being shown. There might also be some suggestions of appropriate costume jewelry, flowers, or toiletries. In a typically European display, there might also be a draper or costumer in the window—on the platform, behind the layered jacket, with a coat, hat, scarf,

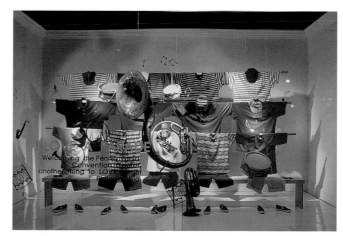

Figure 10.13 A rod pulled through the arms of T-shirts is all it took to create this grandstand display of assorted colorful tops. The short pants are partially resting on the benches. This is an amusing way to show off a line of casual wear. *Strawbridge & Clothier, Philadelphia.*

and so forth. A soft roll of tissue paper or a bendable tube can be inserted inside the sleeve to make the "arm" seem more believable.

Lay-down Techniques

The art of lay-down is all in the folding, the pleating, and the placement of garment next to garment and of accessories next to the featured garments. It requires all the basics of good composition: color, line, texture, balance, and the ability to direct the viewer's eye from object to

Figure 10.14 Forms, torsos, and bits and pieces of mannequins can effectively be used in a helter–skelter manner when the merchandise is fun, casual, and/or sporty. For this denim display the bodies come apart to float or stand—unrelated to each other—to show off some of the store's stock. *Barneys, Madison Avenue, New York.*

and possibly a pointing, rolled-up umbrella leading to the arrangement below.

This type of merchandise presentation does not suggest "image" as we usually think of it. With this type of display, it is assumed that the customer knows what is wanted and liked, and that he or she will be able to select and put together an outfit from the various alternatives suggested.

In most effective lay-down displays, a color theme is promoted and various alternate choices may be offered to tie in with a general scheme. If two or three different color "stories" are to be promoted in a single display window—or with a single basic outfit—each story could be effectively separated from the others by placing each on

a different level or platform and by allowing the basic or neutral color to carry through from group to group. The major color promoted on the uppermost level could become the accent at the center level, and the color "lead" from the middle could become the accessory color at the lowest level. Let us translate this into an actual example: A navy suit is trimmed with red on level one. On level two, a gray outfit is highlighted with the navy from level one. On level three, a red dress is trimmed with the gray from level two.

Lay-down requires that the merchandise be pressed or steamed and in perfect condition—just as the merchandise should be for any presentation. Here, however, the trimmer cannot "fake it" by hoping the mannequin or form underneath will smooth out the wrinkles, or by pushing the crease aside. In this form of display, the garments are usually brought up very close to the viewer, allowing perusal. The buttonholes, the stitching, the matching of plaids and patterns, the meeting of the collar, the dimple in the tie—they are all up front.

The nature of the garment fabric should be "explained" by the type of lay-down used. If the fabric is soft and flowing, it should be allowed to spread out gracefully, to float or drape. If it is hard, crisp, and tailored, the lines should be sharp and precise.

Another form of lay-down is the draping of garments over furniture, on tables, or "sitting" on chairs. With this method, the body of a dress (or jacket), for example, is pinned or draped over a chair back. The sleeves are placed on the chair's armrests or they are posed on the "lap" of the garment. The skirt (or pants) starts on the chair seat and hangs over the edge. Hosiery or pantyhose can be used to fill in the gap between the skirt and the

shoes that are sitting on the floor, looking natural and at ease. A hat can sit on top of the chair back, a scarf and/or jewelry can be shown at the neckline, and a bag can be hooked from the arm of the chair. Or, in a men's wear display, a shirt may sit against the chair back wearing a properly knotted tie. An auxiliary accessory grouping can be arranged on the floor near the shoes. This arrangement is young and trendy and can work for separates as well as dresses—for men as well as women. Lingerie could be draped over a chaise longue, or sunwear out on a beach chair. The possibilities are endless and the results should be amusing.

Pinup Techniques

Pinup techniques make use of a panel, wall, or some vertical surface onto which a garment can be pinned, shaped, and dimensionalized. A form or mannequin is not used; pads, tissue, and straight pins are. The garment is pinned onto the panel and then the tissue is crumpled

Figure 10.15 Pin and fly. Outfits are pinned and wired to suggest figures in action. Some parts of the garments are pinned on to the rear wall while others, like the sleeves, are pulled out into space by means of invisible wire or plastic fishing reel thread. *Macy's, Herald Square, New York.*

Figure 10.16 Scarves, bags, hats, and other fashion accessories are artfully draped and hung on the stylish, cut-out foam core figures for an interesting presentation of the add-ons that make an outfit. *H-Bendel, Fifth Avenue, New York.*

and added to fill out the garment where form is needed: the bust, the shoulders, possibly in a sleeve or at the hips. Accessories are pinned on at appropriate locations; shoes are included on the floor in front of the "dressed" panel.

Humor and wit can help with this type of presentation. Since it is obvious that there is no "body," the more animated and "realistic" the position of the pinned-up garment, the better. Sleeves can be slipped into pockets or waistbands. They may be folded to hold flowers, a bag, or just wave "bye-bye." Gloves can be pinned inside the sleeves for "hands," and rolled-up tissue, slipped inside each finger, can give form and action to the glove. A shoulder bag might be slung over the shoulder. A hat

might be pinned, brim down and crown out, to simulate a missing head. Pantyhose can be used to suggest legs—especially if the toes end up inside shoes on the floor and if the shoes are properly positioned, not just set there. When the outfit includes trousers or pants, the legs can be crossed, bent, dipped, or spread for action poses. The excess fabric of the trouser leg can be tucked inside boots or shoes, or rolled in undulating waves like a French croissant, or pinned down on the floor next to the appropriate shoes. The important thing to remember here is the condition of the merchandise to be pinned. Nothing short of perfection should do! It is possible for a garment to lose an unwanted crease in a pinup technique, but do not depend on it.

Sometimes an outfit can be pinned up in an abstract geometric arrangement similar to the paintings of Piet Mondrian. It is comparable to a lay-down presentation except that it is pinned to a board and shown vertically rather than horizontally. This type of pinup presentation is especially effective when shown on an easel with something soft, such as a coat and scarf, draped off the side and leading down to an auxiliary lay-down arrangement.

Another simple, semi-pinup arrangement uses a traditional hat stand or coatrack. The garments are draped off the hooks on top, but padded, rounded out, and pinned to provide some feeling of depth, form, and detail. If the shoulder and front of a jacket are important, the padding should emphasize these features and the garments should be positioned on the rack to show these parts prominently. The skirt (or pants) could be pinned into the jacket so that the complete outfit is "hung" on the rack. It would also be fitting for a coat, scarf, hat, and umbrella to be hooked onto the stand, to complete the outfit.

Ideally, the use of pinup or lay-down techniques should alternate with mannequin presentations for a change of pace, for a different look, to surprise and amuse the customer, and to suggest that something new is happening. Using only pinup or lay-down methods can be as dull as using the same mannequins or forms over and over again. Either of these two techniques could be used in conjunction with a mannequin or dressmaker form. Variety and change are the essence of fashion and fashion presentation.

Flying Techniques

Flying is a display technique whereby the merchandise is pulled, stretched, and manipulated by means of almost-invisible fishing line or very fine piano wire. The wire is attached to the hem, sleeve, shoulder, and so on, of the garment and then pulled back and secured by pinning or nailing it into the ceiling, floor, a side wall, or back wall. This stretching pulls the garment into abstract shapes with little resemblance to the way it would look in actual use. Flying basically provides an angular and crisp presentation that could be very effective for active sportswear, separates, and fun and trendy merchandise, but could be a detriment to soft, flowing garments when the fabric is pulled taut.

In this type of display, the merchandise "flies" and floats in the open window space. One garment often visually overlaps or flies in front of another garment. The viewer sees a pattern of bits and pieces, but not quite a whole garment or an outfit. Flying is not recommended if the merchandise to be presented is an outfit made up of parts and accessories. It works better where a line of merchandise is shown: all sweaters, all slips, all skirts. It can be effective if the main feature of the merchandise is pattern or color—not shape or form. A window of flying towels or pillows and/or pillowcases, or scarves, caftans, or T-shirts, could be a change-of-pace display that works when done well.

Glossary of Other Forms

Most of the following forms are made of vinyl and are vacuum-formed or, in some cases, made of rubber-maché and cast in a mold.

blouse form See *bust form.*

body trunk A male form that starts at the diaphragm (above the waistline) and continues to just below the knees. Shorter forms, however, will be cut at mid-thigh. It is used to show shorts, underwear, swimwear, and so on. Also called a *trunk form.*

bra form A headless, armless form that ends just below a defined bustline, with or without shoulders. The forms are usually scaled to wear a size 34B. Junior bra forms are proportioned for a 32A bust.

bust form An armless, headless form that ends just below the waistline. It has a defined bust and is used to show ladies' blouses and sweaters. Also called a *blouse* or *sweater form.*

coat form A headless, usually armless male form that starts at the neck and ends around the hips. Used to present suits, jackets, and sweaters. Arm pads or bendable rod arms may be used with this form. It also comes with an adjustable rod and base. Also called a **suit form.** (See Chapter 11 on "Rigging a Suit Form.")

leg form See *stocking form.*

pants form A male or female form that goes from the waistline down to, and including, the feet. Men's forms will usually wear size 30 trousers with a 32-inch inseam. Female pants forms are designed to wear a size 8. If the legs are crossed, one leg will be removable to facilitate dressing the form. It is often provided with a foot spike that will hold the form in a standing position. Also called a *slacks form.*

panty form A waist-to-knees form for showing panties, girdles, or bikini bottoms. These forms are about 2 feet tall and are usually used for counter and ledge displays.

pantyhose form A lightweight, female form that extends from waist to toes. The toe can be set into a toe bracket, permitting the form to stand in an upright position. It may also be inverted to rest on its waist with the legs up. The same form can also display stretch tights and pants.

shell form A half-round, lightweight, partial torso form similar to a bra, blouse, or sweater form. The front is fully sculpted, but the back is "scooped out."

shirt form The male version of the bust, or blouse, form. See *bust form.*

slacks form See *pants form.*

stocking form A form in the shape of a leg used for merchandising hosiery. It has a hollow top into which the top of the hose can be inserted. The form is available in assorted lengths depending on the merchandise to be displayed, such as thigh-high, knee-high, or calf-high. Also called *leg form.*

sweater form See *bust form.*

trunk form See *body trunk.*

Alternatives to the Mannequin: A Recap

- Many European stores set out their wares in simple-to-see and easy-to-relate-to arrangements rather than complicated displays.

- A number of shoppers in the United States seem to be intimidated by the wide range of choices and may be influenced by quick-changing fads and fashion, while European shoppers seem to make their own decisions and consider each purchase an investment and part of an ongoing wardrobe rather than part of an individual outfit.

- In European cities, it is not unusual for stores to close after lunch on Saturday and remain closed until noon on Monday. However, their windows will remain lit and the merchandise will remain on view all weekend, giving strolling pedestrians time to see and evaluate merchandise at their leisure.

- In many shopping centers and malls in the United States, strolling is not encouraged. When the stores are open, they consist of large, gaping openings ready to swallow shoppers. When closed, they are covered by grids, grills, and assorted meshes. Some malls, however, are designed with stores that have windows, storefronts, and actual entrances. In these malls, strolling is encouraged, even after closing, by promenades, cafes, restaurants, and even theaters operating through the evenings and weekends.

- A mannequin occasionally needs a new coat of paint, a new wig, new makeup, or a general makeover to keep looking its best.

- Using the same or a similar mannequin over and over again will become boring and make the merchandise invisible.

- Using a hanger, draper, or inflatable form is significantly less expensive than using a mannequin.

- Apparel and accessories can be shown without a mannequin by using the following: three-quarter forms, soft-sculpted figures, articulated abstract figures, dress and suit forms, and cutout figures.

- The display person may choose to use a lay-down technique instead of mannequins.

- The lay-down technique involves the folding, pleating, and placement of garment next to garment, or accessories next to featured garment.

- Lay-down can be used in windows, on ledges, in cases, pinned onto boards, and against walls and columns.

- Pinup technique makes use of a panel, wall, or some vertical surface onto which a garment can be pinned, shaped, and dimensionalized.

- Flying is a display technique whereby the merchandise is pulled, stretched, and manipulated by means of almost-invisible fishing line or very fine piano wire, and pulls the garment into abstract shapes that present an angular and crisp presentation.

Questions for Review and Discussion

1. In what ways do shoppers and visual presentations in Europe often differ from customers and visual presentations in the United States? Provide some specific examples.

2. Why are alternatives to mannequins being used more frequently by stores?

3. Based on the descriptions provided, use books, trade magazines, catalogs from fixture suppliers, or photographs from stores to find an example of each type of form mentioned in the chapter.

4. How do cutout figures differ from the abstract mannequins mentioned in the previous chapter?

5. What are inflatables and how are they most frequently used to display?

6. Explain the difference between the use of a draper and a hanger in display.

7. Describe a display of men's wear using lay-down techniques.

8. How is flying merchandise accomplished?

chapter eleven

Dressing the Three-Dimensional Form

AFTER YOU HAVE READ THIS CHAPTER,
YOU WILL BE ABLE TO DISCUSS:

- The steps to be taken in dressing a mannequin.
- The methods in which mannequins may be attached to a base for standing.
- The edges of rigging a suit form.
- The process of dressing a shirt form.

DRESSING THE THREE-DIMENSIONAL FORM: TRADE TALK

ankle-rod fittings
butt-rod fittings
quick cuff
shirt board
shirt form
suit form

Dressing a Mannequin

In order to dress a mannequin, it must first be taken apart and then carefully reassembled as the various items or merchandise are put on the figure. After "dressing" a mannequin for some time, the display person will develop his or her own technique for handling the mannequin and assembling the parts. For the beginner, the following steps will serve as a convenient way to start.

If a mannequin has a removable wig, it should be carefully taken off the head and set aside so that it will not be crushed while garments are being pulled over the figure's head. If the wig on the mannequin cannot be removed, or if the display person does not choose to remove it, a plastic bag, slipped over the head before the dressing starts, will help protect the wig.

The head and neck are part of the bust or torso, and this upper half is usually removable at the waist or hips from the legs below. To remove the top from the bottom, one simply holds the torso securely, gently rotates it to the right, and then lifts it up. The fitting that connects the parts consists of a peg extending up from the lower half, and another element, similar to a keyhole, buried in the base of the upper half.

If the hands are removable, hold the arm securely with one hand and rotate the mannequin's wrist to the right in order to disconnect the hand from the arm. The hand has a peg or extension that locks into the keyhole slot in the base of the arm. To avoid confusion when reassembling, it is important that the dresser keep track of which side the various parts came from (e.g., right hand replaced on right arm).

The arms are hooked into keyhole slots in the shoulders of the mannequins. Holding the torso securely, move the arm a bit to free it from the socket in which it is hooked, then raise the arm up and out of the socket.

If the mannequin is to wear shorts, pants, or pantyhose, one leg will probably need to be removed. The legs are hooked into the torso, and are usually removed from it in the same manner as the hands.

The assorted parts should now be lying before the dresser, on a clean, soft carpet or drop cloth. Of course, the dresser's hands should also be clean. Even though most mannequins do have washable finishes, they should be handled very carefully. Some display persons cover their hands with soft paper or clean cloths during the dismantling and reassembling of the mannequin.

The lower half of the mannequin is usually dressed first. The pantyhose or hosiery (of the proper shade to go with the outfit) is put on first. Invert the lower half of the form and remove one leg, if possible. With this lower half in the inverted position, pull the hose and/or trouser leg over the leg still attached to the torso. Insert the "free" leg into the other leg of the hose or trousers. Secure the detached leg and pull the hose and trousers up to the waist.

If the mannequin has a **butt-rod fitting** (an attachment on the buttocks into which the floor rod is inserted so that the mannequin can stand), an opening has to be provided in the crotch or the seam in the back of the pantyhose (or trousers or shorts) to permit the butt rod to slide into the fitting. (If the shorts or pants have wide enough legs, it might be possible to have the rod go up through the garment leg into the fitting without opening the seam.)

Many new mannequins, particularly those designed primarily to wear pants or active sportswear, are equipped with **ankle-rod fittings.** In this case, the fitting for the supporting rod is inserted into a piece of hardware attached to the back of the mannequin's leg, above the ankle. Another alternative is for the display person to wire or nail the mannequin to the ledge or into the window, and thus do away with the need for any supporting rods.

A skirt, if the mannequin will be wearing one, is put on next. If the outfit includes a top that will be tucked into the waistband, the skirt opening is not closed at this time.

The mannequin is now ready for shoes. When a mannequin is purchased, the manufacturer will supply in-

Figure 11.1 The dress form is the symbol of custom-made and designer label clothes. In this simple display the forms are dressed to appear casual and relaxed so that one can almost feel the fabric. The screen serves to separate the forms from the store beyond, and the picture frames and chair turn this small corner space into a vignette setting of a townhouse. *Wallach's, Livingston, New Jersey.*

formation concerning the appropriate shoe size and heel height. If the store does not carry shoes in stock, the display person or management could try to make arrangements with a local shoe store to have them supply the right type and color of shoes in the right size to go with the ensemble being presented. Often, this sort of arrangement can be accomplished in exchange for a credit in the window that states: "Shoes courtesy of. . . ." If such an arrangement is not possible, the display department should invest in purchasing several pairs of basic shoes in basic colors—but in the current season's

style—to use on the mannequins. A mannequin's feet are no longer bound in ribbons, and it is not proper for an elegantly dressed and accessorized mannequin to appear in public without shoes.

With the shoes securely on, the dressed lower portion of the mannequin can be set into the butt or ankle rod, which is attached to a floor plate. If the mannequin will eventually be wired in place, lean the dressed lower half against a soft, clean, nonabrasive surface, until the upper portion of the mannequin is ready.

To attach the top half to the bottom, place the two parts together so that the projecting peg, on the top of the lower part, fits into the keyhole slot at the base of the upper torso. Turn the torso gently to lock it in place. The two parts will now make a smooth, even line.

If a sweater or over-the-head blouse or top is to be displayed, pull it on and slide the detached arms up through the sleeves. Fit the peg on the end of the arm into the keyhole slot at the shoulder. Do not force it. Be sure to insert the right arm into the right slot and the left arm into the left slot.

If the garment is a button-up-the-front (or back) type, put it on over the shoulders. Next, fit the "action arm" (the one with the most bend or twist) in through

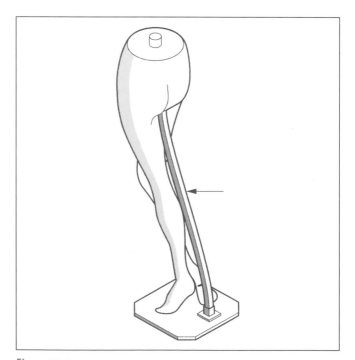

Figure 11.2 A butt rod.

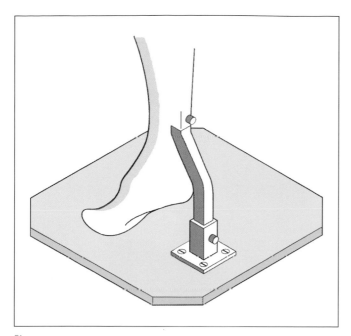

Figure 11.3 An ankle rod.

be put on before the shirt is buttoned—and it should be smoothed down to avoid any unsightly lumps.

Any beads, necklaces, chains, or over-the-head jewelry are added before the mannequin's wig is set back in place. The other accessories (handbags, gloves, pins, brooches, sunglasses, ribbons, and so on) can be added after the wig is replaced.

A mannequin that is to wear a dress, gown, or all-in-one garment may have the garment dropped over its shoulders after the pantyhose have been put on and the mannequin is standing erect. Other garments such as skirts will be easier to put on by "stepping" the mannequin into them and pulling them up from the bottom,

the proper sleeve and into its slot. Follow with the other arm. Lock the second arm into place and then button up the garment. If a tie or neck scarf is used, this is the time to put it on the mannequin.

If the ensemble includes a jacket, cardigan, or coat over the sweater or shirt, the outer garments should be slipped on over the shirt or sweater before the arms are inserted into the sleeves and locked into the shoulder joints. In this case, it is simpler to slip the sleeves through each other and then introduce the arm through the armhole opening with the wrist-end down. The arm is then ready to fit into the shoulder slot. When the arms are positioned and the shirt cuffs are buttoned down or turned back, the hands are then joined to the slot in the wrist and turned into place. The cuff is then pulled down. (If a bangle bracelet is part of the accessory setup, it is slipped on before the hand is set in place.)

Smooth down the front of the blouse, shirt, or jacket, and gently tuck any excess fabric around to the sides (preferably under the arms, since the back may also be viewed). If the costume requires it, pull the skirt or slacks up over the bottom of the shirt, close the top of the skirt or pants, and smooth down the seams. If a scarf or ascot is to be worn under the shirt, blouse, or sweater, it should

Figure 11.4 Dressed hangers on the wall are layered with menswear and the pants are pinned to the wall under the draped shirt. On the low platform another outfit is laid out casually—but carefully—to show how the pieces all go together. *Herbert Stock, Dusseldorf, Germany.*

Figure 11.5 The suit form can have arms attached so that the sleeves of the jackets can be positioned to appear more natural and relaxed. The "hands" appear to be in the pocket so that the pose suggests someone totally at ease. The trousers are pinned onto the form at the waist and allowed to drape naturally to where they meet the shoes. The scorched and shredded mattresses in the background—à la modern art—add a surreal note to the display. *Barneys, Madison Avenue, New York.*

before the removable leg has been secured. This would depend on the top opening of the garment.

Some costumes will require a slip or a petticoat to fill out the dress property. Others may require some padding or puffing with tissue paper or soft pads.

A mannequin that is dressed in one area and then transported to the display space or window should not be moved with the butt or ankle rod attached to the mannequin and the floor base. After the mannequin is located where it will be set up, the supporting rod should be set into the proper attachment on the mannequin and then on the floor or platform. The mannequin, up to this point, is treated just like one that will be wired or nailed into place.

Rigging a Suit Form

The man's **suit form** is traditionally a gray jersey-covered torso made of papier-mâché. It is headless, legless, and often armless. The unit is supported by a rod that is attached to a base. The neck is a straight cut, sometimes capped with a neck-plate of chrome, brass, or covered with fabric. Some coat or suit forms are equipped with ball-jointed arms that can be bent into realistic positions. More often than not, the trimmer who dresses, or rigs, a suit form will have to rely on padded sleeve inserts to give substance to the loose, limp, hanging jacket sleeves.

As a form of economy, some display persons or retail store owners use plastic dickeys (false shirt fronts with collar and tie definition molded in) to fill the jacket opening. From the point of view of merchandising and display, it would seem to be a false economy. If the store does sell shirts and ties, this would be an excellent place to show these wares. Shirts and ties are accessories to a man's costume, just as blouses and scarves are to a woman's ensemble. The showing of a complete outfit can lead to extra sales. Many men will buy a shirt and tie to coordinate with a selected suit.

If an actual shirt is used, it is put on over the bare suit form. The collar button is left open until the tie is placed under the shirt collar; the collar is then closed. The tie should be tied neatly and securely, and "dimpled" to sit perfectly in the inverted "V" of the collar and to hang straight down over the shirtfront. Many trimmers still prefer the very neat and symmetrical Windsor knot; others use more casual or more fashionable ways of knotting a tie.

Some classic trimmers or riggers tuck the sleeves back, out of sight, while they carefully pin, in the back, all the extra shirt fabric in two equal folds or pleats. This will create a smooth, wrinkle-free shirtfront. If a vest is to be shown, it is now put on the form and then buttoned. Some trimmers allow the shirt sleeve to go through the sleeve jacket and then extend about $1/2$ inch below the cuff of the jacket.

A jacket will hang below the usual hipline of the suit form. In order to make the jacket lie just right and not flap in the open space below the elevated form, the rigger will sometimes cut out cardboard shields to pin onto the "hips" of the form. These will conform to the line of the bottom of the jacket. The jacket is now placed over the well-smoothed-out shirt and the cardboard cutouts.

If arm pads, or sleeve pads, are used, they are pinned to the inside of the jacket at the shoulder and then brought down through the sleeve. If the cuff of the shirtsleeve is seen below the jacket cuff, the shirtsleeve will be behind the padding. The sleeve pad can then be pinned to the form for a smooth, close-fitting line with the suit form. Some trimmers prefer a more casual or relaxed kind of rigging. They will not pin the sleeve or sleeve pad to the form. Instead, they may prefer to fold the sleeve, bend it, or suggest some form of animation. Shaped rolls or wads of tissue can also be used in place of sleeve pads.

Once the jacket is centered and set perfectly and squarely on the form, the dresser will often anchor the jacket in place by means of some pins placed in back, under the collar, and in front, under the lapels. If the suit has been properly pressed and/or steamed, and is wrinkle-free, the trimmer should not have too much trouble smoothing down the jacket fabric so that it will mold itself to the shape of the form beneath it. This might require an assist from a handheld steamer. Pins may be used along the way to hold the jacket in place, but they should be hidden and employed only when necessary.

If pants are to be displayed with the jacket, they can be pinned underneath the form and then draped over the surface on which the suit form has been placed. They can then be rolled, cascaded, rippled, or just sharply folded over the table, riser, or ledge, or allowed to stop just above the floor.

Instead of cutting off the excess fabric of the trouser legs or sewing an invisible hem—or anything else such as taping that would permanently shorten the pant legs—the display person could turn the excess fabric back inside the trouser leg, simulating a finished pants leg. This is called a **quick cuff.** The proper pair of shoes, set below, could meet the turned back cuff; or the pants may be shown with the waistline at the bottom, using that opportunity to show a belt worked through the belt loops. Depending on the space, the store's stock, and the

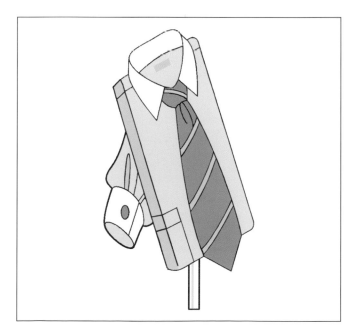

Figure 11.6 This shirt and tie are pinned and shaped for display over a shirt board.

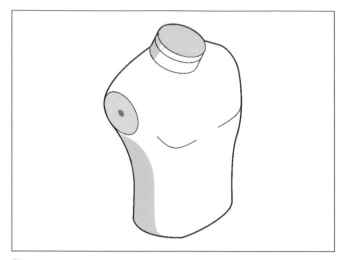

Figure 11.7 This shirt form is capped with a neck-block.

Figure 11.8 The shirt form does not extend down to the hips as the suit form does. Usually the shirt tails are tucked up inside the form and pinned or taped to stay hidden. Here the shirt sleeve is pinned to the shirt front so that the trumpet can be cradled in the bent arm. The music stand and music sheets add to the musical motif. *A&S, King of Prussia, Pennsylvania.*

availability of alternate accessories, the trimmer can do many things, in many ways, with the space below and around the form.

Shirt Board

Displaying a shirt with a jacket presents other problems. Some display persons will opt for a **shirt board** (a flat board about 10 inches by 14 inches), onto which a shirt can be folded with only the shirtfront and perhaps a folded-over sleeve cuff visible. The board can then be pinned onto a wall or panel. An easel, slightly angled and set behind the shirt, makes it possible to show the shirt on the floor, counter, ledge, or inside a showcase.

Shirt Forms

When a **shirt form** is used, the shirt is carefully pressed to get out all the fold lines before it is placed on the form. If a tie is to be included, it is slipped under the collar, and the shirt is then buttoned. The first pin is inserted (into the form) at the top button to keep the shirt in place. The shirtfront is then pulled taut and another pin is placed near the bottom button. The shirt is then smoothed out over and around the shoulders. Two more pins are inserted in the back yoke of the shirt to keep it from sliding. The excess fabric is gathered around in the back and arranged into two symmetrical folds or pleats, which are then pinned. The pins should be as invisible as possible and worked underneath. The shirttail and any excess hanging from the bottom of the shirt is then folded up and, in small, neat, tight pleats, pinned to the underside of the form. Long-sleeved shirts can either have the sleeves pinned at the cuff, close to the body of the form, or treated more casually with pleats, ripples, or even "postured" to give some semblance of reality.

Forms and Customer Attitude

The more sophisticated and expensive the merchandise, and the more educated and selective the customer, the more abstract and nonrealistic the mannequin and the merchandise presentation can be. The display person may not have to define the shape or fit of the garment, but instead may have to spend more time showing the fabric, the details, and the accessories.

The more popular or moderately priced the merchandise, the more realistic and literal the merchandise display must be. The customers of the popularly priced store want to see it all—all the variations and combinations. They will not necessarily be impressed with clever tricks of folding, pinning, or placing clothes on the floor, on panels, or on flat cutouts. They want to see the form, the fit, what goes where, and who is wearing it.

Whichever mannequin, form, or dimensional device is used, its selection must be determined by what it will do for the merchandise and how it will affect the customer's attitude toward the merchandise and the store that is selling the goods. It always comes back to the store image.

Dressing the Three-Dimensional Form: A Recap

- A mannequin must first be taken apart and then carefully reassembled as items of merchandise are put on the figure.

- The lower half of the mannequin is usually dressed first.

- To dress the mannequin, first remove the wig and the upper half of the mannequin. Remove arms from the upper half. If the mannequin is to wear shorts, pants, or pantyhose, one leg will need to be removed. Pantyhose or hosiery should go on first, then trousers or a skirt. If the mannequin has a butt-rod fitting, an opening needs to be provided in the crotch or seam of shorts or pants. Shoes are put on next, and then the dressed lower portion can be set into the butt or ankle rod, which is attached to a floor plate. The top half of the mannequin is attached and dressed, and then arms may be slid up through sleeves and attached to the torso. Outer garments such as coats or jackets should be slipped over the inner garments before arms are attached. Accessories and jewelry are added and the wig is set in place.

- In rigging a suit form, the shirt is put on first, and the collar button is left open until the tie is placed under the shirt collar. The sleeves may be tucked back and extra shirt fabric is pinned back in two equal folds, to create a smooth shirtfront. The vest is put on next, and then the jacket. If sleeve pads are used, they can be pinned to the inside of the jacket at the shoulder and brought through the sleeve. If pants are to be displayed, they can be pinned underneath the form and then draped over the surface on which the suit form has been placed. Excess fabric is tucked inside the trouser leg to simulate a finished pants leg.

- A shirt board is a flat board about 10 inches by 14 inches onto which a shirt can be folded, leaving only the shirtfront, and possibly a folded-over sleeve cuff visible.

- In dressing a shirt form, the shirt must be pressed to get out all the wrinkles. If a tie is included, it is slipped under the collar and the shirt is then buttoned. The first pin is inserted at the top button. The shirtfront is then pulled taut and another pin is placed near the bottom. The shirt is smoothed out over and around the shoulders and pinned in the back at the yoke. Excess fabric is gathered in the back and arranged in two symmetrical folds, which are pinned. Any excess fabric hanging from the bottom is folded up and pinned to the underside of the form in small, neat pleats. All pins should be invisible. Long sleeves can be pinned at the cuffs close to the body form, or may be pleated or "postured" to simulate reality.

Questions for Review and Discussion

1. How might a pair of pants be displayed with a jacket on a suit form? Mention at least two creative methods.

2. How might a suit form be rigged to achieve a casual look?

3. Explain the correlation between mannequins or other three-dimensional forms and customer sophistication.

CHAPTER TWELVE

Fixtures

AFTER YOU HAVE READ THIS CHAPTER,
YOU WILL BE ABLE TO DISCUSS:

- The fixtures often used in window displays, on counters, on ledges, and as floor fixtures.
- The common materials and finishes used in the manufacture of display fixtures.
- How stands are assembled and used for displays.
- The differences among costumers, valets, and drapers.
- How some fixtures can be "pilfer-proof."
- Criteria for the selection of fixtures.

FIXTURES: TRADE TALK

bins	gondola	round rack
brass	half-circle rack	S-rack
bronze	hanger top	semicircular rack
chrome	kiosk	showcase
copper	ledge fixtures	small elevations
costumer	mirror	spiral costumer
counter	mirror chrome	stand
C-rack	nickel-plated	three-part rack
draper	outpost	trays
easel	painted finishes	T-stand
elevations	"pilfer-proof" fixtures	valet
étagere	pipe rack	vitrine
fixture	platforms	waterfalled
floor fixtures	polished chrome	wood fixtures
four-way face-out	quad rack	
freestanding fixtures	risers	

A store without fixtures is a store that is not finished! It is not ready to accept, hold, stock, and show merchandise. It is not equipped to transact sales, take money and make change, and wrap the purchase. There would be nothing in the store to tell you what is being offered, what the selection is, and what alternatives and/or accessories are available. Simply, a fixtureless store is one that is not equipped to function. (Mannequins, figures, and forms are also fixtures of a kind—a very important kind. Thus, they have rated separate chapters (refer to Chapters 9 to 11).

A display window without fixtures is merely a box with walls—one of which happens to be all glass. The merchandise placed in a fixtureless window probably will have to be laid out on the window floor, all at the same level, all in the same line—unless the display person knows about flying techniques. (See Chapter 10.) Even when pinning, draping, and shaping a garment, a **fixture** has to be present to hold the merchandise. Fixtures are not necessarily only frames, stands, easels, rods extending up from weighted bases, hangers, and racks made of chrome, wood, or acrylic. Fixtures can be many things—things that were never originally conceived to raise up, hold, show, and contain a selection of merchandise.

Fixturing can be compared to interior designing. It is the selection of the "furniture" for the selling area of an establishment. It is this selection of the right "accessories" and details that creates the personality or the image of that selling space. A sofa, which might dominate a living room, might be compared to the larger stocking racks, gondolas, or perimeter wall hang-rods. Just as a sofa ordinarily will seat the most guests and disappear under the load, so will these larger fixtures carry the most stock and become invisible under and behind the merchandise they carry. T-stands, counter fixtures, and specialty units are the "individual chairs," and they show a smaller and more select group of merchandise. The featured displays; the displayers; the drapers, costumers, and valets; the merchandise pinned on the fascia—these are the "pictures on the walls" and the "accessories" that add charm, life, excitement, and personality to an environment.

There are certain basic fixtures used in window display that may also be used in the interior of the store, on ledges, or on the selling floor. They include: stands; platforms and elevations; costumers, drapers, and valets; easels; and pipe racks.

These basic fixtures can be metal or plastic fabrications specifically designed to hold or elevate a pair of shoes, a shirt, or a skirt; or they can be props or decorative elements that can work effectively as drapers or costumers. These fixtures elevate merchandise; they hold up and/or give body form to the merchandise.

Stands

The **stand** is a very widely used, basic fixture. It comes with an assortment of tops that may be slipped interchangeably into an adjustable rod set on a weighted base. The base sits securely on the floor (or on a platform, elevation, counter, or ledge) and the rod may be adjusted to the desired height for presenting the merchandise.

The top element can be a straight rod, like the top stroke of a "T," and can hold an assortment of scarves, ties, towels, or any soft, drapable merchandise. The **hanger top** consists of a gentle curve (like the arc of a coat or dress hanger), and serves to show a dress, sweater, jacket, and so on. This fixture is also called a draper. Another kind of hanger top ends with two reverse curves (like a handlebar moustache). It serves to display lingerie and other sleeveless garments that hang from straps and do not have sleeves or shoulders to keep the garment from slipping off a regular hanger top. There are also special attachments for hosiery, shirts, shoes, millinery, and so forth.

Stands are usually used in a variety or assortment window as a means of building up—from the glass line to the back of the display window—a variety of merchandise. The smaller items are set low and up front. As they get larger, the merchandise gets higher and set farther back. A truly elegant and beautifully designed base can provide a drape-away point for a lovely piece of lin-

Figure 12.1 Fixtures are the furniture of the retail store. The "furniture" comes in an assortment of sizes to serve a variety of purposes and can be arranged to create an open and airy look, or to affect a cluttered and more intimate space. What they are made of and how they are designed and used does affect the image of the store and the merchandise being offered. *Paws 'n' Claws, New Jersey. Design: JGA.*

gerie in a one-item or a related merchandise window presentation. (See Chapter 5 Types of Displays and Display Settings).

Platforms and Elevations

Platforms and **elevations** are buildups used to provide interest and to help separate merchandise in mass displays. They can be cubes, cylinders, or saddles of any size or shape. Elevations can be tables and chairs and other pieces of furniture that can be used to raise up a mannequin, a form, a stand, or an arrangement of merchandise. An elevation can also be a platform that covers a large portion of a display floor.

Platforms or elevations are used to separate mannequins in a window or on a traffic aisle inside a store, so that each figure can be seen in its own "space," at its own level. The use of elevations is also discussed in Chapter 5 under "Buildups."

Costumers, Valets, and Drapers

Costumers, valets, and drapers are important fixtures that show coordinates or complete costumes on a single stand.

The **costumer** is a freestanding fixturing unit used on a floor, ledge, or counter, depending on its size. It has a hanger set onto the top of an adjustable upright, which is set into a weighted base. The unit usually has a skirt bar which makes it possible to display a pair of pants or a skirt under a blouse or jacket.

The **valet,** very similar to the costumer, has a heavier and wider hanger along with a slacks bar, which makes this fixture especially useful for men's wear. As in most fixtures designed today, the hanger and the slacks or skirt bar attachment is adjustable, riding up and down on the vertical rod. Sometimes, it includes a shoe platform raised off the floor, but still attached to the same vertical rod on which all the other pieces are assembled. When using either fixture, a scarf, jewelry, a handbag, a tie, and maybe even a hat can be draped over the various parts of the collected costume. In a specialty store, a boutique, a one-item-type window, or even a related merchandise presentation in a limited space, the costumer and valet are excellent and reliable fixtures.

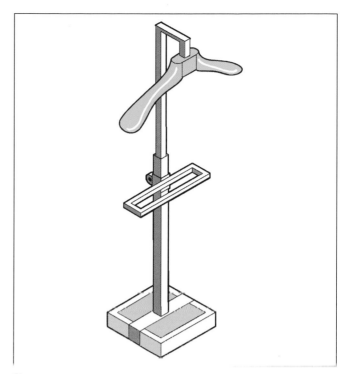

Figure 12.3 A valet fixture is especially useful for men's wear.

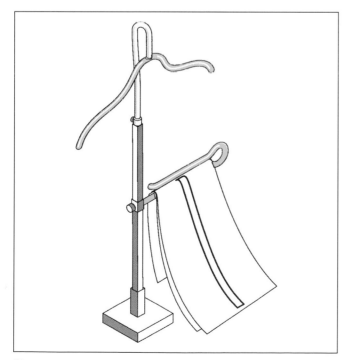

Figure 12.2 A costumer with a skirt/slacks bar attachment.

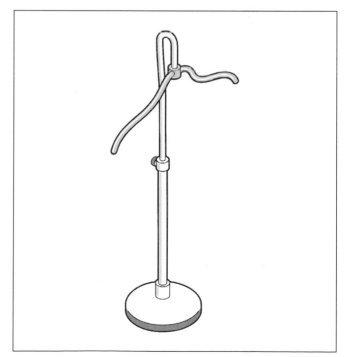

Figure 12.4 A hanger top or draper.

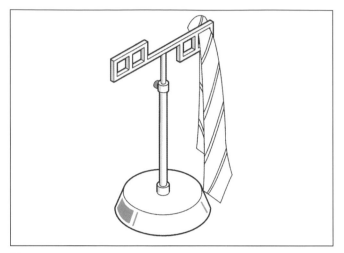

Figure 12.5 A tie displayer.

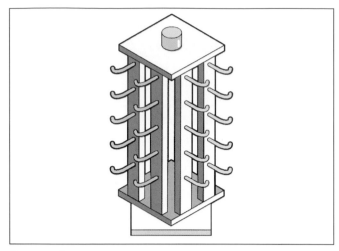

Figure 12.8 A hook stand. A counter unit that can hold bagged or carded merchandise, chains, etc.

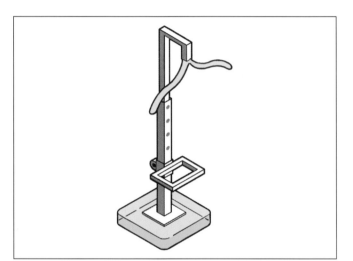

Figure 12.6 A costumer with a hanger set on the top of an adjustable upright.

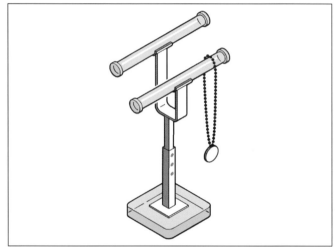

Figure 12.9 A rope displayer. A counter unit designed to show necklaces, chains, etc.

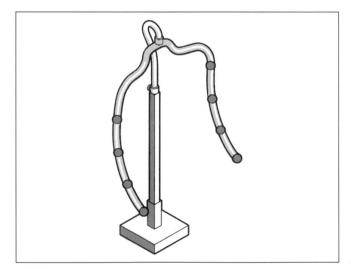

Figure 12.7 A flex-arm displayer. The hanger continues down into flexible cable "arms" which can be bent into animated positions.

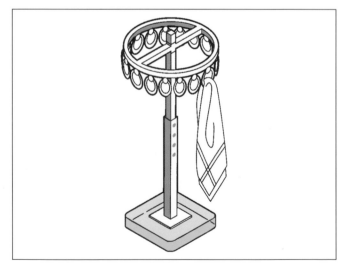

Figure 12.10 A circular, spinning, scarf wheel.

The **draper** is also a hanger on a stand, adjustable in height, but without a skirt or slacks bar. It is usually smaller than the costumer and the valet—a compact unit meant to be used on a counter or on a buildup. It may be produced with a bendable armature that allows the sleeves of the garment to be positioned after the jacket, blouse, or sweater is hung or buttoned over the top hanger. Coordinating skirts or slacks can be laid out at the base of the draper.

Easels

An **easel** is an adjustable folding frame or tripod. Small easels may be used in a display or in a store window to hold a price card or message. Larger ones are designed specifically to hold a shirt and tie at an angle. A very large artist's easel can also be used; a fully accessorized outfit, pinned up on a board can be placed on this size easel. A coat, bag, and/or scarf can be draped from the top of the easel.

In some "arty" type operations, this very recognizable unit will do wonderfully well at suggesting the unique and aesthetic design value of the merchandise. In the one-item display, the single garment is shown as a "mas-

Figure 12.11 The artist's easel is a multi-purpose fixture. It can be a sign holder, a support for a painting or canvas, or serve as a pin-up surface for pinned and draped garments and/or accessories. The trio shown here features a special collection of hand-painted plates. The easel immediately tells the shopper that "art" is somehow involved in the products being shown. The easels also contain the small items in the large space and raise them closer to the viewer's eye level. *Gump's, San Francisco. Bob Mahoney.*

terpiece"—"one-of-a-kind." In a related merchandise display, an ensemble is gathered together and presented as a total composition. The outfit may be labeled "The Designer's Touch," "The Choice Collection," "Composition in Blue" (or in "Red," "Gray," and so on).

Easels also serve effectively off aisles, as a lead-in to a department or special shop. They can be companions to mannequins on ledges, on T-wall platforms, or on islands to show alternate choices or other accessories. The smaller easels serve as supports; they present merchandise in a perpendicular plane and keep small items such as handbags, books, prepackaged goods, and so on, upright or at a slight incline for better viewing.

Pipe Racks

A **pipe rack** is a utilitarian fixture, with wheels, made of round tubing and resembling an inverted "U." It may have a flat wooden base to which the wheels are attached.

Sometimes, for special attention or to promote a clearance sale or to suggest a great diversity of merchandise (e.g., in a line-of-goods window), a pipe rack or a simple A-frame will be used in a window. It really does not "show off" the merchandise. It is another recognizable symbol for workshops, studios, ateliers, and other places where clothes are made and hung on the rack, ready to go. It is also used as a vehicle to move clothes from one place to another. The pipe rack can suggest clothes in the process of being made or clothes being delivered. It also has a negative connotation, suggesting "cheap," "discount," or "mass" production. If the store is saying, "We are getting rid of everything—everything goes," the pipe rack in the window will imply the drastic price reductions and the movement out of the store. This is really an example of using a fixture as a "prop" rather than simply as a showing or holding device.

Counters or Showcases

Counters are important areas within the store in need of fixturing. They are points-of-purchase, where sales are actually made. It is here that the customer can be convinced—have his or her mind changed or miss the point entirely. The counter is the selling field where the give-

Figure 12.12 Stacking tables are space savers and they also effectively separate and present folded garments into horizontal bands. The tables can be constructed of wood, metal, plastic, or any combination of the above, and the styling and detailing of the tables reflect the look of the store and merchandise set out on them. *Maison Simon, Quebec, Canada. Design: Watts International.*

and-take between salesperson and customer can be improved and the sale expedited by the use of good and sufficient counter fixtures.

The **counter** or **showcase** is out on the floor and stands on its own but is not traditionally part of what is called "floor fixturing." These pieces of furniture—for

Figure 12.13 The lowly clothes rack is used to move merchandise from the receiving area to the stock room and then out on to the floor. Here it becomes an amusing. The rack, on wheels, not only carries some women's suit jackets but supports one of the mannequins on the lower hang rod. *Marshall Field, State Street, Chicago.*

showing, holding, and selling merchandise—combine the storage capacities of a cabinet, the selling surface of a table, and the display potentials of a shadow box. The unit may be made entirely of glass, with everything under it on view. It can be all wood, laminated, or combined with metal and look like a closed cabinet.

Until the end of the 1960s, the counter or showcase was all but rooted into the floor of the selling area—large, immovable units that were set out to stay. With stores in need of greater mobility, flexibility, and the ability to rearrange their layout as merchandise changes, the counters become lighter looking and, in some instances, almost table-like. The feeling of "floating" furniture has taken over on many of the main floors of department and specialty stores. To reinforce the light airy look, some units have indirect lights located below the counters in order to light the floor beneath.

The counter fixture is small; the base is balanced or weighted to keep the fixture from toppling when fully stocked. Ideally, a fixture is no more than 24 inches tall and rarely goes over 36 inches when adjusted to its greatest height. A taller one would be an insurmountable barrier to the give-and-take between customer and salesperson.

One of the major problems in retailing today is theft. The counter fixture puts the merchandise right out on top of the counter and invites the potential customer to touch it, try it, and eventually purchase it. However, fully dressed counter fixtures that extend much higher than the salesperson's eye level are invitations to shoplifters to take without being seen. The size of the counter fixture is crucially important.

Assorted Counter Fixtures

The counter fixture is a displayer as well as a holder of merchandise. There are a great many fixtures available today that are designed to show and hold specific merchandise, although a display person could make one fixture "do" for another. Assorted fixture tops are made to hold certain items or accessories in a way that will show them off to their best advantage and keep them from slipping off, or in the case of "pilfer-proof" units, keep them from "walking off." Figures 12.5 through 12.10 show some of the usual counter fixtures required to furnish counters in various departments adequately.

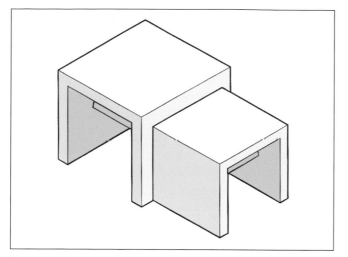

Figure 12.14 Risers and saddles are buildups, groupings of geometric shapes and forms to create multi-levels for the display of small associate merchandise, such as cosmetics, toiletries, small leather goods, and shoes.

Figure 12.16 Ledge fixtures are being used here to display merchandise above a bin exit.

There are other "furnishings" required and used on counters. In cosmetic and jewelry areas, a **mirror** is a must. A customer may try something on and want to see how it looks. A hand mirror can and probably will disappear. A mirror on a nearby wall or column might do, but it means the customer must leave the sphere of influence and the watchful eye of the salesperson. A weighted mirror, with an adjustable or tilt-table frame is needed. A lamp will usually be close by. The lamp, with a peachy, incandescent light emanating from it, adds warmth necessary to the sale of cosmetics, perfumes, and sometimes jewelry. The lamp also supplies a high point to an otherwise horizontal look and a highlight to the general, overall lighting around the counter.

Trays or **bins** may be useful adjuncts to counter selling. **Risers** or **small elevations** will add interest to a display of small items (such as toiletries and cosmetics). More and more often, a bowl of fresh flowers or a thriv-

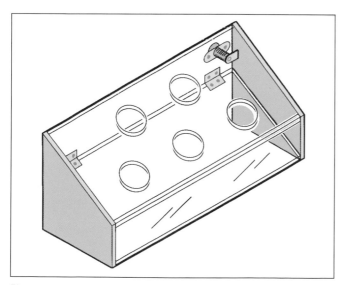

Figure 12.15 A security, or a pilfer-proof case.

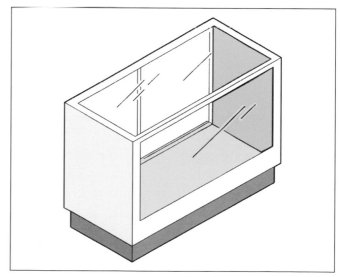

Figure 12.17 A typical showcase with glass top and front.

ing plant is becoming a counter "fixture." It enhances the merchandise, it relaxes the customer, adds to the ambience, and affects the eventual sale.

"Pilfer-Proof" Fixtures

With **pilfer-proof fixtures,** the basic concept is to lock in the merchandise. The customer can see it, but cannot freely touch it. For example, perfume testers are placed on counters, and the customer is invited to spray herself with any of the featured perfumes. Large, "dummy" bottles of perfume, filled with colored water, may be placed on the counter, next to the tester, but the actual perfume for sale is kept below—inside the counter.

Better jewelry and handbags are now being locked in fixtures that require a salesperson with a key to open and to take the item out of the fixture for the customer's closer examination. Merchandise in pilfer-proof fixtures should not look as though it has been locked up with chains and padlocks. The security measures should be artfully camouflaged and discreet.

Ledge Fixtures

Ledge fixtures are larger and more imposing than counter fixtures. Most are placed where the customer cannot reach or touch them. A costumer or a valet, mentioned earlier as window fixtures, will show a completely accessorized outfit on a ledge, as will a torso, three-quarter and even, possibly, a dressmaker form. These fixtures require a space at least 5 feet high.

Some ledge fixtures are set at or above eye level and are not necessarily barriers or screens. When the display person feels a particular ledge unit can become a safety shield for pilferers, he or she should trim the unit, leaving look-through areas in the merchandise arrangement, or alternatively, should select a lower unit. The same fixture used to top the ledge will also be found on top of the upholstered or laminated cubes and platforms that are interspersed on the selling floor. If the unit is set on or adjacent to an aisle, its height should not block the merchandise presentation inside the department or shop.

Units that show and hold merchandise on counters, platforms, or ledges within reach of the customer require constant care and attention. The merchandise will be handled and manhandled—and a softly draped scarf over an outfit on a draper will be fingered and moved about. This type of display is an open invitation to touch, and the display person or the salespersons in the area must be responsible for the upkeep of the merchandise on view. More and more stores now have a visual merchandise program set up to help their sales staffs understand how important it is for all merchandise to be set up at its visual best. The display person's job does not end with setting up the display. It requires follow-up attention and "repairing" of displays that are within touching distance. Some stores are enclosing their displays within glass or plastic cubes in order to prevent the need for some of that upkeep.

Floor and Freestanding Fixtures

Floor fixtures and **freestanding fixtures** are units designed to hold and show merchandise out on the floor—where the traffic is. The major types of fixtures include: round racks, T-stands, quad racks or four-way face-outs, as well as other types of floor fixtures. (The dressing and stocking of fixtures is discussed in the next chapter.)

Round Racks

More traditionally a floor fixture than the counter, and probably the "granddaddy" of commonly used fixtures, is the **round rack.** This unit usually consists of a circu-

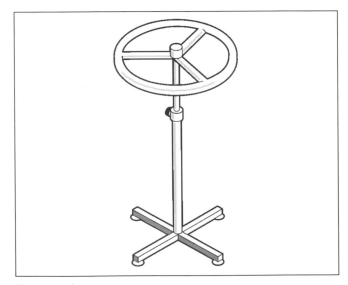

Figure 12.18 A round rack.

lar hang-rod, 3 feet in diameter, raised anywhere from 45 inches to over 6 feet off the ground. It is set on an adjustable upright that is securely attached to a wide, weighted base, which is stable and holds the floor, even when fully weighted down with merchandise.

The round rack, when fully stocked, carries almost 115 inches of shoulder-out merchandise in an area less than 5 feet by 5 feet. This is, at the same time, the big advantage as well as being the big disadvantage. It is good to be able to show a great deal of merchandise in a small area of selling space, but all with shoulders out? This disadvantage of not being able to see more than the sleeve of a garment can be remedied by setting a draper on top of the round rack, as a superstructure, and displaying fully one of the garments from the collection sandwiched in below (see Fig. 12.19).

For some classifications of merchandise—for example children's wear, bras and panties, bikini swimsuits, prepackaged goods, and so forth—the round rack may be ordered with two or even three tiers of hang-rods. Merchandise should not be indiscriminantly loaded onto the round rack just because it is a mass unit. It should be carefully arranged by color and style.

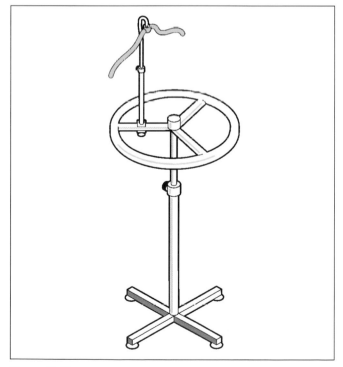

Figure 12.19 The superstructure on top of this round rack is used to display one of the garments stocked below.

T-Stands

At the other end of floor fixturing from the round rack is the **T-stand.** It is a specialty unit—a highlighter or accent piece. It is small, light, carries a minimal amount of merchandise, and makes "big" fashion statements. Originally, the T-stand was simply an upright rod attached to a heavy base with a cross bar (like the top of a "T") on top of which about a dozen garments could be hung. These "lightweights" were set out on the selling floor to show what was new and what was being featured. They were, and still are, used along an aisle to explain what kind of merchandise is being housed in the area beyond.

There have been many improvements and sophisticated changes in T-stand construction. They are adjustable and may have two or more arms to show merchandise in two or more directions as well as at different levels. The arms can be **waterfalled** (i.e., merchandise can be presented on hangers in descending order on a sloping arm; evenly spaced hooks, knobs, or notches keep the hangers from sliding down). A T-stand can even incorporate a dress form, a draper, or a costumer with an arm bracket or a waterfall. In this way, a sample of the garment can be shown dimensionally on a form, and a supply of the same garment—in a range of sizes and/or colors—can be stocked in back. The T-stand is versatile and most effective when used for emphasis.

Quad Racks or Four-Way Face-Outs

A **quad rack** or **four-way face-out** unit stands somewhere between the T-stand and the round rack, in use

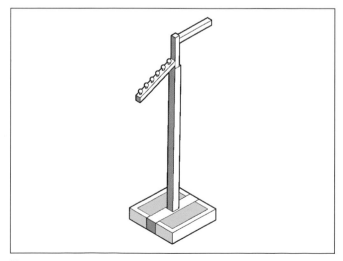

Figure 12.20 A T-stand with one straight arm and one waterfall.

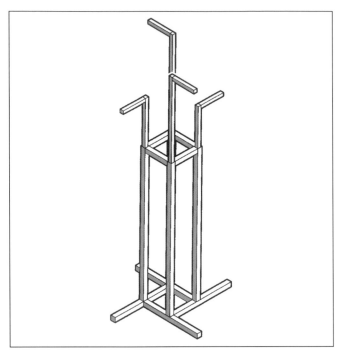

Figure 12.21 A quad rack, or four-way face-out.

and in size, on the selling floor. Basically, it is a four-armed fixture with each arm extending out from a central core. Most often, each arm is turned out at right angles from the center or upright; in a floor plan, this configuration will look like a pinwheel or a swastika. The idea behind this design is that, from certain angles or approaches, the customer sees a shoulder-out arrangement of the collected merchandise, but when coming at the

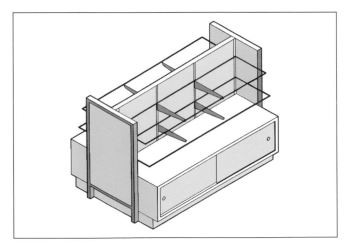

Figure 12.22 A typical gondola, with adjustable shelves and storage space below.

unit straight on, the facing arm will present a "face-out" or "front-forward" view. The potential customer will be able to see the front of the first garment on that particular arm. The arms that extend out in the four directions are often individually adjustable, up and down, so that the merchandise can be seen at four different levels. Some manufacturers are making quad racks in which some or all of the arms are waterfalled. The viewer sees not only the entire front of the first garment, but can see the upper part of the following garments in ascending order.

Because the quad-rack unit is designed with four separate views, it is ideal for showing separates or coordinate fashions. On one fixture, it is possible to show skirts, pants, jackets, and blouses that go together. The pants should be hung from the highest arm to accommodate the extra hang space necessary, and the blouses (or vests or sweaters) will probably be hung on the lowest level. The four arms can also be used to tell coordinated color stories. This will be discussed in Chapter 13.

Other Floor Fixtures

A **gondola** is a long, flat-bottomed merchandiser usually with straight, upright sides. This fixture is sometimes designed with adjustable shelves combined with a table surface and storage cabinet or drawer space below. Since it has a central dividing panel (perpendicular to and equidistant from the end uprights), the gondola is two-sided. The unit is frequently used in groups on the selling floor and oriented perpendicular to the traffic aisles. The ends of the gondolas can be turned into valuable display areas. Gondolas are often found in linen, housewares, china and glass departments, and most commonly in grocery stores. The shelves of the gondola are particularly adaptable to stackable and prepackaged merchandise.

A French term for a displayer shelf unit, an **étagere** is an open, multishelf display fixture. It is most often used to show china, glass, home furnishings accessories, and small gifts.

A **kiosk** is a self-standing booth or structure on the selling floor that may accommodate a salesperson as well as merchandise. It can be used as a miniboutique, an outpost, or for an enclosed information or special-events desk.

An **outpost** is a freestanding, self-contained selling unit that contains a stock of a given type of merchandise,

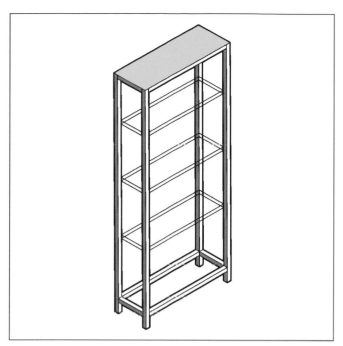

Figure 12.23 An étagère.

along with display and signing relevant to that merchandise. The outpost features merchandise not ordinarily sold in the department in which it is set up (e.g., a cosmetics outpost in a junior department; handbags in a shoe department).

A **three-part rack** is a round rack comprised of three separate but equal arcs. Usually, the height of each arc is individually adjustable. It is more effective for showing separates, coordinates, or assorted colors and styles of a particular item.

A **C-rack** is basically one-half of a round rack. (It is also called a **semicircular rack** or **a half-circle rack.**) It consists of an arc-shaped base with a similarly arc-shaped hang-rod above it. The two arcs are connected by two adjustable uprights. A pair of C-racks can be combined to form a two-part round rack. If each arc of the two-part round rack is set at a different height, it is possible to get greater variety in the merchandise presentation. Two C-racks, placed end to opposing end, make an **S-rack,** which also has a greater potential for variety of merchandise presentation. The C-rack can be used for dresses, coats, suits, and coordinates.

A **vitrine** is a glass-enclosed, shelved cabinet or showcase. It often has glass shelves and partitions. A vitrine is usually a decorative piece, sometimes made to look antique. Like the étagere, it is used to display small, "precious" items or accessories.

A **spiral costumer** is a corkscrewing or descending waterfall extended out from a central upright or post. The merchandise is visible from all around (360 degrees), but the presentation is essentially shoulders out, with an occasional glimpse of the front of some of the merchandise.

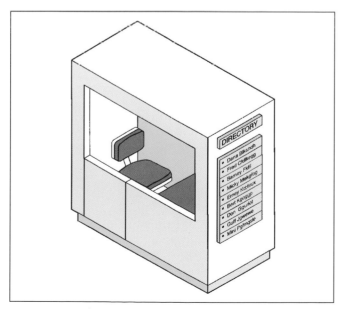

Figure 12.24 An example of a kiosk.

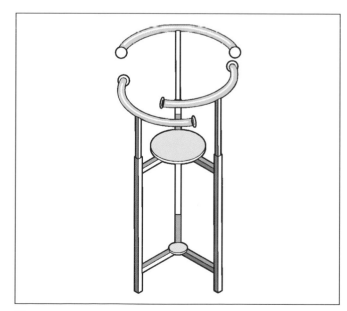

Figure 12.25 A three-part rack.

Selecting a Fixture

In selecting a fixture to use on the selling floor, there are certain criteria or expectations the display person may have with regard to making that selection. The criteria include appearance, construction, end use, upkeep, and finishes.

Appearance

How does the fixture look on the floor? Does it go with the architecture and interior design of the area—the "look," the period—with the other fixtures and furniture already selected or in use? If the interior of the shop attempts to be "quaint and charming" (e.g., Early American), a shiny, slick, chrome fixture would be shockingly out of place and out of character. A weathered wood unit or some other natural or "antique"-type piece would be more fitting, more in keeping with the established image. The new fixture would also have to be in scale and in proportion to the area.

Construction

Is the unit flexible? Is it adjustable? Can the arms that hold the display or stocked merchandise be raised or lowered as hemlines and fashions dictate? Can the fixture be adapted for use with different types of merchan-

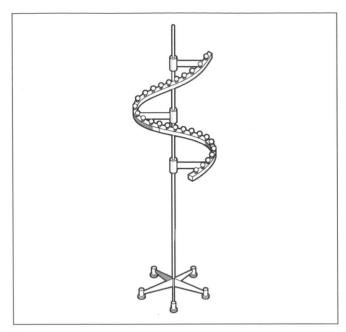

Figure 12.27 A spiral costumer.

dise if the shop is a seasonal one and sells anything from swimsuits to full-length stormcoats—and everything in between? Are the parts or elements of the fixture rearrangeable and adaptable? It is not absolutely necessary that one fixture do everything, but in a small shop with a limited fixture budget, the more versatile the fixture, the better.

End Use

Ask yourself the following questions to determine if the fixture meets the intended end use: Does the unit make fall use of the valuable area of the selling floor that the fixture will occupy? Does it hold as much merchandise as necessary and show it in the most desirable manner? Can the unit be adjusted to double or triple hang, if the merchandise is small (e.g., children's wear) or short (e.g., shorts, miniskirts), or can the hang levels be varied for variety and interest? Is there a way of displaying in all the unused "air space" above the unit, an area that can be seen from many parts of the shop but often goes unused? Is the unit still low enough and open enough to discourage pilfering?

What is the display value of the fixture? Does it have maximum merchandise exposure? Is there some "front-out" viewing of the collected stock? Can the featured

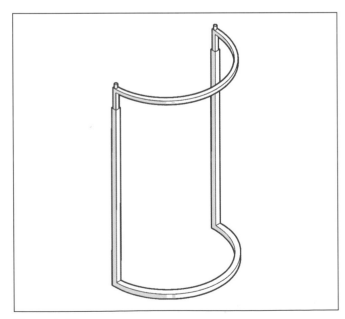

Figure 12.26 A C-rack.

garment be dressed and accessorized? Does the fixture lend itself to creating color and style excitement? Does it allow for the coordination and combination of merchandise? Does it "show and sell?"

Is the unit a self-selector, one that the customer can "shop" by himself or herself and still find what is being looked for? Is it self-explanatory? Can the merchandise be removed and replaced on the fixture without too much difficulty for the customer? Does the fixture contain and hold the merchandise—safely and securely—with few ill effects to the merchandise, or does it create "as is" merchandise by increasing wear and tear?

Upkeep

Is the fixture serviceable, dependable, reliable, and safe? Will it stand and not topple when loaded with merchandise or used as a swing by a customer's child? Does it require constant care, repair, polishing, and housekeeping? Are the parts replaceable and easy to get? How good, how reliable, how dependable is the manufacturer/supplier? Will they stand behind their product with some sort of warranty?

Finishes

What the fixture is constructed of and how it is finished will not only affect its "floor life," but its appearance on the floor.

Chrome is currently the most popular finish for fixtures used for counters, floors, and walls. It is made by electroplating chromium onto another metal. Stronger and often superior fixtures have a base of steel with an electrolytic deposit of chromium on it. Fixtures can also be made of brass or nickel and then given the bright, silvery, chrome finish. **Polished chrome** and **mirror chrome** are only two of the standard names for this shiny finish. The more care given to the preparation of the welded steel, nickel, or brass—the polishing and cleaning of the raw metal framework—the better the chrome finish will be.

Generally, chrome fixtures can be moderate in cost and are usually quite durable. A good finish is uniform, smooth, unblemished, and without the pinkish or coppery discolorations that may occur in welded corners. Chrome-plating does not require an outer lacquer coating to prevent discoloration or tarnishing from oxidation as other finishes may require. A chrome finish will resist scratching and scarring from normal use, such as stacking and moving metal hangers along chrome hang-rods. It is a popular look in department store fixturing.

A variety of finishes in chrome is available. They are referred to as antique, rubbed, satin, and brushed finishes. The surface to be chrome-plated is first treated with an abrasive material to roughen it. This, in turn, will tend to dull the shine on the final chrome-plated surface, but will still maintain the silvery quality. These duller and more satiny looks can be quite elegant and are considered more "masculine" than the usual high shine. With the addition of some color rubs, the resulting toned-down and deeper silver-gray surfaces are referred to as either a stainless-steel finish or a pewter finish.

Nickel-plated surfaces are similar in appearance to chrome-plated surfaces, but that is about as far as it goes. It is not as durable or efficient a finish; it will oxidize and discolor after some period of exposure to the air. Nickel does require a coat of lacquer to seal the finish and protect it from air and moisture. As with most metals treated with a coating of lacquer, it will eventually scratch and scar—the air will get through—and there will be discoloration. Nickel-plating is not frequently used for better fixtures. The nickel finish may have a yellowish cast when compared to the cool, silvery-blue color of chrome.

Brass fixture finishes are second in popularity to chrome, but this finish does need extra protection and care. The bright, golden gleam of a brass finish can be applied over steel or nickel, or even on soft brass itself. Brass metal, not the finish, is rarely used to make large floor fixtures, though it is used in counter fixture construction. The metal is too soft and too easily scarred, dented, or bent. When a brass look is desired, a sturdy and dependable steel is usually brass-plated.

Brass finishes are subject to oxidation and air discoloration, just as brass metal is. Lacquer must be applied to seal it. Harder, more scratch-resistant lacquer finishes are "bake-dried" in ovens rather than dried in the air as with most other coatings. The brass finish is only as durable as the lacquer coating on it; once the protective coating is nicked or scratched, it no longer protects the finish. Air gets through and tarnishing begins. Dark brown lines and spots develop where the lacquer was rubbed away by the erosive movement of hangers, metal clips, and such. Some manufacturers produce brass-finished fixtures that feature chrome hang rods or metal arms where there is constant rubbing and friction. The fixture "glows" because most of it is in brass, but the "working" parts are protected in chrome.

Brass is also available in satin finishes; soft, low-luster finishes that can be very smart, elegant, and particularly attractive in wood-filled men's departments. Deep walnut and mahogany tones are enhanced by rubbed, antiqued, darker brass finishes. Creamy whites and very light neutral tones look even more refined with the soft gleam of satin-finished brass—very feminine and very expensive looking.

Copper and **bronze** finishes also need special care, special handling, and special lighting on the selling floor if they are to resemble copper or brass closely. A copper finish tends to be a pink or rusty-gold color; the bronze is often brown and dark with just a mere metallic glint. On the selling floor, bronze may go black and lifeless and copper may become dull. These finishes must also be protected with a baked-on coat of lacquer if they are to resist discoloration. The oxidation, however, would not be as obvious because of their darker and duller finishes.

Both finishes are usually "special order," that is, they must be ordered. They are more expensive to fabricate and are in no way as foolproof as chrome-plating. The color of the copper and bronze may vary from plating run to plating run, and thus a group of bronze counter fixtures could go from light to dark brown over the series of plating runs it would take to complete the whole order. These two finishes, in the right areas, with the right lighting, and on or near the right colors, can be very different and fashionable. A copper finish goes well with natural, light woods and could create an earthy, traditional, provincial, or masculine setting.

Painted finishes include baked enamel, lacquered, and epoxy paint finishes. All of these methods are used to create fixtures with color. The metal or wood that is to be colored has to be cleaned, sealed, primed, and prepared before being given the particular color coating, and allowed to dry in specially heat-maintained ovens or kilns.

More and more colored units are appearing in children's, junior, and active sportswear shops and/or departments. They are also becoming increasingly popular in hardware, gourmet, and kitchen supply areas. For many years, painted fixtures were white, black, or metallic gold, but today there is no limit to the range of colors available. The use of colored fixtures adds to the ambience of a shop or area, cuts down on the sharp and sometimes shrill quality of chrome, and creates a "unique" or very fashion-oriented statement. How and where one uses color on fixtures will depend largely on the type of merchandise involved. Most painted finishes will eventually scar, scratch, or scrape off. Enamel painting is the cheapest and least durable finish, but even enamel can be made more efficient if it is applied electrostatically.

Wood Fixtures and Store Fittings

After a decade or two of living with the shimmer and shine of chrome and the sparkle of smooth, clear plastics, today's stores see a continued emphasis on richness and refinement begun in the 1990s. This return to classicism finds store designers specifying that most luxurious and versatile of materials endowed by nature—wood. With an infinite variety of patterns and grains available in an expansive palette of tints and shades of neutral brown, wood can complement almost any design.

In the 1970s and early 1980s, one had to venture to EuroShop, a trade show held in Dusseldorf, Germany, to see wood wall systems. But the styling and finishes of those systems often precluded their use for anything other than housewares, children's clothing, and possibly active sportswear. By the mid-1980s, improved finishes and more detailed woodwork, moldings, and enrichments appeared on wall systems and the floor units designed to complement them. Today, store designers and visual merchandisers have many excellent, adaptable systems available to them with a wide choice of woods, finishes, and accessories.

At industry trade shows today, record numbers of companies are showing **wood fixtures** and furniture. Many manufacturers are fashioning elaborate furniture/fixturing memorabilia. Items reflecting the 1920s and 1930s and even earlier are designed for use as props and fixtures. Booths are filled by manufacturers of country-style or provincial furniture specifically designed to function as primary fixtures. There are units that can be strategically placed to add interest, character, and visual exclamation points to spaces otherwise functional and "undecorated."

Figure 12.28 The Timberland vendor's shop can be distinguished in the department store by its fixtures, graphics, and signage—all provided by Timberland. In order to control how Timberland products are shown, the company has designed modular fixtures, so that depending upon the available space and location of the shop-within-the-shop, sufficient fixtures, fittings and decoratives can be provided to the retailer. *Timberland Vendor Shop. Design: Fitch.*

In addition, there are furniture-like fixtures that could easily blend with residential store design. Panel- and molding-enriched wall units as well as modular elements can be used to span an entire wall or to highlight a part of it, serving as a visual break.

Even fixture manufacturers who have traditionally designed and produced ever more adaptable and adjustable floor fixtures with better and more interesting metal finishes also are offering wood-enveloped designs. Units are available with bases and uprights sheathed in wood and only hang rods or arms of exposed metal. To go with these functional units, manufacturers now offer coordinated "show-offs" that can serve up front to present or display a single featured outfit. There was a time when it seemed that wood fixtures worked only in men's areas, but thanks to new designs and exciting finishes, the wood-enclosed elements are even adaptable to better women's sportswear or designer clothes.

Wood is natural—it's real—it fosters an aura of warmth and comfort. Wood can suggest the now-popular Southwest look with natural timbers accented against pastel-tinted stucco surfaces, or it can create the handsome, country-casual atmosphere of a Ralph Lauren Polo shop. Likewise, a Laura Ashley shop is characterized by the use of provincial finishes on built-in fixtures and well-placed furnishings. When it comes to elegant designer settings, it's the smooth, rubbed wax sheen on wood moldings and floors that reinforces the designer's message.

Some specialty stores will continue to opt for a wood chalet or log cabin look because of the customers they appeal to and the merchandise they sell. That, however, doesn't mean we're reverting to the 1950s- and 1960s-styled store, when a wood-sheathed selling space resembled either a cedar-lined closet or a Scandinavian sauna. We're also surpassing the 1970s "return to nature" design, when it wasn't unusual for shoppers to fight through a jungle of hanging plants to be finally entrapped by yellowish planks of nearly raw wood installed in a chevron pattern. Nor are we reinstating the once-popular men's wear store design that suggested a late-19th century men's club with paneled or coffered walls of fumed oak and redolent with maroon leather and moldy green velvet.

Dubbed "The Decade of the Home," the 1990s trend toward residential design, epitomized by Ralph Lauren's Polo shops in the mid-1980s, has influenced department and specialty stores to imitate this intimate style. A look at the department and specialty stores being designed today reveals several themes and motifs. One is a desire for intimacy, for a setting that is warm, comfortable, and human in scale and feeling.

Just as homes are furnished, not fixtured, actual furniture is being used more and more as permanent fixtures in department stores' shops-within-shops and specialty stores. Large pieces of furniture such as cupboards, hutches, tables, and chests are juxtaposed with fixtures to create home-like vignettes.

Once, the "up-front" fixture stationed off a main aisle in a large store was a gleaming chrome T-stand. Today, it's more likely that shoppers are greeted by a table—albeit one that's longer and taller than those found in one's home—displaying folded and stacked merchandise. These fixtures, more often than not, are made of solid wood and are finished like actual furniture, making them appear more substantial, less mass-produced, and less hi-tech. Rounding out the setting might be a pair of chairs, not there for the weary shopper, but artfully draped with featured garments.

Today, a boutique may have nothing more than an armoire or wardrobe, refitted to accommodate hung or folded garments. Accessories or other garments can be displayed on opened doors. With the addition of an armoire, wardrobe, or hutch, what might have been only a wall furnished with standards and brackets is now a more interesting, personalized, and intimate shop.

Wooden fixtures, however, don't have to be traditional pieces of furniture. With some classifications of merchandise, modular wood floor and wall systems can provide a sense of warmth and color in a more open and spontaneous store that complements the merchandise. Floor and wall fixturing systems also contribute to current interior design statements. Consider a Laura Ashley or Polo shop's wall with furniture-finished wood shelves, bins, or floor fixtures sitting on the herringbone-patterned wood floor—both become as visually strong as traditional furniture.

Wood's natural timelessness says home, hearth, and security. "Humanizing" the store through the use of wood in construction, finishing, or furnishings provides the means of achieving a warm and inviting ambiance.

Fixtures: A Recap

- The major functions of store fixtures are to accept, hold, stock, and show merchandise.

- Basic fixtures used in window displays include stands, platforms and elevators, costumers, drapers and valets, easels, and pipe racks.

- Common materials used in the manufacture of basic fixtures are metal and plastic.

- A stand comes with an assortment of tops that may be slipped interchangeably into an adjustable rod set on a weighted base. The base sits securely on a floor, platform, counter, or ledge, and the rod may be adjusted to the desired height for presentation of merchandise.

- The valet, although similar to the costumer, has a heavier and wider hanger and a slacks bar, which makes it especially useful for men's wear.

- The draper is also a hanger on a stand, adjustable in height, but without a shirt or slacks bar. It is usually smaller than the costumer and the valet and meant to be used on a counter or buildup.

- Counter fixtures are important because they are at points-of-purchase, and this is where a customer can be influenced to buy. The counter fixture is also small and does not interfere with the give-and-take between the customer and the salesperson. However, a counter fixture much higher than the salesperson's eye level is an invitation to shoplifters to take items without being seen.

- In pilfer-proof fixturing, the basic concept is to protect or lock in the merchandise. For example, on perfume counters only dummy bottles with colored water are displayed on top, except for the actual perfume tester. The real bottles are kept inside the counter. Jewelry and handbags can be locked in fixtures that require a salesperson with a key to open the fixture and remove the item.

- Ledge fixtures are larger and more imposing than counter fixtures and are placed where they cannot be reached or touched by the customer.

- The major types of floor fixtures include the counter or showcase, round rack, T-stand, and quad rack or four-way faceout.

- A round rack consists of a circular hang-rod, 3 feet in diameter, raised anywhere from 45 inches to over 6 feet above the ground, set on an adjustable upright and securely attached to a weighted base.

- A C-rack is basically one-half of a round rack. A pair of C-racks can be combined to form a two-part round rack, that can be set at different heights.

- A three-part rack is a round rack comprised of separate but equal arcs. The height of each arc is usually adjustable individually.

- Criteria for selecting a fixture include appearance, construction, end use, upkeep, and finish.

- Finishes available for fixtures include chrome, nickel plate, brass, copper, bronze, paint, and wood.

Questions for Review and Discussion

1. Explain the correlation of fixturing to interior design with fixtures being the furniture for the store.

2. List the types of top elements available for stand fixtures. Explain the use for each type.

3. What is an easel and how can it be used in display?

4. What is a counter fixture? Why? Is proper height so vital in the selection of counter fixtures?

5. List fixtures suitable for use on ledges. Explain how each could be used in a merchandise presentation.

6. How do the showcases of today differ from those of the past?

7. Describe the use of each of the following floor fixtures, then identify its advantages and disadvantages:
   a. round rack
   b. T-stand
   c. quad rack
   d. gondola

8. List and explain the criteria visual merchandisers should use for selecting fixtures.

9. Discuss the strengths and weaknesses of the various fixture finishes mentioned in the chapter. Which is currently the most popular type of fixture finish? Why?

10. Why are wooden fixtures gaining popularity?

CHAPTER THIRTEEN

Visual Merchandising and Dressing Fixtures

AFTER YOU HAVE READ THIS CHAPTER,
YOU WILL BE ABLE TO DISCUSS:

- Visual merchandising and how it differs from visual presentation.
- Seven objectives of visual merchandising.
- Six factors that can be used to provide a dominant emphasis in visual display.
- Techniques for stocking merchandise so it reflects the dominance factor.
- Seven benefits of visual merchandising for the retailer.
- The various ways in which clothing may be dressed on T-stands, stock-holders, front-to-back racks, and hang-rods.

VISUAL MERCHANDISING AND DRESSING FIXTURES: TRADE TALK

aisle table	front-to-back display
back wall	gondolas
bargain square	hang-rods
brand names	price
color	quad racks
coordination	shoulder-out hanging
dominance factor	single-rod hanging
double-rod hanging	size
dressed leader	stock-holders
dump table	taste
economy square	three-part racks
end displays	T-stands
end use	vertical presentation
face-out hanging	visual presentation
feature table	

Visual merchandising takes place where the shopper and the product come together in a real, hands-on situation: It is the presentation of the stock on the selling floor. Visual merchandising is not quite a science nor is it solely an art. Though it is possible to draw up plans, draft diagrams, make schedules, and turn the merchandising techniques into a series of graphs and charts, visual merchandising is more than these elements. It takes a feeling for color and mass, for adapting volume to space, for arrangement and balance. It takes everything that goes into making a good composition. Taste and talent are required if the result is to be more than just neatly stacked shelves. It takes a sense of knowing when to be daring, when to be different, and when to surprise if the presentation is to be different from the competition's look—especially if they are following the same "graphs and charts."

To produce good visual merchandising, the display person must understand what good visual merchandising is and must know both the product and the shopper to whom the retailer hopes to appeal. Often a store's visual merchandising is only as good as the fixtures and fittings the display person has to use. Good visual merchandising produces a neat, easy-to-see, easy-to-follow, easy-to-shop sales floor. It involves arranging merchandise in a manner that will not only make fashion sense to the shopper but will also help the shopper to buy quickly, efficiently, and comfortably—and hopefully more than he or she planned to. Simply stated, visual merchandising seeks to achieve the following objectives:

1. To make it easier for the shopper to locate the desired merchandise.
2. To make it easier for the shopper to self-select.
3. To make it possible for the shopper to coordinate and accessorize on his or her own.
4. To provide information on sizes, colors, prices, and such.
5. To take the stress out of shopping.
6. To save the shopper time.
7. To make the shopping experience more comfortable, convenient, and customer friendly.

Customer-Oriented Visual Merchandising

Visual merchandising works best when it is customer oriented! One can only sell when one knows to whom one is selling and when the merchandise is explained clearly and visually to that targeted market. The product must be shown in a way that makes it relate to that shopper's needs, preferences, and aspirations—his or her lifestyle and/or fashion attitude. Only then are the wares being properly marketed.

Do make the shopping experience an adventure. Provide the shopper with a sense of discovery and not one of confusion or frustration. Visual merchandising is effective when it brings together the shopper and the product in a comfortable and convenient manner that also contains an element of surprise or wonderment—a uniqueness that may startle or delight the shopper with its novelty. It is even better when the display person/visual merchandiser can include the coordinates, the alternatives, and the accessories into the same space or setting. The number of items that can actually be seen, studied, and appreciated is often more important than the actual number of items stocked on the sales floor. Several dozen folded and stacked shirts arranged in rising tiers of shelves will read as so many ribbons of a color to the shopper's eye. The number of garments that stretch across a wall in a shoulder-out lineup are just so many slivers of sleeves. A single garment brought forward on a draper/hanger or form, given depth and dimension, well lit, and maybe even accessorized, can do more to sell the product than the staggering piles and endless sleeves that surround it. Sometimes, depending on the store's image, seeing too many of the same product or garment can actually devalue the item or make it less attractive, especially when the merchandise is upscaled, expensive, or designer labeled. Volume may be fine for popular-priced stores and for promotional events, but too many of the same item can be a disaster for some fashion images.

When preparing a visual merchandising layout, it is desirable that the display person/visual merchandiser give emphasis to some special aspect of the product. It can be the color, the coordinates, the brand name, the size, the price, the end use. This emphasis is the **dominance factor.**

Dominance by Color

Color dominance is the simplest, the most direct, and usually the most effective way to visually present products. People see *color!* People buy *color! Color is what sells!* Effective visual merchandising means, first and foremost, folding, stacking, and hanging products by color. Color takes precedence over style and size. Thus, in a display of variously colored items, all the red items are shown in a cluster or group. Within that cluster, items are arranged by size and/or style—for example, all the red

colored "smalls" are grouped together followed by the red "mediums" and the red "large" items. If red short-sleeved shirts as well as red long-sleeved shirts are to be displayed, line up all the short-sleeved red shirts by size—from small to extra-large—and then repeat the procedure with the long-sleeved garments. In this way, the shopper can immediately locate the color he or she wants, can then differentiate between the styles, and finally can find the desired size within the presentation. When stacking folded garments, arrange them from small to large, usually with the larger sizes on the bottom and the smaller on top. Because smaller garments seem to be more attractive in proportion, they are usually placed at eye level or just above eye level. However, logically, the people who wear the smaller sizes are often too short to comfortably reach up for their selections. If the signage clearly identifies which size is on which shelf,

Figure 13.1 Long vertical bands of color decorate the Hanes Spectrum shop and also make the color selection of the assembled sportswear simpler for the shopper. The "folded" garments way up on top–above the shopper's reach–are "dummies" while the "real" things are below where the shopper can self-select from the offerings. *Hanes Spectrum, St. Louis, Missouri.*

then it doesn't really matter if the small goes on top—or on the bottom.

If separates are being shown and there are skirts and pants that go with the red shirts in the previous example, the logical and customer-friendly way to show them is the same. Arrange the red skirts together—from the smallest to the largest sizes—followed by the red pants in the same size order. If the garments are hung on the wall, use two hang-rods. Show the shirts on the upper rod and the coordinated skirts and pants below on the lower rod. The more orderly the arrangement of merchandise on the wall, the easier it is for the shopper to see the whole range of products and then focus on what he or she really is interested in.

When stocking and presenting by color, the display person/visual merchandiser can show a single color either horizontally—on a hang-rod or on a long shelf—or vertically in boxes, cubes, or a series of descending shelves. When there is a range of colors to promote, try to follow the color wheel—or the rainbow—by showing colors with their traditional neighboring colors. This provides a natural and gentle progression from white to cream to beige to yellow, orange, red, and so on. Within each color, items would thus progress from the palest tint to the deepest shade; for example, in the orange family, colors would move from the pastel peaches to the dominant oranges to the subdued and subtle terra-cotta and deep earth tones. In the red family, items would be arranged from pink to red to dubonnet and maroon. The subtler the show of the total range of colors, the more upscaled and sophisticated the fashion look.

For more popular and promotional effects (e.g., casual wear, sportswear, fun-wear), the colors might be blocked—especially in the vertical arrangements—so that red is seen next to its complement green. By putting the clashing colors together, the reds appear redder and the greens are greener; the sharp contrast also creates an animated pattern on the wall or fixture. Yellow complements violet, orange is the complement of blue and, of course, black and white are the perfect contrasts. The use of conflicting colors next to one another will make a stronger, more exciting and colorful wall design—so use it only when that is what you really want. Where colors may "clash" and a tamer effect is desired, place neutrals between the fighting colors.

For certain seasons or holidays, consider altering the color arrangement on the floor so that the overall ambience is more festive or more in keeping with an overall color scheme. If the merchandise is mainly white, gray, and black, perhaps intersperse some red garments to enliven the space and also tie in this area with the rest of the color-filled floor. By using accents and accessories, the display person/visual merchandiser can add sparkle to what would otherwise be an uninteresting space.

Dominance by Coordination

Merchandise can also be presented with the emphasis on **coordination.** In any visual program, it is always effective to coordinate merchandise. The shopper sees how pieces can be matched or mixed—coordinated to go together to create a wardrobe of alternative outfits. In this case, instead of a single color being dominant, it can be a team or a group of colors or patterns or prints plus solids that are organized for easy shopping.

Dominance by coordination can be achieved using a wall system on which garments are hung to show how the various pieces can be arranged or rearranged in a variety of ways. Rather than hanging all the garments in a long, continuous, eye-wearying row, the hang-rods can be staggered in height—set at different levels—and even interrupted occasionally to show off a fully accessorized, coordinated outfit.

Figure 13.2 When the stock can be coordinated by color and/or pattern, the presentation is greatly enhanced if it is shown in use. Here the headless dressed form wears an outfit made up of yellow, brown, and blue coordinated pieces, and the assorted coordinates are displayed in the cabinet next to it. Note how the prints and the stripes hold all the colors together and how the solid separates are used to keep the patterns and stripes apart in the wall unit. *Marccain, Toronto, Ontario, Canada.*

A single quad rack or four-way floor unit can also carry the components of several different coordinated outfits. A single fixture can carry the pants, skirts, blouses, and jackets—dressed in a color-coordinated way (red/white/blue; yellow/black/black and yellow print on white; red/pink/green floral print plus solids in red, pink, and/or green). A combination of prints, patterns, or plaids can be presented with the solid-colored coordinates that were designed to go with the prints. Where prints and patterns need to be separated for the overall look of the area—or to make it easier for the shopper to see what he or she is looking for—the solid garments should be used as "spacers" or separators between the conflicting prints.

Whether the merchandise is presented on a wall unit or on a floor fixture, it is desirable that there be a **dressed leader** on the fixture. The dressed leader can be either the first face-out hanger on a four-way fixture or the first garment shown on a waterfall off of a wall system. That first hanger can be the visual explanation of how the assorted parts come together and how the prints and solids can be combined to create a variety of looks. Skirts or pants can be attached to the bar of the hanger, and a shirt or blouse added, topped by the jacket. The costume, depending on where it is located and what type of store it is in, may even be accessorized with a scarf or a piece of costume jewelry. If a draper is set atop the floor fixture, it can carry the coordinated ensemble and the display can be enhanced with folded alternatives and accessories like hats, bags, and shoes.

Dominance by coordination is easily adapted and applied to home furnishings and fashions like bed and bath linens, and kitchen requisites. Bring the merchandise together by color or pattern with compatible solids and highlight the presentation with a display vignette showing all the pieces together. Though the merchandise is coordinated, the display is still promoting color because color is what sells.

Dominance by Brand Name

All of us are aware of how important **brand names** and designer labels are in the competitive retail field. In the vendor shops (see Chapter 25, Visual Merchandising and the Changing Face of Retail), the manufacturer often provides not only the fixtures and the promotional graphics but the visual merchandising and display directives as well. Other stores may want to feature or merchandise products by brand-name dominance—perhaps highlighting the company's own brands. The display person/visual merchandiser may want to create a "boutique" or "shop-within-a-shop" where such brand-name products are visually presented to help promote and sell the name, the product line, and the compatible accessories.

Dominance by Size

In some stores, especially specialty stores, the **size** is the determining factor when a purchase is planned. This is especially so in the larger-size women's wear, the "big and tall" men's shops, and, of course, in children's clothing stores. Here, size can be dominant in the visual merchandising program. But it can be more difficult to create a harmonious and easy-to-shop space out of what can look like visual chaos. One effective technique is to use—as previously outlined—solid or almost-solid colored garments as separators. If, for example, the merchandise consists of printed or patterned dresses—whether they are sizes 14W to 22W or children's sizes 3 to 6X—arrange the garments first by size with the smallest sizes up front. Then—within the same size group—arrange the garments by color using the dominant color or color family in the print as the criteria. A red/pink floral print on a white background accented with assorted greens would be placed in a red or pink cluster and then, wherever possible, red, pink, or white dresses would be used to separate this floral from—let us say—a red/pink and green plaid dress. The solid or almost-solid colored garments allow the shopper's eye to rest before attacking or being assaulted by the next pattern or print. Here, as in color dominance, the dresses should be grouped from lightest to the darkest within a single size and, whenever possible, the color clusters should follow the rainbow.

Dominance by Price

If this translates into inexpensive, bargain, or sale merchandise where the discounted or slashed **price** is first and foremost, then maybe this is the time to turn the area into a "bazaar" or open marketplace. Let the volume of the product and the savings be dominant, and support the concept with banners, awnings, kiosks, and colorfully skirted tables that groan under the load of merchandise "tossed" upon it. Make it a "treasure hunt" where bargain hunters can rummage through the merchandise in hopes of finding a noted designer's label or famous brand name somewhere in the midst of the visual mayhem. In an upscale shop, this technique will only work on rare occasions and for very special promotions. If you do it, do it with flair—with fun and imagination—and with the customer's sense of taste always in the forefront.

Dominance by End Use

This kind of merchandising is very much like dominance by coordination, but here the term is mainly applied to white goods and hard goods. Just as the merchandiser may group fashion separates and apparel together with accessories for multiple sales, so may the visual merchandiser or merchant show and stock items that go together or complement each other but are not clothing items.

Sheets, pillowcases, throw cushions, quilts, blankets, duvets, floor mats, and even bed trays could be shown in color- and/or pattern-coordinated clusters since their **end use** will be in the bedroom. Assorted towels, shower curtains, mats, scales, cups, toothbrush holders, tissue boxes, and soaps will eventually have their end use in the bathroom; thus, they could logically be shown arranged by colors or patterns that go together. The basic concept is simple: if the products will end up being used together or will appear near each other, then it is effective merchandising to show how they fit together. The concept of end use dominance explains why it is usual to show table settings of china, glassware, tablecloths, place mats, napkins and napkin rings, serving pieces, and even cutlery, and then stock those items together to make it simpler for the shopper to purchase what she sees knowing that they all are coordinated.

Front-to-Back Visual Merchandising

No matter what the dominance factor, when creating a visual merchandising pattern in any area of the store, it is best to show the stock in a **front-to-back display;** from the main aisle to the rear wall of the space. A few of the garments or products should be featured up front, facing the main traffic aisle on either a table, an aisle liner, a T-stand, or even a mannequin or a mannequin alternative. This is where the item is "introduced," and it should be coordinated, accessorized, and well illuminated. If a mannequin or form is used, the outfit should be presented as a totality and alternatives or coordinates should be shown close by on T-stands or as lay-downs on a table or any other light-looking piece of furniture.

As the shopper steps into the area—past the introduction—the garments or products should be displayed in a range of sizes and colors on floor fixtures that are not too densely or heavily merchandised. Here, the total concept of coordination and the mix and matchability of the items can be shown. The lighting here doesn't need to accentuate the items as strongly as on the aisle display, nor should it be as bright as that on the rear wall, which is usually heavily stocked. This is where the dominance factor is most important. The well-lit rear wall not only brings the shoppers into the area or department, it is where the final selection of what will go with what is made.

At the start of a season, when there is the most stock in the store, merchandise may be shown shoulder-out or side-out with some face-out garments featured to show what the garment looks like and also to break up the run of sleeves or sides. As the stock starts to dwindle, a good visual merchandiser—before completely compressing the space—will display more face-out merchandise using waterfalls and fewer shoulder-out garments on the rear wall. It takes fewer garments to fill the space—and it makes the area look as though the stock is still viable and in style. The shop doesn't look "empty," and the stock doesn't look like "leftovers."

Visual Presentation

Visual merchandising is the orderly, systematic, logical, and intelligent placement of putting stock on the sales floor. So, if the display person can logically chart what to do and what not to do, how to organize the perimeter walls, arrange the floor fixtures and dress them, stock the tables and aisle liners—where is the "difference"? How can Brand-X products be shown in a way that appears more fashionable, enticing, and desirable than the same Brand-X products being shown down the street in a competitor's store? How does one store get that special look, that unique fashion image, that one-of-a-kind ambience that the shopper remembers and returns to? Where is the difference—and how is it created?

Display is the difference! Display is the imaginative, the unexpected, the fun and the flash, the panache that turns good visual merchandising into exciting and stimulating **visual presentation.** We are more than showing—we are presenting! We are adding highlighting lights, color, flattering illumination, and the lights that bring the shopper back into the space. These are the lights that bring the shopper off of the aisle and closer to the actual merchandise assortment.

Visual merchandising goes beyond putting out stacks of product when we add display. We animate the stock—

we activate it. We add form and figures, depth and dimension, and sometimes atmospheric, lifestyle decor. We add a personality, a fashion image, a lifestyle feeling, and wish fulfillment. We "humanize" the product and breathe life and excitement into it. The accessories, like the props we use, can be unusual and unexpected or subtly elegant and understated. The color combinations can be outrageous and avant-garde, or stylish and classic. It is how we present and display the product that makes the difference. Here, there are no rules, no charts, no guidelines. Here, the display person/visual merchandiser relies on knowledge of the customer's tastes, lifestyles, and attitudes as well as the store's fashion image. What can be

Figure 13.3 The interactive fixtures and stations in the Encompass by Shell store show off products as well as provide information. Television screens, monitors, video consoles, and computer keyboards are integrated into the units so that shoppers can be informed—and entertained—at the same time. *Encompass by Shell, Dallas. Design: Michael Malone Architects.*

"on target" for one store in one particular location may be all wrong for the same store in a different location with a different market makeup even though both stores are selling the exact same items. There must always be some criteria for **taste:** what is right for the store, for the product, for the customer, and for the location.

Visual Merchandising and the Retailer

We have discussed what visual merchandising can do for the shopper, but how does it benefit the retailer? Why should the retailer invest in the talents of a display person/visual merchandiser, buy special fixtures, pay for additional lighting, and perhaps even keep some of the stock off the sales floor? Visual merchandising can benefit the retailer in the following ways:

1. By resulting in increased sales, especially in add-on sales.
2. By promoting operational efficiency in the store.
3. By motivating and activating the sales force and making it easier for them to satisfy the customer's needs in the least amount of time.
4. By saving both the salesperson's and the shopper's time.
5. By making the salesperson more effective and more efficient.
6. By providing a "silent salesperson" that can give shoppers all sorts of information and suggest ways in which the product can be worn or used until the salesperson is available.
7. By simplifying the inventory process.

Dressing Fixtures

Stores and even departments in the same store may vary in format and image, but there are certain methods that are generally followed for dressing fixtures with the merchandise they are to hold and display. Some stores will display their merchandise by size, and in that size arrangement will show a variety of styles, patterns, and colors. Other stores or departments will show by color or by pattern and style. In the latter situations, it is simpler to get a good, sharp merchandise presentation as well as a pleasant, overall ambience in the selling space. It is not quite as simple when the merchandise is varied

Figure 13.4 The Miller Group designed these basic "show and sell" units for Wrangler to use in their vendor shops. There are short and wide units as well as tall and narrow fixtures so there can be a sense of variation in the shops. The taller unit incorporates space for a "dressed" form or hanger. Like the shorter one, hang rods, shelves and bin accessories can be used on the fixtures as needed. *Design: The Miller Group.*

and multicolored, multipatterned, long and short, and in between.

T-Stands

The **T-stand** is an aisle-facer. It is a feature presentation unit that should be trimmed lightly and emphasize a look, a color, or a special style. It is even more effective if it is located near a mannequin where the garment is shown dimensionally. If there are spacers on the arms, only one hanger per hook should be used, and all the changers should be the same.

Table 13.1 Architectural elements/floor fixtures and furniture for "dressed" fixtures (with garments allow 2 inches for the width of the garments; 1 inch to either side of the hang-rod or waterfall).

Fixture	Dimensions
Counter	39" high × 6'–8' long × 24' deep
Cash/Wrap Desk	39" high × 6'–8' long × 24"–30" deep
Museum Case	4'6"–5'6" high × 2' square
Floor Table	
Round	30"–42" diameter × 30"–36" high
Rectangle	30" high × 4'–5' long × 24"–36" deep
Chair Seat	
(from floor)	18" high × 16"–20" square
Platform	8"–24" high × 2'–5' long × 18"–30" deep
Mannequin	6' tall (approx.) × 2' wide × 18" deep
Mannequin Base	12"–15" square
T-stand	4'–6' adjust. × 2' in each direction when dressed
Round Rack	4'–6' adjust. × 3"–3 1/2' diameter; 5'–5 1/2' when dressed
Quad Rack	4"–6" adjust. × 3' square; 3' square when dressed
A- or H-Rack	
(one rod)	3'6"–4' high × 4"–8" long × 2' for single hang-rod
A- or H-Rack	
(two rods)	3'6"–4' high × 4"–8" long × 30"–36" wide for two hang-rods; 48" wide when dressed
Gondola	4'–6'6" high × 6'–8' long × 3'–4' wide
Door	
Single	7' high × 28"–42" wide
Double	7'–8' high × 5'–6' wide
Step	8" high (riser) × 10"–12" deep (tread); width varies

Whether the T-stand has a simple, straight arm at the top or an angled waterfall, the garment that faces out toward the approaching shopper should be dressed; this lead garment should be completely trimmed. If the T-stand is showing navy suits and the skirt is clipped onto the jacket hanger, a coordinating blouse should be shown under the jacket of the first suit. There could be a scarf tied on, a piece of costume jewelry, and maybe even a shoulder bag. The first garment can almost be treated as if it were a costumer, and a special hanger might be used on the lead garment to allow more of the skirt (or pants) to show below the jacket. Some T-stands are fashioned with a draper or dress form as part of the unit.

If this navy suit is also available in gray and red, then all three colors might be shown on the single T-stand—the lead garment making the most effective statement for

Table 13.2 Units of "shoulder-out" garments per foot of hang-rod.

	Type of Garment	Number of Units
Women's Wear	Raincoats *(lightweight)*	8
	Cloth Coats	8–9
	Fur-collared Coats	6–7
	Fur Coats	2–3
	Dresses	9
	Formal Dresses	3–4
	Bridal Gowns	2–3
	Nightgowns/Lingerie/PJs	8
	Robes	8
	Slips	9–10
	Jackets	8
	Slacks/Jeans	9
	Skirts	8–9
	Blouses	7–10
Men's Wear	Outer Jackets *(depending upon weight)*	7–9
	Coats	8
	Suits/Formal Wear	8+
	Sport Coats	8
	Slacks/Jeans	9
	Knit Shirts	11
	Sport Shirts	9–10
	Robes	6–9
Girls' Wear/ Infants' Wear	Coats	8+
	Dresses	9
	Gowns	8–10
	Slacks/Jeans	9
	Skirts/Blouses	9–10
	Knit Tops	10+
	Slips	10–12
	Coats	8
	Jackets	
	Heavyweight	8
	Lightweight	9
Boys' Wear	Suits	8
	Sport Coats	8+
	Slacks/Jeans	9
	Dress Shirts	7–8
	Knit Shirts	8–9
	Shorts	9–10

Table 13.3 Hang lengths of garments including hanger.	
Type of Garment (including Hanger)	**Length**
Coats	4'6"–5'6"
Jackets	3'–6'
Gowns/Formal Wear/Jumpsuits	6'–6'6"
Pants	
Folded Over	2'–6'
Waist Clipped	4'+
Shirts/Sweaters	3'+
Bras/Panties/Bikinis	18"–24"

Table 13.4 Floor fixtures for specific merchandise	
Merchandise Category	**Number of Pieces**
Belts	240 units
Ties	144 units
Underwear	108 packages of 3
Socks	60 dozen pairs
Hosiery	60 pieces, boxed
Scarves	x60–72
Shawls	45–50

Table 13.5 Folded and stacked merchandise per five feet of shelf *		
	Type of Merchandise	**Number of Units**
Apparel and Accessories	Shirts (folded 8" × 14")	30–36
	Sweaters (folded 10" × 16")	24–30
	Men's Hats	25
	Handbags	10
	Briefcases	24
Domestics	Bedspreads	24
	Blankets (folded)	30
	Bedsheets (folded and packaged)	200
	Pillowcases (folded and packaged)	60
	Towels	
	Bath	60
	Body	48–52
	Hand/Face	72
Housewares	Three-piece Casual Dinnerware	4 place settings
	Three-piece Fine China	3 place settings
	Stemware	
	Single style item presentation	8–10
	Bulk style	24–36
	Silverware	
	4" × 11" setting package	14
Electronics	Portable Radios	8–12
	Tape Players	4–6
	Record Players	3–4

*Shelves can vary in depth from 8", 10", 12", 14", 16". The length will vary with wall spaces or gondola units.

the design as well as the area. The red garment might have the most attention-getting color, but if navy is the color being presented in this area, the front outfit should be navy, followed by the gray, with the red garment bringing up the rear. If a descending waterfall arm is used on the T-stand, the lower garments should be navy, followed by gray, and ending with the red on top. The navy garment would get the full, front-dressed treatment.

If blouses or sportswear—all of the same design, but in assorted colors—were to be shown on a T-stand with a waterfall, the usual technique would be to follow the rainbow and go from the neutral off-whites to cream and ivory to beige-tan and brown into the warm colors—yellow, gold, orange, peach, rust, pink, red, cerise, lavender, and violet; and then into the cool colors, ending up with blues, greens, grays, and black.

Now, that is a lot of color for a little T-stand to hold, so limit the amount of merchandise and the colors on each T-stand but follow the basic scheme. Again, if the area is featuring a lot of red, the lead garment should be red; then go on to the red-violets; into the violets, blues, greens; then yellow, orange, and so forth. It is a logical use of the rainbow—adapted to the promotion. Following the spectrum works! People think of and see colors in that pattern and, as mentioned in Chapter 2, the analogous color scheme is an easy one to live with; neighboring colors coexist and lend each other character and color.

A final reminder: Merchandise on T-stands should be changed frequently. There should always be a new "show."

Stock-Holders

Stock-holders are "bread-and-butter" fixtures, the "workhorses" that actually hold the selling stock. They may display—and they should display—but primarily they are "stockers." Two examples are the quad rack and the round rack.

Almost all stock-holders are used in the following manner: Merchandise is hung from left to right—the way most people read or scan—from the lightest colors to the deepest, from the warmest to the coolest, from the smallest sizes to the largest. Color is the big "come-on," the single most important attention-getter. When a variety of styles are shown, the assorted styles are grouped by color. If there are six styles of blouses available in red, then style A, in red, will be hung from the smallest to the largest size available; followed by style B (also in red), sized from smallest to largest; and so on until all six styles are shown in red. The procedure will begin anew with the next color available that follows red; a red-violet, a lavender, a purple, or whatever. Remember, this is not a rule! This is a technique that works in stores involved with mass merchandising and with a popular appeal. It works where there is a great deal of merchandise to get out on the selling floor and a minimum of sales help to fetch, carry, and answer questions.

Quad Racks

The **quad rack** or **four-way face-out fixture** is usually placed just past the T-stand, in the front of the selling area. Though the quad rack is a "mass merchandiser"—when and where the merchandise and stock permit—it is used to show coordinates or special promotional merchandise. The design of the quad rack allows four frontal views of the displayed garments. From whatever angle the customer approaches, one arm should basically be facing in that direction (see Fig. 12.21).

The main idea of showing coordinates on the single fixture, with each arm holding another component of the outfit, is that from this single fixture a customer can put together a complete ensemble of three or four parts. All the parts that are displayed "go together," are grouped by color and by size, and unless a particular piece is not available on the rack in the customer's size, the customer can make his or her selection and bring it to the cash/wrap desk without any sales assistance. Again, the lead garment—a jacket, for example—could be "dressed" with all the component parts of the outfit.

A draper set in the middle of the quad rack and elevated over the stocked arm could also effectively display the "total look." The use of some elevated points in a merchandise presentation is good, when they attract attention and help lead the viewer from area to area. However, a landscape of "peaks" with hardly a "valley" in view can be quite demanding—and deadly—as a selling ambience. The use of too many high points means nothing is really highlighted. It can also cause an obstructed view of the back of the selling space.

Round Racks

Round racks are the real, no-nonsense, all-shoulder-out, mass-merchandising fixtures (see Fig. 12.18). When the quantity of stock decreases, the merchandise can be consolidated and some of these fixtures can be removed from the central area. It is better to have fewer fully stocked fixtures than many partially filled ones. Psychologically, when the fixtures are sparsely stocked, it looks as though what remains are "leftovers" and, therefore, less desirable or saleable.

Although round racks may be used for sale merchandise or clearance items as much as possible, the following setup is probably best for the customer's convenience and comprehension and for the general look of the area. When a single "rounder" carries assorted coordinates, they can be presented in the following order: pants, being the longest, are first, followed by skirts. Next come long-sleeve jackets, then short-sleeve jackets, and vests.

Figure 13.5 The wall fixtures on the perimeter walls of the Sean John boutique in New York combine adjustable shelves for folded garments with rods for hung ones. The bays of merchandise are broken up or interrupted by display areas where the semi-realistic mannequins show off the neighboring separates in complete outfits. In keeping with the store's upscale design, the shelves, partitions, and frames are made of a dark imported wood accented with nickel. *Sean Jean Boutique, Fifth Avenue, New York. Design: In Site.*

Sweaters, solid-colored blouses, and printed blouses finish the round rack and, thus, bring the viewer and the merchandise full circle. It goes from long to short, from solid to print, and from the smallest to the largest. If a single classification of merchandise is being shown, color again is uppermost: warm to cool to neutral. The strongest, most attention-getting, or most saleable color faces the front of the area or the store.

When color-coordinated groupings are arranged on the round rack, they go, within the single color, from the viewer's left to right: tops, jackets, vests, and bottoms (skirts, slacks). This is followed by another color grouping in the same order. Between the two color groupings, print blouses that can be used with either of the color coordinates may be shown. For example: A red color-coordinated group followed by blouses printed in red, white, and blue on a gray ground may be followed by a coordinated group of gray merchandise. This, in turn, may be followed by more printed blouses, this time, gray, white, and blue printed on a red ground. Either of the groups of blouses will work with the red ensemble or the gray one. This arrangement informs the customer that an extra gray skirt with the red-coordinated group will greatly increase the outfit's use and versatility. The trimmed rack is doing what a salesperson would ordinarily do: It is making suggestions and

assisting the customer in putting together the right colors and parts.

Some round racks, called **three-part racks,** are made up of three equal arcs or segments (see Fig. 12.25). The height of each arc may be individually adjustable. These units can conveniently show three separate groups of color coordinates on a single unit. They can also show pants on one level (the highest), jackets on another, and shirts or vests on the third arc. Each arc should be treated by color—light to dark, warm to cool to neutral—and by size—small to large. The treatment all depends on the type of merchandise, the amount of stock, and the kind of department.

Where the merchandise that is to be presented is small or short, it is possible to use a two- or three-tier rounder. If two levels of shorts are being shown, for example, the color range should still go from left to right, with the shorts grouped by color and by size within each color. But—and this is an emphatic "but"—the smaller sizes of a color should be hung on the top tier and the larger sizes of the same color should be hung directly below, on the bottom tier. This is called **vertical presentation.** Should the merchandise consist of color-coordinated bras and panties, for example, the mauve bras would be on top and the matching mauve panties would be placed directly below —always from small size to large within a given color.

Sale merchandise is usually located between the aisle and the perimeter or back wall of a selling area. Advertised sale or promotional merchandise should be prominently located and properly signed for quick identification. Clearance merchandise is usually set further back in the area and signed. When the merchandise for clearance or sale consists of odd pieces and broken-size lots, it might be better merchandising to arrange the offerings by size rather than color. However, if color groupings can also be done, do it; it looks so much better.

Back Wall

There is a psychology in the presentation and buildup of stock in an area of a shop or a department. The lowest fixtures are up front; the next area, or midsection, is next in fixture height; and the **back wall** is the highest merchandising area.

The basic idea is to make the back wall visible from the aisle or the front of the shop or area. The stocking of the back wall should not be minimized or disregarded. Store planners will wash the back walls with light for added emphasis. They will use light under the fascia for attention and attraction, even spotlighting some of the superwall (the area over the stocked merchandise).

The back wall is best used for coordinates with top over bottoms, or to create an impact for the classification of the merchandise contained within this area. The walls, whether they are used for hanging, shelving, binning, or combinations of all these, are also treated in the light-to-dark, small-to-large, left-to-right manner of merchandising. Because the lowest hang-rods, shelves, or bins will not be visible from up front, a vertical presentation is used. Ordinarily, the lower part of the back wall is all but hidden by fixtures, sales help, and customers collected in front of it. The merchandise that is to be hung on the two levels of the vertical presentation will be shown red over red, yellow over yellow, and so on; the larger sizes on the bottom, smaller sizes on top; blouses on top, skirts and trousers on the bottom.

Ideally, the back wall should be broken into coordinated groupings or color patterns to stimulate the customer, please the viewer's eye, and alleviate the curse of uniformity and boredom. Endless rows of sweaters or jackets hung at the same level or binned without a break tend to be boring.

By using slotted standards set into the wall and the wide variety of brackets available to secure into the slotted uprights, the visual merchandiser can raise or lower hang-rods, occasionally setting in a waterfall or face-out rod to break up the all-shoulder look. Displays can be set up on a shelf or pinned directly onto the wall in order to explain the merchandise around and below the display. Even row after row of binning on the perimeter wall can be broken up by devoting one of the bins to a dimensional presentation of some of the merchandise that is neatly folded or bagged around it.

Sometimes merchandise will be presented on the wall at a level that is too high to be reached comfortably by the customer. This top level may be reserved for the display of color-coordinated accessories that go with the merchandise below, or it could be used for reserve stock. These visual focal points, or displays, on the heavily stocked back wall area are absolutely necessary to stress the "new" and the "special" contained within and below.

Gondolas

Where there are **gondolas** on the selling floor and they are shelved or binned (see Fig. 12.22), it is advisable to carry through the same aforementioned "color-size"

procedure. A gondola, carrying a complete color and size range of women's socks, for example, could show a rainbow of the colors across the unit, while at the same time, each color would be vertically presented according to length. The vertical lineup of a single color presented in a horizontal rainbow of color is effective. It is easy to look at, and more important, it is easy to shop.

Since the merchandise that is usually stocked on the gondola is either folded or bagged, display is desirable. A draper set on top of the gondola can be used, or a displayer specifically designed for the type of merchandise (e.g., a towel displayer, a bust form for sweaters or blouses).

The display person can also set up an end table, a bracket, or a fixture to cover the flat, unmerchandized end of the gondola. **End displays** are especially effective when the gondolas are set perpendicular to the aisle; this is what the customer sees as he or she approaches the area. The end display can be anything from the merchandise itself simply unbagged or opened up, fluffed out, draped, and shaped, all the way to a mini-environmental setting that shows towels, for example, with a bathroom sink and all sorts of decorative go-togethers displayed in a semirealistic scene: a draped shower curtain as a background, a wastepaper basket, a drinking glass and matching soap dish, a makeup mirror, and maybe, if space and material

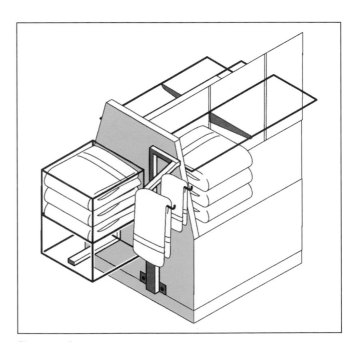

Figure 13.6 A combination bin and displayer attached to the end of a gondola. This end unit may show the feature color and/or pattern as well as a group of related items.

permit, a laundry hamper with more towels neatly tied and stacked on top. A softly draped towel will always "sell" better than a folded one, but it is the neatly folded one that the customer wants to take home.

Aisle Tables

Aisle tables are promotional or **feature tables** set in an aisle for impact selling. They may be elegant—skirted, flounced, and covered with cloth, or perhaps highlighted with an attention-getting lamp; they may even be beautifully arranged with a draper and platforms or risers to form a "wedding cake." Or, they may simply be **dump tables,** a term that sounds just about as awful as the end result may be. They can be arranged to form a **bargain square,** or an **economy square,** conveying the image of "come and get it," "what you see is what you get," "there

isn't any more." The dump table may be piled with merchandise that looks as though it had gone through a wind tunnel, and then been jumbled and plopped down on the table. To the aesthete, this is a very inferior display, one that certainly does not add to the store's image. But is it really so bad?

Many people, and that includes those with money, love a bargain. There is adventure, excitement, and a sense of discovery in shopping in bazaars, flea markets, and garage sales. Occasionally—and only occasionally—a dump table can be an effective merchandising device, but it takes a good and talented visual merchandiser to make it fun, exciting, and an adventure in scavenging rather than a demeaning, ragpicking task.

If the concept is used as a "special sale" technique and then "displayed," it will work and can even enhance the

Figure 13.7 Aisle tables or stacking tables can be anything from "bargain squares" with a jumble of sale items tossed about on them to furniture-like units that combine merchandise with display. In this men's area the lower tables are inverted wood "U"s edged in stainless steel, and the taller tables stand on square legs of stainless steel and are topped with glass. The "U"s up front are finished with the same wood used in the multi-tier fixture in the middle of the department. *Hecht's Short Pump, Virginia. Design: Pavlik Design Group.*

store's image. Imagine a main aisle treated as a street fair with stands, push carts, and fold-up displayers adding to the "look" as well as holding the merchandise. How about converting an aisle into a Near Eastern bazaar with billowing and swagged tents, and the merchandise tumbling out onto Oriental-type rugs or falling out of tubs, vats, or overscaled straw baskets? It could be an import event with stenciled crates and shredded packing materials supplying the holding space and the proper ambience.

Stores that pride themselves on their "better" or more expensive images, should tuck away the out-and-out "clearance" or "as is" tables toward the rear of the department. In popular price and discount operations, however, they are expected—right out in the open—in the middle of things.

Clothing on Hang-Rods

Shoulder-out Hanging

The hang-rod should be about 12 inches away from the wall when **shoulder-out hanging.** Allow approximately 2 inches for the width per garment; 1 inch to either side of the hang-rod.

Face-out Hanging

In **face-out hanging,** the hang-rod should be 4 to 6 inches away from the wall. Add approximately 2 inches to the width of the garment; 1 inch to either side of the rod or waterfall.

Hang-rods are usually 3 to 4 feet long; longer rods (unsupported) may dip or optically sag. Heavier garments such as leather and fur coats and jackets are best hung on shorter, supported rods.

Single-Rod Hanging

If using **single-rod hanging,** rods should be from 5 to 6 feet, 6 inches from the floor depending upon the length of the garments being hung.

Double-Rod Hanging (one rod over the other)

The top rod should be from 6 feet, 6 inches to 6 feet, 9 inches from the floor when **double-rod hanging.** The lower rod should be 42 inches from the floor.

Visual Merchandising and Dressing Fixtures: A Recap

- Visual merchandising is the presentation of stock on the selling floor. It takes place where the shopper and the product come together in a real, hands-on situation.

- To produce good visual merchandising, the display person must know both the product and the shopper, and be able to arrange the merchandise in a customer-friendly way that makes sense to the shopper.

- Visual merchandising seeks to make it easier for the shopper to locate, self-select, and accessorize merchandise; to provide information on sizes, colors, prices, and such; to take the stress out of shopping; to save the shopper time; and to make the shopping experience more comfortable, convenient, and customer-friendly.

- When preparing a visual merchandising layout, it is desirable to give emphasis to some special aspect of the product—this is the dominance factor. Dominance may involve color, coordination, brand name, size, price, or end use.

- In a display that emphasizes dominance by color, all of the same-color items of a particular style should be presented together, grouped by size from smallest to largest. Then the next style should be presented.

- In a display that emphasizes dominance by coordination, various items that can be mixed and matched to create an outfit are grouped together by color or pattern.

- The best visual merchandising pattern is one that shows stock from the front to the back; from the main aisle to the rear wall.

- Visual presentation is more than just an orderly, systematic, logical placement of stock on the floor—it is display: the imaginative use of atmospheric lighting, color, and arrangement that breathes life and excitement into the product.

- Visual merchandising benefits retailers by: resulting in increased sales, especially add-ons; promoting efficiency; motivating the sales force and making it easier to satisfy customers' needs; saving time (for salesperson and shopper); making salespeople more effective; providing a "silent salesperson" to give information about and suggest uses for the product; simplifying the inventory process.

- The T-stand is an aisle-facer that should be trimmed lightly to emphasize a look, a collection, or a specific style. The garment that faces outward toward the approaching shopper should be completely trimmed. If garments of different colors are to be shown on a waterfall, the rainbow technique should be used.

- The primary types of stock-holders are the quad rack and the round rack.

- When using stock-holders, merchandise is hung from left to right, from the lightest color to the deepest, from the warmest color to the coolest, from the smallest to the largest.

- A quad rack is a four-way face-out fixture usually found just past the T-stand in the front of the selling area. It allows four frontal views of the merchandise, and is especially useful in displaying coordinated ensembles because each of the four arms can hold a component of the coordinated outfit.

- When color-coordinated groupings are arranged on the round rack, they go within the single color, from the viewer's left to right: tops, jackets, vest, and bottoms. This is followed by another color grouping in the same order. Between the two groupings, print tops that may be used with either of the coordinates may be shown.

- The back wall is best used for coordinates with top over bottom or to create an impact for the classification of the merchandise contained within the area. A vertical presentation is used.

- A gondola should be merchandised using the color-size procedure and a rainbow technique. Since merchandise on a gondola is usually folded or bagged, display is desirable, either on top or using an end display.

- Display tables are promotional and are set in an aisle for impact selling. They can bring attention to a particular item, or can be used to indicate a sale or bargain merchandise.

- Clothing on hang-rods can be displayed shoulder out or face out on either single-rod hangers or double-rod hangers.

Questions for Review and Discussion

1. List the seven objectives of visual merchandising.

2. How could a display of different-colored skirts and coordinating print tops be stocked to demonstrate dominance by coordination?

3. Identify seven benefits of visual merchandising for the retailer.

4. How and with what types of merchandise should a T-stand be dressed? Why should merchandise on T-stands be changed frequently?

5. Explain the procedure for merchandising stockholders. Why is this technique commonly used?

6. For what kind of apparel is the quad rack best suited? Why?

7. What is vertical presentation? When is it most effectively used?

8. Where should advertised sale merchandise be displayed? Where is clearance sale merchandise best positioned?

9. Illustrate how you would merchandise the back wall with a coordinated group of misses red, white, and blue summer sportswear. The group includes shorts, pants, T-shirts, tank tops, and jackets. What types of fixtures would you use on the wall? How would the merchandise be arranged with regard to color and size?

10. What type of table would you select to convey a prestigious image? Why? What type of table would you select to convey a bargain basement image? Why?

Chapter Fourteen

Modular Fixtures and Systems in Store Planning

AFTER YOU HAVE READ THIS CHAPTER,
YOU WILL BE ABLE TO DISCUSS:

- The major types of modular fixtures and systems in store planning.

- The advantages of modular fixtures in creating a store design for a chain-store retailer.

- The benefits of display systems.

- What items to consider when purchasing a display system.

MODULAR FIXTURES AND SYSTEMS IN STORE PLANNING:
TRADE TALK

   clamps
   extruded uprights
   hollow tubes with finger fittings
   L-joints
   modular fixtures
   modules
   outriggers
   roll out
   slotted joiners
   slotted uprights
   system
   T-joints
   X-joints

Use of Modular Fixtures

As you travel across the country and visit malls and shopping centers in the different cities, you discover that some things never change. A Gap is always a Gap, a Banana Republic is always a Banana Republic, and The Limited in a different city somehow looks just like the one back home. When a chain-store operation calls upon a store designer to create a retail setting that will be recognized anywhere —in any mall or on any fashion street—the first step is the creation of a prototype store. The prototype is the first constructed unit; once it has been customer tested and any problems worked out, the design is ready for **roll out.** This means using the same design for all of the retailer's stores, but adapting it to the new locations.

In order for the same look—the same fixtures, materials, graphics, and lighting—to be consistent despite retail spaces that may vary in height, in length, in width, and maybe even in shape, the store's design and everything in it are planned to be made in **modules.** The modular concept means the pieces will be adaptable, movable, and rearrangable—and also cheaper to produce. By using the same basic measurements, shapes, and details, it is simpler and less expensive to run off a number of units at the same time.

Think of a module as a building block. Let us imagine a building block that is 2 feet wide by 2 feet tall by 2 feet deep. Using these 2-foot-square modules, we could place five cubes in a row to make a unit that is 10-feet wide by 2 feet tall by 2 feet deep. It is also possible to add blocks vertically. By stacking the cubes three high, the result is a "wall" that is now 10 feet wide by 6 feet tall by 2 feet deep.

Most designers and store planners prefer to use 7 feet as the usual height for wall cabinets or fixtures, though these elements can go higher. If the merchandise is placed over 7 feet from the floor, it is almost impossible for most shoppers to comfortably reach up to get it. A very tall salesperson—or a salesperson and a ladder— are required to reach merchandise stacked from 7 feet to 12 feet off the ground. As for the width of the modules, the most popular sizes are 3 feet and 4 feet, though the fixture designer/store designer may also add 18-inch and 24-inch modules to go with the 3-foot and 4-foot units. Two 18-inch modules will make up one 3-foot module while two 24-inch units equal one 4-foot piece. So, within one module we have smaller modules that can be combined to make up the module.

Figure 14.1 A modular system is one designed in sections or pieces that can be added to or subtracted from as needed. This Vitrashop wall system combines 4' wall panels with 2' panels and they are connected by vertical slotted standards that hold the assorted hardware available for the system: hang rods, shelf brackets, hooks, bins, etc. In addition, the panels are finished with drilled holes so that hangers or forms can be pegged into them for merchandise display. *Vitrashop.*

If storage space is required, the designers may design a cabinet unit that is 3 feet wide by 30 inches tall by 24 inches deep. Placed on top of this storage unit can be another shelf/hang-rod unit that is also 3 feet wide but only 4¹/₂ feet tall and 15 inches or 18 inches deep. Together, they become a 3-foot by 7-foot module that can be mixed with other 3-foot by 7-foot modules. The 18-inch module can be used when there isn't enough room for a full 3-foot module.

Modules are most frequently constructed of wood and designed to be adaptable and convertible. The same frame will adapt to holding shelves or hang-rods, so depending on the merchandise mix, the time of the year, and the amount of stock at any time, the **modular fixtures** can be changed to show off what is available. In adapting the prototype design to a particular roll-out location, the store designer or the company architect will fit in the 3-foot and 18-inch modules along the perimeter walls—using the smaller pieces to break up long runs of 3-foot modules.

Often the floor units are also designed as modules. This is especially true for selling and display counters and cash/wrap desks. There may be a single 6-foot module (twice the 3-foot module) plus 3-foot add-ons. There may also be 18-inch corner or end pieces. Depending on the available floor space, the store layout person may create a 6-foot or 9-foot counter with an 18-inch end piece at either end.

With graphics so very popular as a decorative and lifestyle form of display (see Chapter 21), many designs will include a 3-foot by 7-foot framed panel that holds a large photo blowup or a light box of the same size for color transparencies. In one roll out, the designer may use two photo frames while in another, depending on the store's merchandising needs, the designer may use one graphic frame and one shelf module. It is also not unusual for changing rooms or dressing rooms to be designed to fit within the same module to improve efficiency and simplicity when implementing the roll-out plans.

As we will see in Chapter 25, vendor shops have become more and more important as boutiques within department and specialty stores. The designers of vendor shops work almost exclusively with modules, since the spaces allotted to the shops in these stores will vary. The space may or may not have a perimeter wall; it may be an island between two aisles. In addition, the merchandise mix may vary from one store to another. With so many variables, the only effective and economical approach to getting the same look and image for the vendor shop—no matter how large or small—is to use modular fixtures and fittings.

Use of Systems

A **system** can resemble a set of building blocks, a sophisticated tinker toy, a nursery school jungle gym, or a "Lincoln Log" construction, grown to life size or larger. It can be a collection of rods, tubes, panels, or vertical and horizontal elements that are assembled by means of assorted joints, joiners, and connectors. It can be clips or slotted joiners that secure plastic panels or sheets of glass, wood, or composition board. Systems are manufactured in steel, aluminum, wood, and various plastics. They can be fragile, web-like constructions that are all but invisible; or they can also be heavy-duty scaffolding able to rise two or three stories and sustain a heavy load.

What most good and practical systems have in common is the ability to be easily assembled, disassembled, reassembled, and rearranged in new and different ways, in new and different places. A good system is stable, versatile, adaptable, modular, and is designed with many

Figure 14.2 This wall system is not attached to the wall but is designed to be self-standing with the upright slotted tubes holding the patterned metal panels. This system can also be adapted to shelving, hang rods, bin attachments, etc. The logo panels on the top shield the fluorescent tubes that light up the garments displayed on the panels. *The Adidas Shop.*

accessories that enhance the unit in the store aesthetically and functionally.

A system can be used to make a displayer, a fixture, and a stocking and selling merchandiser. It can be assembled to create a complete wall of hang-rods, bins, shelves, and even dressing rooms. It may be designed to contain its own lighting and signing elements. With a system, the store planner/display person can start with the perimeter wall and erect a whole selling environment without once needing to nail or screw into the wall, bolt down into the floor, or suspend or reinforce from the ceiling. A system may supply the wall hanging or the on-floor stocking. It may serve as a feature unit, or be devised as counters, tables, and cash/wrap desks.

The most remarkable thing about using systems is the relative ease with which one can put them together and

take them apart. It usually requires few tools; the ones most frequently used are a soft mallet (for pounding the finger joints into the tubes) and a regular or Phillips screwdriver. A few systems require an Allen or hex wrench. The display person has to study the system, get to know what parts are available, and determine what the unit can do. We will outline below some of the major categories of structural systems available today.

Types of Systems

Hollow Tubes with Finger Fittings

It is possible to obtain metal or plastic systems consisting of precut or standard lengths of hollow rods or tubes, round or square, and joiners or connectors that look like fingers. These **hollow tubes with finger fittings** fit into the open end of the tube and thus effectively "plug up" that end. At the same time, another finger in the same connector joint will fit into another tube. A two-pronged or fingered joint can be used to form a right angle, or an L. Four equal lengths of tube joined by four **L-joints** will form a rectangle.

A T-shaped connector will join three pieces of tube in one plane. This will form what is essentially one long line with one line bisecting it. Another type of **T-joint** has two extensions at right angles to each other, and the third

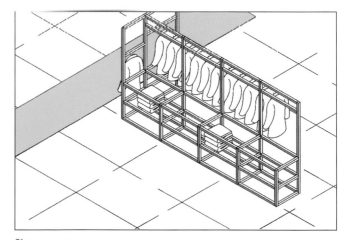

Figure 14.4 A modular system consists of same size, interchangeable units or elements that can be combined to make up a specified modular size, e.g., a two-foot module made up of a single two-foot unit or two one-foot elements. Most important in a modular system is the strict adherence to the dimensions, the detailing of the connections and connectors, the availability of accessories, and the ability to rearrange parts visually and easily.

finger extends up or down. In effect, a corner can be turned with this joint, and a continuation made with an open tube above or below. A cube could be constructed by combining twelve tubes with eight of these right-angle **T-joints.**

An **X-joint** brings together four lengths of pipe into a cross or X shape. Another four-pronged joiner forms a right angle and connects with rods above and below the angle. A five-fingered joint forms the X and has one finger open to connect above or below. A six-pronged joint forms the X and receives tubes or rods above and below the X.

There are many variations on this type of system. Some use round tubes from $1/2$ inch up to 2 or 3 inches in diameter. The sizes of the square tube systems are just as varied. The following are some of the better promoted and easily available finger systems: Kason's Rocker-Lok and Anchor-Lok, Abstracta, Unicube System, Metrex Display System, MEG "Moduline 11," and Kiddie Merchandise Equipment Group.

Clamps

A vast collection of systems are available based on variations of a clamping device that holds or joins round rods or tubes. Often these **clamps** are hollowed out spheres that come apart. They have shaped contours that will accommodate the proper size rod or tube. The rods are set into the proper "pocket" in the clamp and secured

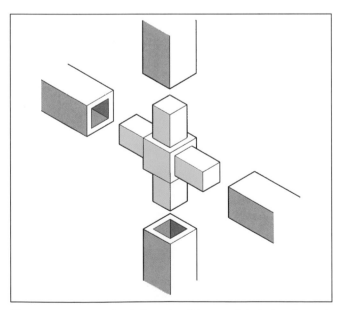

Figure 14.5 When the four hollow tubes slide over to join the four-fingered fitting, a cross or "X" is formed.

in place by means of setting a screw that closes the two or three parts of the come-apart clamp.

Other systems have clamps that are external units. Still other systems have vise-like clamps that work with sheets of plastic, glass, wood, or composition board. These joiners function like hinges and connect the panels at various angles so they can stand as walls, screens, or dividers. Some systems are available with colored tubes, but their painted surfaces are easily scuffed or scratched.

Some clamp systems are: Opto Clamp System, Tris and Tris Block from Societa Italiana, Multi-Blok, Klem System, and Viava System from International Promotional Shops.

Extruded Uprights

This group of modular systems is based on vertical multi-faceted and multislotted metal or plastic lengths into which horizontal elements, brackets, panels, or other structural elements are slipped and then secured. Some of these extruded metal (often aluminum) tubes are designed with four sides for assembling. Some have six sides, and others have as many as eight; with these, it is possible to form hexagonal or even octagonal structures. The store planner/display person is not limited to right angle turns only. Again, the more accessories to be displayed, the greater the possibilities for variations in systems.

Following are some of the **extruded uprights** available: Allied Trend Systems, Cardinal Shopfitting System, Syma Structures, Technal of America Universal Aluminum System, Standex Structural Aluminum Design, Daymond Modular System, and System Standex.

Slotted Joiners

These are like Tinker Toys, only bigger, and are produced in an infinite variety of shapes, sizes, and materials. Basically, they are either cubes, or spheres that are precision-slotted or drilled with holes. Some **slotted joiners** are designed to accommodate sheets of glass, plastic, or composition board to form shelves, bins, or rectangular structures. Others work with rods and tubes to make skeletal frames.

There are many varieties available today because they are simple to use and even simpler to disassemble and store. Among the most commonly used are: Ultima, Glass Cubes (J.C. Moag Corp.), Stackable Q-Bits (Sutton Designs), Natural Wood System (Coastal Trader), Twist-Lock Connectors (Cal-Tuf Glass Corp.), Unistrut (Mero-

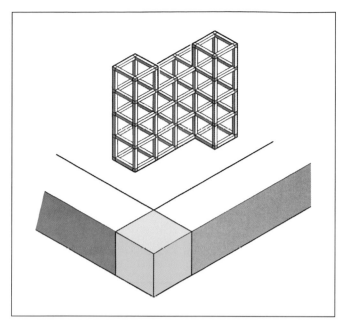

Figure 14.6 The system shown here uses square tubing of various lengths with finger projecting connectors of many configurations. It allows two to six tubes to connect at a single junction (see detail).

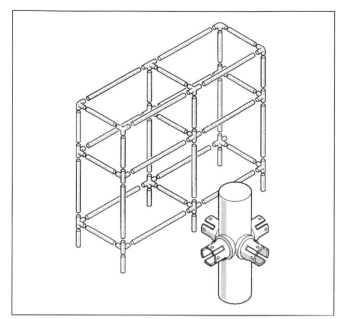

Figure 14.7 This system combines round metal tubes by means of fingered fittings (detailed in lower right).

form), Clip Master System (Outwater Plastics Inc.), Deco-Project, Raum Technik Studio System, and Voluma Connector System.

Slotted Uprights

Slotted uprights are not quite a system in the same way as those mentioned above, but they are certainly simple, adaptable building devices for fixturing and store planning. Slotted uprights are usually steel or aluminum squared tubes that are precision slotted on one, two, or four faces. The convenience and myriad uses of slotted upright standards that are secured onto walls and partitions have already been discussed in Chapter 13. These slotted uprights can be used with the finger joints to make self-standing units, or can be secured at the floor and at the ceiling, or spaced away from a wall or column by means of **outriggers** (horizontal members, attached to a wall or column, which serve to support and keep a horizontal or vertical element away from the bearing surface). The great variety of brackets and attachments that work with the slotted wall uprights will, in most cases, work on these square vertical poles.

Slotted upright standards are made by Garcy, Kason, Crown Metal, International Promotional Shops (Kissystem), and Ready Metal ("Z" Wall).

Selecting a System

There are other specialized systems on the market that cannot be put into one broad category or another. The display person would be wise to send for the manufacturer's literature, which not only states what the system will do, but will usually provide illustrations of the many components, attachments, and refinements. Some systems are produced in different diameters, assorted colors, and with accessories that might be available in some sizes, but not in others.

To use a system effectively, the display person or store planner must know what it will and will not do. Since each system is somewhat different and has its advantages and disadvantages, more or fewer accessories, and different degrees of adaptability, the display person should consider the following aspects before selecting a system for a specific use.

Looks

How will it look in the designated space? Will it look right with the type of merchandise that will be shown? How does it go with the store's image? Will the system be too "spidery," too kiddie-cute, too metallic, or too woody? Will the system appear overwhelming in the

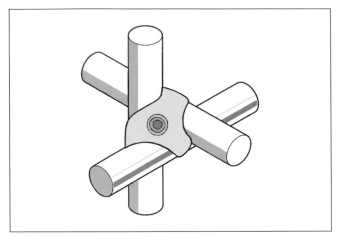

Figure 14.8 The Opto tube and clamp system.

space it will fill? Will it blend with other fixtures or architectural elements already in the area? Will it scale properly with the architecture and the merchandise?

End Use

How long will this particular system be used in the specific area? If it is to be a semipermanent arrangement that may only require occasional, minor adjustments, but will, essentially be installed until the "shop" is changed, the store planner or display person may wish to consider a system that locks or may be secured rather permanently.

Construction

How much weight will this assemblage have to sustain? Will it be carrying children's clothing, lingerie, separates, or will it be used for heavy outer-wear and leather coats? Will the hang-rods and shelves be sturdy enough for the load intended, or will they sag or bow? Does the designer have to plan to use more uprights or shorter hang-rods to sustain the weight?

Upkeep

Will the materials used in the manufacturing of this system hold up in daily use over a prolonged period of time? If it is made of metal, will the finish stay bright and shiny, or will it require polishing or replating? If it has been painted or lacquered, will the painted surfaces be subjected to rubs, scars, strains, and stains? Can the surfaces be retouched? If the system is made of wood, is it hard and scuff-resistant? Can scratches, scars, and blem-

ishes be easily removed in the store? If the shelves or bins are made of plastic or glass, will they break easily, discolor, sag, or bow? Will the edges be resistant to chipping? Will the exposed corners present a problem?

Adaptability

Is the system simple to assemble and reassemble? Is it too simple? Will unauthorized individuals undo what a display person has done? Are new washers or fillers needed every time a unit has to be put together? Does it require special bolts, screws, or nuts that can cause untold problems when a screw is missing? Are the replacement parts easy to get? Will the basic size and scale of this system work in most areas in a store, or is the system too spe-

Figure 14.9 OPTO's system can be used against a perimeter wall, or used to create a free-standing partition or construct counters and floor fixtures. The assortments of parts and accessories make it possible to create an entire shop of compatible elements all constructed out of the OPTO system parts. *OPTO International, Inc.*

cific? How safe is the unit? Will it stand without being reinforced into the floor, wall, or ceiling?

Price

Since price is such a variable, the selection must be based on the projected use and adaptability of the particular system.

It is only in the last few years that systems have been more commonly used by store planners and display persons in the United States. Since the early 1970s, environmental selling spaces and seasonal shops have become the responsibility of the merchandise presentation department. They are expected to come up with clever, charming, ambience-filled boutiques or "shops" in no time at all, often at a minimum cost. Display persons are beginning to recognize the great advantage of these collapsible systems that can be quickly converted from a bunch of rods, tubes, and connectors into a three-dimensional entity housing and showing merchandise—and even carrying its own decorative "skin," signing, and lights.

Systems are practical because they are so versatile. Study the systems that are available. Consider all the advantages and disadvantages. Select the most convenient, practical, and adaptable one—for the price—and remember, save the parts. A system will serve only as long as the bits, parts, and pieces are cared for properly. Keep track of all elements, store them carefully, mark the cartons and boxes, and your system will be a worthwhile investment.

Modular Fixtures and Systems in Store Planning: A Recap

- Modular fixtures—constructed of module building blocks in standard sizes—provide designers and store planners with flexible, adaptable units that can fit differently sized retail spaces.

- These units enable store designers to create an identifiable "look" when rolling out—introducing a new design for a chain-store retailer.

- Modules are usually made of wood.

- A system can be used to make a displayer, a fixture, or a stocking-and-selling merchandiser. It can be assembled to create a complete wall of hang-rods, bins, shelves, and even dressing rooms. It may also contain its own lighting and signing elements.

- With a system, a store planner or display person can start with the perimeter wall and erect a whole selling environment without once needing to nail or screw into the wall, bolt down into the floor, or suspend or reinforce the ceiling.

- A system requires relatively few tools and is fairly easy to put together and take apart.

- Major types of systems include hollow tubes with finger fittings; clamps; extended uprights; slotted joiners; and slotted uprights.

- A display person should consider the following aspects before purchasing a display system: looks, end use, construction, upkeep, adaptability, and price.

Questions for Review and Discussion

1. How would the use of modular fixtures help a store designer create a standard design for two differently sized retail spaces?

2. What are display systems? What materials are used to manufacture display systems?

3. What are the advantages of using display systems in store planning as opposed to using traditional display fixtures?

4. Why has there been an increase in the use of display systems over the past several years?

5. If you were in charge of the selection and purchase of a display system for the young men's sportswear department of an upscale department store, what factors would you consider? Describe the type of system you would select.

CHAPTER FIFTEEN

Furniture as Props

AFTER YOU HAVE READ THIS CHAPTER,
YOU WILL BE ABLE TO DISCUSS:

- How furniture can be used to set the mood in a display.
- Uses for various types of chairs in visual presentations.
- Types of merchandise suitable for tabletop display.
- How the interior of an armoire or chifforobe can be "fitted" to accommodate a variety of merchandise.

FURNITURE AS PROPS: TRADE TALK

Adirondack chair	fauteuil
armoire	folding chairs
Art Deco chairs	freestanding closets
beach chairs	ice-cream parlor chairs
bergère	Louis XV chairs
captain's chairs	Louis XVI chairs
chifforobes	peacock chairs
Chippendale chairs	posture chairs
country or provincial chairs	rattan chairs
	swivel chairs
deck chair	tables
desk chairs	tavern chairs
director's chairs	Victorian chairs
drawer units	wicker chairs
Empire chairs	yacht chairs

We will explore the concept of using furniture as attention-getting props further in Chapter 16. In this chapter, we will develop that idea and show how furniture can be much more. This chapter, among other things, will show you how a chair can be more than a support for a seated mannequin!

Furniture can be a prop or fixture, and often both at the same time. Furniture should not be saved only for window displays because, as you will see in the following discussion, chairs, tables, armoires, and chests are just as effective in mall openings, on the aisles, or on ledges and platforms inside the store. Not only can they bring charm, but they can also provide interest at the all-important point-of-sale.

Chairs

A chair can be the essence of a whole room, of an entire period or style or time, of a culture. A simple, single, easily obtainable **director's chair** of colored canvas and wood can imply the glamour and excitement of Hollywood, of stars and famous names, and all of that in the confines of the display area. It doesn't take a whole sleek steamship to suggest "Going Cruising"—a slatted **deck chair,** a bit of railing with a lifesaver attached (or painted on the front glass), and a single "floating" porthole somewhere in the background will more than imply that this is the top deck of a luxury liner. Instead of attempting to recreate an entire designer's salon, a single elegant Louis XV or Louis XVI **fauteuil**[1] or **bergère**[2] (two names for French-styled chairs with and without arms) can become what the shopper imagines that salon would look

like. Ralph Lauren Polo and the image created in the Polo shops are easily identified by the classic Americana and late 18th-century furniture used in retail spaces, just as Early American pine chairs and furniture can be the visual essence of fine country classic woolens and tweeds. Thus, a chair can be more than a chair!

There are numerous types and styles of chairs in a variety of furniture periods and finishes available—often for the borrowing from local furniture stores, antique shops, or local historical societies. All it takes is a smile, a "please," and a "courtesy card" in the window that identifies the donor or the source for the chair in the display.

If there is space, a chair can be "accessorized" and the display area further enhanced by adding a table or a plant in an appropriate planter. The director's chair can become part of a "fashion-shoot layout" with the addition of a camera on a tripod and several white or silver reflector umbrellas from a willing camera shop. The result is a "studio"! To complete the illusion, add some gray, white, or sky-blue seamless paper rolled down behind the dressed mannequin that is being "photographed" for a fashion magazine.

Figure 15.1 Furniture is readily available and is also the most versatile of props. A single chair can set a "look," a "time," or a "place," provide a seat for a mannequin, elevate a display of accessories off the window floor, replace a mannequin by serving as a "form" upon which an outfit can be set out, or be used to balance an asymmetrical composition. *Barneys, Madison Avenue, New York.*

---

[1]fauteuil—French for armchair. An upholstered armchair with open sides, usually with upholstered arm or elbow pads.

[2]bergère—An all-upholstered low armchair, usually with exposed wood frame and enclosed sides. The upholstered arms are shorter than the length of the seat, and a soft loose pillow rests on a fabric-covered seat.

Figure 15.2 To show off a collection of small but fine clocks and crystal, this small window has been turned into a library or study, and the big, cushy chair and ottoman serves as the anchor for the vignette setting. The piles of books—at various heights—serve as elevations for the small products and the bookcase wallpaper furthers the library imagery. *Stueben, Fifth Avenue, New York.*

To promote swimsuits, cover-ups, and beachwear, use a canvas and wood **beach chair.** It could be color-keyed to match or complement the garment being shown. The mannequin doesn't have to stretch out on the chair; the chair could serve as an elevation for related merchandise or fashion accessories like jewelry, cosmetics, or beach bags. To enhance the setting, drape a colorful but coordinated towel over the chair, add some inflatable plastic beach balls, a bright float, and maybe, on the floor, some scattered sand with or without pails and shovels. The pails can also hold the small accessories. If the display

area is large, one can make a bigger splash with the addition of a large canvas beach umbrella. Beach chairs and beach umbrellas can be used to create a window setting, on an interior ledge, or on a platform in front of a swim-suit shop.

A **yacht chair,** another type of director's chair, can provide the desired ambience for active sportswear. This is the wood framed chair with the changeable canvas seat and back, and with legs that scissor front and rear. It is usually available with a wide range of colored canvas accessories. If the chair is set on a green grass mat or strip of green indoor-outdoor carpeting, it becomes part of an outdoor or lawn setting. On a "wood" floor, it becomes part of a ship's deck. It is natural and logical to drape coordinates and accessories over the chair back, on the arms, or use the seat as an elevation to bring the accessories closer to the viewer's eye level. To expand or open up the setting, add more chairs and some sporting equipment such as golf clubs, tennis racquets, a croquet set, or even a bow and some arrows, and a big bull's eye target. Most of these "props" are also available from sporting goods shops in exchange for a credit sign in the display.

A rattan **peacock chair** can become the major prop for summer and resort wear, for "Town & Country" casuals, for a touch of the exotic, and the suggestion of far-away places. The peacock chair is a tall, woven chair with a high sweeping back that immediately flashes a tropical message to the viewer on the other side of the glass. The chair is often 5 or more feet tall, and it almost begs for a few palm plants (the indoor variety) as an accompaniment. **Wicker** and/or **rattan chairs,** either plain or fancy, bistro-type, or off the Victorian front porch, or out of a 1920s setting are all harbingers of nostalgia, and the "good old days." They can create a lovely period setting for soft filmy dresses, especially if they are romantic in attitude and a bit retro in design. Often the wicker pieces are finished in white, which is a fine complement for summery pastels. To expand the scene, try a round table covered with an appropriately colored cloth that extends down to the floor. On the table, place a pitcher filled with lemonade, some tall glasses with straws, and maybe a bowl filled with fruits (real or artificial) that are also color-keyed to the merchandise being presented. If the dresses have white lace accents, set the table for a party and add an artificial cake for tabletop interest. With the

Figure 15.3 Even old, worn, or broken pieces of furniture can be effective display props. In this window the chairs are wrapped and tied up with the traditional yellow tape measures associated with custom tailoring. The jacket is a work-in-progress and tells the "made to measure" story. The pin cushions and other tapes just underscore the message. *Dunhill's, Fifth Avenue, New York.*

showing off maternity clothes for a Mother's Day promotion or for at-home leisure wear and nightgowns.

The slatboard **Adirondack chairs** are strong and sturdy and are representative of the great outdoors. They are designed to withstand the seasons, to go from autumn to spring, from spring through summer. They can show off sportswear, casual wear, sweaters, skirts, slacks, and men's wear. Usually the Adirondack chair is left in its natural woody state, but it can be whitewashed for summery events or pastel-tinted for special occasions. Not quite as rustic, but also slatted and extremely adaptable is the familiar **folding chair** that, in multiples can create instant seating for a PTA meeting, a social club, an evening of summer stock, or for a bunch of guys planning football strategy. A group of folding chairs could also be an evening concert in the park. These small chairs are, obviously, most effective when clustered in groups of three, five, seven, and so on. If used in a window display, they can be lined up next to the front glass and hold a variety of fashion accessories on the seats and over the chair backs. Each chair can tell a complete, color-related story. Also great for storytelling in color are the metal folding chairs that are already finished in shiny, enameled colors.

What is more nostalgic than **ice-cream parlor chairs?** What could be more summery than ice-cream sundaes and sodas? These quaint wire chairs, all twisted and fragile looking, are excellent for a "parfait perfect" theme. White ice-cream parlor chairs set the mood and place for pretty pastel-colored outfits. To complete the scene, add a white marble-topped table to match the chairs and some soda glasses and sundae dishes to "fill" with colorful accents and accessories like scarves, belts, and costume jewelry. For Valentine's Day, wouldn't it be romantic if the cushions on the seats were red and if a red-and-white cloth covered the table?

Fall and back-to-college bring thoughts of traditional and tailored outfits to mind. One associates the career woman with her career-oriented clothes and **desk chairs, swivel chairs,** or ergonomically designed **posture chairs.** There are executive chairs for the board rooms, big desks and round tables for the top-echelon woman executive. The display "set" designer can add water coolers and file cabinets. When showing women's suits and going-to-work outfits, the scene could be filled with folding chairs, **tavern chairs,** or **captain's chairs** to suggest that "doing lunch" is part of the workday schedule.

addition of a wedding cake and pastel pinks, the setting could be perfect for a summer bridal display. While we're still on the porch, imagine what can be done with rockers and porch swings.

While "dressing for easy living," place a straw basket filled with yarns and knitting needles next to the rocker. Add some human interest with a fluffy, stuffed tabby cat from the toy store. The scene could be further elaborated with flowers or plants (live or silk) in terra-cotta planters set on the floor along with a homespun area rug under the rocker. The rocker could also be the major prop for

Figure 15.4 Nostalgia is always attention getting and it can also be fun. The old beauty parlor chairs—circa 1950s—set the retro theme that is further carried out by the very cumbersome and dated hair dryers. The pink plastic combs on the wall add another fun touch. *North Beach Leather, Boston.*

"gothic" are often better suited to suits, tailored outfits, simpler designs and, of course, men's wear. These chairs are usually finished in mahogany or walnut, and the upholstery is often deep and rich in color, while their French counterparts are mostly topped with pastel-colored, satiny upholstery. Add graceful palm plants or a wide-spreading lacy fern plant in a brass planter to fill the window.

Another lovely "light" touch could be a chandelier in brass or bronze, curly and swirly, dripping with prisms or swagged with crystal chains. It isn't necessary that the display person match the chandelier to the chair, what is important is that the scale and proportion of one go with the other and that they look right and comfortable together.

Figure 15.5 The slightly wrinkled white cotton-covered sofa sets the scene for the cut-out seated figures and the ones standing behind it. This designer boutique is not showing any of its costumes, just providing an in-your-face, attitude filled expression of who they are and what they do—and still getting the shopper to come closer to figure out what's going on. *Moschino, Madison Avenue, New York.*

Let's switch to "going out"—to a night on the town—from dressy on up to formal wear. The right chair or cluster of chairs can set the scene and create the desired ambience. French **Louis XV** (Rococo), Louis XVI (Neoclassic), and **Empire chair** designs are all elegant and lovely, and so right with formal wear and bridal wear. The small, light-scaled chairs—often accented with gilt or rubbed with antique white—can be used to hold items or they can play host to an artfully draped fur coat or a display of evening bags, gloves, slippers, scarves, perfumes, and jewelry. The mid- to late-18th-century chair designs of England are also elegant and refined, but not as "fine" in scale as the French pieces. **Chippendale chairs** that range from "ribband back" to "Oriental" to with the aura of the countryside—and the essence of the landed gentry. No light and lacy palms or crystal chandeliers here! These chairs call for sturdier, leafy plants like geraniums, begonias, colorful asters, mums, and marigolds. Fireplaces, mantles, and trophies can further enhance the settings.

Today, anything that is Art Deco is considered chic, and since the silhouettes of the thirties, along with the shapes and details, are reappearing in designer clothes and men's suits, the **Art Deco chair** (original or reproduction) chair can effectively sell the idea that something unique and of-the-moment is happening in the display space. **Victorian chairs** are just the thing for nostalgia trips; for marking off anniversaries, for the good

Figure 15.6 There is no question as to the time of the year! The two outdoor lounge chairs, covered in Bendel's signature brown and white stripe, carry the assorted accoutrements for a "weekend getaway." The white lattice panel and green mat complete the illusion and also partially back up the action in this open-back window. *H-Bendel, Fifth Avenue, New York.*

Figure 15.7 The beach umbrella and the canvas-backed yacht chair put the headless mannequin in the swim suit near the beach—or pool. The shimmering blue plastic floor mat suggests water with the yellow and white beach balls "floating" on it. *H-Bendel, Fifth Avenue, New York.*

Let's not overlook the **country** or **provincial chair** styles: country French, country English, and Early American. These chairs are less detailed, simpler, country cousins of the more ornate court styles mentioned above. These styles are usually interpreted in light-colored, natural woods, sometimes rubbed with white or gray, and upholstered in textured fabrics in solids, plaids, and small allover prints. These sophisticated rustics are complements for fine woolens, tweeds, and cashmeres, for designer separates for autumn and winter. They can add the Ralph Lauren or Laura Ashley look to a display

Figure 15.8 "Retro elegance" is what this display is all about and the "antique" natural wicker chair helps to create the right ambiance for the realistic mannequins. The moss-covered floor with scattered stones brings the setting out of doors and the violet flowers pick up and help promote the violet in the print dresses on the figures. The "garden" is further suggested by the floral background pattern. *Macy's, Herald Square, New York.*

old days, and especially with lacy and beribboned frothy confections, trimmed with ruffles, and full flowing lines. Whether the merchandise is up-to-the-neck nighties or peignoirs, little-girl dresses, or romantic wedding gowns, the Victorian-style chair will work just fine.

Tables

Tables are not only props, they are fixtures too. These everyday pieces of furniture can create a sense of time and place; they can show off or hold merchandise in a more interesting, more personal, and intimate manner than a cold, steely fixture does. A table is an elevated platform. In a traditional window, it will raise merchandise 30 inches off the floor of the window, which can be another 18 inches off the street level. Where the window floor is level with the floor of the shop, tables definitely bring whatever is set out on them closer to the shopper's eye level. And to restate that old retail adage, "eye level is buy level." Small items or fashion accessories are more easily seen and appreciated if shown on top of a table. An arrangement of shoes, gloves, bags, scarves, jewelry, and cosmetics, plus a vase filled with live (or silk) flowers will create a decorative still life, and it will also let the shop-

per know what goes with what. If the 30-inch-high table is too tall, use a 16-inch "cocktail" table. The lower table is especially effective for the presentation of shoes and handbags.

As previously discussed with respect to chairs, the period, style, and finish of the piece of furniture can help identify the class of merchandise as well as suggest where the items can be worn. A period piece may work wonderfully for dressy shoes, but casual or sporty shoes could be set out on provincial, Early American, or even rustic, rough-barked cobbler benches. Low woven wicker or rattan tables can present casual or sporty shoes

Figure 15.9 An abstract atelier or workshop is suggested in this window with the assorted chairs, chest, and tables painted red. One mannequin is stretched out on the chest while another stands on top of it along with a chair. On the floor the standing chairs are used to seat the mannequin and also raise a framed picture to the viewer's eye. The "forced perspective" of the "woodwork" and "ceiling" make the window look much deeper than it really is. *Bergdorf Goodman, Fifth Avenue, New York.*

Figure 15.10 The console table and matching stool, borrowed from a furniture gallery, help to create an elegant setting in this small window that features assorted designer accessories and exquisite crystal. *Lalique, Madison Avenue, New York.*

tral-colored cloths, the color of the rug or the walls, and use smaller accent-colored cloths over them. Some fabric stores or theatrical supply houses carry muslin in 8-foot widths (96 inches) and even 9-foot widths, in white, natural, and sky-blue. Fabric this wide can be made to cover 3-foot tables without joining or patching pieces of fabric. However, there is still a long hem to sew, even if one works with white glue instead of needle and thread. Felt is an excellent material to work with since it does come in 6-foot widths. A 2-yard square of fabric, cut in a circle, will make a colorful overcloth to drop, for a color accent over a neutral cloth. Search out discount fabric shops that carry odd lengths of fabrics and mill-ends of prints and solids in 48-, 54-, and 60-inch widths that can be hemmed and used as squares (48 by 48 inches or 54 by 54 inches) over the basic long round cloths. Imagine a black-and-white polka-dotted overlay cloth when the merchandise is black and white, and the accent is polka dots. Or try a checkered overlap with checkered accessories. A floral print in the same or complementary colors of the feature merchandise could be a display in itself for spring or summer prints, just as burlap or heavy homespun textures would be for autumn display.

Armoires and Cabinets

Armoires, chifforobes, and **freestanding closets** all afford the shopper a glimpse at a coordinated lifestyle. It is like looking into the wardrobe of an organized, color-aware, color-conscious friend. In it, one can see sweaters, blouses, skirts, slacks, and jackets just asking to be mixed or matched. If the closet is well designed, the top shelf will hold hats and handbags, while shoes will be lined up on the lowest shelf or on the floor of the closet. An armoire or chifforobe is an excellent sometime window prop, and an often-time prop on the selling floor with featured merchandise. An armoire usually combines shelf space with hang space, while the chifforobe provides the hang space with drawers that can be partially opened and filled. In an open-back window, the armoire becomes the break or partition between the display space up front and the store's selling space beyond. Inside the store, on the selling floor, the armoire can be a mini-boutique or a specialized "shop" within the shop, or the focal display area at the end of an aisle. It can even

for cruise and summer. A steamer trunk, lying on its side or back, could suggest shoes that travel places.

Any old, beat-up, and battered table can be used successfully by draping a cloth over it. Cloths are available ready-made in many sizes, colors, textures, and patterns in linen shops. What size to use? A standard table is 30 inches tall, so double the height and add the diameter of a table for the correct size for a down-to-the-floor tablecloth. A 30-inch round table (30-inch diameter) requires a cloth that is twice 30 inches tall plus 30 inches in diameter, or a 90-inch round cloth.

If tables can be used inside the store for feature presentations, on or off the aisles, it pays to invest in neu-

Figure 15.11 This is the dinner party to end all dinner parties! However, it does get to show off some smart and sophisticated going-to-party outfits on some really spirited, realistic mannequins. Note how the spindly ballroom chairs have been cut down, as have the table legs, so that the tabletop with its display of fine china, crystal, and linens is at a convenient height for the viewer on the street to see all the beautiful "stuff"—up close. *Bergdorf Goodman, Fifth Avenue, New York.*

be the entrance into a particular selling area. In a really small shop that sells mostly ready-to-wear, the open armoire can be the accessory "wall" with belts on an open, exposed inner door, scarves on the other, and on the shelves an assortment of the accessories carried in stock.

To be really effective, this "fixture" should not be crammed full of merchandise. This is a display unit and the garments need more breathing space—more space to show off. They need to be viewed. Coordinate a single color or color scheme, add a scarf or a belt, and then turn the hanger on the rod so that the shopper gets an almost full frontal view of the outfit. Search out secondhand stores and used furniture depots for salvageable wrecks that can be painted a soft neutral color that will almost "disappear" into the surroundings. What really counts is

what is on the inside, so do clever and interesting things with the interior and throw open the doors to reveal the contents. The inner sides of the doors and the interior space can be painted a contrasting color or papered. Panels can be cut of board that can be wallpapered or covered with fabrics, and serve as liners for the doors and closet interior. Interchangeable panels make it possible to change the color, the texture, or pattern of the armoire with the changing merchandise. Moiré fabric or papers that look like watered taffeta will make an elegant interior against which one can show gowns, furs, and fine intimate apparel. A soft, subdued allover paisley might be very handsome with woolens and cashmeres. Try ticking or stripes with casual sportswear and floral prints with pastel-colored garments. Though the basic piece is al-

Figure 15.12 Barneys has created a bedroom you can move into if you like everything "wallpapered" in the same repetitive pattern. It may not work at home but it certainly works here to show off the black and white designer fashions. Note the humorous touches that keep the shopper's nose up against the glass, like the paper-wrapped cat and canary—and the canary's cage. *Barneys, Madison Avenue, New York.*

ways the same, the interior, where the display goes, can be a changing stage set.

The original rods and shelves can be removed and replaced with slotted standards (see discussion of "back wall" in Chapter 13, Visual Merchandising and Dressing Fixtures). These slotted standards can be almost hidden by the replaceable liner panels just mentioned. It is then possible to create different hanging and shelving arrangements. The wide range of brackets and accessories that fit into the standards will make it possible to have varying heights and lengths of hang-rods and shelves.

The style or period of the armoire, chifforobe, cupboard, or hutch can say something about the merchandise within. The provincial or country styles are better suited to sportswear and separates, to country-style woolens and tweeds, and to classic casual garments. The more elegant period pieces are especially well adapted to lingerie, better dresses, and gowns.

Drawer Units

Drawer units—chests, bureaus, anything with pull-out surfaces—can be put to work in presentation and display, from tall units to low units, from highboys to low-

boys, to night stands. A closed drawer is a secretive thing and piques the viewer's interest and curiosity. An open drawer shows all, tells all, and can sell almost all. What do you put in drawers? Drawers are filled with small, all-important separates and fashion accessories from shirts and ties, to T-shirts, to sweaters and scarves, socks, stockings, and all kinds of underwear.

When you pull open a drawer, you make a statement. Whether it is a color, a color scheme, or a full spectrum, it must combine show with stock. If showing blouses or sweaters, stack the neatly folded garments in the color range in the drawer while one open garment "casually drips" out of the drawer onto the floor, or reaches up to a dramatic lay-down on the top of the chest. In using drawers for display, the eye level is important. The top drawers of a tall unit will not show off what is in the drawers, so that is the place to drape the single show item. The drawers at and below eye level are where the selling really takes place.

The top of a not-very-tall chest is also a valuable display elevation for a lay-down of garments that are not usually folded away in drawers: slacks, skirts, shoes, handbags, and toiletries. Thus, a traditional 36-inch-tall chest, ideally displayed, would feature garments laid out on top, maybe sharing the space with a vase filled with the appropriate color and kind of flowers (pink carna-

Figure 15.13 What says "wash and wear" as clearly as washing machines? What is just about the last thing you would expect to see in a designer boutique's display window? Washing machines! Moschino's "tongue-in-cheek" display uses them as props and attention-getters, and to get the garments and accessories up to eye level. The laundry basket, up front, carries more of the designer stuff. *Moschino, Madison Avenue, New York.*

Figure 15.14 The country-style hutch not only centers and holds the whole composition together in this on-the-floor display in a house-wares department, it also elevates some of the assorted products up to different viewing levels. The hutch also reinforces the "country casual" theme of the merchandise and display. *Macy's, White Marsh. Maryland.*

tions for Mother's Day, yellow mums for autumn, and so on), or a live plant or a fashion magazine opened to the "right" page, or the store's message in a handsome picture frame. The open drawers below could show off the range of go-with material available. As an example, for

Mother's Day the chest could overflow with lacy things in pastel colors and the vase of carnations could share top surface space with some ribbon-tied gift boxes, some greeting cards, and maybe a framed photograph of "the children."

Drawers are opened for a campus-wear setting with an avalanche of sweaters, scarves, hats, and socks, and piled up on top are books and fashion accessories in precariously built-up stacks. Scattered on the floor along with football memorabilia could be tapes, discs, college handbooks, and maybe even a stereo set courtesy of the local supplier. Add several pieces of open luggage for cruise and resort wear. Luggage can be partially filled with the same merchandise that is filling the drawers. On top of a rattan or wicker chest, add a collection of sun lotions, sunblocks, sunglasses, and hats as well as brochures for faraway ports of call. It is really quite simple and logical. Imagine moving in or moving out, of packing and unpacking, then add some atmosphere for time and place, tell a merchandise story, and it's a display.

In addition to luggage, imagine what can be done with steamer trunks that are bigger. In an open-back window, an upright trunk with drawers pulled out and filled with accessories, and one or two outfits hung on the wardrobe side, not only shows off a wealth of related merchandise, it creates a partial screen of the store's interior. The trunk also suggests a time and a place; it gives the display person a theme to work with. It would be a worthwhile investment to buy a secondhand or used trunk and fix it up with paint, paper, and travel labels. Ignore the scuffs and dents. What trunk is perfect after the first voyage? Paint it or paper it; make it decorative. With some clever draping, it is possible to hide the ravages of age and misuse. Since "theater" is always a great attention-getter, the old steamer trunk could be turned into a theatrical trunk by stenciling on the names of theaters or opera houses or even top musicals on the shiny black finish. Put a big star on the suggestion of a door— and it's "opening night."

Furniture as Props: A Recap

- Furniture can be used as props or fixtures or both at the same time.

- A chair can suggest the essence of a scene.

- Some chairs that can be used as props include the following: director's chair, deck chair, Louis XV or Louis XVI chairs, Early American pine chair, yacht chair, wicker chair, office chair, French country chair, English country chair, and Art Deco chair.

- Tables can also be used as fixtures as well as props.

- Tables can be used for window display to raise the merchandise to eye level.

- Tabletop displays work well with small items and fashion accessories.

- To determine the correct size of a round tablecloth that reaches the floor, double the height of the table and add the diameter.

- Using an armoire, chifforobe, or closet for display can show the shopper a coordinated lifestyle and suggest mix-and-match choices.

- An armoire, chifforobe, or closet display should never be crammed full of merchandise. Items need breathing space and room to show off.

Questions for Review and Discussion

1. Give an example of how a chair can create an image in a window or interior display.

2. Describe the type of merchandise you would display with a wooden deck chair, an upholstered chaise lounge, a porch swing.

3. Explain how the period, style, and furniture finish all come together to suggest the merchandise class and store image. Provide an example to illustrate your understanding.

4. What is the formula for determining the proper size of a table covering? What size cloth would be necessary to completely cover a 36-inch round table?

5. How might an armoire be used as a selling fixture in a lingerie shop? A men's furnishings department? An accessory outpost?

6. Use decorating magazines to find five examples of furniture that could be used in display. Indicate the name and style of each piece, the type of merchandise you would use in the display, how the furniture piece would be incorporated into the display, and the reasons why you feel this piece of furniture would be appropriate for the setting.

PART FOUR

VISUAL MERCHANDISING AND DISPLAY TECHNIQUES

MOST DISPLAYS must capture the attention of passersby in only a few brief seconds. Chapter 16, to this end, provides some great attention-getting tips that are sure to captivate customers. Some of the most popular themes and schemes in visual merchandising and display are set forth in Chapter 17.

Chapter 18 focuses on the variety of materials used for masking and proscenia. One of the most universal events in retailing is a "sale"; ideas for effectively promoting sales in a myriad of inventive ways are presented in Chapter 19.

Fashion accessories are best shown in use. Chapter 20 focuses on how to show accessories in co-ordinated groupings and how to handle displaying accessories without outfits. Chapter 21 relates the unique techniques used for displaying home fashions, hard goods, and foods.

Graphics and signs are used to communicate with customers and stimulate the desire to buy the merchandise on display. Chapter 22 discusses the use of graphics in display and the essentials for store signage from size and color to techniques and manufacturing processes.

CHAPTER SIXTEEN

Attention-Getting Devices

AFTER YOU HAVE READ THIS CHAPTER,
YOU WILL BE ABLE TO DISCUSS:

- The purpose of using attention-getting devices in displays.
- Twelve attention-getting devices commonly used in display.
- How a store could use humor to attract customers.
- The ways in which motion can be created in a display.
- The careful use of shock as an attention-getting device.
- Sources of props for visual displays.

ATTENTION-GETTING DEVICES: TRADE TALK

color
contrast
humor
lighting
line and composition
mirrors
motion or movement
nostalgia
props
repetition
scale and proportion
surprise and shock

Be it a one-window, one-item display in an ultra-exclusive shop, or a wild, variety assortment in the multiwindow display of a mass merchandiser, the display was put there to be seen! The basic concept of display is to show and to *see* what is shown—and then to *sell*. One of the main problems in setting up a window display is how to attract attention in order to bring the prospective shopper closer to the window and then to convince him or her to enter the store.

In the past, merchandise tumbled out from the shop into the street to greet and envelop the shopper. Or, as is still practiced in some bazaars and markets today, the salesperson would physically "collar" the shopper and cajole him or her into buying something. This is hardly the recommended approach for sophisticated, fashion-wise storekeepers.

The display must be the "psst" that is loud enough to be heard on a heavily trafficked street, but not so loud as to scare off the shopper. How the display says "psst" will depend on the merchandise and the image the store is trying to project. The display of a very chic and soft-sell type of shop may politely "clear its throat," and the "ahem" may be enough to be noticed by someone tuned in to the sophisticated—and the soft-sell. On the other hand, the popularly priced "shock 'em and sock 'em" operation may yell out a "Hey, you!" What they both want is the shopper's attention for a brief but important moment.

Sometimes, the most effective way to get attention is by not raising one's voice at all. Silence, the absence of sound, can in some cases make a very loud "noise." Also, it should be remembered that getting the shopper's attention sometimes will depend on what neighboring stores are doing.

There are many devices that can be used to attract the shopper's attention. Some of these include:

- Color
- Lighting
- Line and composition
- Scale
- Contrast
- Repetition
- Humor
- Mirrors
- Nostalgia
- Motion
- Surprise and shock
- Props

Color, line and composition, and lighting are discussed in greater detail in Chapters 2, 3, and 4, respectively. Additional information dealing with props can be found in Chapter 15, Furniture as Props.

Color

Color is still the big attraction. It is what we see first, what attracts us to an object. A big, hot pink promotion can be dazzling in its intensity on a cool, gray day—the warmth of the color pink, flowing and gushing out from the window, can draw the passerby like a magnet.

An all-black-and-white window makes a really strong color statement even though the colors are neutral. Here, the power to attract is in the absence of color,

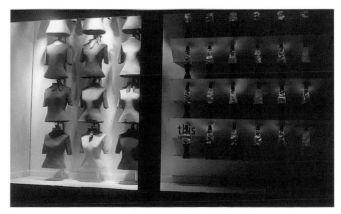

Figure 16.1 Color is still the big attraction! It is what we see first and what attracts us to a display. The many colored T-shirts are balanced by the equally bright and colorful display of retro lava lamps in this color laden display. The expert lighting helps to emphasize and enhance the many colors on view. *Macy's West 34th Street, New York.*

Figure 16.2 Color attracts, especially when it is red! This window is saturated with red—all red—from the garment to the drapery to the hot, hot lighting. The light makes the red appear even richer and more intense. *Saks Fifth Avenue, New York.*

especially since the display will be surrounded by a multicolor explosion of people moving back and forth in front of it.

Thus, a sharp color contrast will do it: black and white, red and yellow, and so on. Even in a window filled with dozens of related or assorted items, if all the merchandise is telling the same color story, in unison, the display will have the power to attract!

Lighting

Lighting is another device used to draw shoppers to both window and interior displays. Effective display lighting can be the jolt that catches the eye and carries it to the product. A forceful spotlight in a subtly lit display area can be as attention-getting as a yank on the collar.

A display bathed in fiery red or eerie green or dramatic blue light can effectively intrude into the gray environment of concrete sidewalks and building facades. Brilliantly colored lights can command instant eye contact. A window, or any interior display without lighting, might just as well be a window with a drawn curtain or merchandise left hanging in a closet. Even a drawn shade can elicit more curiosity or interest than an unlit window.

Line and Composition

Line and composition can be valuable attention-directors after color and lighting have done their parts. The use of vertical, horizontal, curved, and diagonal lines can help determine the effectiveness of a merchandise presentation. Each type of line suggests something different (e.g., vertical lines: height, dignity, strength; horizontal

Figure 16.3 Bright, strong accent lights can catch the viewer's eye and those lights seem even brighter when the rest of the window is in semi-darkness. Notice how the shaft of clear white light washes gently over enough of the mannequin to define what she is wearing while the steamy red in the rest of the window highlights the "Heat Up" theme. *Bloomingdale's, Lexington Avenue, New York.*

Figure 16.4 The repetition of the black and white "eye"—on the walls and floor of the window—creates a dynamic draw for the featured black and white outfits. The multi-graphed sheets of $8^1/2'' \times 11''$ paper with the eye motif reinforce the theme "25 Years of Pure Vision." By alternating the sheets on the walls and floor, a strong repeat pattern is created. *Barneys, Madison Avenue, New York.*

lines: width, elegance, tranquility; curved lines: softness, grace; diagonal lines: action, force, excitement). Each can be used in different ways to arrest the attention of the passerby to the display.

Composition is the arrangement of different visual elements in order to achieve a unity and wholeness. When brought together effectively, line and composition lead the eye around the design of the display, through the patterns created by the mannequins and the merchandise, around props and platforms, until the sales "spiel" is given and the scenic route is completed. In this way, the attention of the shopper is brought to the entire display as well as to each of its parts.

Scale

A change of proportion, an abnormal size relationship, is an attention-getter. Something overly large makes an average-size object appear tiny, while something tiny (e.g., miniatures or models) makes something average in size (e.g., a mannequin) appear to swell and soar to superhuman size. These are examples of playing with **scale and proportion.**

Our eye accepts objects in relation to other objects. We know approximately how tall a door is because we know about where an average human being would stand in relation to that door. As the relationship between a known object and a known figure (e.g., a mannequin) changes, and slight differences are replaced with glaring differences, the look or size of the object to the figure, and vice versa, appears to change as well. Next to a door scaled up 12 feet, a 6-foot mannequin seems to shrink to about 4 feet. The human figure is dwarfed by comparison.

Place a full-size mannequin in a setting of child-scaled furniture, and the figure grows in stature and in appearance. The change from the traditional or usual proportion is the attention-getting technique. It is an are the types of jolts that cause the eye to react and relay a message to the mind which says "something different is going on here, something special."

A beach or resort wear display, glowing with sunshine, blue skies, and palm trees is particularly effective when the street outside is mired in slush and dismal winter gloom. That is an example of contrast too.

Repetition

Repetition of an idea over and over again will make an impact—and the message will sink in. In a fashionable, but not haute couture operation, the same dress worn by three mannequins, each in the same pose but with different makeup and hairstyles, can be an attention-getter. Three different garments made of the same pattern or print, on mannequins in the same pose, will also score. A lineup of props of the same size and color, strung across a display and ending up with a single piece of merchandise, will be effective too.

Three windows in a bank, or group, reiterating the same color or promotional theme have more impact than a single, isolated window. They are also much more emphatic than three windows, each different, with different merchandise, each in competition for the shopper's attention. Seven coats (odd numbers seem to work better than even numbers) hung on hangers, all at the same height, will dramatize a coat story, especially if the different coats are all in the same color family, or are presented in a dramatic, light-to-dark grouping of color.

If something is worth repeating, repeat it several times over. It could be just the attention-getting device for which the display person is looking.

Figure 16.5 The pile of accordion-pleated paper hearts clustered on the floor, complemented by the smaller ones on the white wall, is all it takes to make a Valentine's Day display. The red light that washes over the display contrasts with the clear white light that accentuates the yellow garments on the stylized mannequins. *Burberry, East 57th Street, New York.*

"irritant"; the viewer knows the mannequin is not shrinking and that the door is overscaled, but the unexpected sight of a normal figure "growing" or "shrinking" will draw attention.

Contrast

Contrast accomplishes with light and color what a change of scale or proportion accomplishes with line and form. A white gown against a black background, or a white spotlight on an otherwise dark display—these

Humor

A smiling shopper can be converted into a customer much sooner, and with much less effort, than a frowning or grumpy shopper. If a "show me" attitude can be replaced with a "that's funny" or "isn't that cute" outlook, a sale may not be far off. People will laugh at themselves and human foibles. Show the human and humorous side of life in display; show the "happily-ever-after" type of display. Freeze a moment out of the "soap opera"—an

Figure 16.6 Being outrageous and somewhat off-the-wall works for the Barneys image, and its smart and sophisticated clients seem to enjoy the humor often generated in the windows. This retro setting plays up fashions that were old—but new again. The display recalls the "good old days" in a gentle, good-natured, and good-humored way. *Barneys, Madison Avenue, New York.*

embarrassing situation or an awkward scene. Most people love to laugh at the harmless discomfort of others.

Examples of uses of **humor** include a man in full evening dress, but also wearing sneakers or a T-shirt. Imagine a dignified woman in fur coat, hat, gloves, and "sensible" pumps astride a motorcycle; or soft-sculptured figures dressed like humans sitting at a realistic breakfast table while discussing a white sale, with cartoon-style bubbles over their heads containing the script. Another people-pleaser is children playing at being grown up in grown-up clothes. All that the successful, humorous display need elicit is a smile and a relaxation of the tense feelings of some shoppers.

Mirrors

Mirrors are marvelous. They can add depth, width, and height to a display. They can reveal new angles and attitudes, show hidden backs and sides, and turn a setting into a full-round presentation. They reflect light and sparkle. They add flashes and unexpected splinters of light as a spotlight hits the surface of the mirror and sends out a spectrum of rainbow-colored sparks.

Mirrors, however, can also show the unfinished backs of objects and props, and the pinning and pulling together of nonfitting garments. They allow the shopper to see the backside of the window, the undressed, unglamourous side: the lights, cords, construction, and collected bits and pieces that perhaps never got swept out. Mirrors may also expose overhead and side lights, causing them to shoot back eye-stinging reflections into the viewer's eyes.

Mirrors can be the undoing of the presentation in other ways as well. People may become fascinated looking at their own reflections, completely overlooking the merchandise being presented. A good display person will angle a mirror to show only that which is supposed to be

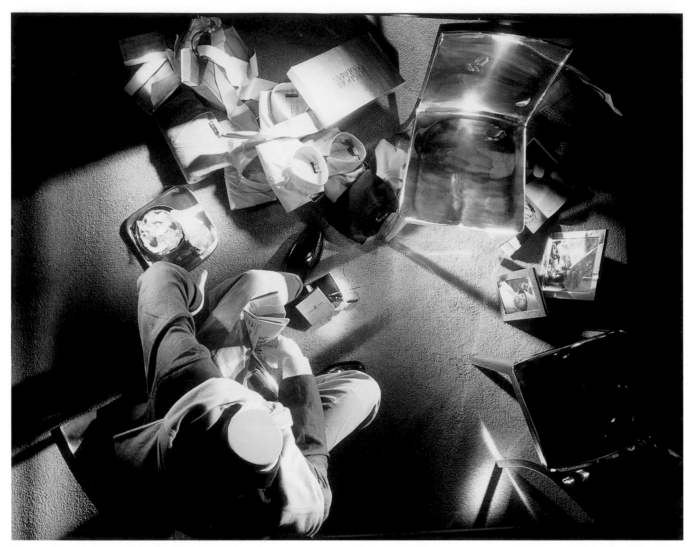

Figure 16.7 Expect the unexpected to create interest and draw the shopper over to the window. In this "gravity defying" feat the back wall becomes the floor of the window and all the props and the mannequins are set perpendicular to it for a shocking, out-of-space experience that has the viewer wondering, "How did they do that?" A great effect but it takes talent—and lots of time and effort to accomplish it successfully. *Bergdorf Goodman, Fifth Avenue, New York.*

seen. Mirrors should highlight, explain, repeat, or show a new slant on a fashion look.

Nostalgia

Nostalgia sells! Many people dream of the "good old days," which probably were not all that good and are not really so long gone. They find a backward glance to the fashions of the 1940s, 1950s, and 1960s as special as looking back to those of the 1880s and 1890s. We prefer to think that those were the golden days, days of charm and romance, when everything was "lovely."

The very old can be used to sell the very new. Antiques and antique reproductions can add class and character to garments that still have to make their mark. By association with a classic, a new classic is born.

People also love to see elements of "before and after." Show an old-time chemise, bustle, or crinoline in relation to today's teddy or other scanty undergarments. A line drawing or a photo blowup of a turn-of-the-century lady in the proper tennis attire of her day—all starched and buttoned up, from her high-standing collar to her highbuttoned boots, would make an interesting counterpoise for a long and lissome modern mannequin in an abbreviated tennis outfit. An old, wood-burning, an animated Christmas display. An institutional spectacular does not become spectacular until some inanimate doll turns and bows, or a stuffed teddy bear toots a horn, or an angel sings as part of a heavenly choir.

Motion can be created by a whole line of electric fans across a window, whirring and stirring up a small hurricane to emphasize the cool, cool wonder of the clothes on the mannequin lined up behind the rotating fans. A single, old-fashioned ceiling fan, right out of the film *Casablanca*, lazily spinning above a tropical setting, can move a palm tree or two below. (This display would be a combination of movement and nostalgia.) A fan, way off to the side and out of the shopper's view, can send a

Figure 16.8 Humor always works! It doesn't have to be a "knee slapper" or a "belly laugh"; a smile will do. Dogs are sure attractions and with the cartoon drawing behind it, along with the perfectly dressed mannequin—it is sure to get a pleasing reaction. *Lord & Taylor, Fifth Avenue, New York.*

kitchen stove as a back-up for a microwave oven could show how far technology has come.

Nostalgic props and scenes of the "good old days" can be used to lend their charm and acceptability to unknown and untested merchandise.

Motion

Motion or movement within a display area will get attention. A passerby is made suddenly aware, out of the corner of his or her eye, that something moved in an otherwise static setup. People of all ages will line up just to walk by and savor, for a few minutes, the delights of

Figure 16.9 Mirrors can be great gimmicks but they are also tricky. Sometimes the reflections become more important than the object being reflected, or the shopper gets more involved with how she looks than in the merchandise on display. Here the various mirror panels are set at different angles to create a dazzling but dizzying, funhouse look for urban fashions. The controlled color palette of red, white, and black helps to keep things from getting completely out of hand. *Marshall Field, State Street, Chicago.*

Figure 16.10 Nostalgia and a return to the past to play up the present. The old-fashioned camera on the tripod stand with black cloth is really antique but also says "photography"—black and white photography especially. This display also served to salute the work of the legendary photographer Edward Steichen and a museum showing of his work. It thus became a promotional display for the garments on view and an institutional display with its public service message. *Bergdorf Goodman, Fifth Avenue, New York.*

soft wind wafting through a window display just enough to play gently with the grace and lightness of a chiffon gown, or to set a scarf in motion.

Just as it can be attractive, motion can also be disturbing—irritating and distracting. Blinking light and strobes have the impact of motion, but can be unpleasant and may do nothing positive for the presentation of the merchandise. The motion is intended to draw and attract the curious over to the window for a better view of the merchandise. It is generally not intended to be the whole show, except in those animated displays where no merchandise is being shown (e.g., Christmas institutional displays).

A turntable will make a garment visible full round. It can show a variety of items as they come into view, each in its own space and each getting its moment in the spotlight. A turntable is relatively inexpensive to buy, easy to use, and versatile enough to use over and over again, in and out of the windows. Inside the store, it can add excitement to a gift display or individual place settings complete with linens, china, and crystal on a feature table, for example. A mannequin on a turntable which, in turn, has been set on a platform, will move around and show off some back interest. Shoppers will be interested enough in the turning movement to stop and watch the full 360-degree showing.

Although it requires careful supervision by the display person, a display filled with battery-operated, stuffed animals can be fun. They can be made to carry on and carouse all over the display area. However, the batteries will eventually run down, abruptly causing an end to the movement in this motion-filled display.

What gets more "oohs" and "ahs" than that "little doggie in the window?" A word of warning, however: *please* use care and discretion with live animals in a display. Windows heat up from the lights and the sun, air usually does not circulate adequately, and it can be disconcerting for the animals to have people constantly tapping on the glass for attention. There are also sanitation and odor problems that must be controlled. In many cases, it would be wiser and kinder to use cute, furry reproductions of live animals.

Some stores, usually those with open-back windows, have found that a live mannequin, walking into, around, and out of the display window—like a miniature fashion show—will draw crowds to the window. Any live action in a window—a mime, a juggler, a disc jockey, a demonstrator, or even the display person setting up a window—is a great attention-getter. All the store is a stage and everything that moves—or looks as though it might move—becomes a player, attracting the attention of an audience of shoppers.

Surprise and Shock

Much of what has been described in the various techniques outlined above will succeed in attracting attention because the elements of surprise or shock are in-

A **surprise** can be fun. It can be a pleasant or amusing, unexpected moment frozen in time. A surprising display can be one with chairs on the ceiling or a 7-foot "take-out" food container from a Chinese restaurant (a combination of surprise and scale), or an elegantly dressed mannequin "wearing" a cream pie on its face, with more pie splattered against the window and on the floor below.

A surprise can also be surrealistic or a bit of fantasy—the juxtaposing of people or objects out of a proper place or time sequence. For example, grown-ups acting like children, or "flying" off the ground like Mary Poppins or Peter Pan, will also get a second look from a passerby. The sign or copy card would clarify the "mix-up."

Figure 16.11 Surprise, shock, and stretched beyond belief! Taking advantage of its extra tall windows, the mannequin with stilt-like legs disappears through the ceiling of the window while the long trouser legs are still firmly planted on the floor of the window. The viewer's eye goes up, up, up and gets to take in the Pucci designs along the way. *Bergdorf Goodman, Fifth Avenue, New York.*

volved. A smashed window with a brick flying through it will stop a viewer in his or her tracks. The controlled mayhem of an overturned table, broken crockery, and a mannequin standing on top of a chair to escape from a mouse that looks like it just escaped from a Disney cartoon—will be answered by a viewer with a smile or a grin. Windows, floors, and props splashed with paints of all colors can be shocking and confusing, but a "come-on" all the same. However, there is always the safety of the glass between the viewer and the display to separate the shopper from the shocking or surprising goings-on under all those lights.

Figure 16.12 Familiar masterpieces of art replicated but not reproduced! Most people will recognize the neutral colored painting of Whistler's Mother, but in this adaptation, mother is off her rocking chair and has given up knitting in favor of getting out in a smart and stylish outfit. This display calls for a second look—and is sure to get a knowing smile. *Saks Fifth Avenue, New York.*

Shock goes beyond surprise. It must be used sparingly and carefully. It is a shakeup that can work against the store and its merchandise even though it does attract attention. If not handled properly, a display aimed to shock can be upsetting, distasteful, or just plain bad taste. Showing a mugger in the process of stealing a handbag, for example, will gain attention, and then generate unfavorable comments from long-standing, but now, irritated customers. Several years ago, a store on Fifth Avenue in New York, showed a murder scene in a window presentation, calling it *street art.* Fortunately, it was reserved for a side window. However the "murderous" setting still caused quite a controversy.

Surprises can be delightful and ingratiating, capable of charming and amusing their audiences. They can become topics of conversation: "Did you see what they did in X's window?" They can and will be remembered, and if the display is done well, the merchandise will be remembered too.

Props

There is a whole industry that does nothing but produce **props,** devices, and gimmicks to enhance merchandise presentations. There are manufacturers who specialize in mannequins and forms; some produce fixtures and displayer units, others create painted or photographically reproduced backgrounds; and still others collect tinsel, glitter, ornaments, and other assorted material from all over the world and supply them to the display person. There are some who are specialists in foliage, while still another group supplies the raw materials, the decorative papers, and fabrics that become whatever the display person's imagination, time, and ability will allow him or her to create.

There is, however, another world out there—one for the display person with little or no budget, but with imagination, drive, time, and the desire to be "different." Basically, it is a world of "beg, borrow, and make do." Even large retail operations must come over to this side of display when budgets shrink, which happens more and more often in times of inflation. Times like these test the display person's ability to improvise, be clever, creative, and see "splendor in the trash."

No store is an island unto itself. It is part of a street, a mall, a neighborhood, a community. Just as neighbors go next door and ask to borrow a cup of sugar or an egg, so the display person of a dress shop, for example, can step over and ask a noncompeting hardware store to borrow a stepladder, some unopened cans of paint, paint rollers, and dropcloths. The display person can then combine the ladder, paints, rollers, and dropcloths with mannequins dressed in bright yellow sportswear to promote a "fresh yellow paint" story. A card in the window could give credit and thanks to the neighborly hardware store for its contribution. After the display is "struck," the unopened cans of paint and the clean dropcloths would be returned to the hardware store.

Figure 16.13 What is more current or in the news than what is in the newspaper? In this display the word is out as is the latest thing to wear. The background consists of blowups of want ads while piles of actual newspapers reiterate the theme and act as elevations for accessories. The black and white of the newspapers also plays up the black and white garment accented with a red bag. *Macy's, Herald Square, New York.*

A Philadelphia store created a brilliant rainwear window by filling the floor space with clean, galvanized pails—the metal buckets traditionally used to catch leaks from the rain. The buckets were from a hardware supply house. And what could be simpler and more effective for certain promotions than artist's easels, paints, and brushes, plus empty frames to accent and delineate merchandise or accessories? These useful props are only as far as the nearest art supply store. All one has to do is ask politely. Someday, the display person may repay the "debt" to the art store with the loan of a be-smocked mannequin playing the artist, or without clothing—playing the model.

Cartons and crates can say anything from "import" to "new arrivals," "open stock," or "ready for delivery." Brooms and shovels convey the concept of "clearance," "swept away with . . . ," "getting ready for . . .". Brooms might even be used to supply a slightly giddy ride for mannequins on Halloween.

Ladders of all kinds and sizes are a great way to elevate a mannequin or even an assortment of small merchandise, like shoes "stepping up" in the fashion world or cosmetics "making the grade." Scarves, belts, and floral accents can cascade down the step. Planks, set horizontally between ladders, can become shelving units for sales promotions. Wire hangers, by the hundreds, can be woven into a fantasy that is still familiar—an abstract pattern created out of a fashion symbol. Show boxes can be risers, platforms, or spiraling stairways. They can also become building blocks or a big-city skyline in miniature.

Other sources for props include furniture stores, which can be a great source for such props as beach chairs, bentwood chairs, ice-cream parlor and opera chairs, folding chairs, director's chairs, and all kinds and sizes of tables. "Raid" toy stores for stuffed animals, model railroad trains, planes, racing cars, building blocks, and pull wagons. There are also go-carts; supermarket shopping carts; golf carts, golf bags, clubs, balls, and tees; tennis rackets and tennis nets; bows, arrows, and targets—or anything from friendly and "giving" sporting goods, hunting, and camping goods stores.

Visit your local garden supply center for flower pots, rakes, hoes, lawn mowers, seed spreaders, packets of seeds, picket fences, plants and bushes in burlap bags,

Figure 16.14 Artwork, sketches, caricatures, and line drawings can create window or in-store settings with flair and a sense of style or humor. These elegant ladies with highly stylized heads are perfectly at ease in this street corner setting. The watercolor-like drawing of the newsstand, behind, features real papers on a wire frame stand as well as sketches of top fashion magazines. Note how cleverly the drawing of the sidewalk on the window's floor pads meshes with the sidewalk on the drawn background panel. *Lord & Taylor, Fifth Avenue, New York.*

picnic tables and benches, beach and sun umbrellas, garden and patio furniture, barbecue grills and hibachis, firewood and logs. There are also clotheslines, clothespins, and clothes dryers. For travel and vacation promotions, use posters and giveaways from airlines, tourists offices, and foreign trade bureaus. See the importers in town who are looking for a place to show their wares. Luggage shops are a treasure trove of all those things that

Figure 16.15 Props can be found in the most unexpected places. What makes them so special is what the designer does with them. The object is to turn the ordinary into the extraordinary. This is often accomplished by juxtaposing everyday objects with special designs, as in this outdoors display featuring designer-dressed mannequins involved with everyday barbeque equipment. *Barneys, Madison Avenue, New York.*

say "travel," "vacation," and suggest movement and direction. There are potential treasures in antique shops, secondhand shops, and clock stores. From building-supply houses, "beg" bricks, cement blocks, terra-cotta blocks, gravel, rain drains, copper and brass pipes, joints, elbows, even the bathroom sink. Try tinsmiths, welders, ironmongers, and scrap-metal dealers.

Even galleries, art shops, and handicraft stores might welcome some extra exposure. Explore art schools for young artists looking for a showcase; a store window might be just such a vehicle. Imagine the magic of a window filled with a display of military band instruments, gleaming and golden, and all courtesy of the local music store; collections of music boxes, and music stands to hold sheets of music, copy cards, or fashion accessories; a metronome to suggest a timely move in fashion; and score sheets to play up a black-and-white sonata for spring.

Appliance centers have television sets and radios that will add color, light, movement, and interest. Fans, freezers, toasters, and coffee brewers can promote anything from cool summer clothes to beige or brown fashion colors. Extension cords, worklights, droplights, emergency lights—all spell "highlights."

There can be a display in a barber's chair, a dentist's chair, or a child's high chair. Piles of old newspapers can be as timely as the headline on the top sheet. A real refrigerator or ice maker can set a coiling pattern in a merchandise presentation. A water cooler, a desk, and some metal office files are all it takes to make an office setting —and they can all come from the office supply house.

An architect's table, some high stools, a drafting lamp, and a taboret have the makings of a career scene for men and women. Store shopping bags and boxes make marvelous sales and clearance displays.

A housewares department has the ingredients for dozens of merchandise presentations: pins, brooches, or earrings in plastic egg containers; cooling balms and toiletries in vegetable crispers; hot-colored accessories in steamers. Why not a "sizzling hot" item in a frying pan? How about using colanders filled with spaghetti to show Italian imported shoes and bags? The possibilities are limitless! A few loaves of bread may last a week or more and add color and interest; slice one apart and make a "heroic" presentation with all the trimmings. A spray coat of lacquer may keep the bread looking fresh a little longer and retard any mold. Some fresh fruits and vege-

tables will have a window life of a week or two, but a few pounds of produce can go a long way in creating an effective, interesting display.

Do not pass up garage sales, "white elephant" sales, auctions, or house razings. Potentially, there are dozens of window displays and display props in all those objects that others want to dispose of. All you have to do is have the imagination and creativity to see the glitter amidst the ruins. Do not look at things for what they are, but for what they can be. Buy classics. Buy things that can be used again and again and that always look different and can do different things. Buy objects that can be repainted, retrimmed, and/or rearranged.

When a house is being torn down, go prospecting. There are doors, mantles, railings, architectural details, and even old bricks. A window frame, for example, has

Figure 16.16 The closest outdoor sporting goods store provided the props for this seaside display. The fully inflated yellow rafts serve to close off some of the open-back window while setting the scene. The red life vests are more than fashion accessories: they tie the assorted headless mannequins into a single composition while the oars, ropes, and such tie the various levels of display together. *H-Bendel, Fifth Avenue, New York.*

many uses. It could be used as a surrealistic, architectural frame, or realistically curtained and draped to create a vignette setting; a painted landscape can be inserted behind the open frame; or it can be used with drawn blinds, with perhaps a slat or two askew, to provoke the interest of some passerby. The outlined window could also become a framework for a geometric presentation of merchandise and accessories with some colored pinup panels placed behind it. It can also be used in an open-back window to frame the mannequin or the presentation in the selling area. As an additional touch, a few flower pots sitting on the ledge could be added for seasonal accent.

Imagine what could be done with a segment of a row of seats from an old, torn down movie house. Think of all the vignette settings in which those seats could be featured. Old, but not necessarily antique, curio cabinets and closets, strange and odd pieces of furniture with doors, drawers, and/or shelves—can be revived and rejuvenated quickly with a coat of paint. Investigate what is available from local theaters, theater groups, and movie houses. There can be display potential in the king-size poster for a current movie or play, ballet, concert, or opera that is passing through your city. It can add a touch of culture and more than a smattering of what is current and special in town. There are local, municipal, and state institutions like museums, libraries, and historic preservation societies that can supply material on loan. Search out the local sources—and ask. How about traffic and road signs, bus and train signs, directionals and such?

You never know what can be had for the asking until you ask! Remember, the possibilities are endless. The only real limitation is a lack of initiative, creativity, and imagination.

Attention-Getting Devices: A Recap

- The basic concept of a display is to show, and to see what is shown.

- Some important eye-catching devices include, color, lighting, line and composition, scale, contrast, repetition, humor, mirrors, nostalgia, motion, surprise and shock, and props.

- Color is what the eye sees first.

- Effective lighting can catch the eye and lead it to the product.

- Different types of lines, such as vertical, horizontal, and diagonal, can arrest attention.

- Composition is the arrangement of visual elements to achieve unity.

- Scale, as in an abnormal size relationship or a change in proportion, is an attention-getter.

- Contrast uses light and color to attract the eye.

- Repeating an idea over and over makes an impact.

- Although the use of mirrors can add depth to or show new angles in a display, they must be used carefully, so as not to show anything at a disadvantage. Poor placement of mirrors can show pinned-in clothing, unfinished backs, light cords, debris, and so on.

- Nostalgic props are a pleasant reminder of the "good old days" to the viewer.

- Motion, something moving in an otherwise static setup, will always catch the eye, but too much motion can distract the viewer from the merchandise.

- The element of surprise in a display can be fun or surreal. Shock goes beyond surprise and must be used carefully, so as not to upset or irritate the viewer.

- Props for display is an entire industry unto itself. Props can be bought, rented, borrowed, or improvised from whatever is on hand.

- Many props can be found in local stores, such as appliance centers, hardware and paint stores, antique shops, travel offices, toy stores, and others.

Questions for Review and Discussion

1. Explain the importance of attention-getting devices in the creation of visual presentations.

2. Describe a display that effectively combines any three of the attention-getting devices discussed in this chapter. Include in your descriptions the display location within the store, the merchandise, and the props that you would select.

3. How can a nostalgic feeling be introduced into a visual presentation? For what types of displays would nostalgia be most appropriate?

4. Where can a visual merchandiser acquire display props that are both interesting and cost-effective?

5. List three household items that could be creatively used as props in a jewelry display. Explain how you would utilize these items to support your display theme.

CHAPTER SEVENTEEN

Familiar Symbols

AFTER YOU HAVE READ THIS CHAPTER
YOU WILL BE ABLE TO DISCUSS:

- The major seasons, holidays, clothing lines, and store events for which visual merchandisers must prepare.
- Appropriate settings, props, and display themes for major seasons, holidays, and store events.

FAMILIAR SYMBOLS: TRADE TALK

anniversaries	fall
back-to-school	Father's Day
bridal	formals
career fashions	lingerie
Christmas	Mother's Day
clearance sales	patriotic
clichés	spring
cruise and resort	Valentine's Day
Easter	

Because they are used over and over again, certain familiar symbols used in display presentations are so commonplace that they have become clichés. **Clichés** are the symbols and images that telegraph the message, sometimes more readily than the copy. One has to read to understand copy, but these symbols are like old, familiar friends; they announce and explain themselves. We have previously mentioned how certain colors or color combinations are recognizable as representing holidays or events; for example, red and green for Christmas; red and pink for Valentine's Day; red, white, and blue for presidential sales or the Fourth of July, and so on.

The following are everyday—and not so everyday—things that can be used to set a display scene, to trim a case, to accompany a mannequin on a ledge or platform, to accent a column or fascia trim, to illustrate a copy line, or to illuminate an event or promotion. They are simply ideas and "word pictures" that hopefully will stimulate the display person's imagination.

Anniversaries

Anniversaries can be symbolized by anything old or antique, from bicycles to ice-cream makers, from brass headboards to foot warmers and kerosene lanterns. Birthday cakes and wedding cakes, multitiered and many candled, say "anniversary," as do wedding bells and old-fashioned belles and costumes, fashion drawings, and etchings. Songs and song sheets from the past and the musical instruments of bygone days, the old gramophone and the player piano, can set the theme with musical overtones. Old kitchen appliances, coal stoves, iceboxes, ice tongs, mangles, hot irons, coal scuttles, and such are also reminders of bygone days. The toys and games of the past can be dusted off and revived for another go-around as can the tintypes and daguerreotypes of an anonymous ancestor.

Antiques or reproductions of period furniture from another century can create truly period settings. What-ever one might hope to find in some long, undisturbed attic can be used, with or without the cobwebs: ornate picture frames, trunks, carpetbags, strapped satchels, discarded clothes, hats, and hat racks. Blow up some line illustrations from old newspapers or fashion catalogs, or original store brochures or broadsides from years long gone. These are attention-getters and scene-setters. Check through the lettering books and the catalogs of the

Figure 17.1 Special events, holidays, and sales—they all call for special displays to entice and excite the shopper. They make the shopper aware of some special day on the calendar and alert them to the fact that the day is approaching. Fortunoff celebrates its own anniversary with a sale but suggests gifts that would be right for other people who celebrate anniversaries in June. *Fortunoff, Fifth Avenue, New York.*

pressure-sensitive type suppliers for those typefaces that suggest "The Gay Nineties"—gaslights, tassels and fringes, red velvet swags and drapes. Suggest the wasp-waisted or shirtwaisted beauties of that period—the bustled, bosomy, bowed, and buttoned-up belles of 100 years ago. People looking in may not actually remember "the good old days," but they will definitely recognize them.

Back-to-School and College

It happens every fall, starting with alphabet blocks and advancing to busts of Caesar and Shakespeare. Symbols of **back-to-school** also include owls, foxes, and squirrels storing up knowledge, and blackboards, chalkboards, and mortarboards for the graduates. It is the little red school house complete with a smiling sun and an un-furled flag, the school bus, the dunce cap and the stool in the corner, an apple for the teacher, teacher's pet, and teachers of all sizes and shapes. Don't forget pencils, pens, rulers, and erasers, nursery rhymes and easy-to-read readers, the old school bell, books, pads of paper, note-books, desks and chairs, and the inkwells that are now no longer used—these are all still symbols of school.

And then the student grows up: halls of ivy and walls of red brick. This can be the time to show spiral pads, date books, telephones, and intramural sports. And speaking of sports, don't forget banners, pennants,

Figure 17.2 Back to school doesn't usually make kids happy, but this cheerful, fun-filled display can almost convince them that getting new clothes can be okay. The upside down, pinned-up outfits add to the light-hearted, colorful approach to this promotion. *Woodward & Lothrop, Washington, DC.*

cheerleaders, and megaphones. Try pompoms, confetti streamers, the football hero, or "the most likely to succeed." For setting the scene, there is the ice-cream parlor, the junior hop, and the senior prom. In the classrooms are the classics: dictionaries open to the right word for fall fashion, books, bookcases, and the calendar to mark off the time.

Bridal

Bridal symbols include: "Here Comes the Bride" and "The Wedding March," the bridal aisle, the strains of an organ, love songs, golden rings, and hearts entwined. White roses and lilies of the valley become nosegays or bridal bouquets flowing with ribbons and streamers. A petal-strewn carpet leads the way and is outlined with woven baskets billowing over with floral and foliage cascades, heroic-sized candles in gleaming golden candlesticks, lattice work, gazebos, or even a rose-covered bower. Floating wisps of net and tulle fill the air as do white doves and white paper cherubs. Louis XV and Louis XVI tables and chairs set the scene while a rococo standing mirror is used to frame and reflect the bride's gown.

If a groom is not in evidence, suggest him at least with a supply of top hats and canes. Try a blow-up of a wedding invitation; or the garden party setting for the reception that follows: green grass, blue skies, and a pink-and-white awning or marquee. A stained glass window, an arch, a column—these are some of the minimal appurtenances necessary to suggest church architecture. The display can be set in a forest fantasy of entwining branches that form a leafy arcade. It can be a true-to-life setting with the mother-of-the-bride fussing with the veil, or Dad beaming. Perhaps a forties vignette of the bridal procession with flower girls, train bearers, and dainty gold chairs lined up to review the romantic affair. A bridal window should always imply, "and they lived happily ever after."

Career Fashions

This is the world of "9-to-5," of getting to work, coffee breaks, of lunchtime, personal and business calls, and dinner dates. It is filled with desks, chairs, files, and computers, and a cluster around a water cooler or a coffee

Figure 17.3 Bridal promotions are usually scheduled in the winter for the spring and June brides and in early fall for winter brides. This one-of-a-kind display has the bride stepping over top hats to get to the altar. The simple but effective hat trick adds a touch of humor—and elegance. *H-Bendel, West 57th Street, New York.*

brewer. **Career fashions** can appear at an architect's table, a doctor's office, or the conference table for the chairperson of the board. Computers can take over the window and spew out yards and yards of impressive looking data. Graphs and charts look very professional, as do doors with impressive titles lettered on them.

A law-office setting can be depicted by stacks of thick volumes and a stepladder to reach the top. A designer can be recognized by an easel, palette, drawing boards, swatches and swatchbooks covering the floor, and drawings pinned up on the walls. A giant phone or super-scaled Rolodex file means business. Portfolios, envelopes, briefcases, and attaché cases also mean business. The world of big business is made up of newspapers and headlines, calculators, cellular phones, appointment books and calendars, clocks and watches, timepieces of all types to tick off the business hours and the appointed times. Careers that can be depicted include: commerce, law, medicine, engineering, designing, computer programming, politics, and theater—and all are unisex.

Christmas

The **Christmas** list is endless. It starts with Santa Claus, a sleigh, elves and deer, and then continues with trees, garlands, swags and drops of evergreens sprinkled with snow and "diamond dust" or glittering with ornaments, paper chains, or strings of cranberries and popcorn. It is a "sweet" time: peppermint canes, bonbons, and candies gay with stripes and swirls. It is cakes and cookies, gingerbread boys and girls and little houses, all iced and sugarcoated. This holiday can shimmer with snow and snowflakes, ice and icicles, stars and comets, the fireplace and the hearth, families and friends, and gifts and gift boxes, opened or ribbon-tied.

Christmas is the poem, "A Visit from St. Nicholas" by Clement Moore, a hundred children's fairy tales, and the sweetest dreams come true. Christmas can be "sung"

Figure 17.4 Christmas is all glitter and glow—all red and more red. Here the festivities begin with a mirrored disco ball serving as a giant Christmas ornament, with more of the glittery balls scattered on the red mirrored floor. Black and red holiday dresses are shown in the red setting. *Escada, East 57th Street, New York.*

with songs such as carols by characters out of Dickens' England, "Silent Night" or "Rudolph the Red-Nosed Reindeer." Musical instruments, music boxes, dancing ballerinas, and toy soldiers all suggest Christmas. It is a time for stuffed animals falling out of overstuffed stockings, model trains and planes, old-fashioned baby dolls, and chrome-plated computerized robots. Set the scene with chimneys or roof tops on which red-suited strangers can prance about.

For the religious emphasis of this holiday, try stained glass windows or a crèche, organ pipes, oversized candles, and a choir of angels or angelic choirboys holding sheets of music dotted with familiar songs. Santa is Pere Noel and Father Christmas. It is also time for piñata parties, Mrs. Claus, signs directing the viewer to the North Pole, letters to Santa, and endless lists of gifts. It is a party time as well as a time for "peace on earth" and "goodwill to all."

Clearance Sales

The posters say, "And away it goes" or "Gone with the wind," but not necessarily with antebellum houses and magnolia trees. The cleanup of a **clearance sale** can be represented by brooms, mops, pails, shovels, big plastic bags, oversized crates and cartons, wrapping paper, and twine. It also could be shopping bags and store boxes "walking," "riding," or "flying" out of the display area loaded with the sale goodies. A window filled with assorted mannequins and forms, stripped down to fig leafs or palmetto fans, for modesty's sake—or dressed in big brown paper bags because everything is gone—can be fun.

A few pipe-rack fixtures festooned with a few forlorn and naked hangers—some already lying on the floor—says "Going, going, gone!" Giant scissors cry out that "prices have been cut—or slashed" as does a setting of shelves or bins, denuded of merchandise with boxes scattered helter-skelter. The big iron ball used to smash down buildings could be "breaking" into the plate-glass window—with "cracks" beginning to appear, and announcing, "We're making way for the new season." Clearance sales demand dynamics—action and movement—diagonals and direction. It's the only way to go.

Figure 17.5 A clearance sale can be smart and stylish, especially if the merchandise is upscale to start with. Red sails announce the sale in this display and the red, white, and blue color scheme carries over to the outfits on the stylized mannequins. *Burberry, East 57th Street, New York.*

Cruisewear, Resortwear, Sunwear, and Swimwear

Summer is a time for the great outdoors: blue skies, picture-postcard scenery, green grass, and blue water. Over all sits a big, bright, yellow ball of sunshine to spread its warmth over everything. Cover floors with green grass mats or sandy stretches (the dunes can be painted on the background), and add some sea grass, seaweed, and seascapes. Palm trees and palmetto leaves, rain capes, thatch, tatami mats, and tapa cloths are the textures of summer, **cruise and resort** wear. It is the South of France

Figure 17.6 White paper cut, scored, and folded becomes the palm leaves and tropical foliage in this cruise/resort setting. The foliage frames the window and the stylized figures in their assorted beach outfits. The all-white proscenium serves to accentuate the garments on view. *H-Bendel, Fifth Avenue, New York.*

and the South Seas. Get playful with beach umbrellas, beach blankets, beach balls, and beach chairs; yacht chairs and canvas sling chairs; outdoor furniture; fishnets and tennis nets. Try travel posters, steamer trunks, steamboats, sailboats, model boats, and boating supplies; or anchors, oars, lifesavers, rubber rafts and rubber ducks, gangplanks and boardwalk planks.

Summertime is sports time and spectator time—baseball innings and outings, golf and golf carts, bleachers and poolside sitting, tennis matches, lemonade and ice-cube coolers, picnic benches, barbecues, and grills. Daisies and cucumbers are considered to be "coolers," as are electric fans, ceiling fans and hand-held fans, air conditioners and body conditioners. It is all part of outdoor living.

Easter

What would **Easter** be without soft, cuddly, pastel plush bunnies (the more the merrier), decorated eggs in a rainbow of colors, or stately, elegant, and pristine white lilies on slender stalks? What would this holiday season be without daffodils, tulips, and gift wrappings in yellow, pink, and lavender? What about Irving Berlin's "Easter Parade" and the "Easter bonnet with all the frills upon it"?

Easter is also fluffy yellow chicks, ducklings, and other baby denizens of the farm and forest. It is the time of rebirth and renewal.

There is also the spiritual side of Easter: sunrise services, pipe organs, stained glass windows, architectural vignettes of a church or cathedral, choirboys, and the

Figure 17.7 The addition of simple bunny face masks over traditional child mannequins turns this into a fun Easter display for children's wear. The naive cut-out, foam core cloud overhead, and the blades of grass up front create a child's view of a garden. *Godchaux, New Orleans.*

essence of the Renaissance. Easter may have its origins in pagan lore, but today it is a Christian holiday that sometimes shares the calendar with the Jewish Passover holiday. It is a time for dressing up and getting out, a time for families to gather and dine together.

Often Easter gets absorbed into the general spring trim, but it could rate an institutional window—in memory of what the holiday is all about. The window can be "religious" without using religious symbols. Show the beauty of nature and the natural growth of plants and flowers, which is spiritual, yet nondenominational.

Fall

Fall is the "ripest" season of the year, the time for harvesting fruits and vegetables of rich, warm, and earthy colors; vines and vineyards, grapes and wines. Fall leaves are painted all red, gold, and glowing. The season is a bouquet of asters, mums, marigolds, and other flowers of rich ambers and rusts.

People expect to see pumpkins, gourds, jack-o'-lanterns, scarecrows, squirrels, and owls. It is the time for rakes and hoes, bushels and baskets, and all sorts of earthy materials and textures. Fall is a medley of music: "September Song," "Autumn Leaves," and "Autumn Serenade"—and everybody is "Falling in Love." It also hap-

pens to be the time for going back to school and when career fashions make their statements.

Father's Day

Make it a celebration for George, "Father of His Country," or to that "Great Guy," dad, pop, poppa, pater, or father. Dad is everything: male, macho, sentimental, amusing. The sentiment should not be contrived, but touched with humor. Familiar symbols associated with **Father's Day** are: chess pieces; oversized playing cards (with dad as the king); trophies, medals, awards, citations, and certificates for years of service and years of

Figure 17.8 Fall leaves would be all it takes to say "autumn has arrived," but the addition of lawn rakes adds interest to the composition. The leaves are contained in a chicken wire cylinder though some of the leaves have dropped down into a tidy little pile on the floor. The details make it different. *Saks Fifth Avenue, New York.*

giving. Dad is shown as "champ," as a winner, a leader, "tops." Dad can be portrayed on a facsimile cover of *Life* or *Time*. He can be the super-sportsman, the breadwinner, the careerist, and also a cartoonist's delight.

Father's Day can be remembered by marking the day on a calendar or in an appointment book. Show Dad right out of an old photo album. Dad can bring back memories of the "good old days," bicycles built for two, Model T's, and barbershop quartets, even though Dad's father probably was not even a father back then!

Formals

Dressing up can be classy and classic or fun and funky. It can be an elegant, smart, and sophisticated dinner party, complete with crystal, silver, lace tablecloth, prismed chandeliers, candlelight, centerpieces of rosebuds and baby's breath, and potted palms in the background. It can be a realistic setting with fine boiserie panels or flocked damask wallpaper and Oriental rugs, or a vignette setting that suggests as much but does not include all the details.

Formals could mean a night at the opera or ballet, a charity concert, a fund-raising celebration. A few well-selected posters and props could set the scene: railings, balustrades, columns, arches, stairways with red velvet runners, brass stanchions swinging velvet-covered ropes, marquees or canopies, photomurals of famous opera houses or concert halls, or some gold opera chairs set about to simulate a box at the opera, with the addition of some velvet swags and drapes and a program or two.

Figure 17.9 April showers? A day at the beach? A color statement? Umbrellas can work at almost any time of the year to set a scene, back up a mannequin, or serve as a clever divider between the display area and the store in an open-back window. *Barneys, Madison Avenue, New York.*

Figure 17.10 Father's Day is a salute to Dad and also comes at a time when the retailer wants to show off his line of men's casual wear for summer. This salute puts dad together with eye-appealing photographs of Hollywood pin-ups from the 50s and 60s for a rakish and fun display. The noted photographer whose photos have been enlarged has also produced a book of his work which is featured in this display as well. It is all explained in the sign in the gold frame up front. *Barneys, Madison Avenue, New York.*

A formal setting is a view of a skyline at night, a midnight sky scattered with diamond-like sequins, a garden with ghostly pale sculpture, a fountain, clipped and shaped plants. Furniture can be formal in a setting done in Louis XV, Louis XVI, or French Empire antiques or reasonable reproductions. The scene can be Versailles, Monte Carlo, or a suite at the Ritz.

Antiques may also suggest formal wear. Coromandel screens, Oriental lacquerware, and fine porcelain vases sparingly and artfully filled with branches and blossoms can bespeak formal wear. A man's top hat and cane resting on a small velvet chair says it, and so do opera glasses, theater programs, dance cards, and oversized menus. A champagne cooler and two champagne glasses on a long skirted table can imply the start of something big.

Formal can also be disco, jazz concerts, or jet-setting to "in" places. Dress-up clothes also belong at a New Year's Eve gala with balloons, confetti and colorful streamers, champagne, party hats, party favors, a clock and a countdown to midnight, "Auld Lang Syne," "Cocktails for Two," and more. Father Time and Baby New Year appear together—for one night only! It can also be a gambling casino, dice, and chips galore. Formal wear is synonymous with "going out," gala, grand, gracious, the arts—how the "other half" lives. Formal is fantasy and dreams.

Lingerie

Lingerie is lovely and sexy. It is hidden and secret, but designed to be seen. Show it in the boudoir, sheer and all ribbons and ruffles; sheer curtains can be drawn partly across the window and tied back so that the viewer can get

Figure 17.11 Formal wear is given a simple but elegant treatment in this red-infused window. The mannequin is "framed" by an ornate frame and the pull back red drape adds another dollop of drama to the presentation. The frame focuses the viewer's eye on the dress. *Saks Fifth Avenue, New York.*

Figure 17.12 Halloween may not be a reason to run out and buy a little black dress but it is a popular event and certainly makes an effective setting for black outfits. People seem to enjoy the "scary" fun of black cats, bats, witches, and all sorts of "evil," dark, and mysterious things. *Lord & Taylor, Fifth Avenue, New York.*

a good look at what is going on behind. Or set the scene in a leafy bower, a gazebo in a garden, a powder room, or a bedroom all rococo or faded French provincial.

Lingerie usually suggests pastel colors: pinks, creams, pale lavenders, and other fashionable delicacies. A period screen can suggest privacy or a barrier behind which a woman can change. Use a vase with pretty blossoms set on a festooned table that can also show some choice pieces of merchandise. Lingerie is right for Mother's Day, Valentine's Day, and rates high as Christmas gifts.

Lingerie can be set against a midnight sky and blanched classic columns, or a billowing tent with soft satin pillows filling the floor. Provide a setting for a modern-day

Scheherazade in which she can tell her thousand-and-one tales, or make it the tent of the Sheik of Araby. With a bit of imagination and the merest suggestion of props, the lingerie-attired mannequin can be a fairy princess; turn a long, long blonde wig into a ladder (Rapunzel); use a red apple and a wall mirror (Snow White); a spinning wheel and a floor full of pretty slips, bras, and panties (the fair captive in Rumpelstiltskin). With a crown, a long velvet cape, a satin streamer across a mannequin's chest, and an armful of red roses, it is the American choice, Miss America.

For attention-getting value, for a touch of humor, or to show how things do change or never change, juxtapose a modern, scantily clad figure against a period piece of furniture. Turn the lingerie display into a ballet setting—*Les Sylphides, Giselle,* or any other romantic piece—with the mannequin on pointe to show the freedom of movement, the drape, and the shape of the feminine garment. Use a ballet bar and a large mirror to suggest a practice setting, or let her hold a pair of ballet shoes, with some flowers and sheets of music on the floor. Or, try a theatrical trunk spilling over with more lovely "unmentionables." Add a poster for a ballet company, and say "grace," "charm," and "feminine." Lingerie should be lovely, sexy, and definitely seen.

Mother's Day

Pink carnations may say it all, but it can also be said with pink roses, ribbons, ruffles, laces, lavender, and lilacs. **Mother's Day** is Whistler's Mother and all the other famous mothers of history. It is represented by cameos, lockets, velvet-covered photo albums, tintypes, and ornate, rococo frames. A bell jar protecting a fragile floral arrangement on a moiré or velvet-skirted table or a pink and white boudoir setting can say "mother." Chicks in a nest can be reaching out to a providing mother bird.

Mother's Day is the time to bring out the Victoriana and turn-of-the-century devices that usually enhance anniversary promotions. Even though Mother may be smart, sophisticated, and ultra-chic, on Mother's Day she can become all "lavender and lace," fragile and feminine, and frou-frou. Turn a display setting into a bon-bon dish or a plate of petit fours, or strawberries and cream. Add a giant, lace-edged card dripping with sweet sentiments; Mother will be served, as will the gift merchandise that is usually promoted for her day.

Patriotic

Presidents' Day, Fourth of July, Election Day—these are time when flags are unfurled. It is hooray for the red, white, and blue, and "Stars and Stripes Forever." Now is the time to show pictures of George Washington and Honest Abe, hatchets and cherry trees, log cabins and log fences. Bring out the eagles, the White House, the Capitol, victory wreaths, Columbia, and the Statue Of Liberty. Add fireworks, firecrackers, and the light of the

Figure 17.13 Mother's Day does not have to be sweet and sugary, a day when you treat your mother like someone from "Leave it to Beaver." It can be sophisticated, lovely, or just reek with femininity. The elegant Empire period furniture in white and gold with the large mirror as the dominant element in the composition is softened by the billowing sheets of silk drapery. Revealed are the realistic mannequins in Empire-inspired lingerie. *Bergdorf Goodman, Fifth Avenue, New York.*

"rockets' red glare." Show Betsy Ross sewing away at a star-studded flag, Washington crossing the Delaware, or the three weary Revolutionary fife and drum players in a cloud of dust.

The setting can be a map of the United States, the Declaration of Independence, the Bill of Rights, or the Con-

Figure 17.14 There are times when striking the red, white, and blue colors is just right—like for cruise and resort wear, denims, and anniversary sales. However, there are also times to just be patriotic and proudly show the country's colors. The stars and stripes in this display are a salute to the 4th of July—or some other civic event. Notice the miniature Statues of Liberty used to underscore the theme. *Lord & Taylor, Fifth Avenue, New York.*

stitution. Musically, it is any song by George M. Cohan, from "It's a Grand Old Flag" to "Yankee Doodle Dandy" —or Irving Berlin's tribute, "God Bless America."

The Fourth of July or any **patriotic** promotion could stress brotherhood, liberty, and equality—the "melting pot" concept that is America and its citizenry. Surround the promotion with striped bunting, white stars spattered on a blue field, and gold fringe; shields and frames; campaign buttons, banners, and election-type placards and posters; and balloons—red, white, and blue—confetti and streamers. The viewer will get the message and salute your efforts.

Spring

Green is busting out all over, and the early bloomers are daffodils, jonquils, crocuses, tulips, and hyacinths. Trees are budding and ready to bloom. Grass and shrubs are sprouting and "the red, red robin is bob, bob, bobbin'" all over the place. **Spring** is the time for seeds, rakes, hoes, and lawn equipment; April showers and May flowers, and May poles. It is a period of renaissance and rebirth. Baby birds appear in nests, and bunnies hop onto the scene. All kinds of soft, caressable animals announce "spring is here."

Spring could be represented by a clock made of branches, flowers, and ribbons that say "springtime," or by an oversized song sheet with flower-headed notes to suggest a sing-along of any of the hundreds of spring songs. Try butterflies, dragonflies, and flying kites; flowers and flower pots, vegetable gardens, latticework, garden hoses, and "Everything's Coming Up Roses." Spring can be a woodland nymph, a forest fantasy, or an enchanting setting for a fairy tale. It is a state of mind, a reawakening, and a return to nature.

Valentine's Day

After red hearts, pink hearts, and cerise hearts, it is "sweethearts" all the way: Romeo and Juliet, Tristan and Isolde, Scarlett and Rhett. This is the time for cherubs in

Figure 17.16 It ain't red—but it is still Valentine's Day! While everywhere else the display windows overflow with red hearts, red flowers, and red gift boxes tied up with red satin ribbons and red garments, Banana Republic maintained the heart motif but switched to black and pink for this smart holiday display of black and white spring fashions. The black and white chair keeps the theme going. *Banana Republic, Fifth Avenue, New York.*

Figure 17.15 In New York and Chicago it wouldn't be spring if there wasn't a giant flower show scheduled in a major department store. Live flowering plants take over all the windows and spread out inside the store over ledges, columns, and into the aisles. Every year Macy's Herald Square boasts a gigantic floral tribute to the citizens of New York, and thousands of visitors come to soak up, inhale, and be thrilled by the sight and smell of the blooming plants and flowers and the special fantasy theme that ties it all together. *Macy's, Herald Square, New York.*

pink, white, and gold. Make a hero of Cupid with bow and arrow; or simply show the bows and arrows dripping with ribbons, rosebuds, and lover's knots, and heart-shaped targets to hit.

An oversized deck of playing cards will win a lover's heart, if the display shows a suit of hearts—all kings and queens. Deliver the message with Valentine's cards, both sentimental and humorous, trimmed with ruffles and scrolls, flourishes and furbelows. For a sure reminder, use stuffed animals with arms entwined, and red, red

roses on extra long stems. There are love songs and serenades; madrigals to be accompanied by lutes, lyres, harps, and flutes; and minstrels to sing them.

Tell a fairy tale with a happy ending, or show love poems, love stories, and love letters tied in red ribbons. **Valentine's Day** is a date on the calendar circled with a red heart and surrounded with lipstick kisses, chocolate kisses, and lovebirds. It is a day lovers remember, and a ribbon tied around an elegantly gloved finger would serve as a lovely reminder.

Familiar Symbols: A Recap

- A cliché is a familiar symbol or image that is used constantly and telegraphs a message. The image is so recognizable that it explains itself even without copy.

- Anniversaries can be symbolized by wedding cakes, wedding bells, period furniture, old line drawings from catalogs, old toys and games or appliances, or anything that indicates the "good old days."

- Back-to-school displays are enhanced by alphabet blocks, owls, blackboards, pens and pencils, notebooks, dictionaries, books and bookcases, and dunce caps.

- Bridal displays are promoted by use of wedding music, wedding rings, hearts entwined, bridal bouquets, white doves, top hats, church scenes, stained glass windows, and tulle or net materials. A bridal window should always say, ". . . and they lived happily ever after."

- Career fashions are best displayed by using a professional office setting, a conference room, computers, office equipment, an architectural drawing board, an easel and palette, or graphs and charts.

- Christmas symbols are almost endless and include Santa Claus, garlands, Christmas trees, snow ornaments, snowmen, candy canes, reindeer, sleighs, bells, music boxes, Christmas music, stuffed stockings, and so on. For a religious emphasis, a crèche, stained glass windows, organ pipes, angels, or choirs can be used.

- Clearance sales can be promoted by cleanup symbols such as mops, brooms, pails, crates, plastic bags, and

cartons. Mannequins stripped down or in paper coverings can mean "everything is going." Empty hangers or shelves, or a giant scissors "slashing" prices can be used. Clearance sales demand dynamics—action and movement—and direction.

- Cruisewear, resortwear, sunwear, and swimwear are enhanced by blue skies, green grass, blue water, and bright yellow sunshine. Seascapes, beach and picnic scenery, fans and air conditioners, pool and barbecue equipment, and travel posters are good backgrounds and props for displaying this type of merchandise.

- Easter is perfect for cuddly bunnies and chicks, decorated eggs, Easter bonnets, white lilies, daffodils, and tulips. The spiritual side of an Easter display can involve church scenes, stained-glass windows, sunrise services, and pipe organs. Since Easter sometimes shares the calendar with the Jewish Passover holiday, this can be a good time for a store to make use of an institutional window to commemorate what these holidays are all about.

- Fall is the perfect time for using fruits and vegetables, red and gold fall leaves, asters, mums, and marigolds, and pumpkins, gourds, and jack-o'-lanterns. Baskets, leaves, rakes, and any sort of earthy materials are good for display at this season.

- Father's Day displays should be sentimental, but also touched with humor. Familiar symbols are sports equipment, chess pieces, playing cards (with Dad as "king"), trophies and awards for years of giving. Old-fashioned props, such as a Model T or a barbershop quartet, can bring memories of the "good old days," even if Dad wasn't born yet.

- Formal display settings can be elegant and classy or fun and funky. They can be realistic, as in a finely decorated room, or suggest a scene at the opera or ballet. Or the display can be New Year's Eve, champagne, or jet-setting to "in" places. A top hat and cane or champagne glasses on a table can also indicate a formal setting. Formal is fantasy and dreams, and synonymous with "going out."

- Lingerie should be lovely and sexy. Though it is hidden or secret, it is designed to be seen. It is usually shown in a boudoir with ruffles and ribbons and soft pastel colors, but can be bold and sexy when set against a midnight sky or in a billowing tent with lush satin pillows.

- Mother's Day displays are usually pink carnations or roses, ribbons, ruffles, laces, lavender, and lilac. Mother's Day can be represented by cameos, lockets, ornate frames, Victorian settings, or anything fragile and feminine. Delicate floral arrangements, velvet-covered albums, a white boudoir setting, chicks in a nest reaching out to a mother bird, a giant, lace-edged sentimental card, and various gift items usually associated with Mother's Day will also serve to promote this display.

- Patriotic holiday sales such as those taking place around Presidents' Day, Fourth of July, and Election Day, are best served by using flags, eagles, fireworks, the White House, the Statue of Liberty, George Washington, and Honest Abe. A map of the United States or a reproduction of the Declaration of Independence or the Constitution are good props. A promotion stressing "brotherhood," "patriotism," or the "melting pot" would make a good display. Any red, white, and blue color theme will get the message across.

- Spring is best represented by early-blooming flowers such as daffodils, crocuses, hyacinths, and jonquils. Baby animals will emphasize the season of rebirth. Garden equipment, vegetable patches, flower pots, latticework, butterflies, a flying kite, spring music, or a forest fantasy can also make good displays for spring.

- Valentine's Day is perfect for hearts and for well-known sweethearts such as Romeo and Juliet, Tristan and Isolde, and Scarlett and Rhett. Any props signifying romance can be used: cupid, cherubs, a bow and arrow, heart-shaped targets, lovers' knots, playing cards showing the king and queen of hearts, and so on. Red and pink are the usual colors for a Valentine's display.

Questions for Review and Discussion

1. How does a cliché relate to visual merchandising?

2. What are the color clichés for Valentine's Day? Easter? Fourth of July? Halloween?

3. List three holiday periods for which a visual merchandiser must prepare. Describe the types of displays that might be produced for each.

4. Create a theme and describe supporting props that would successfully portray the following store events:
    a. swimsuit sale
    b. white sale
    c. end-of-summer clearance
    d. Italian import fair

CHAPTER EIGHTEEN

Masking and Proscenia

AFTER YOU HAVE READ THIS CHAPTER,
YOU WILL BE ABLE TO DISCUSS:

- The terms proscenium and masking.
- Uses of proscenia.
- Situations in which a proscenium would be beneficial to use in a display.
- Methods for masking display windows.
- Materials and items that can be used for masking purposes.

MASKING AND PROSCENIA: TRADE TALK

    bamboo blinds

    foamcore

    lath-lattice panels

    masking

    natural materials

    plants

    proscenium (proscenia, plural)

    ribbons and streamers

    venetian blinds

    vertical blinds

    window shades

    wrapping materials

As discussed previously in Chapter 7, **proscenium** is a term used to describe the permanent, often ornamental, framing that goes around the stage in a theater. In store design and window display, the proscenium is the border, usually set against the front glass, that frames the top and sides of the window and contains the display. The proscenia in department and specialty stores in the past were often handcarved or formed out of rich moldings and in some cases were embellished with a medallion with the store's name or logo. Today, a proscenium may be cut out of foamcore or plywood covered with a suitable fabric or paper. It can also be made of garlands and lights or out of several other inexpensive materials. Basically, the proscenia is a frame and is used to.

- Accentuate the display setup behind it.
- Hide the pipes and lighting fixtures that might otherwise disturb or distract the street-side viewers.
- Provide a promotional or seasonal theme for the window.
- Unify and add a dramatic and coherent quality to a group of windows that may be different in size, unrelated, or just architecturally dull.
- Make the window opening suitable to the scale of the merchandise to be presented.

The last reason is probably the most important of all. Often something small and well done will succeed over something big and overblown. A short, sharp, on-target visual statement can carry more sales impact than an overabundance of merchandise shown across a display space. A compact, concentrated merchandise grouping can relay a fashion trend, a look, an attitude, or get a story across better than a mass presentation. In Chapter 7 we briefly touched on proscenia and masking, but here we will more fully develop how masking windows with often improvised proscenia can make the display area more properly suited to the scale and size of the products being shown.

Too often retailers will move into established spaces and "inherit" display windows that were never designed to show off their type of products. A 10-foot-tall window is fine when the display person is using and showing garments on mannequins, but it can be a disastrous disadvantage for showing off shoes, handbags, fine jewelry, or cosmetics. When the window is tall and long and deep, the retailer feels that all of that space must be filled, and the results are often too much merchandise displayed for too long a time. If it takes so many hours to install a display, the retailer hopes to amortize the effort over several weeks. That eventually means an overexposure of the merchandise. In other words, the merchandise has been seen too many times by the same group of shoppers. The merchandise is no longer fresh and exciting, and no longer sends out the right message to the shoppers on the street. It has been overexposed to the heat and light of the spots in the window and possibly the penetrating rays of the sun that blasts down on the window day after day, week after week. Also, a small, specialized presentation makes the product seem more precious, more desirable, and more unique.

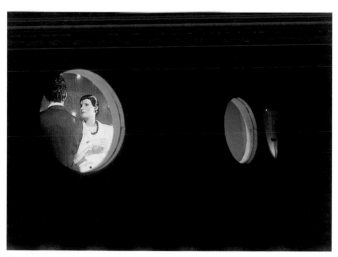

Figure 18.1 The black panels with portholes cut out of them turned this window into a cruise ship so if the shopper on the street came closer she could look through the opening and behold the newest fashions for cruising and resort wear. The strong light coming through the openings was a draw as well as curiosity about finding out what was being blocked off. *Lazarus, Columbus, Ohio.*

Figure 18.2 The window has been blocked off into a series of different size shadow boxes and each box is outlined in bee lights. The mirrored panel behind each opening affects not only the outline lighting but affords shoppers another view of the object on display. *Louis Vuitton, Fifth Avenue, New York.*

while letting each one be special and distinct. By using the mask concept, vertical dividers, set against the glass, can create a series of openings out of the one long stretch of glass. The panels can make one, two, three, or four equal display spaces or maybe create a larger central stage with smaller, and maybe lower ones, to either side for the presentation of the fashion accessories that are much better viewed in confined spaces. By dividing the run-on window into a series of smaller windows, the display person can do a series of related yet different display setups that will bring together one major story, or present a single promotion. For Mother's Day, each framed space could show a different gift idea for Mother, or a different type of mother that requires a more specialized gift. If the dividing panels were foamcore boards covered with pink moiré or paper, they would serve as the "continuity" in the Mother's Day promotion.

A really good mask is removable; it is not a permanent installation that doesn't allow an opportunity to change. A mask is placed against the front glass and can be used whether the store has an open-back window or an enclosed window space. If the window area is actually an extension or a part of the selling floor, as it is in many mall operations, then the mask or proscenium should be finished on both sides since the back will be on view from inside the store. Here are some ideas for masking open-back windows. They are simple and work well, and they are open to reinterpretation by the display person/visual merchandiser.

Masking reduces the size of the window by making an opening for viewing that is smaller. Ordinarily, a window that is 10 feet tall by 12 feet wide would take about three mannequins and several props to fill. If the glass opening was reduced to a space that was 8 feet tall by 6 feet wide, all it would require is a single mannequin or dress form, and a simple prop like a chair, a plant, or a piece of sculpture. In addition, the mask or frame enhances the enclosed presentation and makes it appear more important and more concentrated, just as a mat or frame makes a print or a picture seem more important and impressive.

A run-on window is a long, long, seemingly unending window that presents problems for the retailer and the visual merchandiser. The biggest problem is attempting to show a variety of merchandise categories

Figure 18.3 The long window has been divided into three different viewing areas by the vertical panels. Each headless figure or pair has its own space separate and apart from the others. *Barneys, Madison Avenue, New York.*

Ideas for Masking Open-Back Windows

Venetian Blinds

Venetian blinds or **vertical blinds** will work. The former, horizontal slats of wood or metal, can be ordered in lengths that will extend from the top of the glass line down to the floor of the window. Ideally, the color should be neutral so that it can be a background for applied decorations. Ivy vines could be entwined for an autumn look, snowflakes and ornaments appliquéd for Christmas, red ribbons and hearts interwoven through the slats for Valentine's Day, and so on. Select an off-white, neutral gray, beige, soft coral or rose, or a color that blends in

Figure 18.4 The walls, ceiling, and floor are black. By lighting up only one part of the window, the part where the bride stands and is reflected in the pier mirror, the designer has cleverly masked off the rest of the space and left it undecorated. The viewer's eye is literally forced to the focal element in the window—the bride and her gown. *G. Fox, Hartford, Connecticut.*

with the interior of the store because, from the interior, it is part of the store. A deep gray, black, or dark brown will make a more dramatic statement. It will be a "statement" that the shopper will remember. The darker, deeper neutrals could be kept in reserve for special occasions when a dynamic frame is needed for a black dress presentation, formal wear, or furs. Silver, copper and brass blinds are also "dramatic statements" that can be and should be used for special occasions like Christmas, New Year's Eve, and other glitter and glitz displays.

Once the display person has installed the top mechanism for the blinds against the top of the glass, it is simple enough to change the blinds from gray to black to metallic, to highlight an occasion or the merchandise. Should the display person want to change the display space for a particular event, the blinds can be pulled way up and the mask disappears. Blinds also make it possible for the retailer to control the light that comes into the store and the visibility of the selling floor from the street or the mall. Matching or contrasting blinds can be used as backgrounds for the display setups in the open-back window. They cut off the view from the store but can allow some of the light to seep through. Here, too, when an open-into-the-store look is desired, the pulled-up blind hugs the ceiling line and is out of view.

Wooden blinds are so old-fashioned that they are new again and, though they are expensive to install, they do add an architectural quality that can enhance some categories of merchandise like men's wear, women's tailored clothes, designer wear, and better sportswear. The wood tone should be compatible with any wood that appears inside the store, on the walls, on the floor, or in the furnishings and fixtures. Particularly rich, handsome, and traditional is the use of the natural wood blinds with a wood floor in the window. For bridal wear and very feminine up-scale merchandise, there is a selection of pickled or pastel-colored rubbed woods available as blinds.

Important! Blinds do get dusty and they must be maintained if they are to add to the good looks of the display without suggesting neglectful housekeeping and downright sloppiness. Dust doesn't look good for the merchandise or the store's image.

Window Shades

It is possible to achieve the same effect with **window shades.** The rollers can be attached to the ceiling and the

Figure 18.5 Giant panels of russet toned fall leaves fill in the sides, top, and bottom of the window to create a limited focal area in the center where the realistic mannequins seem to be stepping out of the surrounding foam core "forest". The "leaves" form a frame around them and block out the rest of the display area. The same deep orange color is used to cover the floor pads of this open-back window. *Holland & Holland, West 57th Street, New York.*

green or red shades can span the glass between the side vertical panels to form a proscenium for the front.

Imagine red shades with applied white letters that spell out S-A-L-E to serve as an emphatic reminder once or twice a year; hot pink shades for Mother's Day or Valentine's Day; neutral shades of rough burlap or homespun fabric for autumn. Brightly striped canvas shades can herald summertime living and dressing, while black-and-white polka dots can be just the thing to add sparkle to a black-and-white merchandise presentation. All it takes is a few yards of fabric—cut to the desired length and width and hemmed—and a staple gun to attach the fabric to the roller. Of course, using a ceiling grid

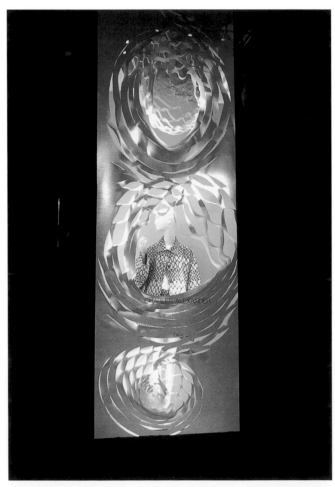

Figure 18.6 A black proscenium frames the entire front glass, thus cutting the viewing area into a long, vertical slot. Another panel with cut-out openings appears behind the window mask and is trimmed with sculptured paper "wreaths." The central opening is exaggerated so that the viewer can actually see the object that has been so enshrined. *Bergdorf Goodman, Fifth Avenue, New York.*

shades can be raised or lowered as desired. For the sake of interest and change, the shades can be pulled down to different levels. If the display person wanted to show shoes and handbags next to a display of dressed mannequins, the shade can be pulled down to 4 or 5 feet from the floor of the window and the small fashion accessories can be shown on platforms or stepped elevations. Once the roller-receiver is in place, it is simple and inexpensive to have an assortment of different-colored and patterned shades to use with the changing seasons, color promotions, or even sales events. All it takes is stapling a new length of fabric onto the roller. A Christmas window can be created with this technique by using bright red or green, narrow ceiling-to-floor shades, and wide

Figure 18.7 A semi-transparent sheet of fine wire netting swirls its way down the side of the window, thus masking off part of the glass opening. The shimmering metallic material forms a partial frame that sets off the realistic figures in the open-back window. *Pilar Rossi, Madison Avenue, New York.*

that is installed in the window, the display person could hang matching panels to serve as background for the up-front displays in the open-back windows.

Foamcore and Board

Probably the simplest and most efficient mask or proscenium can be made of **foamcore.** The material is available in 4-foot by 8-foot panels. It is lightweight and fairly rigid, especially in the thicker sheets. There are also newer, denser, and more rigid styrene-covered boards on the market that will work. The material is available in thicknesses up to $^3/_4$ inches and can be cut with an X-acto knife, a mat knife, or a single-edged blade. What-

ever cutting tool is used, it should be a new, fresh blade because the material can crumble or rip with a dull blade. The most traditional use would be to cut the panels to the desired height and width and, if more height is needed, add on a piece and brace it with a 1-inch by 2-inch strip of lumber. The panel can be covered with colored felt (in convenient 5-foot widths) or fabrics (48- to 54-inch widths). Vinyls, contact papers, and even decorative wallcoverings can make effective, semipermanent prosceniums, but the whole idea behind masks and prosceniums is to make them an integral part of the changing display scene.

For Christmas and special events, the foamcore can be pierced and bee lights pushed through to add pinpoints of twinkling light to the frame. Larger openings can be cut out and Christmas ornaments can be integrated into the frame or added like ball fringe along the inner edge of the frame—the sides closest to the display setup. It takes more time and effort but the frame board can be scalloped or shaped to resemble a pull-back drapery on the sides and a swagged valance across the top. This more dramatic treatment works for dress-up displays as well as holidays. Also, the drapery look will unify a group of dissimilar windows that are awkward or too small to need a mask. They can still be given a dramatic impact by the use of a narrow overhead valance and a one-side-only pull-back drapery. The edge of the "drapery" could be embellished with actual fringe or a string of bee lights.

Lath-Lattice Panels

Another rather inexpensive, but open and double-faced masking construction material, is **lath-lattice panels.** They are available in lumber yards and in garden supply stores. The crisscross of narrow strips of thin wood can make a lacy proscenium or a three-sided frame for lingerie, bridal wear, summer, and resort clothes, or any soft merchandise. It will take some joining, nailing, and bracing to create the arboresque frame, but the result can be well worth the time and effort. This frame will allow the light to go through and it will not hide the store's interior, but it does limit the glass opening for the display. The lattice should, again, be white or a light neutral or pale pastel, and if a definite color emphasis is desired, fabric or paper can be stapled behind the lattice to cut down on the see-through effect and also get the impact

Figure 18.8 The soft drapery hanging off the suspended rod not only blocks off part of the shop beyond, it also provides a dramatic setting for the crystal candelabra on the sleek black pedestal. *Baccarat, Madison Avenue, New York.*

of formal wear, bridalwear, better dresses, and furs. The planters should be the same or similar; all terra-cotta, all brass, or all white, but preferably neutral. The foliage also creates a semi-barrier in an open-back window and the display person may even find a local florist or plant nursery that will "lend" some plants for a two-week window exposure in exchange for a card saying "Plants courtesy of —." Cactus plants can provide the right ambience for resort sportswear and separates, for western wear, as well as subtle desert-tone promotions. Blossoming plants will work at almost any time of the year for a seasonal display; lilies, daffodils, and tulips for spring and Easter; poinsettias (red or white) for Christmas; asters, mums, and marigolds for autumn; daisies and geraniums for summer. The small bushy plants may have to be backed with 5 to 6 feet of leafy green to effectively serve as a divider.

Ribbons and Streamers

Many interesting and colorful things can be done with assorted widths and lengths of **ribbons and streamers.** The ribbons can be stapled onto long strips of lath or 1-inch by 1-inch wood strips that are then tacked into the molding over the front window. The long, to-the-floor streamers at either end of the window serve to mask off the width of the front glass, while the shorter fringe on top, in the center and between them, takes care of any unwanted extra height. The ribbons can be cut in equal lengths or can be cut to different lengths to create an arc or a sweep and form an arch in the window. The ends of the ribbons can be cut and finished in a dovetail or inverted-V design.

Ribbon curtains and frames can work year-round. For Mother's Day use several shades of pink; for Valentine's Day, red and cerise; for Easter, mix pretty pastels; use cotton streamers for summer and sportswear; burlap and/or velvet ribbons for autumn—whatever suits the merchandise best. There are dozens of ways to use black satin or velvet ribbon to add class and elegance to formal wear display, while white satin ribbons could frame almost any bride and bridal party, especially with some pink rosebuds or lily-of-the-valley sprays tied together with bowknots.

Try mixing widths and textures as well as colors. For the best price—and they are quite inexpensive—try

of the colored accent. For a handsome effect that does take some extra effort, the lattice can be backed with colored tissue papers or translucent gels then lit from behind for a stained glass effect.

Plants

Turning to something less formal and structured, an arrangement of assorted **plants** can create a greenbelt or a growing divider that will separate a large window into smaller, separated areas. A few large, lacy-leafed plants such as palms or schefflera—5- to 6-feet tall, in simple planters—can add dignity and class to showing the strip of lath in ribbon, then attach the beribboned strip to the ceiling grid.

Imagine the possibilities of white cotton roping for cruisewear, resortwear, swimwear, and summer sportswear, or hemp rope and twine for autumn wear, outerwear, and western wear. What could be cheaper, more colorful, more exciting, and filled with more happy memories than paper streamers and confetti. Turn the window into a festival for New Year's Eve or Mardi Gras with coils of twirling paper streamers framing the front glass. For a special sale, for an anniversary promotion—it is simple and effective.

Figure 18.9 The zigzag screen, part white and part black, breaks up the window space into two distinct areas of merchandise. In one section a headless mannequin appears while in the other a partial form is used and raised up on blocks of the same construction as the screen to bring it up to the same visual height as its neighbor. *Chanel, Fifth Avenue, New York.*

Figure 18.10 The ultimate mask! The total and complete blocking of a window display area! A red velvet curtain is dropped—very theatrically—against the front glass. In three pools of light on the floor three pairs of shoes seem to be sneaking out from behind to take their curtain calls. Clever, amusing, and it tests the shopper. Why is the window closed? Why the red velvet curtain? What's in those spotlights on the floor? *Saks Fifth Avenue, New York.*

shopping for ribbons at the floral supply stores where the ribbons are available in 100-yard rolls. To provide a background for an open-back window—or even a closed-back one—add a ribbon curtain behind the display, or have your mannequins interspersed between streamers. The curtains are light and airy, but they do stop and hold the viewer's eye. If the window has a ceiling grid, staple the ribbons onto a 3- or 4-foot strip of lath that has been painted to match the ribbon, or wrap

Bamboo Blinds

Frames and masks can also be made of inexpensive split **bamboo blinds.** A top border can be made by cutting up one long blind into several pieces of different lengths while at the ends the long, floor-to-ceiling blinds would finish the frame. The blinds can be cut with a mat knife and the pieces can be stapled or glued together with hot glue or white carpenter's glue to the desired lengths or widths. The glue also keeps the cut cords from unraveling. The small bamboo slats are especially good for cruise/resort and jungle treatments for animal-print fashions and safari-inspired neutrals. Backlighting, through the blinds, can enhance the mood and the ambience.

Wrapping Materials

Corrugated **wrapping material** and brown wrapping paper are also adaptable for creating window masks. By just covering the entire front glass with brown paper and cutting a few well-spaced "knot holes" at eye level, the display person has not only masked the space, he or she has created a great "come-on." Everybody is curious, and when a window is blocked out with a light shining through in spots, the viewer is more and more interested and is impelled to step closer and look through the keyhole at what has been "hidden." One curious shopper leads to a lineup of curious bodies just waiting for a peek at what lies beyond.

Imagine the window as a gift-wrapped box and the center "torn out" so that what lies behind—in the light—is revealed. Or make a series of diagonal passes through the window using corrugated board—one from upper left to lower right and the other from upper right to lower left. The mannequin, set between the two opposing diagonals, is framed in an angular arch. This also creates a much smaller and more concentrated window space. With good lighting, the mannequin can be picked out quickly.

Natural Materials

Natural twigs and branches nailed on 1-inch by 2-inch strips of wood can also be used to create window frames. The branches can be left natural or sprayed white or a pretty pastel, or accented with shimmering "snow" for winter or Christmas, or glittery gold and silver diamond dust for formal wear and holidays. What could a display person do with branches sprayed shiny black, or bright red enamel? Strings of bee lights could be entwined in the jumble of branches. Green leaves cut out of tissue paper could be attached with spray glue for a spring opening, as could buds and colored confetti. Try hanging pale pink, lavender, and yellow eggs with matching ribbons off of the branches for Easter. Add orange, red, and gold leaves to the otherwise bare, brown branches for an autumn setting. Valentine's Day could be red hearts on white or pink branches, and lingerie could be shown with white lace paper-doily flowers on the pastel branches. Depending on where the display person is located, the basic **natural material,** like the branches, can cost almost nothing. The sides of country roads and the forests beyond usually have surplus branches and twigs just lying around waiting to be picked up. A deal with a local tree trimmer could provide you with enough branches to turn the store into a forest too.

It should be evident by this point that all it takes is some imagination and some not-very-expensive or difficult-to-get materials to make most masks or frames for display windows. The idea is to frame, to bring whatever is on display into focus, and to scale the display area to the size of the merchandise. It is so much better when we can add a seasonal or promotional quality to the mask or frame. If one picture is worth a thousand words, imagine how much more expressive and definitive the picture is when it has been properly framed.

Masking and Proscenia: A Recap

- Proscenium is a term used to describe the permanent framing that goes around a stage in a theater.

- In a window display, the proscenium is the border, usually set against the front glass, that frames the top and sides of a window and contains the display.

- The proscenium is used to accent the display, hide pipes and fixtures, provide a promotional or seasonal theme, add a coherent quality to a group of different-size windows, and make a window suitable to the scale of the merchandise presented.

- A short, sharp, on-target visual statement can carry more sales impact than an overabundance of merchandise.

- A run-on window is a long, seemingly unending window. This type of window presents a problem when attempting to show a variety of merchandise categories while letting each one be separate and distinct.

- A really good mask is removable and able to be changed.

- For masking open-back windows, the display person can use the following: venetian blinds, window shades, foamcore and boards, lath-lattice panels, plants, ribbons, bamboo blinds, wrapping materials, and natural materials such as twigs and branches sprayed in colors or wrapped in tiny lights.

Questions for Review and Discussion

1. What is proscenium and for what purposes is it sometimes used?

2. Explain the subtle differences between masking and proscenium.

3. Describe a display setting where venetian blinds could be used effectively as window masking. Include the type of merchandise, theme, props, and specific types of blinds to be used in the window display.

4. What is foamcore and how can it be used as a window proscenium or mask?

5. For each of the four seasons, make a separate list of materials related to that season that could be used for creatively masking windows.

CHAPTER NINETEEN

Sale Ideas

AFTER YOU HAVE READ THIS CHAPTER,
YOU WILL BE ABLE TO DISCUSS:

- How a store's image can be maintained while promoting a sale event.

- Unique sale themes.

- How mannequins and props can be used to effectively promote sales events.

SALE IDEAS: TRADE TALK

    graphics

    magic

    sale

nto each retailer's life "a little **sale**" or even a big sale must fall. It is not necessarily indicative of poor business acumen or planning, but a cycle in retail life that is used to clear the shelves and hang-rods when a season is over to make room for new merchandise. It does not have to be a sign of defeat, it can just be an event that marks a passing and heralds a new opportunity. A good display person with an imagination and a sense of humor can turn what is often a distress signal into something special. A sale can be a real event—a celebration—a promotion in the business cycle that serves to bring in the shoppers who really were not thinking of buying. Thus, to be successful, a sale needs as much planning and preparation as any other fashion promotion and, as always, the accent is on *fashion* and on maintaining the store's *image*.

Too many retailers think that customers equate a sale with drastic reductions, and with the blood and gore that accompanies the slashing of the prices. Too many also have stored away in some musty closet amid mops, brooms, and burnt-out fluorescent lamps a rolled up sweep of seamless paper with a blood curdling S-A-L-E scrawled across it in sanguine red. The sale officially begins when the tired, tattered, and battle-scarred banner is unfurled in the front window. It also seems to be the cue to shovel in samplings of everything that is on sale. This really is not necessary. There are ways of promoting a sale without turning the window into a warehouse of forlorn frocks and despairing dresses.

The store's image—fashion-wise and business-wise —must be maintained at the time of a sale promotion. If the merchandise is traditionally presented with taste, discretion, and quiet dignity, that same attitude should prevail when the sale is in progress. Dignity does not equate with deadly dull. For the very upscale shopper, a "reminder" may be all that it takes. That reminder can be an easily perceived "message," maybe something graphic that says "out with the not-too-old and in with the very new." The "old" should never suggest something that is lacking in taste and value, or something that is no longer desirable or worth owning. The retailer is not "dump-ing" the merchandise, only moving it to make room for something fresher. The message can be delivered with a well-lettered, well-situated sign or, depending upon the store's location and clientele, in a humorous manner. If, however, the store's merchandise is light, bright, and trendy, the displays may be more explosive, more fun, more daring and shocking, and tongue-in-cheek. Here the display person can let go with startling displays that are a little wild and crazy.

However, no matter what the style or image of the merchandise being offered, a sale event should not be dull and repetitious. Just as nobody believed the boy who cried wolf, nobody wants to see the same dreary banner proclaiming what seems to be the same ongoing, never ending sale. They just will not believe it. If the message continues to be presented in the same way, the impact is lost to a "familiarity breeds disbelief" mentality. Nobody is looking!

Mannequins

Starting with ideas that use mannequins, realistic or abstract, here are some points of departure that should suggest some effective adaptations. "Everything Must Go." "Down to the Bare Essentials," "Stripping for Action" are fitting words that could be themes for sale displays. The display could feature an "Eve," with or without her fig-leafed "Adam," or Adam could be represented by a cutout caricature in black and white, and the copy could be in a balloon, like in the comics. She could be standing in her altogetherness, but with parts censored by the artfully arranged tresses made of hempen rope, or cotton roping, or even a wig of paper-sculpted curls or confetti streamers attached to a skull-hugging bathing cap. "Not a thing to wear!" The Garden of Eden setting could be a "forest" of empty hangers or just a few choice sale items could be lovingly draped, snake-like, around a cutout tree or an actual branch. "Let us tempt you!" Or an oversized apple with the word S-A-L-E spelled out on it could be hanging off a tree limb, dangling in front of style baggy trousers (one on each leg and tied at the waist and at the ankles). Tie them into turbans or fantasy headdresses and it is " 1001 Delights—and all on sale"; or with an Aladdin's lamp or genie-in-a-bottle prop— "Make dreams come true at great savings"—or "Wishes do come true during our wish-fulfilling sale."

As a prop, a palm tree can be made by wrapping the plastic material around a cardboard tube with leaves that are cut out of seamless paper and fringed. The fruit of the tree can carry the sale insignia. Simply pull a garment bag with the store's logo emblazoned on it over the mannequin's head, cut slits so that the arms can be attached,

Figure 19.1 The sign says "SALE" and somewhere in that dense collage of merino sweaters hanging from the strange, striate patterned "tree," there must be one for the shopper drawn by the bright colors and unusual setting. In case the shopper missed the notice on the front glass, there is another message on the tree. *H-Bendel, Fifth Avenue, New York.*

Figure 19.2 Character mannequins that appeal to trendy teens and twenty-somethings wear white coveralls with the "50% OFF" logo graphic on their breast pockets. These logos match the signs that appear within the shop. For this event all the mannequins that are usually spread out throughout the store were ganged up near the windows for impact. *Chicago.*

her, enticing her to enter the store. Want to add some humor? Borrow an assortment of stuffed animals to inhabit the vignetted Eden and have them showing off a few items on the green grass mat floor. "At these prices, why go naked?" "Make a fresh start." Keep the themes upbeat, suggest reasons for shopping, and don't even mention the fact that the merchandise is being moved out.

It is not necessary to show any merchandise in the display to get the message across. Dress, drape, wrap, or package the otherwise nude mannequin with the store's distinctive plastic garment bags or wrapping material. Make them into halters or bras, into skirts or harem-

and boldly stencil the word S-A-L-E on the front and back of the bag-dress. To further emphasize the "Going-Going-Gone" of the sale merchandise, fill the floor of the display area with more store shopping bags and boxes, store name showing, filled either with suggested sale buys or with colorful poufs of tissue. Same idea but different: Dress the mannequin in a giant-sized store shopping bag made of folded and stapled seamless paper and set the actual bags in a tumble on the floor. Using store-branded bags and boxes creates a background by stapling them in a collage on the rear wall of the window. If it is an open-back window, simply attach them onto a 4-by 8-foot panel that is used as a screen to semi-block the store from the street or the mall. Make a stencil with the word S-A-L-E boldly lettered and then proceed to stencil the word on the bags, on the front window glass, on the floor after it has been covered with a sweep of seamless paper or even plain brown wrapping paper. It can also be stenciled on inexpensive aprons or smocks and worn by the salespeople while the event is going on. Should there be a tired and soon-to-be-retired mannequin available, or a realistic one that is about to become semiabstract with a solid coat of paint, give her one last fling and tattoo her body all over with "sale" in technicolor (red, yellow, blue, green, and violet). If she is too good to despoil, wrap her in a prestenciled sheet of white muslin, mummy-style, with only her face showing. For fun, tie her up with brightly colored cotton roping.

Dressing a mannequin for a sale? How about undressing her and using that old cliché of a wooden barrel, only this time imprinted with S-A-L-E. A pair of bright red ribbon suspenders will keep the barrel in place as she greets the shoppers from the window or standing on a platform on the selling floor. Though not previously emphasized, what's happening on the outside or up front should be reinforced on the inside, on the selling floor, at the point of sale. Many of the aforementioned concepts will work as well inside the store.

Less extreme and softer, and really quite inexpensive, is an oversized T-shirt stenciled with the word "sale" or four T-shirts with the individual letters spelling out the

Figure 19.4 Specially sculpted papier mâchè heads set atop dressed forms create a street scene in the window. The people "queuing up" in the window replay the shoppers out on Regent Street in London waiting for the bus. The window people are already loaded down with the sale merchandise they have picked up. *Burberry, Regent Street, London.*

Figure 19.3 Blinking danger lights on the floor hold back traffic while the mannequins dressed in Kenneth Cole outfits carry some of the giant cutout letters that spell "SALE." In the white window, the red letters make the desired statement. *Kenneth Cole, Michigan Boulevard, Chicago.*

Figure 19.5 "They're playing our song" or "Going for a song!" Whatever—the tuneful display of floating music notes and sheets of music tell you that a sale is going "My Way" at Hugo Boss. The music stand with the single shirt and tie sort of explain the theme. *Hugo Boss, Washington, DC.*

message. These can be worn by the mannequins, put over pipe forms or even floated from suspended hangers tied to the ceiling grid by red satin ribbons. Print up some extra T-shirts for the willing salespeople to sport on the floor during the event. If the sleep tees are used, the mannequins do not need any other clothes. Also fun and inexpensive are the disposable painter's coveralls with the word "sale" emblazoned on the front or the back. "What's Cooking?" or "What's Hot?" It's a SALE and the mannequins can wear those white-bibbed sale aprons over red and white outfits. Top them off with the high, white chef hats and some kitchen supplies for a "Come and Get It" celebration. For the more daring, let the aprons be the only coverings for the mannequins.

Another thought on wrapping the mannequin: Cover it with brown wrapping paper and tie with rope or twine. Stencil the message either on the wrapping or on a "card" attached to the "package"—"Unwrapping the

Sale of the Year." They'll get the message. Cover your barely dressed mannequin, or even suit or dress form, with sale sign boards connected with over-the-shoulder ribbons. Let it carry the message for all to see.

It does not really require a mannequin to do a sale window, sometimes it can be done with just an arm or a leg. This could be the time when the mannequins get a much-needed rest from their overexposure in the display arena and the display person relies on **graphics.**

Graphics

If it has not been done over and over again in the same way, a simple sign can be sufficient. It can be stenciled on the front glass, backed up with bags and boxes and/or an empty clothes rack with only a few wire hangers left on it and lots more empty hangers scattered on the floor.

Figure 19.7 The hatchet is there in full sight and so are the trees. This is a real price chopping event and the viewer cannot only see the "chopped" tree in this forest but can also "hear" the prices falling. A novel sale twist. *Macy's, Herald Square, New York.*

Figure 19.6 Giant dimensional letters are toppling through the open and spacious corner window. If the shoppers didn't read "SALE" coming down they would see it as a horizontal "SALE" if they looked from another angle. *Hugo Boss, Fifth Avenue, New York.*

The window can be a "nightmare" of hangers suspended and swooping through the air and pinned onto this variation of Alfred Hitchcock's *The Birds*. With a ceiling grid this is simple and easy: "Off and Flying," "Take-off-Time," "What a Way to Go," and "Away We Go." These displays don't require a single piece of merchandise.

The promotion could consist of a fabric panel with "the word" lettered on it, or it could be a collection of Crayola-colored felt triangles, like at the football games, only here the team is SALE and the winner is the customer. Confetti streamers and balloons wouldn't hurt the rah-rah look.

It is a pun and puns can be amusing, so how about a play of "sale" with "sail." "We're off and Sale-ing," "Sale along with us." If the nautical theme is appealing, cut out sails of foamcore or white muslin with lath strips to hold them in the "breeze." Maybe a rotating fan, just out of view will get the fabric to billow in the artificially induced breeze. Make the sailboat or borrow one of those light and colorful ones the teenagers take to the waves with from a local sports supply store in the neighborhood. Models of sailboats will also work.

Make it a "SALE-abration" with balloons (stenciled or screened), along with confetti and streamers. Fireworks will make it a SALE-A-POPPIN and all that it takes is lengths of red-covered cardboard tubes of varying dimensions with white cotton rope "wicks" sticking out of the tops. With all that pop, crackle, and sparkle it could be the Fourth of July, and that's a great time for a sale. Make it red, white and blue, add stars and stripes, and

Figure 19.8 Going! Going! Gone!! The fashion closet is being "outed" and so are the names of the designers and top brand names whose wares are on sale. The empty hangers are covered only with designer names and they hang on the rod in the open armoire and from the overhead grid, and lie scattered on the floor along with pictures of the "outed" designers. A fun display targeted directly at the store's clientele who know all about "being outed". *Barneys, Madison Avenue, New York.*

Figure 19.9 Bendels waves its signature colors proudly—the brown and the white—to herald their sale. The dress forms are lined up across the front window and each is monogrammed with a single letter that when read together explains where all the merchandise has gone. *H-Bendel, Fifth Avenue, New York.*

blast off with pizzazz. Make it a SELL-abration or a SELL-sation: "Three-Ring Excitement," and "Season Blast-Off." Keep the excitement going inside the store with helium-filled balloons and confetti-strewn cases and counters. Wrap columns and up-front platform presentations with streamers and let the forms or dressed mannequins "hold" the balloons. Columns could be wrapped in red seamless paper and turned into giant Roman candles or firecrackers.

Magic

How about a **magic** theme: "Watch Them Disappear," "Nothing Up Our Sleeves—Nothing Under Our Hats— Everything Goes," "The New Cut-in-Half Trick." All it takes are black top hats (from the novelty supply house), giant-size playing cards (made of foamcore and appliquéd with cut-out diamonds, hearts, and spades), over-scaled price tickets cut or "sawed" in half, long strings of colored silk squares and, maybe, some trick mirrors. Dress one mannequin as a magician in a top hat, white tie, and tails and another mannequin as the sequined, scantily clad assistant, or use a cardboard cutout for either one, and let the cards fly with the overhead grid and invisible wire to do the trick: "It's the have-to-see-it-to-believe-it-sale," "Now you see it—tomorrow you won't," "Watch Things Disappear."

A giant 4-foot round crystal ball, drawn caricaturestyle on white foamcore, with the word S-A-L-E appearing upside down in the ball suggests "There's a Sale In Your Future" or "The Future Is Now." For extra sparkle, pull out

Figure 19.11 The bold red and white panels that partially block the open-back window are quite emphatic. Nothing subtle—they just spell it out. The red and white shopping bags complete the graphic concept and reiterate "The Sale" message over and over again. *Express, The Fashion Show Mall, Las Vegas.*

Figure 19.10 How obvious do you have to be? The red and white striped curtain offers a hint but the red paint-dipped paint brushes dangling from above, and the cans of red paint on the white drop cloth covered floor indicate that this is a "red letter event." The refined script banner across the white dress form politely delivers the message. *H-Bendel, Fifth Avenue, New York.*

Figure 19.12 *(right)* Cleaning up or clearing out. It is all the same when it is a sale promotion. The utter havoc and "destruction" in the window—completely devoid of merchandise—tells the shopper that there is an upheaval in the store. With the signature shopping bags filled with poufs of tissue it must mean "SALE." Could it be anything else? *H-Bendel, Fifth Avenue, New York.*

the Christmas tree bee lights and swing them across the display area or use them to outline the window frame.

Cleaning Up

A "Clearance Sale" can be fun even when it is painful for the retailer: "The Great Giveaway," "The Big Sweep," "A Clean Sweep," "Making Way For Tomorrow," "Clean Up At Our Sale"; and all that is needed are these easy-to-procure "props" that are probably tucked away somewhere in the store or at home in a closet or in another local shop. It takes vacuum cleaners or electric sweepers working their way across a path of lay-down garments with long electric cords snaking along behind. Mannequins can be working with brooms, mops, pails,

dustpans, and shovels, "cleaning up" the way to the sale. Or, without mannequins, tissue-stuffed work gloves can be wrapped around the broom, and mop sticks can "sweep away" thanks to the invisible wires that hold them suspended in mid-air. The invisible sweepers and moppers can be great attention-getters. Whatever the technique used by the display person, the garments must look fresh and desirable and not like rejects from a rummage sale.

Creating a display for a sale event should be done with style, taste, imagination, and humor. There must always be the respect for the shopper and for the merchandise being offered. If the retailer doesn't think much of the merchandise, why should the shopper? Even if a sale hurts, put a smile in the display; it works wonders for the display and for business.

Sale Ideas: A Recap

- A sale represents a cycle in retail life that is used to clear the shelves and hang-rods when a season is over in order to make room for new merchandise.

- A store's image can be maintained during a sale by presenting the merchandise with the same kind of taste, discretion, and dignity that the store traditionally presents.

- Mannequins can be adapted to fit certain types of sales. For example, an "Everything Must Go" sale can use mannequins representing Adam and/or Eve stripped to the bare essentials.

- Displays can be done graphically without using merchandise, by using simple signs or props.

Questions for Review and Discussion

1. How can an upscale store aggressively promote a sale without damaging its reputation?

2. What is the effect of continual promotion of sale events on a store?

3. Suggest creative themes and display ideas for the following types of sale events:
   a. a white sale
   b. an end-of-season clearance sale
   c. a Mother's Day sale
   d. an anniversary sale

4. Collect sale flyers and newspaper ads promoting sales for local department and specialty stores. Suggest ways that the stores could carry through with their sale themes using the store window and interior displays.

Chapter Twenty

Fashion Accessories

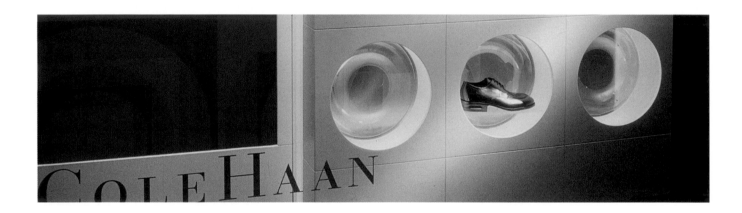

AFTER YOU HAVE READ THIS CHAPTER,
YOU WILL BE ABLE TO DISCUSS:

- The importance of accessorizing in fashion displays.
- Effective props for displaying accessories.
- Display techniques used in jewelry presentations.
- The importance of lighting in accessory display.

FASHION ACCESSORIES: TRADE TALK

    courtesy or credit sign

    props

    struck mannequin

ashion accessories are the little things that mean a lot. They complete an outfit. They add color where there was no color. They provide the panache and daring that can turn a simple "nothing" dress or suit into a stylish outfit. The right accessories can update a dress or revitalize a suit and add sparkle to last year's outfit with the shimmer and shine that appears in this month's *Harper's Bazaar* or *Vogue*. The fashion accessories—the shoes, bag, gloves, belt, hat, and the costume or fine jewelry—are the exclamation point of a fashion statement!

The best way to show fashion accessories is as part of a look—part of a total costume. Symbiotically it helps the dress or suit as much as being shown with a dress or suit helps the accessory by providing a background or setting for those accessories; it creates a sense of time, place, occasion—and a look. The difference between a dress or suit carefully fitted on a form and the display of that same garment accessorized with a scarf, "in" jewelry, and a bag slung over the shoulder along with the right style and color of shoes is the difference between "just a dress or suit" and a "total outfit." What was merely a garment on a three-dimensional form is magically transformed into a display, an idealized presentation of what the garment can be and look like when properly accessorized.

If the shop or store doesn't sell or stock shoes, hats, bags, and the other accents, the store owner, visual merchandiser, or display person should take advantage of the shops and stores that do specialize in those classifications of merchandise. They should reach out to local shoe salons, millinery and fashion accessory shops, and "borrow" the desired pieces in exchange for a **courtesy or credit sign** in the display setup. The courtesy sign will credit the store or stores who provided the "borrowed" pieces. This way the shopper knows where she can go to complete her outfit. Of course, some stores that use mannequins will have a wardrobe of classic "pumps"—good for any occasion—in navy, black, brown, and cream. The more stylish and trendier stores will arrange to get the right shoe that not only covers the mannequin's feet, but also adds to the totality of the outfit and the look. All it

takes is time and planning; it takes making amicable "deals" with neighbors that can be mutually beneficial. That is the really important point; it does as much for the scarf, bag, or hat to be shown with the suit as it does for the suit to be fully and properly accessorized. What could make the "borrowing" even more agreeable and even more successful for all parties is if the dress or suit retailer could occasionally provide an outfit on a form or mannequin to the fashion accessory shop to feature in its display window. For the ready-to-wear store, it is an extra exposure for the merchandise in an unexpected setting where the suit/dress becomes the star attraction and attention-getter and the courtesy card in the corner of the window advertises where the garment can be obtained.

Let us continue with the specialty store or department store that not only sells ready-to-wear, but also has a stock of up-to-the-minute fashion accessories. In addition to accessorizing the mannequin or form, the display person/visual merchandiser can add a secondary arrangement of fashion accessories into the display area. It can be an additional bag, gloves, and costume jewelry. The display person/visual merchandiser may even use a bottle of cologne or perfume in a small still-life arrangement set out on a casually (but artistically) draped scarf at the foot of the mannequin (or form) that is already accessorized. The grouping on the floor can—for greater effectiveness—be raised onto a low table or pedestal, onto a transparent cube or cylinder, a classic capital or a piece of a column, a log or tree stump if the merchandise and the season and the texture are all right, a mound of moss, a pile of flower pots in either the natural terra-cotta or painted to blend in or complement the assemblage, a "rock," a construction of bricks or glass blocks, a low piece of furniture. The possibilities are endless. Not only can the elevation step the merchandise up off the floor and bring the merchandise closer to the viewer's eye level, it can also add a seasonal touch to the whole display setup or promote the image of the material or even complement the color and texture of what is being offered.

In men's wear displays, and in some cases with women's wear—especially pant outfits—a complete suit or outfit

Figure 20.1 It is all about shoes! This display is like a "Where's Waldo?" picture in which the shopper is invited to join the ladies in a game of finding the shoes hidden in the design. The small, very special shoes need the large scale of the figures to hold the small objects together—and to bring the shopper closer to the glass. *Stuart Weitzman, Madison Avenue, New York.*

can be rigged on a suit or dress form or even off a hanger. The display person can create the illusion of a total figure—headless—with just a form, a rod, and a base. An auxiliary setup of fashion accessories, including shoes, can then be neatly arranged in a lay-down or build-up next to the base on the floor. A good visual presenter will then be sure to highlight the floor composition as well as "chest light" the suit, shirt, tie, and so on. Where drapers or hangers are used, the trousers may hang off or over the slack bar and reach down almost to the floor of the

display area where the shoes and other accessories can be clustered. The viewer's eye will travel from the jacket, shirt, and tie down the length of the draped trousers to the accessory grouping on the floor.

In England and some other parts of Europe, mannequins are usually equipped with foot spikes rather than butt or leg rods—or *struck* with taut wires and no rod or base at all. The spike rod goes up through the sole of the mannequin's foot into the leg cavity and thus holds the figure erect. A **struck mannequin** conversely is wired into a standing position by means of invisible wires attached to the figure, then is pulled taut and nailed into the floor of the display. It is not unusual, therefore, in Europe to see a beautifully accessorized, realistic mannequin—wearing hat, bag, gloves, scarf, jewelry, and so on—standing shoeless in the window, since display persons aren't willing or able to drill holes through the shoes, which could then be put on the mannequin. The right and fashionable shoes are often shown standing on the floor next to the dressed figure. Since it happens so frequently, it is only surprising to people who have been brought up on mannequins with butt rods or those that are struck in the window or on the ledge.

Some mannequin manufacturers who do produce figures with spiked bases do make plastic shoes with predrilled holes available as a mannequin accessory. Usually they are classic pumps in traditional colors not necessarily on the cutting edge of the fashion season. Other manufacturers will sculpt the pumps right onto the mannequin's feet and they will often be sprayed the body color of the mannequin. These shoes have heels and the suggestion of a design but disappear in the total presentation. When the specialty shop has the right shoes in stock, they will be set down next to the sculpted ones.

As previously mentioned, it is important to light the auxiliary accessory group in a display whether it is on the floor, on a chair, on a table, or arranged within empty picture frames as a still-life composition. The display person will usually light up the chest area of a dressed figure and the aura of light will take in any neck, lapel jewelry or earrings, shirts/blouses, and scarves/ties.

Let us turn now to the store or shop that specializes in fashion accessories without the ready-to-wear. One of the major problems faced by these retailers is that the products are usually small and often there are many styles, variations, and colors to show. Most products look best at eye-level—at 3 to 5 feet above the ground level. Elevations are effective in raising the products and putting them together into lifestyle clusters or compositions.

A raked or ramped floor (see Chapter 7) is an excellent device for raising the product off the ground. The inclined level of the raked floor puts the rear of the space at a higher level than the space up front near the glass. The viewer on the street can see more comfortably the

Figure 20.2 The simulated open "wardrobe" in the window has garments hanging on the rod and also shows off to excellent advantage the collection of designer accessories that include shoes, bags, and scarves. *Ferragamo, Fifth Avenue, New York.*

pieces displayed in the back. Finally, window masking (see Chapter 18) may be another excellent way of focusing on small pieces. A traditional show window may begin about 2 feet off the ground and the glass opening can be about 10 feet tall by 10 to 12 feet wide. That is just too much window—too wide, too tall, and too deep to really show off items such as shoes, bags, gloves, jewelry, and so forth. The large window can be divided into two or three smaller windows with a frame or proscenium and with the floor of the new windows raised up and the ceiling dropped. This way the new windows are more than shadow-box windows but also much less than a tradi-

Figure 20.3 The "accent" is on accessories and the fully dressed and accessorized, stylized mannequin proves the point. In this display the color turquoise is featured and the variety of turquoise tinted scarves, bags, costume jewelry, and other accessories are set out for the street shopper's approval. *Lord & Taylor, Fifth Avenue, New York.*

tional show window more suited to ready-to-wear. By dividing the space with masks into smaller windows, it is now possible to cluster and group individual color stories or fashion looks that in one larger window would conflict with each other. The large window would probably not do justice to any of the accessories. It is now possible to use the smaller areas and create either a totally red or blue and white display or a casual or formal display. Each will be separated by a frame or proscenium.

When working with small items, in order to get the desired viewer's or shopper's attention, it is often effective to resort to contrast and scale (see Chapter 3). An array of white shoes shown against a black, dark gray, or deep green setting will "pop" and be easily seen. Diamonds are brilliant and more intense in sparkling color when viewed against a deep, dark matte surface like velvet, faille, or even a wool crepe.

Importance of Props to Display Fashion Accessories

Props are the decorative elements in a display that add image and enhance the illusion of time and place and the appropriateness of merchandise to setting. They can and do get the shopper to stop and look at the display and at

the merchandise being offered. In a display of fashion accessories, the prop can, by its size and scale, serve to unify the assorted smaller pieces into a total, comprehensive composition. The prop, therefore, not only serves to attract the shopper; it is the presence and force that "holds" the various elements together in an easy-to-see, easy-to-comprehend manner. In Chapter 15, Furniture as Props, we discussed just how a chair, a table, a chest of drawers, an armoire, a piece of luggage, or a trunk can hold the assemblage of accessories and coordinates while also elevating them off the floor to a better height for viewing from out in the street or in the mall. But there are also many other everyday items that can serve the same purpose. A good example is a folding stepladder, where each step presents another group or cluster—a scarf can trail and drape down several steps with gloves and a bag on one step, shoes a step below with maybe a hat or jewelry, and a flower or bottle of cologne a step above. A 5-foot folding wood ladder left natural for fall or painted white for summer or resort, pastel tones for spring, and maybe glittery gold for Christmas can fill up the main space of a window and contain a variety of small merchandise. It also helps to elevate the fashion accessories. For a larger display, a pair of folding ladders can be used—maybe of different heights for interest—and planks of wood or

Figure 20.4 While the abstract mannequin turns to study the beautifully hung, pinned and draped outfits on the wall panels, the assortment of accessories and coordinates are arranged on floating shelves on the center panel. Another choice of accessories and coordinates are presented on the raised platform along with a different outfit on a suit form with an egg head attached. *Max Mara, Como, Italy.*

There is nothing wrong with the soft, limp drape of gloves casually displayed over a bag or in a lay-down arrangement, but sometimes a little "animation" is called for, a little humanizing. The glove can be holding a piece of jewelry or the end of a draped scarf. It can be gripping a shoulder strap or clutching some foliage. All it takes is time and imagination.

Strips of tissue can be rolled into pencil-thin shapes and inserted into the individual fingers of the glove. For a little more control, the tissue can be wrapped around a piece of bendable wire or even some pipe-cleaners. There are hand forms available on the market but the really good ones with the articulated and bendable fingers are quite expensive while the other ones may be "lifeless," or difficult to pull the gloves over. The rigid hand form may also stretch or distort a fragile glove and affect its possible sale when it is removed from the form and returned to the selling floor.

Jewelry

If the jewelry sparkles and shimmers—if it has a metallic glint—it is best shown against a flat, matte surface like velvet, felt, or jersey. Usually dark, deep, and rich colors are best for showing off the sparkling pieces.

Pearls, however, will be enhanced by being shown against warm peach or pinkish fabrics. Avoid using fabrics in yellows or cream colors since these colors may make the pearls look yellowish and dingy rather than lustrous. If you want to show jewelry on a head or form, use an abstract head or one that has been painted a single, deep matte color. Don't make the jewelry compete against skin tones and makeup colors. There are forms available covered in jersey or flocked in a velvet-like finish that work very well. You could try pulling an opaque stocking over a head and then twisting the toe part into a decorative topknot. With this technique, you can change the color by changing the color of the opaque stocking. If you are using tights you will have to be extra clever in converting the other leg of the hosiery into a chignon or braid or hair-roll.

Some presentation people prefer to "locate" the pieces on body forms—showing where they can be worn. Personally, I am not particularly fond of seeing bits and pieces of human anatomy used as display props, such as arms, a dismembered hand, or an ear. I prefer to see more

Figure 20.5 Think pink! Shoppers are invited to inspect—up close in the shadow box window—the selection of pink fashion accessories arranged like a dimensional "still life." A painted modern art canvas—in shades and tints of pink—adds to the arty look of the display. *Lord & Taylor, Fifth Avenue, New York.*

glass shelves can be stretched between them, supported by the steps, to show off a greater array of accessories in appropriate groupings.

Gloves and Bags

Just as handbags are usually comfortably padded with tissues to fill out the hollow interior and show off the bag at its best, so can gloves be enhanced with some "stuffing."

Figure 20.6 Scale + Humor = An attention-getting display for small fashion accessories. In this oversized window the gigantic red ribbon "wig" centers and anchors the different wig heads arranged on pedestals of assorted heights. These heads feature some of the myriad hair accessories being offered. *H-Bendel, Fifth Avenue, New York.*

abstract or sculptural forms used—something not quite so realistic. There are also jewelry pads and bibs that are marketed that can be used to show off pieces of jewelry.

Draped fabrics can be used to "simulate" a jacket or dress for a pin or brooch to be pinned onto or even to lay a necklace on. Bracelets can be shown over gloves that are flat or stuffed and rings can be displayed over a glove with tissue-stuffed fingers. Velvet or fine kid gloves are especially good for the presentation of diamonds and other sparkling stones.

Fine pieces of jewelry or very expensive pieces of costume jewelry can be given a "Tiffany" treatment. The pieces can be "dropped" into a shadow-box setting along

with an attention-getting prop like a piece of sculpture, a vase, a piece of quartz, a small painting, a collection of rare leather-bound books—or with any prop that says "unique," "one-of-a-kind." By limiting the display space and accentuating the featured piece of jewelry in a beam of light and by using subtle illumination of the prop and the background, the jewelry stands out. The piece can be draped over the books, sit atop a ridge of quartz, be displayed casually in front of the sculpture, or even be immersed inside a clear crystal vase (supported by invisible wires). However you do it, the viewer will see it and appreciate the class statement. A one-of-a-kind display usually means "expensive."

Silver and pewter jewelry can be treated more casually. They can be displayed against coarser-textured fabrics like tweeds, burlap, wools, and linens. They can be laid out on floors covered with sand, pebbles, bricks, pavement tiles, or beautiful polished black stones. With the Southwest look so popular and with Native American jewelry always in demand, why not show silver and silver and turquoise jewelry on sand "dunes" accented with cactus plants—real or artificial. Real cactus needs so little watering or watching, you can use the real thing. Native American artifacts like bowls, baskets, and woven blankets can also add to the ambience while underscoring the authenticity of the jewelry. The props can also be used as elevations and as a means of separating clusters of material into easier-to-see-and-understand groupings.

Lighting in a Jewelry Display

Lighting is of the utmost importance in the presentation of jewelry. Cold fluorescent lamps may be fine for blue-white diamonds but they can be awful for gold settings and other colored stones. It certainly does not flatter skin tones when the diamond is tried on. Today, the small tensor lights—the sharp, brilliant MR16 lamps—have an excellent color rendition and are ideal for jewelry displays. The narrow beams of light can be focused on the piece or pieces being featured and add fire to the brilliance of the stones and the setting. MR16 lamps can be used in shadow-box displays, in regular windows (maybe extended down on pipes), or in museum cases on the floor. They are small, available in various housings, and can be easily adapted to the showing of jewelry.

Figure 20.7 The boldly patterned, striped, and dotted background in Bendel's store colors is counteracted by the floating shelf up near the glass. It crosses the long window and presents, at eye level, an assortment of toiletries/cosmetics to shoppers on the street. The striped brown and white packages of store brand toiletries appear throughout the space along with polka dotted ones. *H-Bendel, Fifth Avenue, New York.*

Figure 20.8 *(left)* The foam core panel has been patterned with assorted cut-out square and rectangular openings. A lime green panel with another pattern of cutouts backs the one up front. A variety of shoes and bags are attached or bracketed off the white front panel so that each object can be viewed within its own opening. *Ferragamo, Fifth Avenue, New York.*

Figure 20.9 *(right)* The panel of cut-out circles capped with half-round plastic domes steps forward from the red "op art" panel that also carries the store name. Some of the new men's shoes appear—under glass—in the central domes. *Cole Haan, Madison Avenue, New York.*

Figure 20.10 The spindly ballroom chairs with red seat pads—to match the partial diving wall—raise up the coordinated clusters of accessories to the shopper's eye level. The chairs also organize the assorted leather products into color stories. *Coach, Fifth Avenue, New York.*

Figure 20.11 The ties are draped over one of the suit form's "arms." The other "arm" leads to the umbrella that is angled and directs the viewer to the assortment of accessories and coordinates artfully arranged on the textured floor pad. Another painting, on the floor, carries through the art theme. *Aston & Gunn, Hamilton, Bermuda.*

Figure 20.12 Outdoor dining. The à la carte menu is serving up leather accessories in this vignette bistro setting. The striped awning and topiary trees set the scene and the accessories are raised into prominence on the wire frame chairs and table. *Cole Haan, Fifth Avenue, New York.*

Figure 20.13 Though the emphasis is on "SUIT POWER" and the dressed hangers suspended mid-window, it is the dynamic pattern created by the ties and shoes that really capture the shopper's eye. The repetition of ties applied to the three walls and suspended throughout the window as well as the lines of ties and shoes on the floor make this display memorable. *Barneys, Madison Avenue, New York.*

Fashion Accessories: A Recap

Fashion accessories are best shown in use—as part of a costume. Fashion accessories should be shown together in coordinated groupings either in a lay-down next to the costumed form or figure or raised up on a platform, elevation, piece of furniture, and such. When fashion accessories are presented without outfits try to:

- Reduce the window glass by masking into a smaller opening or into a series of shadow boxes.

- Raise the floor level or use a ramp or raked floor.

- Bring the merchandise up closer to the viewer's eye level.

- Use props to unify small objects or to bring attention to the small piece shown in a large space. Props can hold, elevate, show off, contrast, complement, or even suggest the value and prestige of the pieces being offered.

- Use the right lighting and put the strongest light on the merchandise while downplaying the ambient light. Colored lights can be used to "paint" the background and also enhance the merchandise.

Questions for Review and Discussion

1. What are the key functions of fashion accessories?

2. If the store does not stock accessory items, what is the best way to obtain such items for displays?

3. Describe fashion accessory displays you could create around each of the following key props:

    a. an empty wooden picture frame
    b. a beach chair and umbrella
    c. artificial ice cubes

4. How can large window displays be made smaller so as not to diminish small accessory items on display?

5. Explain the importance of contrast in the display of accessories.

6. What tips and pointers would you give to an individual creating his or her first accessory display?

CHAPTER TWENTY-ONE

Home Fashions, Hard Goods, and Food Displays

AFTER YOU HAVE READ THIS CHAPTER,
YOU WILL BE ABLE TO DISCUSS:

- Effective methods for home fashions display.
- The importance of creating lifestyle situations in hard goods presentation.
- Techniques used in food displays.

HOME FASHIONS, HARD GOODS, AND FOOD DISPLAYS:
TRADE TALK

color or color and pattern story
lifestyle presentations
lifestyle situations
mixing and matching
natural
terra-cotta
tone
vignette settings

isplay persons and visual merchandisers working with home fashions, hard goods, and foods can use many of same the techniques that are used in fashion display. It is important to approach this type of display keeping in mind that the buyer of fashion items and of home goods is the same person. An effective method for home fashions displays is the creation of vignette settings that unify assorted elements into a theme. Linens and accessories can be mixed and matched, and can be the focal point of a display or accoutrements for other home fashions. When working with hard goods, whether they are large or small items, it is important to create lifestyle situations for the products. This can be done through the use of props that will grab the attention of the shopper and eventual user.

Food displays need skillful lighting. Produce should be presented to convey a message of natural and country fresh and look as if bathed in sunlight. The clientele must always be considered, however. A more sophisticated rather than rustic look may be desired with upscale customers. Depending on the target market, the displayer can set the look and tone by selectively using certain accessories. In either case, a food display will benefit from presenting the goods in a way that allows shoppers to envision their use.

Home Fashions

The very name "Home Fashions" turns ordinary sheets, pillowcases, quilts, lamps, and throw pillows into a product line that calls for fashion-oriented windows. Here we have the numerous items that can be used to give a distinct personality to a home; products that definitely need **lifestyle presentations.** They call for displays that bring assorted materials together into a single theme, and that theme usually fits a particular lifestyle.

Color and pattern are most important here. No matter if the products can be used in the living room, den, bedroom, bath, or kitchen, they can all be pulled together in a **color or color and pattern story.** The strength of the display of these assorted products depends upon the overall color story that reaches out beyond the glass. With many designers and brand name national labels like Ralph Lauren Polo, Calvin Klein,

Figure 21.1 Butterflies are the theme that tie together the assorted linens and bed/bath/kitchen accessories. A butterfly patterned sheet is clothespinned onto a common clothesline that swings across the back of the window, and more pieces are pinned onto another line just in front of it. A wrought iron garden chair serves as an elevation and a draper while the wicker basket adds yet another out-of-doors touch. The flowers tie in with the garden setting and play up the color palette of white, soft green, and peach. *Park Smith, Fifth Avenue, New York.*

Figure 21.2 *(left)* In its open-back window, Crate & Barrel assembles a variety of products from departments throughout the store, and with an assist from a chair and a bed frame, show off an array of color coordinated home fashions in fabric, glass, and metal. The analogous color scheme of yellow, orange, and lime green keep it all together. The fabric panels in the background cut off some of the store activity beyond but also reiterate the color scheme. *Crate & Barrel, Madison Avenue, New York.*

Figure 21.3 You have to know your customer! This sort of risqué, humorous approach for the display of bed linens is right on target for this store's smart and sophisticated shoppers. The cartoon drawings work effectively in creating the "room" and also add to the light-hearted appeal. For some stores and their clients this could be considered "X-rated"! *Bloomingdale's, Lexington Avenue, New York.*

Figure 21.4 The elegant furniture sets the look for the gift items set out in this window. The garden theme is carried out with foliage and vines draped and twisted over the period pieces and layered on the shelves upon which the gifts are displayed. Crumbled cork chips and upturned and out-turned fern plants and terra-cotta pots add to the sophisticated "fantasy" look of the window. *Bergdorf Goodman, Fifth Avenue, New York.*

Eddie Bauer, and others extending out beyond their clothing lines into home furnishings, linens are definitely "fashionable" and can be presented in clever, amusing, and unexpected ways. We are long past the time when linens were white and were stacked in neat piles, tied with ribbons and thus displayed. There is so much more color today, many more patterns, and lots and lots of **mixing and matching** of bed and bath linens and the go-with accessories. Here, again, simple **vignette settings** can set the scene with back panels, or draperies or even shower curtains serving as backgrounds and to accentuate the color/pattern arrangement up front.

Propping can add to the lifestyle setting as well as serve as risers or elevations for some of the smaller ob-

jects being offered. As mentioned in Chapter 15, Furniture as Props, the use of tables, chairs, chests, armoires, outdoor furniture, bedsteads, etc. can all help to affect a vignette setting for a particular lifestyle and the clientele or target market for that look. They also provide a variety of levels in the display to showcase the assorted clusters of products. As previously mentioned and as restated here, the display person must, usually because of budget restraints, learn to "beg, borrow, and credit" the props they want to use. Tie-in with neighboring retailers in the mall or on the street who are non-competitive—who do not sell what you sell. Develop a system where they lend you some of their stock for use in your window display; and in exchange you place in the window a card

Figure 21.5 Cut-out foam core figures dominate in this eye-catching window display. Most people respond to cartoons and caricatures and are curious enough to read the words that appear in the floating balloons. The artwork tablecloth covers the riser that brings the assorted crystal wine glasses up closer to the viewer's eye. *Gumps, San Francisco. Robert Mahoney.*

that credits the lender of these "props." It serves them—the neighbors—by giving their merchandise window exposure in a different location. Their merchandise will be shown in a different way and used in a way they never could have.

Since many of the products are often soft, drape-able, and textile in nature, the display person should approach the display with the same attitude and make use of the

same attention-getting devices suggested in Chapter 16. The non-textile items are "fashion accessories" of the home rather than an outfit, and should be layered into the composition in the same way one would add fashion accessories, only here they are part of a room or a place. The accompanying illustrations should help, and if the reader will go back and scan some of the other illustrations, he or she will see how it has been done, and see how fashion accessories can be adapted to home fashions and the particular market.

Hard Goods

Some people feel that the presentation of fashion is all glamour and fun because that is where the display per-

Figure 21.6 Bridal gifts are arranged on a series of levels in this white-on-white display. The crystal draped black branches tie this window into a series of vignettes that make up "The Book of Love." Each shelf or bracket holds a cluster of related items. *Marshall Field, State Street, Chicago.*

Figure 21.7 If a flickering or picture-filled TV set wasn't enough to bring curious shoppers closer to the window, the bright colors would. The two unusually colored kids add a human touch and a sense of scale to the assorted small Sony products in the window. The multi-colored gumdrop couch acts as an elevation for the small pieces. *Sony, Madison Avenue, New York.*

Figure 21.9   Repetition works! The hand-held electric Mix Masters are lined up like soldiers—in echelon—in this oversized shadow box. The graphic on the back wall and the over-scaled "beaters" suspended in front of it serve to draw—and explain—what this amusing set up is all about. The lighting is bright and right on target. *Macy's, West 34th Street, New York.*

Figure 21.8   Swimming in between the shimmering strings of CDs that act as the "air bubbles" in this sunny underwater display are the yellow, bat-like fishes that support an array of small Sony products. Swimming at different levels, they bring the products up closer to the viewer's eye level. More Sony products are displayed on the yellow floor and the contrast of the black against the yellow is remarkable. *Sony, Madison Avenue, New York.*

son can really take off and be different, unique, and do strange and wonderful things. Some of these people look at the prospect of displaying "Hard Goods"—non-fashion products—as dull and boring. Refrigerators, vacuum cleaners, auto parts, TVs, cell phones, and all sorts of small, hand-held electronic devices aren't "fun." Yet, as you may have noticed looking through this book, many of these "boring" and "dull" everyday objects have been used by talented visual merchandisers to add life and excitement to their fashion presentations. It is important to note that although there is a difference between a casual

sports outfit and an upright vacuum cleaner, it is the same shopper who buys both. The approach to the display of hard goods is therefore to treat them the same way you would a fashion product: humanize it and dramatize it—add color and texture—and use whatever display techniques you would use with clothes to attract the shopper and get him or her interested in the product.

Create Lifestyle Situations

Big, bulky appliances, and small hand-held electronic and digital devices need the same thing in a display; they need to be humanized. They need to be shown in relation to the eventual user by creating **lifestyle situations.** Scale is important! While large units can often stand on their own, smaller units need to have something dominant in the display composition—some focal element— that will catch the viewer's eye and bring him or her closer to where the smaller items can be more readily seen. In the case of hand-held and small products, they also need to be brought up as close to eye-level as possible, which means the use of risers, pedestals, or props that will elevate them off the floor. The dominant element can be a mannequin shown "using" the product or an enlarged lifestyle photograph showing the small unit in a gigantic, overblown size, or in use. If possible, an over-scaled model of the product, either dimensional, or even rendered in black and white as a line drawing on foam core, cut out and suspended in space, will work. The important thing to remember is the targeted shopper and his or her interest. Who is the shopper? What is the shopper looking for? How can this product be presented so that it appears to enrich or enhance the shopper's life—and lifestyle? So, we are back to lifestyle.

Small Items

Create everyday situations in the display space. Humor usually works best, even when the product is expensive. If the products are small or hand-held, like electric shavers, cell phones, iPods, etc., try turning them into "people" by adding "arms" and "legs" made out of thick chenille pipe cleaners or wire, or even use cut out figures, à la Keith Haring drawings, where the "head" or the "body" is the actual unit applied directly over the sketch. Have these make-believe people doing activities such as the eventual shopper may be involved in: working at the office, cooking at home, jogging in the park, etc. To make these "scenes" work, try masking the display window into a shadow box (see Chapter 18) and raise the floor of the shadow box up closer to eye-level. The little bendable, wooden artist's manikins that artists use to get the look of a body in motion are readily available in art supply shops and are not only inexpensive—they can always be used in interior cases as well. Have these "Lilliputian" mini-people carrying on everyday activities as they carry these hand-held products. The settings for these little people can be furnished and propped with materials found in dollhouse supply catalogs. This will add another light touch as well. If the reader goes back to Chapter 20, Fashion Accessories, he or she will find many suggestions that are applicable here.

Large Items

For the larger and often bulkier units, try to set them into lifestyle settings as well. Vignettes will do. You don't need to create the whole kitchen or the entire outdoors when a suggestion will do. A piece of picket fence, a grass mat for the floor pad, and maybe some flower heads and a watering hose will certainly do to create a backyard setting for barbeque equipment or outdoor furniture. Of course, it could be more attention-getting with some humanizing details, like adding a life size figure to the composition. If it isn't possible to "borrow" a casually dressed

Figure 21.10 Individually the knobs, handles, faucets, and other decorative pieces of hardware would be lost in a window of this size. Anne Kong has created a decorative flower stand, and on the shelves, raised up from the green grass mat covered floor, she has cleverly turned the hardware into bouquets of flowers. They are combined with silk foliage to complete the illusion. The store's china waste baskets become the flower holders and the yellow and blue printed fabric that cover the steps are made up into a variety of bathroom accessories also available in the store. *Sherle Wagner, East 57th Street, New York.*

mannequin from a neighboring retailer, a cut-out foam core figure can probably work as well—or even better—depending upon the target market. If the window is too large, try masking the glass with foliage drawn as a frame around the window or set cut-out foliage drawings against the front glass. Maybe hang a line of "wash" across the back, if the window is open-back, and write the "message" on the "wash." Add some atmosphere like children's toys, lounge chairs, a doghouse—whatever you can "borrow" from local suppliers of outdoor furnishings in exchange for a "credit" card in the window.

Treat the object itself as part of the lifestyle. Make it seem "human," or turn it into an object of "awe and wonderment." Imagine an artist with a paint palette and canvas-covered easel painting the portrait of a refrigerator set up on a platform with drapery behind it. Add a "kid's" drawing of the Mona Lisa to the door—for extra interest. Open the refrigerator door and fill it with unexpected objects like baubles, bangles, beads, and lots of "bling" (shiny sparkling stuff)—"rocks" overflowing the ice cube trays on the shelves.

Using foam core panels, cut them so that they fit around the appliance or large unit and thus create an all-in-one setting with the product. Use colors to bring out the color or lack of color of the product, draw a suggested room or place setting on the panels, but don't be too realistic or rational. Be flighty, have fun, be a little over the top if it will work with the store's image and the customer's lifestyle.

Play with words or sayings to get eye-catching displays: "Play it Cool," "Baby! It's colder inside," "Easy Living," "The Easy Life," "This is Living!"

Food Displays

People have always been interested in food and how food looked, but lately, food presentation—raw or cooked, fresh or frozen, right out of the garden or off the chef's

Figure 21.11 Greeting the shopper is this array of fresh fruits and vegetables presented in a variety of baskets, bushels, barrels, and burlap bags. They all reinforce the "fresh-from-the-farm" theme. The crusty breads, in their own baskets, add yet another color and texture to the already color-filled opening statement. *Dean & DeLuca, Prince Street, New York.*

Figure 21.12 Lighting is very important and to prove the point, Amerlux—a major lighting distributor—showed visitors at a trade show what a difference the right sort of lighting can have on an assortment of fruits that ran the color spectrum from yellow, orange, and red to green and purple. *Amerlux, New Jersey.*

stove—has become a profession. Food magazine spreads, TV commercials, cooking programs, in-store displays, and demonstrations all require the visual merchandiser's know-how, talent, and imagination. Whether the food is in the supermarket or in a gourmet food shop, on a roadside stand or in a specialty shop, being set up for photography or viewing by a TV audience, it is not enough to just show the food; it must be visually merchandised—and presented!

Fresh Produce
The imagery usually associated with the display of fruits and vegetables is of "country fresh," "just picked," "from

the farm." It is **natural** and of the country; it is farmer's markets, roadside stands, orchards, and gardens. It is about color and texture, and it is mainly about light. Ideally, it is sunlight. Fruits and vegetables glow under warm yellow light so avoid, if at all possible, cool fluorescent lamps. Incandescents are fine as are some of the super warm fluorescents, but the MR16 tungsten lamps are better still in the rendition of crisp greens to rich reds and purples.

Like in merchandising clothing it does make a difference which colors are presented next to each other. Sometimes an analogous theme will work with lemons next to limes that are next to oranges and red apples. However, to make fresh produce—and foods—appear richer and fresher, it helps to complement the products with colors and textures. The rougher-skinned ones make the smooth-skinned ones seem more velvety by comparison. Green leaves or green foliage used to frame or highlight red apples, purple grapes, and any of the warm-colored produce will help them look richer and redder.

To reinforce the "country fresh" or "just picked" concept try to accessorize the produce with coarse linen or heavy checkered cotton napkins, burlap bags, baskets of natural wicker or rattan, raw wood baskets, bushels and barrels. Twigs, branches, raffia, and straw all work to promote the outdoor, country-fresh look. Arrange fruits and vegetables in the assorted baskets and bushels lined with provincial printed napkins of complementary colors and set them out on tiered, weathered timber shelves or food stands, or use bushel baskets—upright and upended—for a variety of heights. Put them out in baskets laid out on country-style tables or rustic hutches accented with colored fabric cloths. Add some "natural" elements—like sprays of leaves or flowers for color accents.

Prepared Foods
When setting out prepared foods and edible delicacies, depending upon the type of store and the clientele, the displayer can set the **tone** and look with the choice of accessories—the types of linens, plates and platters, serving pieces, glassware, flowers, napkins, etc. They are all part of the selling story. If the shop caters to a sophisticated, upscale market that thinks "country" is "kitsch," avoid the rustic and provincial look and go for smart and stylish with lots of white, stainless steel, glass, cool colors, and smooth surfaces. Bring out the silver wine coolers, the

Figure 21.13 So pretty it is almost a crime to bite into any of these beautifully prepared and presented items of "take-out" food. Each item is treated as a "painting" and the colors and textures are balanced and enhanced. Lace paper doilies are placed under some of the less "ornate" items to "soften" the effect while the sunflowers, green leaves, and cut-in-half tomatoes add colorful accents throughout. The all-white platters bring out the color of the foods and reflect the light from above. *Traiteur Gillet, Chalon, France.*

Figure 21.14 More prepared foods with slices of oranges and cucumbers added to the sunflowers for a more colorful display. The use of natural materials—like other fruits, vegetables, flowers, and foliage—help maintain the "fresh" and "wholesome" look of the foods. *Traiteur Gillet, Chalon, France.*

Figure 21.15 The meat shown here is uncooked but ready-to-go. The rich red color of the meat is enhanced by the warm light in the counter and from overhead. The touches of green also compliment the red to make it seem redder. A red and white rustic checkered cloth, in the background, also adds a sense of "country fresh" to the meat presentation. *Butcher Shop, Milan, Italy.*

Figure 21.16 The meat is cooked/baked/whatever and ready to take home and be served. The simple white platters are decorated with greens, sprays of rosemary, and accented with cherry tomatoes. The greens again serve to enhance the red in the meat. *Traiteur Gillet, Chalon, France.*

candlesticks and floral centerpieces. Use the designer china and tableware, all the linens and other accoutrements that you can possibly "borrow" or rent. Be ready to serve up the very best where only the very best will do.

You can also go casual—and still be smart and stylish—with hand decorated pottery dishes and serving platters, colorful napery and linens—not too rough but not too smooth either—and add some **terra-cotta** touches throughout for a nice, earthy quality. Maybe use terra-cotta floor tiles under the serving pieces or add some terra-cotta garden statuary to the set ups. When

you set out the prepared foods it should look as though company is coming—real friends whom you are trying to impress. Table settings with an imaginative mix of colors, textures, and materials work best. Flowers, leaves, fruits, and vegetables—all natural—make wonderful decorative accents for prepared foods.

For inspiration check out food publications like *Gourmet* and *Bazaar* as well as catalogs from Williams-Sonoma, Crate & Barrel, and other upscale household and houseware stores. They are filled with ideas and products that will enhance your displays.

Home Fashions, Hard Goods, and Food Display: A Recap

- Lifestyle presentations bring assorted materials together into a unified theme.

- Colors and patterns can be used to tell a color or color and pattern story. Linens and accessories can be mixed and matched against vignette settings to accentuate the arrangement up front.

- Lifestyle situations, which show hard goods like vacuum cleaners in use by mannequins or other creative human forms, can dramatize the products for shoppers. The important thing is to remember the targeted shopper, and to make a presentation that demonstrates the viewer's relation to the products.

- Food displays benefit from natural and country fresh images. Lighting that resembles sunlight is particularly effective for fruits and vegetables.

- Colors and textures are important for the composition of food displays. Rougher skinned fruits can make smooth fruits appear even more so by comparison.

- Accessories like burlap bags, wood baskets, and colored fabric cloths will enhance the country fresh image.

- A more sophisticated or stylish approach may sometimes be desired. Designer china and tablecloths with some terra-cotta touches can give the display an earthy quality while allowing shoppers to envision home and dinner scenes with company over.

Questions for Review and Discussion

1. How is a color or color and pattern story created for a home fashions display?

2. What display methods can be used to humanize small or hand-held items? Large and bulk units?

3. What imagery is associated with produce? List some accessories that are effective in conveying such a message.

4. In the presentation of food, what methods should be used to prepare the proper look and tone for different clientele?

CHAPTER TWENTY-TWO
Graphics and Signage

AFTER YOU HAVE READ THIS CHAPTER,
YOU WILL BE ABLE TO DISCUSS:

- The term graphics as it relates to store design and display.
- The use of lifestyle graphics and artwork in store displays.
- Methods of manufacturing signs.

GRAPHICS AND SIGNAGE: TRADE TALK

bleeding	points
blowup	pressure-sensitive letters
calligraphy	proof press
card topper	punchboard sign machine
category card	quarter sheet
contrast	run
copy	selling sign
copy card	signage
croquis	silk-screening
cutout letters	squeegee
font	standard full sheet
graphics	stock
half sheet	tusche
institutional sign	
lifestyle graphics	

What Are Graphics?

The term graphics is defined as "referring to drawings, paintings and lettering or the reproductive arts of engraving, etching, lithography, etc." In today's store design and display, graphics more often than not refers to oversized photographs, blowups, or light box art, although artwork, sketches, and enlarged prints are also used.

Pictures, pictographs, logos, and stylized drawings can be "read" by anyone, when a specific language may not. A traveler to a strange and exotic country can still find a place to eat or a hotel room guided by international symbols for these places and services. Pictographs "speak" to people of all ages and still leave room for personal interpretation. People so often are bombarded by visual images—on TV, in the movies, in ads—that they tend to react to these images rather than to the printed words that often accompany them. Display designers and store designers using color and artwork are letting graphics do the selling job.

Graphics and Lifestyle

Graphics, today, is almost synonymous with lifestyle, and lifestyle graphics are appearing in window displays, interior displays, on fascias over stocked merchandise and even integrated with the merchandise in wall displays. Usually the graphics are photo blowups of people doing things and dressed for the occasion: bicycling on an autumn day, strolling through a park in April, a prom date, a family picnic, a power lunch in a smart restaurant, or a romantic, candlelight dinner. The graphics show people living a particular kind of life and dressing in that life's style. The lifestyle can be real or imagined. It can be camping, skiing, swimming—or even climbing Mt. Everest or trekking through the Amazon jungle. It can be a romantic moment or a hilarious one like stomping in a fountain in formal wear. Lifestyle is what

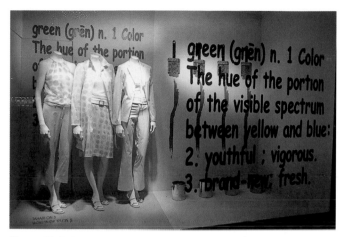

Figure 22.1 The printed material "explains" and complements the garments on display. The assorted styles of letters in the signage are also decorative and serve as a patterned background for the three outfits in the featured color. The two-dimensional paint brushes and the three-dimensional paint cans help to further the "color" theme. *Macy's, West 34th Street, New York.*

we think we would like to be—and we at least dress as though we were living the style. The graphics suggest a place, a time, and the right wardrobe for the moment.

Many of the graphics in the chain specialty stores like Gap, Eddie Bauer, and Club Monaco are actually over sized enlargements of ads that appear in fashion magazines, or are clipped out of TV commercials or reproductions from a current catalog or store mailing. Having seen the picture before—on TV, in an ad, or in a catalog—gives the viewer an even greater visual impression and an association with the product.

Graphics in Retail Stores

The lifestyle photo **blowup** often appears either as a framed or unframed background panel or in a light box illuminated from behind. In the more effective displays, the mannequins or forms in the foreground are dressed in exactly the same outfit reproduced at more than life size behind or beside them. The display creates a double impression. The photo may also show some alternative

Figure 22.2 The giant, super, super graphic of the young girl completely fills the oversized window and creates a startling contrast to the child-size dressed forms in the foreground. Since this store is on a major traffic street the graphic becomes a beckoning billboard and identifies the target market and color keys into the featured garments. *The Gap, Michigan Boulevard, Chicago.*

and/or coordinating items, which the display person can introduce on the floor in a lay-down or raised up on a platform, chair, table, or other prop. In some instances, the photo blowup is the display and the pictured outfit is shown in a lay-down—below eye level. This draws the viewer to where he or she will eventually see the actual garment. When showing small fashion accessories like shoes, handbags, pieces of jewelry, and even cosmetics, the photo enlargement of the product used as a background also helps by showing details and unique touches that aren't visible through the glass.

In vendor shops (described more fully in Chapter 26), the graphics will reiterate and reinforce a current advertising campaign or special promotion. In specialty stores, a particular photograph or piece of artwork may be the basis for an entire promotion. It will appear in the store mailing and catalog, as posters and card toppers in the store, and even—blown up to heroic proportions—as the window background. This will work with either open-back or closed-back windows.

The **lifestyle graphic** is a selling tool. It will explain how an outfit goes together and where it can be used. Imagine a photographic background panel of some attractive women in career outfits conferring around a computer station—or seated at a boardroom table or

even a drafting table. Better than a sign that says "suits," the graphic also says something about the variety of merchandise and how the suits can be accessorized or personalized. Show a mannequin in front of the graphic panel along with the right style of chairs (an ergonomic chair, a leather captain-of-industry chair, or a drafting stool) to carry some of the alternates and accessories and you have a display with the message built in. Inside the store, the lifestyle graphics often replace traditional signage. If the shopper sees a photo above eye level, on a perimeter wall, of a woman on a bicycle wearing shorts and a short-sleeved shirt, with a sweater flung over her shoulders, and with a gentle breeze blowing through her hair, the shopper knows that this is the place for sportswear separates. The lifestyle graphic says—"this could be you—this could be your life."

Signage

Despite a picture being "worth a thousand words," some display persons and store designers—like men who wear belts and suspenders—want to be sure that the message is read as well as seen, so they add some words to the graphic display. The fewer words the better: the more simply stated, the more effective! Don't complicate matters or confuse the shopper. Posters are used much less

Figure 22.3 The oversized sketches on the back wall add a fresh, young, and carefree feeling to the merchandise on the abstract mannequin. Also adding to the young feeling are the colorful surf boards that tie in with the "surfs up!" copy. *H-Bendel, Fifth Avenue, New York.*

Figure 22.4 The strong, brushed-on lettering across the front glass demands immediate attention from the shopper on the street. The black and white design is highlighted with the red star outline (the store's logo) and the red dress on the mannequin pushing the food cart. The cart is filled with "necessities" and the black copy provides "reminders" of what the busy lady still has to do. This could be adapted into an effective sale window. *Macy's, Herald Square, New York.*

frequently now than they once were. There was a time when spring, back-to-school, and fall brought out a snowstorm of 22-inch by 28-inch cardboard posters hanging off of columns, from the ceiling, standing on ledges, supported on floor fixtures, and layered atop the fascia over the merchandise stock. Today, a graphic sym-

Figure 22.5 The word is "refresh" and other cooling words appear with it in this crisp setting. The featured words are used to pattern the background for the casual fashions. The same "printed" text is used on fabric to upholster the suit form that appears in the cluster of dressed forms on the right. The Burberry name, in red/orange, pops out from the gray letters and the same strong color is used on another form to highlight other outfits being featured. *Burberry, Michigan Avenue, Chicago.*

bol or decorative element, often screened on fabric and used as banners and streamers, will say with color and design as much as the posters did. In addition, these banners are adding a festive look to the shop interior. The flag or banner says "celebration," "holiday," and "special event," while adding color accents to the floor. These elements will be replaced by a new color scheme and a new graphic symbol for the next seasonal or promotional event. The same screened banners and flags can be integrated into the window displays or the external trim of the store.

A sale is a sale is a sale, but a sale need not be an act of desperation or a last resort. It can be a bright, colorful, and fun event. Banners, flags, and streamers with just the word "sale" can be enough to stir up some activity.

There is a negative side to **signage** and it can apply to graphics as well. It is overkill! It is when "too much" is much too much. It is a case of visual clutter: a window or a store swamped, smothered, and overcome with signage. It is a bombardment of messages and a paper blizzard that chills and then kills the senses. Instead of informing, this barrage has a negative effect and turns off the shopper. How many times must the same message be repeated? If the sale or promotional message is simply, clearly, and colorfully expressed up front—in the window—and the same graphics and materials are used inside, that should do it. It does not have to be repeated every 3 or 4 feet inside the store, where it drenches the shopper in a paper deluge. That is overkill—and that cheapens the merchandise and the event. Shoppers equipped with their sales-oriented antennae just need a few good and clear clues and they will figure out what is going on and where it is happening. The excessive signage may hinder rather than help the shopper in search of bargains.

Graphics combined with some signage can be an effective twosome in window display. The colors used, the style of lettering, the artwork, and the materials all can further the store's and the products' image as well as complement the overall design of the store.

Drawings

A **croquis** or fashion sketch—blown up to life size or bigger—also makes a great display setting for a dressed

Figure 22.6 It does not take a linguist to figure out what is going on! The all but empty rack in the all-white space backs up the copy scrawled on the front glass. The "- 70%" is international, while the copy in Russian Cyrillic letters spells out "Sale." *The Atrium, Moscow, Russia.*

mannequin or form in the same designer outfit. The sketch adds class to the setup and makes the product seem more upscaled and more special.

Artwork, rather than photography, suggests elegance, refinement, and uniqueness. Drawings or etchings, blown up to a larger size, can serve as a background to set a time and a place for the merchandise being featured. The flat panel has depth and dimension drawn in and thus creates the feeling of space in the display area. If the drawing is in forced perspective, then the effect is even more startling. An etching of a classic piece of architecture can create a great display background for a man's suit while a drawing of an old-fashioned gazebo or a formal garden can do wonders behind a mannequin in a formal gown. The drawings bring a certain quality with them that is then instilled into the product in front of them.

Color and Contrast

Some colors "read" better than others. The greater the **contrast** between the color or ground of the board or paper and the copy printed on it, the more readily the copy will come across. Black on white and white on black are two good examples of contrast. The former is more traditional and, therefore, is usually more acceptable. Black on yellow makes a strong statement. Mention has already been made of using red and green as contrasting colors; this combination can and will be a disaster for a sign that has to be read. The proximity of the two colors creates a vibration, the letters jump and jitter over the printed surface.

Metallic paints and inks can be elegant and lovely, but become almost invisible when light strikes the metallics in a certain way, or when there is a glare on the window. Metallic boards look marvelous and super-rich under controlled lighting arrangements, but because of highlights, white lettering can "disappear" from a metallic surface. Black or dark-colored inks or paints do not hold up well on the metallic backgrounds, either.

Sometimes, a light-colored or white letter with a darker outline or shadow will survive under window lighting. Though they may lack excitement, white or pale tints make the best grounds for signs, and black ink, which is convenient and available, can, at times, be replaced by more fashionable or interesting colors that do tie in with a theme or promotion: red for Valentine's Day, green for spring or St. Patrick's Day, royal or flag blue for a presidential sale, brown for Father's Day, and so on.

Sizes for Signs and Cards

The size of a sign will depend on the location or end use of that sign, and how much **copy** or information the sign has to carry. Following are some of the stock, or standard, sizes. **Stock** refers to the usual sizes to which the used in windows and on or off columns. This is the popular choice for storewide promotions, sales, and holidays. The 22-inch by 28-inch sign will usually carry some sort of graphic design or illustration, and a banner or caption indicating the event. A sign of this size will often be silk-screened for use throughout the store and for use in branch stores, if there are any. The poster will also tie in with ads, commercials, and other media, such as store mailings and handouts.

A **half sheet** measures 14 inches by 22 inches and is used for window displays or to identify merchandise in an interior display. A **quarter sheet,** measuring 11 inches by 14 inches, is a smaller, more restrained window reader or feature copy sign. It can be used effectively on the selling floor to explain certain larger pieces of hard goods or

Figure 22.7 Retro-style posters set the scene for the retro-inspired fashions. The many-colored raffia plaited wigs on the mannequins and the color coordinated straw hats on the floor in front of the posters tie in with the look being presented. *H-Bendel, Fifth Avenue, New York.*

boards or cards can be cut down. The cardboard is stored in these sizes or can be purchased precut in these standard dimensions; frame-holders and easels are also available in these same sizes.

Stock also refers to the material (paper or cardboard) to be imprinted. The thickness or rigidity of the stock is designated by **points.** The larger the number of points, the thicker and usually more rigid the material. Of course, the display person can vary from these standard sizes if the new or unusual dimensions will satisfy some special design requirements.

The **standard full sheet,** or poster size, is 22 inches by 28 inches. Most floor frames are designed to accept that size board, usually in 14 point stock, a fairly stiff board that is not too thick or too rigid. This size poster can be

Figure 22.8 Signs and symbols. It is time to hit the road when the light says "GO" and the familiar road signs are indicating which roads to take. This travel-oriented theme plays up the familiar and recognizable symbols to get the idea across. *Bloomingdales, Lexington Avenue, New York.*

Figure 22.9 Magazine covers, newspapers, headlines, printed words, cartoons—all these everyday graphics take on a new meaning when used imaginatively in a display setting. Here a blowup of a New Yorker cover plays up Central Park and the where, what, and why of New Yorkers and tourists go there. The cut-out foam core figures—right out of the background but enlarged to life-size—wear some of the "Summer Essentials" available in the store, carrying through the cartoon concept. *Saks Fifth Avenue, New York.*

furniture. This size is also used in elevators and dressing rooms for signs about store policy, special events, fashion shows, and so on.

Small **copy cards** come in a variety of sizes—7 inches by 11 inches, 5 1/2 inches by 7 inches, and 3 1/2 inches by 5 1/2 inches—in order to fit standard easels and frames for merchandise identification within the store and in windows. The smaller ones usually appear on counters in cosmetics and accessories areas.

An easel may be a plastic holder that is self-standing at a slight angle, or it can be elevated on a metal upright

to extend above the merchandise described. A frame can also be mounted onto a wall or fixture, and the proper copy can be dropped in and changed as the merchandise or the event changes.

Card toppers, usually long and narrow—about 11 inches by 3 1/2 inches or 7 inches by 3 1/2 inches—are used to tie in with storewide events, themes, and promotions. They often have the same color and graphic concept as the promotion's 22-inch by 28-inch store poster, and the same caption or tag line, acting as a reinforcement, for the shopper, that this merchandise is part of the ongoing sale or event. The card topper emphasizes the limited-time concept of the promotion. The sameness and the repetition of the colored and designed card topper on the selling floor can be an effective point-of-sale technique as well as a way of adding a seasonal or holiday look to the area. Card toppers should be short-lived. They should disappear from the floor as soon as the event is over.

The standardization of sizes is convenient for the display person or the store's sign maker. The material can be precut and stocked in specific sizes. All the sizes listed above can be cut from the regularly available 22-inch by 28-inch board without waste. This standardization also helps keep the interior of a well and fully signed store looking neat and orderly. The customer can find and recognize the signs by their shape and size and not be bombarded by a confusion of assorted cards and card toppers.

Other sizes can be used for store signs, but the ones given above are traditional and easy to purchase in various colors and finishes.

Types of Signs and Cards

A **selling sign** is a promotional sign, in that it promotes the sale of a particular item on the selling floor. A good sign should be clear, concise, and comprehensive. If it is "selling" an item, it should say what the item is, what it does, why it should be purchased here and now, and how much it costs. In the fewest possible words and in the most understandable language, it should cover the questions a customer might ask.

When preparing a selling sign, remember the following points: Print only three or four words on a line. Check the facts, the spelling, and the punctuation. Be sure that the overall effect is neat and not crammed with copy. If a relatively great amount of information on the featured merchandise is to be included, use a larger sign. Shoppers on the selling floor do not read "encyclopedias."

If the back of the copy sign will be visible, back it with either another sign or a graphic design. Try to keep all signs that appear in the same area or department consistent in color, size, and layout, so that the customer is not confused by too great a variety of conflicting signage. Be sure the choice of type is clear and readable and in keeping with the merchandise and the store's image.

A **category card** specifies the major classification of the collected merchandise rather than a specific design, pattern, or price. It could read, for example, "Women's Wool Sweaters"; and under that one sign there could be a bin full of an assortment of varying prices, colors, kinds of wools, and manufacturers. As with the selling sign, neatness, accuracy, and simplicity count.

An **institutional sign** lists the services provided by the store: its hours, refund and exchange policies, delivery charges, alteration setup, and so on.

A store should not have too many signs, but items and categories should be identified to provide ease of recognition and relevant information. The more fully a store is "self-service," the more important good signage becomes. The signs help to supply the answers the sales person would ordinarily provide.

Techniques for Preparing Signage

Silk-Screening

Silk-screening is one of the oldest and most dependable stencil reproduction techniques for making signs and posters. With this process, printing is achieved by means of paint or dye forced through a screen which is covered with a fine silk (or synthetic) mesh. Silk-screening is especially effective where there is a considerable quantity to be produced (a **run**), but not enough to warrant the use of expensive plates and lithography.

There have been tremendous advances in the silk-screening or hand-screening processes, including photographic methods for producing the screens, or stencils. This technology eliminates the hours required to cut

each stencil by hand, including all the letters needed for the signs. The hand-cutting of the stencils is an art and a craft, requiring much more than just a steady hand. Many books are available on how to do silk-screening. Briefly, this is the technique.

For each color that is to be printed, a separate stencil is prepared. The stencil is actually a true and rigid wood frame over which a very fine denier of silk (or a synthetic fabric of a similar type) is stretched and pulled taut. A lacquer film is applied to the fabric screen. Only the parts of the design that are to be printed in the specific color are cut out of the film, leaving exposed those areas of the fine screen through which the paint or dye will be forced. The area that is not to be reproduced is left with a protective coating of the lacquer which will resist the paint.

After the screen is prepared, it is carefully set down on the surface to be printed (i.e., the stock). If more than one color will be used, special care must be taken to ensure that the successive screens—for the overlaying colors—will be lined up with each other, so that there will be a minimum of **bleeding** (colors seeping through beyond their intended outline). A "puddle" of paint is placed at one end of the screen and a **squeegee** (a hard, rubber-edged tool, similar to a windshield wiper) is pulled across the screen, forcing the paint through the openings in the fabric. For each color, this process is repeated. All of the stock to be printed is "screened" in the first color before proceeding to the next color.

For smaller runs (several dozen of a single kind), one might make a less sophisticated form of screen, or stencil. The area that is to be printed is left exposed, and the rest of the screen is "printed" with a blocking solution that will not be affected by the paint, lacquer, or dye used for the screening.

Another silk-screening technique involves the use of liquid **tusche** (a substance similar to a crayon that has been dissolved in turpentine) which acts as a blocking agent. In this method, the area that is to be printed is painted with the tusche and allowed to dry. The remaining surface of the screen is sealed off by a glue that is not water-soluble. When the glue dries, the tusche is washed off with water, leaving exposed to the paint only the design to be printed. This is a simpler, more manageable technique because no cutting is required. The results are not as sharp and slick as they might be from a real silk screen, but posters and card toppers printed in this way can still look good and deliver the message in color.

Sign Machines

Some stores have made an investment in sign machines, especially when signing and pricing play an important part in the store's promotional attitudes and selling techniques. For the retail operation with a full sales force, which provides help and answers for shoppers just for the asking, signs may tend to clutter or create confusion on the floor or with the store's image. The more popular-priced the store, the more often the customer will "self-select," and the greater will the need be for the clear, clean, and precise merchandise and pricing information supplied by signs.

There are basically two types of sign machines on the market today. One is a **punchboard sign machine,** which is similar to a "giant" typewriter. It has a flat surface, or "bed," on which is placed the stock to be printed. An alphabet of type, on a roller, is designed to ride up and down and across the bed of the printing machine. A hand press, or punch, brings the selected letter or symbol onto the exact desired location on the stock. Rollers with ink cross over the typeface and keep the letters inked.

After being lined up exactly where it will appear on the printed card, a letter is punched. The ink rollers coat the letter; the letter descends and is imprinted on the card. The next letter or symbol is lined up and the process is repeated. This technique is fast and simple enough to use for one or two signs, or where there is a great variety of signs and prices needed.

A store that uses a dozen or more of the same copy card or price card would do better with a **proof press.** This is a more traditional type of printing press. There is a flat bed or surface on which the copy is set down in bars of type (held in place by a magnetic force), and a roller sweeps across the bed below. The card is printed by placing the face of the stock down on top of the type that has been inked either automatically or manually, and pulling the roller across the back of the card stock, thus causing the inked type to make an impression on the face of the card.

When using a proof press, many cards or readers can be made from the same setting of type. It just takes another pull of the roller over a fresh piece of card stock. With this kind of machine, it is possible to have an in-signia or logo plate made that can be incorporated with the type for a personalized touch.

The punchboard machine is cleaner to operate than the proof press and is generally considered to be more versatile and adaptable. With the punchboard it is possible to print on fabrics, plastics and, in some cases, wood or laminates.

Other Signage Techniques

Cutout letters are available in many **fonts** (a font is an assortment of type all of one size and style), in diverse sizes, thicknesses, and colors. Some cutouts are reusable and, thus, can be a worthwhile investment. There are also rub-on, **pressure-sensitive letters,** which are inexpensive and can be purchased in most art supply houses. They, too, are available in a tremendous assortment of styles and sizes and can be used to make signs with different looks conveying particular images.

With the printing machines described above, the display person, due to the financial outlay, is wedded to a specific style or type of letter. With the pressure-sensitive letters, the display person can use different types for different products, from very elegant, elongated, and ultra-thin letters for fine jewelry and furs, to strong, dark, condensed letters for lawn mowers, power tools, and auto tires. Even in a store that sells only fashion merchandise, different lettering styles for swimwear and bridals, for example, could be used.

Hand-lettering, or **calligraphy** is almost a lost art. It requires a steady hand, infinite patience, and talent. There are many brushes and pen nibs on the market that will assist the letterer in his or her work, but the tools alone do not ensure the desired end result.

The art of calligraphy can enhance special events or promotions, or it can be used to create a look for a logo, a headline, or for an original store signature (a "sig"). In many cases, however, a pressure-sensitive alphabet can be found that "will do." It may lack the color option that is possible in hand-lettering, but it does have the advantage of being predictable, sharp, precise, and mechanically reproducible.

Much of today's signage is created with the aid of a computer. New graphics software packages and color printers are "user friendly" and have made it possible for even the smallest of shops to create professional signage using a personal computer.

Graphics and Signage: A Recap

- Graphics, as used in today's store design and display, refers to the use of oversized photographs, blowups, lightbox art, artwork, sketches, and enlarged prints.

- Lifestyle graphics—photo blowups of people doing things and dressed for the occasion—are an effective selling tool when combined with displays featuring mannequins in those same outfits or some of the accompanying accessories.

- If words are used along with graphics, keep the message short and simple: the fewer words, the more effective. Often a colorful graphic banner can take the place of signage or posters. But avoid overkill: Too many visual elements can overwhelm the viewer.

- Artwork, such as a croquis (fashion sketch) or an etching, suggests elegance, refinement, and uniqueness.

- A store's sign is judged on legibility and comprehension of the message it carries.

- The greater the contrast between the color of the board or paper and the copy printed on it, the more readily the copy will come across.

- Colors such as red and green are contrasting, but the proximity of these two colors creates a vibration and makes letters jump and jitter on a printed surface.

- Metallic ink becomes almost invisible when light strikes it a certain way or if there is a glare.

- The usual size to which a board or card can be cut is called stock size.

- Stock also refers to the paper or cardboard to be imprinted.

- Silk-screening is achieved by means of a paint or dye forced through a screen that is covered with fine silk or synthetic mesh.

- A punchboard machine is a sign machine similar to a giant typewriter. It can print on stock, fabric, plastic and, in some cases, wood or laminate.

- A proof press is a more traditional type of printing press and many cards or readers can be made from the same setting of type.

- Other signage techniques include cutout letters, pressure-sensitive letters, and calligraphy, or hand-lettering.

Questions for Review and Discussion

1. Explain how graphics might be used to enhance a display of women's formal wear.

2. How do the store's signs impact store image?

3. What are the two major criteria on which a sign is judged?

4. Why should colors that are directly opposite each other on the color wheel (such as red and green) not be used together in a sign?

5. Beginning with a standard sheet of 22-inch by 28-inch sign board, explain the standard cuts made to obtain each subsequently smaller standard sign. Cite typical uses for each size of sign board.

6. Provide an example of a selling sign, a category card, and an institutional sign.

7. Describe the silk-screening process. When is silk-screening the most appropriate method for sign making?

8. What is the difference between the punchboard machine and the proof press?

PART FIVE
VISUAL MERCHANDISING AND PLANNING

CHAPTER 23 DISCUSSES THE PRESENTATION of stock on the selling floor and how visual merchandising takes place where the shopper and the product come together in a real, hands-on situation.

Whether a freelance display trimmer or the head of visual merchandising for a large department store, the display person must have appropriate tools and workspace. The requirement for setting up a display workshop are examined in Chapter 24.

Floor space is a primary concern of fixturing. Since a store's success is often computed in terms of sales per square foot of selling space, the floor plan, including the positioning of departments and fixtures within the store is vital to the ultimate success or failure of the store. Guidelines for store planning and interior layout are explored in Chapter 25.

Visual merchandising considerations related to specific retail format—big box stores, discount or factory outlet stores, and vendor stores—are detailed in Chapter 26.

CHAPTER TWENTY-THREE

Visual Merchandise Planning

AFTER YOU HAVE READ THIS CHAPTER,
YOU WILL BE ABLE TO DISCUSS:

- The importance of a display calendar.
- Events that are included in the display calendar. Points of consideration for planning a display.
- Steps in the display planning and installation process.

VISUAL MERCHANDISE PLANNING: TRADE TALK

cooperation
coordination
display calendar
installation
lead time
planning
scheduling
showpiece buying
store promotion

good display is the result of **planning, coordination,** and **cooperation.** The display person must know, in advance, when a particular display will be installed, where it will be installed, and what will be shown and promoted. He or she needs some sort of schedule (which can be altered) or, at least, a master plan.

The execution of a good display comes from knowing in advance what trends, what colors, and what type of merchandise are scheduled for future display so that some thought and preparation can be made for the eventual visual presentation of that new merchandise. It also requires a close working relationship with the retailer or buyer, the promotion department, advertising people, and display manufacturers and suppliers.

Good displays come from the display person's knowledge of what is available and where, what is in stock or in the warehouse, and what can be borrowed or "begged" from neighbors or institutions in the community. It requires an awareness of what is going on in the community, in the city, in the country, and in the world, and then being able to draw on that awareness to create attention-getting, image-building, and merchandise-selling displays.

Display Calendar

A well-thought-out time schedule keeps displays and merchandise moving freely, in and out of the windows and on and off ledges and platforms. These predetermined time slots keep the store looking as new, fresh, and exciting as the new merchandise that keeps coming into the store. The change of windows may be set for every ten days or every two weeks. However, it should most emphatically *not* be any longer than one month between window changes. Even in the smallest store, there should still be a frequent change as well as variations with each change.

The schedule should be worked out with merchants and buyers, determined by when they buy new merchandise, seasonal and holiday promotions, and yearly sale events. There should be built into the plan the flexibility to switch or change a scheduled trim in the event of unexpected problems with merchandise delivery or happenings in the community or in the world. If there are only one or two display windows and several different classifications of merchandise (daytime dresses, evening wear, fur coats, lingerie, active sportswear, and so on), then the schedule should apportion which classification or type of merchandise will be presented, where and when. It can be based on the selling period (e.g., Mother's Day gifts, Christmas, and New Year's Eve formals), or on the arrival of new merchandise (e.g., spring dresses, fall separates, winter outerwear).

The **display calendar** should be roughed out or blocked out a year in advance, based on the previous year's experiences, sales, and promotions. If there is no previous experience on which to base a schedule, the display person might want to refer to the calendar in Table 22.1, which suggests possible events and promotions for a typical year.

Planning a Display

The following are some of the points to consider in planning a display:

1. Is there a theme or an idea that will not only stimulate sales, but stimulate the display person to create an exciting, eye-arresting display based on that theme and idea? Are there to be newspaper advertisements, store mailings, national campaigns in magazines, on radio and television to tie in with the theme for greater impact and exposure? Is the theme new or timely?
2. Will the promotion or display presentation be limited to a single garment; a single classification of garments or merchandise; a single pattern, color, or featured designer? Is the promotion to be storewide or will only one department or type of merchandise be featured? Will the window display be coordinated with the interior of the store: on major ledges, on columns, plat-

Figure 23.1 It's Father's Day—or at least it will be soon—and shoppers are not only reminded of the upcoming day but amusingly presented with gift suggestions for dad. The red and white checkered motif is carried through in the condiments lined up and on the cut-out letters applied to the red back wall, as well as on the merchandise offered for the window shopper's perusal. It's "What's Cooking for Dad!" *Macy's, Herald Square, New York.*

forms, counters, and along the traffic aisles? How will the display person unify all these areas into a cohesive, dramatic, and dynamically flowing presentation? Remember, the simpler and more direct the approach, the easier it will be for the shopper to comprehend the message. Too many ideas, too many "stories," too many items or unrelated colors, can end up in confusion as well as clutter.

3. Ideally, the whole idea or theme of the display should be summed up in a copy card or reader that appears somewhere in the display area. It can be placed on a streamer or consist of raised, cut-out letters resting on the floor. It can be on a card raised up on an easel, or even spread across the front glass or all over the back wall of a window. This is the "key" copy, the catch phrase that tells—and sells—the story. The key message is told in the fewest words and in the most mem-

orable way. It is like a message on a poster: simple and direct. (See Chapter 22, Graphics and Signage.)

4. If there is to be a series of windows, will the merchandise all have the same look? Will there be variations on a theme? Will all the windows show only loungewear and robes, or will it be an emerald green promotion and include men's, women's, and children's fashions and accessories—in green—as well as home furnishings, linens, kitchen gadgets, gift items, and so on, in that featured green? The display person may want to use the same decorative theme in all the windows—no matter what the merchandise classification—or vary the decorative elements from display to display, but retain a flow and easy movement from window to window. The store management will decide how many windows to give to a promotion and how those windows will be apportioned among the

various departments in the store. This is part of scheduling. The schedule indicates which merchandise will be given emphasis and "star" exposure, up front, and which will be subordinated to the secondary windows (on a side or less-trafficked street) or to the shadow boxes.

5. How can this display setup be different from the previous one? Can a different set of mannequins or an alternative to the regular mannequins be used? Can the background and floor colors be changed for this promotion? Can something new be done with the format of a window? Could the window be masked or cut down in size? Could a valance or proscenium be added to create a "come-and-look-at-this" frame around the glass? How about an awning or a change of awnings? Plants added in front of the window or trees or bushes placed between windows could provide a change. Can the type and arrangement of light be varied? How do we get the customer to know that something new and different is going on before they are close enough to really see it? (See Chapter 16 for some suggestions on attention-getting devices.)

6. How do we reinforce the store's image with this display? Is it possible to enhance the store's reputation while promoting the merchandise? Some noted stores today show only image-promoting window displays assuming that shoppers will be fascinated enough to want to enter the store in order to be transformed into what was promised outside—in the window.

The Visual Merchandiser's Part in Store Promotion

Big promotions and big sale events need advance preparation time. They should be developed for possible themes, concepts, slogans, and directions, in cooperation with retailers and the promotion and advertising staffs. It is a good idea to find out if an extra budget allowance exists for some of these promotions. Sometimes, a manufacturer contributes to the promotion and advertising of a product by the store, or the store may be able to tie in with another group, for example, an airline, a foreign trade council, or an industry organization.

The display person should start searching, among his or her regular suppliers as well as elsewhere for props and devices to be used in the coming **store promotion.** Of-

ten, props are available just for the asking or for an acknowledgement card in the display. The visual merchandiser should also question, if he or she does not already know, how much **lead time** (advance planning time) is necessary in order to ensure the on-time delivery of props, backgrounds, and accessories for the promotions. It is then the visual merchandiser's responsibility to get the "go-ahead" and/or the additional funds to get these items into the store and the windows on time.

Ideally, the display person should see or know in advance exactly what merchandise is coming in and what he or she will be required to "show." This means knowing how many pieces of merchandise will be available to the display person, in what colors, patterns, and styles, and what accessories are to be used. It usually does not work out that way, however.

Some stores have a fashion coordinator who pulls or specifies the merchandise and the right accessories before the display is scheduled to go in. Often, however, the display person or a member of the display staff must wander through the store, requisition book in hand, writing out requests or receipts for shoes from one department, scarves from another, jewelry from still another area, and so on. Some stores or fashion coordinators will bring in special merchandise and/or accessories to enhance their display presentation. This is called **showpiece buying.**

Scheduling the Promotion

Let us assume that the basic schedule was blocked out a year in advance and that the theme, copy, and advertising for the promotion were already "roughed out." Three months before the promotion breaks, the display person will order whatever props or backgrounds are necessary from an outside supplier. He or she will then begin **scheduling** those parts of the display presentation to be done in the display studio of the store (e.g., covering floor and wall panels, signs, posters, mounted blowups).

A week or two before "P-Day" (promotion day), the display person and buyer should check that the promotional merchandise is in or on its way, and that everything is set to go as planned. The display person should also check those areas in the store to be tied in with this promotion: the counters, ledges, platforms, and so on, to

Table 23.1 Display Calendar of Sales, Promotions and Tie-In Events

Month	Sales	Promotions	Tie-In Events

January	Post-Christmas
	Pre-Inventory
	White sales (linens, blankets, towels, comforters, spreads, etc.)
	Furniture, bedding and home furnishings
	Foundations and lingerie
		Bridal showings
		Resort and cruisewear
		Pre-Valentine's Day
			Football-Bowl games
			Birthdays
			  Martin Luther King (15)
			  Benjamin Franklin (17)
			  Franklin D. Roosevelt (30)

February	Final winter clearance
	Presidential Birthday sales (Lincoln and Washington)
	Housewares
	Pre-season (for spring)
		Valentine's Day
		New spring fashions and colors
			Birthdays
			  Thomas A. Edison (11)
			  Abraham Lincoln (12)
			  George Washington (22)
			Valentine's Day (14)
			Bachelor's Day (27)

March	Pre-Easter	Spring and Easter for the whole family New season accessories Children's shoes Rainwear Summer bridal fashions Home and garden improvement (fabrics, floor coverings, curtains and draperies, slipcovers, etc.)	St. Patrick's Day (17)
April	Post-Easter Pre-summer fabrics Sleepwear and lingerie	Easter Summer wear Fur storage Early swimwear and sunwear Pre-Mother's Day	April Fool's Day (1) Easter Pan-American Day (14)
May	Baby Week Home furnishings and housewares Spring apparel clearance Memorial Day	Mother's Day Bridal Summer sportswear Change-of-season ready-to-wear Luggage and vacation needs Outdoor living	Mother's Day (second Sunday) First nonstop trans-Atlantic flight/Charles Lindbergh (May 28, 1927) American Red Cross (21) Memorial Day (end of month)
June	Home furnishings and bedding Furniture	Father's Day Graduation Bridal gifts Summer formals Camping clothes and supplies Summer active sportswear Swimwear Sporting goods, cameras Men's wear and furnishings (with Father's Day tie-in)	Father's Day (third Sunday) Flag Day (14)

Table 23.1 Continued

Month	Sales	Promotions	Tie-In Events
July	Independence Day Summer clearance begins White sales	First flurry of fall Fur coats Early back-to-school Christmas in July! Outdoor living	Independance Day (4) Bastille Day (14) First Feminist Convention in U.S. (July 19, 1848)
August	Summer storewide clearance Furniture and bedding Fur sales	New fall fashions Back-to-school and college Career fashions Bridal showings Woolen fabrics	Founding of Red Cross, Geneva, Switzerland (Aug. 22, 1864) 19th Amendment, Women's Suffrage (Aug. 26, 1920)
September	Labor Day	Fall fashions and accessories School supplies Home improvements (china, glass, etc.) Sporting and hunting supplies Introduce coats, suits, outerwear	Labor Day (first Monday)
October	Columbus Day Import Anniversary or special storewide clearance	Introduce Christmas gifts Layaway plans Evening and dress-up wear Furs Ski shop Women's coats and suits Outerwear for the family Gloves and millinery Personalized Christmas cards and gifts	Baseball World Series (might be late September) Columbus Day (12) United Nations Day (24) Statue of Liberty dedicated in 1886 Halloween (31)
November	Thanksgiving Veteran's Day Pre-Christmas Election Day Fur sales	Christmas gifts Home furnishings for the holiday season Evening wear Stay-at-home dress-up Women's coats Men's clothes and furnishings Toyland open—Santa's coming	Election Day Veteran's Day (11) Sadie Hawkins Day (16) Thanksgiving (third Thursday)
December	Pre-inventory clearance Clearance of holiday goods (cards, wrapping, trim, novelties, etc.) Pre- and post-Christmas sales	Christmas gifts and fashions Institutional windows Beach and resortwear Formals and holiday clothes Bridal showings	—

be trimmed. The necessary signage, the pads to be changed in cases and under counters, backgrounds to T-walls, the walls over ledges, and the column treatments also have to be considered.

The following is a suggested checklist for installing a display, be it part of a major promotion or a regularly scheduled display change:

1. Merchandise. Is it in the store? Is it ready for the display: selected, cleaned, and pressed? Is it the merchandise that was expected? Does it, in the full piece, look the same as it did in the color swatches or samples around which the window was designed? If not, will any changes from the original plan be necessary? Have all the accessories been pulled together? Are there any unexpected problems?

2. Mannequins. Have the correct mannequins been selected on which the merchandise is to be displayed? Do they have the correct line, the appropriate look? Will the body positions work with the garments? Are they clean? Have any chipped fingers been repaired? Is any emergency cosmetic treatment required on cracks or rubs on the finish? Are the wigs right: the right style, the right color, and in good condition? Will the shoes fit properly? Does the mannequin's base need any special covering or repair? Are all the parts in one place and ready to be assembled?

3. Lights. Are all the necessary lights working? Does anything need to be replaced? Have the right filters been found and set aside? Are any necessary extra extension cords on hand? (It would be wise to have a few additional spots available should the setup need more lighting than anticipated.)

4. Props, fixtures, and backgrounds. Are all the pieces necessary for the presentation in the store? Does anything still have to be picked up? The display person should refer to his or her floor plan and display checklist, ticking off the items. Are the props, platforms, and risers that are to be used in top condition? Are any scratches, rips, runs, or ragged edges visible? Can a quick paint job or "touch-up" remedy the eyesore? What is the condition of the fixtures to be used? If need be, will camouflage or "display magic" work (e.g., the addition of some ribbons, trimming, netting, or tape)? Are the floor pads covered? Are the wall coverings ready? Will the display window be clean, inside and outside, on the day of the trim? If the walls of the window show, in what condition are they? If there is a permanent carpet on the floor, will a thorough vacuuming be sufficient, or should the display person plan for some decorative ground cover (gravel, pebbles, ground cork, flitter, scatter grass, and so on) to cover any badly worn or soiled areas?

5. Signs. If any price and copy cards will be needed, are they ready?

On the day of the **installation,** the previous trim is "pulled" (removed) and the merchandise is returned to the proper departments. The final countdown includes the following:

1. The merchandise to be installed is given a final check: wrinkles, loose threads, uneven hems, loose buttons, mismatched patterns, and so on.

2. The tool kit is completely fitted, and all the necessary tools and accessories are in it. (See Chapter 24 for specific recommendations for stocking a tool kit.)

3. The lights are clean and working.

4. The windows and floors have been cleaned.

Much of this preparatory work becomes "second nature" once the display person has had some experience planning, setting up, and trimming displays. The best professionals remember to check out and take care of all the little details; most of the "big" ones are obvious and will be easily seen and checked. Remember: Someone out there is looking—judging the merchandise and the store. It is the responsibility of the display person to ensure that everything being shown is presented at its best—in the best of all possible ways.

Visual Merchandise Planning: A Recap

- A good display depends on planning, coordination, and cooperation.

- The display calendar is a well-thought-out time schedule that keeps displays and merchandise moving freely in and out of windows and on and off ledges.

- A change of windows can be set for every ten days to two weeks, but should never be longer than one month.

- The display schedule should be blocked out a year in advance.

- The visual merchandiser should plan advance preparation time for big promotional and sale events. These should be developed in cooperation with retailers and the promotion and advertising staffs for possible themes, slogans, concepts, and directions.

- The display person should order whatever props or backgrounds are necessary about three months before the display is scheduled. The display person will then schedule the parts of the display presentation to be done in the store's display studio.

- A week or two before the promotion day, the display person and buyer should check that the promotional merchandise is in or on its way and that everything is set to go.

- The display person should check the following for planning a new display installation: merchandise, mannequins, lights, props, fixtures, backgrounds, and signs.

- On the day of the installation, the final countdown should include checking the merchandise for loose buttons, uneven hems, and so forth; checking to see that the tool kit is fitted properly and completely; checking to see that the lights are clean and working; and checking that the floors and windows have been cleaned.

Questions for Review and Discussion

1. Why is it important for a visual merchandiser to have local, national, and international awareness?

2. How far in advance should the display schedule be roughed out? What items should be included on the display calendar?

3. Create a year-long display calendar for a small specialty store. Be sure to include all major sale events and seasonal merchandise deliveries.

4. Beginning three months before a promotional event and ending with the installation of a major display, outline the process the display person should follow.

5. In display planning, what questions should the visual merchandiser answer regarding the following items:
  a. merchandise
  b. mannequins
  c. lights
  d. props, fixtures, and background
  e. signs

CHAPTER TWENTY-FOUR

Setting Up a Display Shop

AFTER YOU HAVE READ THIS CHAPTER,
YOU WILL BE ABLE TO DISCUSS:

- The physical requirements for a display workshop.

- Furniture and fixtures used in a display shop.

- Tools, supplies, and trimmings to be kept in inventory in a well-stocked display shop.

- Handy reference materials that might be kept for use in a display shop.

SETTING UP A DISPLAY SHOP: TRADE TALK

    cut awl
    disco ball
    jigsaw
    no-seam paper
    seamless paper
    Skilsaw
    taboret

I f one goes to work for a department store or a large specialty store, there will probably be an established display area or department with tools, tables, bins, and the assorted paraphernalia that gets collected over the years. In the event, however, that such a shop does not exist, one would have to be set up. An effective but minimal shop can be equipped in a minimum space with a small budget for materials and machinery. This shop should provide the basics for a work area to facilitate the planning, designing, detailing, preparation, and the eventual storage of displays—and all that these processes involve.

Physical Requirements

There should be enough space for a worktable, a desk, a drawing table, bins, storage cabinets, and possibly a sign machine or even a sign shop. Also necessary is a sink or some other source of water for mixing water-based latex paints, for doing a watercolor rendering, and for cleanup. Good lighting and lots of electrical outlets are essential. The display person also needs a telephone to keep in close touch with store activities and to provide a line to the outside world and to suppliers.

A decent ceiling height is important since props, rolls of seamless paper, and mannequins cannot be bent. Although hard floors (concrete or vinyl) are not the most comfortable underfoot, they are easier to maintain than carpets. An office apart from the actual shop—a place to plan and draw projects and keep files—is desirable. It can be screened or curtained off, or set off by a 4- or 5-foot partition, but the more private and the more soundproof it is, the better. Shops can and do get noisy.

Furniture

To conduct the business of the department, a desk or other writing surface (not a drawing board) will be necessary. It will be a place to figure costs and work up budgets, to pay bills and find unpaid ones, to open mail and

write correspondence, to study upcoming promotions, peruse fashion magazines and other periodicals relevant to the merchandising being offered by the store. A desk lamp and a good chair or two will also be very useful.

A file cabinet will be needed for the files that must be kept. An organized display person knows what has been ordered, what has come in, and what has to go back. He or she should keep a log or calendar of trims and upcoming events and, if possible, a record of past displays. Ideas for future displays should be filed away along with booklets, brochures, and other collected data that may be used at some future date. Everything should be organized, labeled, and logically filed so that others, if necessary, can locate designs or information.

A drawing table or some sort of drafting setup should be a surface apart from the desk, and used for sketching, drafting, and designing. This surface can be at desk height (29 to 30 inches), counter height (36 inches) or higher, depending upon what suits the display person. He or she might prefer to sit on a posture chair, or to perch on a 24- or 30-inch stool, or perhaps to stand to

Figure 24.1 When all else fails, the display person can always empty out the tool chest and use the tools as props. Ladders, brooms, vacuum cleaners, steamers, whisk brooms, tape measures can all be brought into a fashion window to create arresting displays. Thus, they are props as well as tools of the trade. Here a hatchet and bits of pieces of twigs—all suspended by twine from a grid overhead—create this fall setting for men's suits. *Bergdorf Men, Fifth Avenue, New York.*

draw. A good light source that can be directed to the work surface is a must.

A **taboret,** or small drawer or cabinet unit (perhaps on wheels), should be close to the drawing table. It is necessary for the storage of drawing supplies, tools, templates, paints, pencils, and the other items necessary for the creative process.

A large, clean, unobstructed work surface is also a necessity. It should be at least 4 feet by 8 feet and approachable from all sides. This island in the display shop is used for cutting, scoring, constructing, and even dressing forms or children's mannequins. It should be at least 36 inches high. If possible, the area below the work surface could be a combination of cabinet space and shelf space. The cabinet could hold some of the tools that will be used at the table, and the shelf could be used for oversized cardboard or paper. This worktable should be under a good light fixture. There should be an electrical outlet close by for power tools. The tabletop could be covered with a piece of thick fiberboard or an inexpensive grade of plywood. There should be a roll of inexpensive wrapping paper on hand so that the tabletop has a clean and fresh covering on which to work. It is easier to put a fresh piece of paper down than to replace the tabletop. It also would be a good idea to use a clean, quilted cover (such as that used by furniture movers) to put over the table if it is going to be used for dressing mannequins or forms.

Adequate closets and shelves are essential for the storage of tools and hardware supplies, as well as for basic fabrics and trimmings. Also vital are bins for the storage of mannequins, their spare parts and wigs, and other forms. Ideally, the bins should be padded. Extra arms and/or action legs should be stored with or above the mannequin with which they will be used. If the bins are open, then a curtain should be installed to pull across the stored mannequins in order to keep them free from paint or sawdust while the worktable is in use.

If the construction of bins is too involved, the display person could use a system of slotted uprights (standards) and brackets along one wall. Start these shelves about 6 feet high (i.e., just above a mannequin's head), and use them to store the parts and accessories that go with the figure placed directly below. Pieces of fiberboard, cut into 2-foot by 8-foot panels, can be used as vertical dividers between the shelves and act as separa-tors between forms. The mannequins could also be laid out on shelves, but they would have to be at least 24 inches wide for the mannequins to be secure. The shelf should be lined with a pad or felt, and a protective piece of plastic used as a cover over the reclining form.

The use of several fireproof, metal cabinets is advisable for the storage of flammable paints, dyes, spray cans, and so forth. Paint brushes, rollers, and other painting equipment could also be stored in these cabinets or nearby. When painting, adequate ventilation may be a problem. Never spray paint in an enclosed or unventilated area. If need be, step outside or into any available space with an open window.

It is a good idea to have a simple, inexpensive pipe-rack or two around to hold the merchandise to be collected, pressed and/or steamed, and prepared for display. A pipe-rack can also hold the garments that have been "pulled" (removed from a display) and have yet to be returned to the proper department or area. An inexpensive shoe bag with see-through pockets could be attached permanently to the pipe-rack, and the pockets could hold not only the right shoes for the selected outfit, but the other accessories that will be shown.

A small "dump" wagon, or a box on wheels, facilitates the movement of mannequins, props, tools, and more from the display department to the area to be trimmed.

If the operation is small and the borrowing of fashion accessories is not feasible, a locked cabinet should be provided for the storage of "basic" costume accessories (e.g., shoes of the proper size and heel height, costume jewelry—chains, pearls, colored beads—solid-colored scarves, a few new purses, some neutral-colored gloves). The locked cabinet might even include some basic hat shapes in straw or felt that could be trimmed with ribbons, scarves, or flowers.

Tools and Supplies in the Display Shop

As mentioned in the Preface of this edition, a computer/printer combination is a "must" today and—within the budget—the very largest digital printer one can buy will digitally reproduce material prepared on the computer. Many different types of material can be used for printing: paper, plastic, fabric, etc. At the Fashion Institute of Technology our faculty and students have found that Macintosh and Apple computers are the most adaptable and complementary to the many drawing programs available. Whether the work station is standard desk height or a counter height of 36"–39", it is a good idea to have an ergonomically designed chair to sit on when working at the computer.

Every display person must keep an adequately stocked tool kit containing a staple gun (with extra staples), staple clipper, diagonal cutters (nippers), scissors and/or shears, "X-acto" knife, claw hammer, screwdriver, Allen or hex wrench, Phillips screwdriver, masking tape, cloth tape, cellophane tape, assorted pins (banker, dressmaker, and "T" pins), nylon fishing line, "invisible" piano wire, fine sandpaper (or an emery board), kneaded eraser, needle and "invisible" thread, white glue (Sobo or Elmer's brand), hot glue gun and glue sticks, whisk broom, some clean rags, ruler, tape measure, and extension cord. It is desirable to have a compact clothes steamer and miniature vacuum cleaner to bring into the display area for a final touch-up.

Seamless paper, or **no-seam paper,** is useful, relatively inexpensive, available in many colors, and extremely versatile. A stock of colors should be kept on hand. Seamless paper comes in rolls 9 feet wide by 36 or 50 feet long. Storing these rolls can present a problem. Even if there is enough space to store them upright, it is best to store them parallel to the ground and not stand them on end. The ends could become crushed or wrinkled. If space permits, they could be placed against a long wall, one over the other, and supported on brackets, with the whole selection on view. Since seamless paper is sometimes the medium for a painted or drawn background in a window, a wooden frame should be kept near the stock of paper. If it were necessary to draw a sketch on the seamless paper, all the display person would have to do would be to unroll the desired length of paper, tack it up on the frame, and start to draw.

Panels of fabric, sewn into curtains, could also be stretched out on this open frame to be painted or decorated. The frame can be constructed out of 2-inch by 4-inch lumber, with three vertical members going from floor to ceiling and one top and one bottom member to hold it all together. If there is sufficient wall space available, the frame could be set about 1 foot forward from the wall. The space behind could be used to store templates for wall and floorboards, and so on.

Other basic supplies for the display shop include: casein paints, latex paints, and cans of assorted spray paints; enamels, metallics, and transparent floral dyes; fixatives (varnish sprayed over pencil or chalk drawings to protect them from smearing); spackle and wood filler; flitter (tiny bits of finely chopped brass and tin, which sparkles) and glitter.

Hand Tools

Hand tools include the following: hammer, mallets, assorted screwdrivers (including a Phillips screwdriver), Allen or hex wrench, Stillson wrench, awl, pliers, wire cutters, nippers, plane, brace and bits, hacksaw, coping saw, chisels, staple guns, staple clippers, C-clamps, vise, a Pantograph or blowup machine (to enlarge drawings), mat knife, squares, compass (for big radius drawings), assorted nails, brads, screws, and staples, white glue, rubber cement, and Duco brand cement.

Power Tools

A **cut awl** is a "must." This is a lightweight power tool that is designed to cut out intricate profiles from boards and fabrics of assorted weights. It works best on a padded surface so that the cutting blade, which extends below the flat base surface of the saw, can bite into something disposable after passing through the layer or layers it is cutting. It comes with a variety of blades and attachments, making it very versatile.

Another desirable power tool is the **Skilsaw,** a portable, lightweight circular saw for ripping and crosscutting. It can be used anywhere within reach of an electrical outlet; therefore, with this tool, it is possible to bring the "shop" to the installation. A **jigsaw** is another hand-held power tool which is excellent for cutting curves, scrolls, and irregular patterns. It is possible to adapt this tool to make inside cuts as well as outside cuts. The following power tools are also useful in a display shop: sander, electric hand drill with assorted bits, a router, a power or table saw, an air gun and, possibly, a band saw.

Basic Trimmings

The list of basic trimmings is endless, but for starters, the shop should stock: foamcore in white and assorted colors, ribbons in assorted colors and widths; cotton and hemp rope; dowels and cardboard tubes of assorted lengths and diameters; braid, fringe, and gimp (or guimpe); cloth tapes in assorted colors and widths; millinery wire and covered wire; wrapping papers; assorted yarns and ties; gift boxes and assorted empty boxes, cases, and small crates; tissue paper in a range of colors; felt in as many colors as possible (but rolled rather than folded, the fold creases being hard to eliminate); net, tulle, duck, canvas, and so forth. A couple of fonts of cutout letters could be useful as well.

Save anything architectural or dimensional that is nonspecific, but can be adapted to different uses. For example, corrugated boards and boxes can make interesting backgrounds. Grass mats and assorted types of floor scatter could be useful too.

Lighting Equipment

Start with extension cords, plugs, multi-outlets, electrical tape, wire, and assorted gelatins and colored glass filters with housings to attach to spotlights and floodlights. Add clamp-on holders for spots and floods. A simple, revolving wheel would be useful, as would a mirrored globe, or **disco ball,** and turntables of assorted diameters, heavy enough to hold merchandise and mannequins.

There is no end to the list of things one could collect to fill a display department, but it takes time and money to do. To fill in any missing items, it may be necessary to "beg," borrow, and improvise.

Books, Publications, and Reference Materials

Whether the display person has an office, a studio, a shop, or works out of an attic or basement, some books and publications should be available, always at hand, for ready reference. Collecting books because they look nice, or because they have pretty pictures, is not the answer. Books should be used. They should be handled, read, and studied. It is not necessary to memorize everything contained in these reference books, but the display person should be able to find the information when needed.

Select the books as you would your friends. They will be around for a long time. They can become your allies, your protectors. They are filled with good ideas, suggestions, and answers. They can keep you from looking foolish because of misspelled or improperly used words. A good dictionary is a very worthwhile investment. *Roget's Thesaurus* or another good book of synonyms will give you a choice of words so that you can say the same thing, but in a different way. You can find ideas to "visualize" as displays in *Bartlett's Familiar Quotations.* Also, an encyclopedia will answer all kinds of questions, and can be fun to peruse.

Anyone in the fashion business should have a picture-filled history of costume to trace the derivation of a "new" look, a style, or a "retro" trend. A history of furniture and home furnishings is helpful if one has furniture to sell. Also, because furniture can be the right setting for fashion, it is helpful to know which are the appropriate periods to use in a display. *The Dictionary of Interior Design* illustrates periods and styles of furniture and architecture, and also lists art terms, artists, and artisans. *The Language of Store Planning and Display* is a compilation and explanation of thousands of words the display person hears in the daily business of presenting merchandise in a retail operation.

Display & Design Ideas (DDI) is published monthly by VNU Business Publications (www.ddimagazine.com) and is filled with retail store designs, new product information, and numerous advertisements for new materials and products of interest to the display person/visual merchandiser/store planner. During the year they also have interesting results on opinion polls and research into business practices that are of special interest. *Visual Merchandising & Store Design* (VM+SD), published by Signs of the Times (www.visualstore.com) is another monthly publication that contains articles of interest to the store designer/visual merchandiser, as well as numerous ads for products of value to the person in the design field. VM+SD also sponsors the VM+SD International Retail Design Conference and the SHOPXPO as well as other industry challenges. Signs of the Times publishes books of interest as well. Visual Reference Publications (www.visualreference.com) produces numerous books on all aspects of store design, visual merchandising, and window display. They have a monthly service, Retail Design & Visual Presentation that features new retail stores from around the world, window displays, and interesting interviews with leading designers in the field.

The display person can subscribe to or purchase fashion magazines to keep up with the "scene." Fashion ads are filled with presentation concepts. Read *WWD (Women's Wear Daily),* for the day-to-day activities in the fashion world. The display person should also peruse newspapers for community, national, and world news, and for what is happening in the arts, sciences, and sports.

Other useful references include: illustrated books on the history of art and architecture and travel books or brochures (filed by country) with vistas and views of familiar and recognizable sights, scenes, or symbols for ready reference.

A display person should become addicted to books and never pass up a book sale. One never knows from whence an idea can come. He or she should *never* stop looking, reading, and learning.

Setting Up a Display Shop: A Recap

- A display shop should have enough space for a work-table, a drawing table, bins, storage cabinets, possibly a sign machine or a sign shop, a sink or other source of water, good lighting, a lot of electrical outlets, a high ceiling, and a concrete or vinyl floor. An office apart from the actual shop is desirable.

- Furniture and fixtures necessary for a display shop include: a desk or writing surface other than a drawing board; a desk lamp; a good chair; a file cabinet; a drawing table or drafting setup; a taboret; an unobstructed work surface; adequate closets and shelves; storage bins; fireproof metal cabinets; a pipe-rack; a dump wagon; and a locked storage cabinet.

- An adequate supply of hand tools and power tools should always be kept in the shop.

- The display shop should have two sets of tools—one in the tool kit to move around with the display person and one that always remains in the shop.

- Reference books should include a good dictionary, *Roget's Thesaurus*, *Bartlett's Familiar Quotations*, and a variety of other reference texts. Subscriptions to trade publications such as *Views and Reviews*, *Visual Merchandising and Store Design (VM&SD)*, *Women's Wear Daily (WWD)*, as well as various consumer fashion and general magazines, are another important resource.

Questions for Review and Discussion

1. What things should a basic display work area facilitate?

2. Make recommendations for mannequin storage in a display shop.

3. What special precaution should be taken when spray painting?

4. Describe the need for three different types of power saws in a display shop.

5. Explain the problems of storage of seamless paper.

6. How might a thesaurus be helpful in the creation of a window or interior display? A recent issue of *WWD*? An interior design book?

CHAPTER TWENTY-FIVE

Store Planning and Design

AFTER YOU HAVE READ THIS CHAPTER,
YOU WILL BE ABLE TO DISCUSS:

- The duties and areas of expertise essential to successful store planners.

- Scale in relation to floor planning.

- The concept of store rehabilitation.

- The basic architectural and store planning symbols used in floor plans.

- The differences between an elevation and a floor plan.

STORE PLANNING AND DESIGN: TRADE TALK

architectural symbols   isometric perspective
beam   kneaded eraser
block plan   model
buttress   mullion
clean rag   partial wall
column   pier
compass   rehabilitation
drawing board   ruby eraser
dwarf wall   sale
elevation   scale ruler
floor plan   store planner
french curve   template (templet)
graph paper   triangle
hard pencils   T-square

"Interior designers" have probably been plying their trade as far back as when exotic bazaars and old Persian markets were the shopping centers that attracted the bargain shoppers of days gone by. Someone had to have selected the rugs and tapestries that supplied the rich and colorful ambience. Someone must have decided that raising certain merchandise off the sandy ground and onto a rug-covered platform would make it more visible and more desirable. Where the brass lanterns were hung and where the encrusted candelabras were set did affect the highlights and shadows on the buffed and gleaming merchandise. The casual but carefully orchestrated tumble of merchandise from baskets, barrels, and brass bowls, however, must have been left to the "display person." Thus, for a long time it was the interior architects and designers who created the retail space and supervised its decoration.

In the past few decades, a new breed of architect/designer has appeared on the scene, the **store planner.** This new designer is more than a space planner, decorator, and divider of the selling floor space. This is a designer who is also a merchant and a merchandise presenter. Today's store planner is a designer, an architect, a space "surgeon," a lighting expert, a colorist, and a visual merchandiser with a knowledge of mannequins, fixtures, furniture, and forms, and the "know-how" to sell the merchandise. Most of these individuals we now call store planners have a background in architecture or interior design, but more and more visual merchandisers are bringing their special talents into the store planning field.

It began late in the 1960s when the large department stores were caught up in the "boutique blitz" that exploded in retailing. Management wanted to subdivide the large, open, selling spaces into intimate and exciting minishops, rich in personality and unique flavor. Budgets were barely sufficient for the transformations into these seasonal shops and environmental selling experiences. Thus, the assignments were often turned over to the existing "display departments" with the order to "Make a miracle happen, but don't spend any money!"

Miracles did happen. Fresh, innovative, and intriguing shops and boutiques did appear on the vast, high-ceilinged, and often impersonal floors. They created warm and charming boutiques filled with special mer-

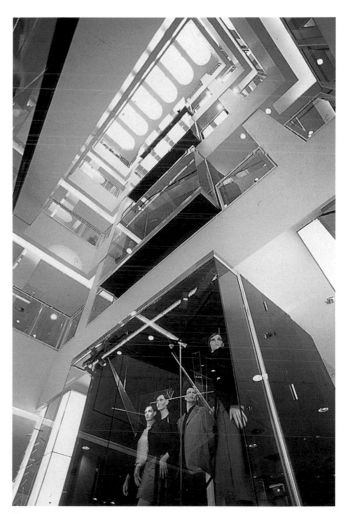

Figure 25.1 With so many department stores being built facing parking lots or with display windows non-existent, display has moved inside the store and, as shown here, the "windows" now face the central, soaring atrium. Shoppers going up or down the escalators are treated to the display of the merchandise being featured on that level either in the enclosed or open display areas facing the atrium, or by mannequins realistically clustered and standing along the balustrade and looking back at the shoppers. *Harvey Nichols, Edinburgh, UK, Four IV.*

Figure 25.2 Platforms with dressed mannequins either step forward into the main traffic aisle or become "islands" that shoppers must navigate around to get to their desired destination. *Maison Simon, Laval, Quebec, Canada, Watts International.*

chandise and spilling over with new and inexpensive methods of housing and displaying that merchandise. Never did so many improvise with so little. It did not take long for the more progressive minds in merchandising to realize that some display persons or visual merchandisers had something extra to offer store planning.

Here were talented and imaginative people that could see beyond the traditional round racks and tired and trite, overexposed methods of merchandising. The visual merchandisers, who became the store planners of the 1970s and the 1980s, have attempted to enhance the merchandise, making an art out of even housing and stocking it.

Functions of the Store Planner

The following are the functions of the store planner involved in store design today:

1. To design an efficient and attractive selling environment that will promote maximum sales and savings in labor and energy.
2. To combine the selling space with the "behind-the-scenes" service area where stock is maintained and the nonselling activities of the store are carried on.
3. To set up traffic patterns that will promote customer movement from areas that get the greatest exposure (near entrances, elevators, and escalators) to remote corners and back areas where the more expensive items are usually located.
4. To promote and sell. To stock and show. The store planner selects the selling vehicle for the specific merchandise being offered.
5. To enhance the store's image and, thereby, add stature to the merchandise being offered.

The store planner works closely with the architect (if there is one), the store management, the merchandisers, and the buyers. Based on previous sales figures, or on projected or anticipated sales figures, the store planner, together with the executives, will prepare a **block plan.** This is the first allocation of space on the ground plan and the designation of selling areas on that selling floor. This apportionment of space is based on the merchandising needs, proposed traffic patterns, proximity to related merchandise, and anticipated sales. By roughly blocking in the areas, management gets a visual picture of how much space is actually needed and how much is left for growth. The "behind-the-scenes" areas (service elevators, storage, employee's changing rooms, toilets, offices, and so on) and the social amenities (rest rooms, vistas, galleries, restaurants, meeting or community rooms, and so on) will then be fit into the remaining space. The floor plans are then redrawn, always in scale, with more and more details and specifications added on.

The final floor plan will have all the counters, cases, tables, and freestanding floor fixtures (round racks, quad racks, T-stands) drawn in place, and will show the aisles, passageways, dressing rooms, exits and entrances, escalators, elevators, and more. Islands for display arrangements, platforms for mannequins, and T-walls to separate areas will be indicated. The store planner will locate the "impulse items" (merchandise purchased on impulse rather than by plan; e.g., cosmetics, candy, inexpensive but faddish novelties) in the high-traffic areas, leaving the customer to find his or her way to the "demand merchandise" (the necessities: household goods, appliances, and so on).

The effective store planner directs the shopping drama that starts right at the entrance. He or she plots the lighting, creates the changes in color and texture as the shopper moves from area to area, and is responsible for the raising or lowering of ceilings over aisles or boutiques. It is also his or her responsibility to place mirrors for reflection or glitter, to suggest changes in flooring materials between aisles and shops, and to arrange for dividers, screens, plants, and artwork. Also, related merchandise is placed close together so, for example, shoes can be matched to a handbag, or skirts to sweaters.

Whether the store planner is designing a small specialty store or dividing up floors or areas in a large department store, the basic responsibilities, as enumerated above, are still the same. However, the small store pres-

Figure 25.4 The structural column on the floor becomes a focal element in the design. It is a merchandising fixture/displayer and an identifying element in this area. The backlit graphic "explains" the garments below and the form, attached to the illuminated translucent panels, shows off an actual garment. *Jockey, Kenosha, Wisconsin, JGA.*

Figure 25.3 The built-in ledge along the wall that separates a "shop" or designer boutique from the general flow of merchandise on the sales floor serves as a "runway" for a fashion showing of garments. On the opposite side of the aisle, the mannequins standing directly on the floor are backed up with a partition or partial wall that carries stock on the side facing the sales floor. *David Jones, Melbourne, Australia, RYA.*

ents particular problems since space is especially precious and each cubic foot is expected to earn a certain amount of dollars in gross sales. In the larger operations, this is still a factor to consider, but sometimes the gracious sweep of a wide aisle or a vista is worth the expenditure of space in favor of store image and the ambience that is achieved.

Rehabilitations

Not all stores are built from the ground up, all new and ready to accommodate the needs of a particular retail operation. Some merchants seem to find it more economical and desirable or, for the sake of a "different" look, more advantageous to start with an existing structure and restyle it to their own requirements. Many department and specialty stores discover that after some years their operations have become dull, dingy, and dated, and they no longer function as efficiently as they did twenty or thirty years earlier. New fashions just do not look "new" in an area whose decor is passé.

When an existing structure is restyled, redecorated, and rearranged, but not necessarily gutted and rebuilt, the store planner/architect is involved in rehabilitation, or "rehab." **Rehabilitation** is the remodeling, redecorating, and refixturing of an existing structure, often by the store planner. The "rehab" will still have the interest, the spirit, and the architectural details and flavor of what it once was, but it comes out fresh and ready to function for today's fashions.

Floor Plans

An architect does not simply buy thousands of bricks and then start to erect a building. An engineer does not take a crew of bulldozers out into a field and say, "Let's try here." And a display person does not walk into an empty window or onto a cleared-off ledge and say, "What shall we do here today?" What they all do is *plan!*

They plan, they make drawings, they consider the details, the special requirements, and the limitations. Most of the problems are usually solved before the start of construction or installation. The display person, like the architect and engineer, is a professional and should not be given to whims and fancies that will not come to terms with reality. He or she must communicate with coworkers, consult with buyers and fashion coordinators, and get construction done through the carpenters and painters before ever stepping into the window or onto the ledge. It takes planning, plotting, and programming. It takes *preparation.*

Just as architects and engineers work with blueprints and mechanical drawings to correct errors before they become full-grown and costly mistakes, the display person should also work with scale drawings of the areas for which he or she is responsible. The display person should not only know how to read and interpret a floor plan or building plan, but should also be capable of drawing a plan—to scale—and with the special "hieroglyphics" used by architects, engineers, and designers.

Today, the display person is often given a set of blueprints for a new store, or a revamped department, or the designated space for a shop-within-a-shop, and told to lay out the fixtures, counters, counter fixtures, furniture, and so forth, to be used, and/or asked to plan the aisles, the traffic flow, and the display areas and, thereby, see what will and will not work in the allotted space. It is also possible, using these preliminary drawings, to estimate the amount of background or flooring material required; the sizes of the platforms or risers; the partitions, dividers, or screens that will be used. It is also possible to preplan the lighting requirements. He or she must be able to render these ideas in scale, in a plan, and sometimes with an elevation, so that the area can be finished by contractors or carpenters.

The computer and several drawing programs, especially CAD, have proven remarkably helpful in this type of work. It is possible to "draw" the space and "move" fixtures, furniture, whatever around in the established parameters to get the desired traffic patterns and merchandise layouts. Some programs even create three-dimensional images of the space, and the designer can "walk" through the space to visualize the flow of movement within the space. Again, we emphasize the point that the computer and the programs do not create the new special design. It is the designer who does it; and he or she uses the computer and the program to execute ideas conceived and developed on paper before sitting down at the computer. It is a wonderful tool: it is a great visualizer and assistant but it is not the designer or the master.

It is simple enough to prepare one sharp, clean, basic plan of each area to be arranged and displayed, and then make dozens of photocopies for use as needed. Sometimes, for a really ambitious undertaking, a **model** is made in proportion to the actual finished design. This is done to get a "visual" image of how things will look, how things will fit, and how they will work.

Let us, first, be sure we understand what a **floor plan** is. It is a flat representation of only two measurements—the length and width (or depth) of an area or object as seen from overhead. It is as though one were viewing the area from far up in the air, and all that could be seen is a flat, graphic representation of height, with everything flattened out.

By using a scaled floor plan, it is possible for the visual merchandiser/display person to experiment on paper, with platforms, fixtures, display cases, and so forth, of assorted sizes and shapes, without ever actually having to lift or push them. The investment of time, money, and effort will more than pay for itself.

Drawing to Scale

When we speak of scale, we are referring to the relative proportion of one object to another. When we say something is "overscaled," we mean it is too big, too overwhelming, too dominant in relation to the objects around it. "Relation" is the key word here. A real, live, 7-foot-tall basketball player visiting a kindergarten class would be overscaled in relation to the children. True, the ball player would be noticed—he would be an attention-getter—but he would also, by contrast, show how very small the children are. **Scale,** in mechanical drawing or in the preparation of floor plans or models, refers to the proportion that is used by the designer or draftsperson to designate the future actual size.

If an architect is going to build on a plot measuring 100 feet by 300 feet, it would be absurd to paste up a single sheet of paper to that size, then lay it out on a football field and start to draw the foundation in the actual measurements. Instead, a scale is selected—a proportion—and the designer works on the assumption that each foot of actual construction will be represented on the drawing by $^1/_8$ of an inch or $^1/_4$ of an inch, for example. The contractor or engineer looks at the corner of the designer's finished drawing—in a special box usually found on the lower right-hand side of the drawing—in order to find the proportion or scale used in the drawing. Thus, at a scale of $^1/_8$ inch = 1 foot, the plan drawing of a plot measuring 100 feet by 300 feet will be drawn at $12^1/_2$ inches by $37^1/_2$ inches. Using this size paper makes it easier to make corrections, overlays, or even prepare new drawings, and it is certainly more convenient to carry around.

Materials Needed to Draw a Floor Plan

Some basic materials are needed to draw a simple floor plan. It is a good idea to start with a **drawing board,** an essentially flat, rectangular surface, usually made of wood, with absolutely straight and true sides. The four corners should be perfect right angles.

In order to draw straight lines, one should have a **T-square,** which looks like a 24- to 36-inch calibrated ruler with a head on top that is perpendicular to the ruler part, forming a "T." When drawing, the top of the T-square lines up with the edge of the drawing board, and thus any lines drawn along the ruling edge will be parallel to one another and perpendicular to the sides of the drawing board.

A **triangle** is a tool having three sides and three angles (30, 45, 60, and so on). It is used to line up vertical and horizontal lines on the drawing board. Triangles are usually made of plastic or metal and are used in connection with a T-square.

If a T-square is lined up with a drawing board and the base of the triangle sits flush on the ruling edge of the T-square, the straight, vertical edge of the triangle will work as a guide for vertical or perpendicular lines. Thus, with a drawing board, a T-square, and a pair of triangles, it is possible to draw straight or angled lines that are true and even.

A **compass** is used to draw circles and arcs of various sizes. This drafting tool consists of two rigid arms—a needle point and a marker arm—hinged to each other at one end. The wider the spread between the arms, the larger the circle or arc that can be drawn.

A **french curve** is a flat, plastic or metal drafting tool consisting of several scroll-like curves and arcs. The desired curve is drawn and reproduced by following the edge of the form at the selected curve. French curves are available in a wide variety of sizes and shapes.

Especially useful in mechanical drawing and essential for reading plans done to scale is a triangular-shaped **scale ruler.** It is slightly over 12 inches long and calibrated in assorted scales. One edge is marked off in $^1/_8$-inch spaces; each line is equal to a single unit in the $^1/_8$-inch scale. On the edge that is marked off for the $^1/_4$-inch scale, the spacing is in $^1/_4$-inch modules; therefore, the designer knows that each $^1/_4$-inch space is equal to a unit, whether that unit be an inch, a foot, or a yard. A scale ruler is also marked off in the following scales: $^3/_{32}$, $^3/_{16}$, $^3/_8$, $^1/_2$, $^3/_4$, (which are all fractions of an inch); and 1, $1^1/_2$, and 3 inches. One face is usually calibrated as a traditional ruler, that is, with markings of sixteenths of an inch. Scale rulers are also available in metric scales.

If you do not want to use a ruler, all is not lost! It is possible to do scale drawings on **graph paper,** paper which has been lightly marked off into squares. Until such time that the United States formally adopts the metric system, be sure to select graph paper that has

Figure 25.5 Some typical floor plans showing the layout of departments, fixtures, and the traffic patterns that direct shoppers through the spaces.

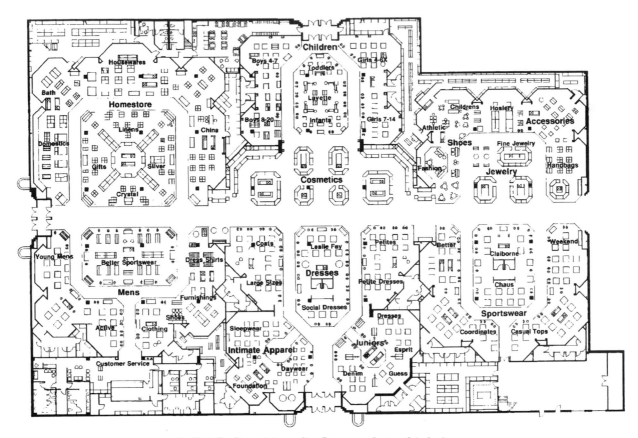

Proffitt's The Shops, Johnson City, Tennessee. Design: Schafer Assoc.

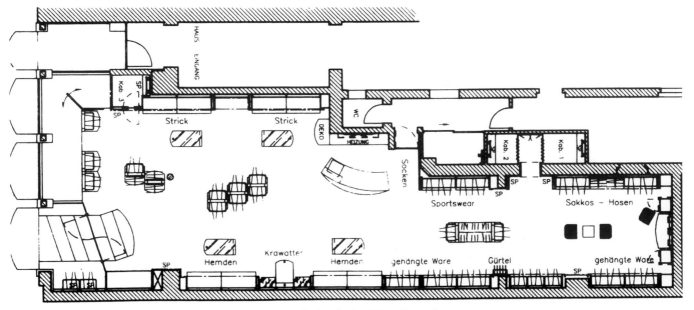

Klucken, Germany. Design: Umdasch Store Fitters, Germany.

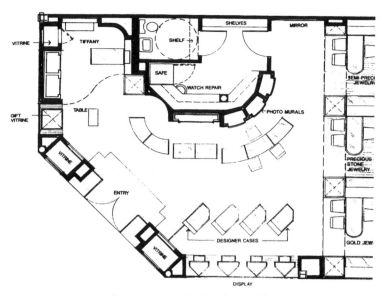

Yamron Jewelers, Design: Brand + Allen Architects Incorporated, Houston, Texas.

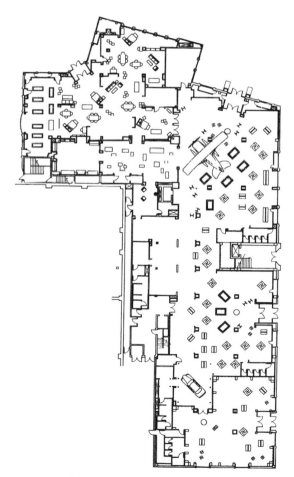

Eddie Bauer, Illinois. Design: Mithun Partners, Seattle, Washington.

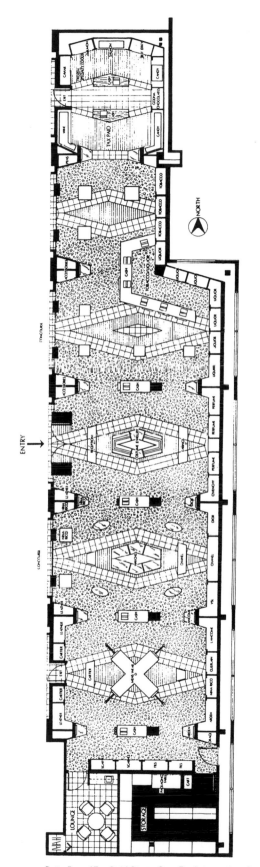

Duty Free / Tax Paid Store, Sea-Tac International Airport. Design: Sunderland.

Figure 25.6 Structural columns divide the space into brand name "shops" on the sales floor. The dressed forms, angled for better viewing from the aisle, help to identify each "boutique" and the brand name on the rear wall further personalizes the manufacturer's or designer's area. With some variations in style but with a consistency of materials and colors, the floor combines the individual brand name shops into a consistent whole that reflects the department store's image. *Lotte, Daejun, Korea, Pavlik Design Group.*

been divided into four or eight boxes to the inch. Four boxes to the inch means that each box is equal to a $^1/_4$-inch. Using graph paper that has eight boxes to the inch gives a $^1/_8$-inch scale. If you want a scale of $^1/_8$ inch = 1 foot, and there are eight boxes to the inch on the paper, then each box is equal to one foot, and half a box is 6 inches. If you want to use the same paper for a drawing with a scale of $^1/_4$-inch = 1 foot, then each box is equal to 6 inches, and it takes two boxes to make 1 foot.

In addition to graph paper, it is recommended that the display person have a good supply of tracing paper to try out variations, moves, and changes. Once a plan is carefully drawn, any corrections and changes deemed necessary can be made on tracing paper laid over the finished drawing. Then, when the final design is approved, the final, corrected scale drawing can be done.

Have a lot of sharpened **hard pencils** designated 4H to H on hand, not those with soft points. Soft pencils (No. 2 and B) make fat lines that smear and rub. A good **ruby eraser** (for erasing lines) and a **kneaded eraser** (for removing smudges) are also necessary adjuncts. It is a good idea to keep a **clean rag** on hand to wipe off the edges of the T-square and the triangles as the drawing

proceeds. The lead of a pencil adheres to the edges of the instruments and can make a drawing messy.

Also, to make scaling and drawing plans simpler, there are dozens of kinds of **templates** (also spelled **templet**) available in art supply and stationery stores. They are thin, plastic or metal plates containing patterns of specific symbols and shapes precisely die-cut out of the plate, leaving an opening one can trace in order to produce a perfectly scaled object. There are templates for home and office, using engineering and architectural symbols as well as basic geometric shapes (circles, ovals, rectangles, and triangles). Templates are available in assorted sizes and scales.

With the materials assembled and scale ruler in hand, the designer is ready to draw symbols and "shorthand" of architectural drawing as they relate to display and store planning are discussed below.

Reading a Floor Plan

Figure 25.7 is a composite of a store floor plan and it gives us the opportunity to point out some of the usual

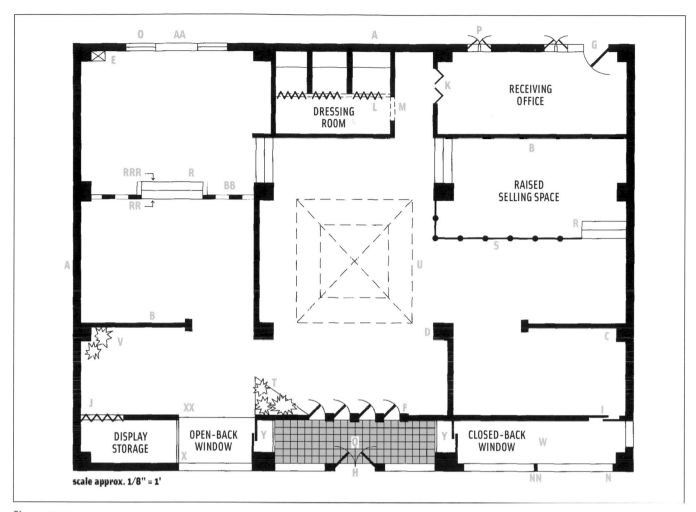

Figure 25.7 A composite floor plan of a small retail operation.

and unusual **architectural symbols** and markings found in floor plans.

Basic Architectural Symbols

A. A heavy solid fine line (or two lines that are not filled in—see AA), indicates a structural, exterior wall. It is a part of the basic construction of the building. (This can also be a common wall that is shared with an adjacent building.)

B. A solid line, thinner than A (sometimes two lines that are not filled in, but closer together than A and indicates a floor-to-ceiling interior wall, partition, or solid divider. The wall or partition may or may not be structural, but usually the columns or piers on the floor plan (see C) will indicate where the weight-bearing, structure-bearing elements can be found. This thin line indicates a di-

vision or separation between departments or areas, as well as where the on-the-floor selling operations end and the "behind-the-scenes" activities begin. In this way, it is possible to recognize how much space has been devoted to fixturing and on-the-floor stock, compared to the area reserved for backup stock, dressing and fitting rooms, receiving, packing, offices, and so forth.

When the partition or wall does not go up to the ceiling, it is represented by narrow lines, partially filled in (BB). This is sometimes called a **partial** or **dwarf wall.**

C. A heavy, solid (or shaded) rectangle extending out from either the thin or heavy solid line, indicates a **pier,** a **beam,** or a **buttress**—reinforcing elements used to add strength to the wall's construction or to help support the weight of the floors above. When the rectangle is attached to an internal or external wall, but is not shaded or filled in, it can represent a vertical conduit or duct for water pipes, electric or gas lines, and so on. This is part of the building's functioning structure and cannot be removed or disregarded by the draftsperson laying out a store or a department.

D. A solid rectangle, out in the middle of the floor, usually in a set grid pattern with other such rectangles, represents a **column.** (A column stands free, out in the open and unattached, while a pier is actually a thickening or an extension out from a constructed wall.) In many cases, interior walls will be constructed to tie in with the independent columns, and thus make them appear as piers. A supporting I-beam will appear on the floor plan looking like the capital letter "I."

E. A rectangle with an "X" through it will usually indicate an unusable area that is part of or essential to the construction and/or maintenance of the building. It is unusable floor space for the purpose of the draftsperson. It is a situation similar to the vertical conduits mentioned previously (see C).

F. A thickening at the end of a wall indicates a door jamb, a molding, or a frame around a window. In either case, the thickening will be to either side of a break in a wall, thus indicating some sort of opening.

G. A thin line plus an arc indicates a traditional door. The line represents the door in plain view; it is hinged to one side or the other of the door jamb or frame. The arc shows the direction and extent of the door swing. This is important to the space planner since it will limit what can be or should be placed on the wall onto which the door will swing back. Traditional doors will vary from 24 inches to 27 inches for closets and toilets, and from 30 inches to 36 inches for main entrances.

H. A double door—two doors that swing open, one to each side—is indicated by a double arc representing two swings. If it is a foyer or vestibule and there are a series of doors—and they all open into the store—all the doors will be hinged, usually swinging in the same direction.

I. For a sliding door, since one panel slides behind the other, there are two lines shown, one for each panel. There is no loss of wall space with this type of door. It is usually used to cover closets or storage space.

J. An accordion fold door—a corrugated vinyl or slatted wood screen that folds back over and over again on itself and often does not extend out beyond the door frame—is represented by an inverted "V". The same symbol could represent a movable, folding wall or partition between areas.

K. A pair of folding doors, hinged to fold back on themselves, is represented the same as an accordion door. These can be solid panels or louvered doors; they may be used as a single pair or two pairs to the single opening. Each pair folds back to the side of the door frame to which it is hinged. Because they fold back on themselves, they take up less back wall space than a traditional door.

L. A curtain closing over a door-way such as might be used in a dressing room area is represented by a double dotted line that indicates a hang-rod; a snaking line is the curtain. (At this point, it should be mentioned that a broken or dotted line usually indicates something that is above ground or floor level, i.e., does not rest directly on the floor, but is still an integral part of the floor plan.)

M. An archway or wall opening that has no door or any other covering or closing device is represented by a broken line. It could also be a pass-through from one area into another, similar to a pass-through between most kitchens and dining rooms. The broken line indicates that there is some wall space above the opening and below the ceiling. If sliding panels or a corrugated screen were installed inside the wall opening, it would be indicated on the floor plan as they appear in I and J. (As previously mentioned in F, the thickening at the end of a wall could indicate a window frame as well as a door jamb. It is much more likely that windows will appear in perimeter or outside walls rather than in internal walls or partitions.)

N. A plate glass window, similar to a "picture" window or a display window that cannot be opened, is represented by two fine lines that abut and fit inside the heavy line representing the exterior wall. Sometimes, three fine lines, close together, will represent the glazed unit inside the thickness of the wall. In architectural drawings, where the wall is not shaded in, the nonopening windows (N) are represented by three lines within the two lines indicating the exterior wall. (See AA.)

NN. A **mullion,** a metal divider between a run of several plate glass windows that facilitates the replacement

Store Planning Symbols

of glass when necessary, is represented in the floor plan by a solid area between the two fine lines of the plate glass window.

O. Windows that can be opened, usually are represented by three fine lines set inside the wall construction. The three lines actually make up the two window frames that can be raised or lowered. (In a casement window, it takes an upper and a lower frame to cover the window area.) The framed windows are usually 30 to 36 inches wide.

P. A casement window with two vertical frames, hinged onto the window frame with windows that swing in and out rather than ride up and down have a symbol that is similar to the one for swinging doors (H) since the action is basically the same.

Q. A tiled floor that could represent vinyl, asphalt, ceramic, or even marble squares set in a geometric pattern is indicated by drawing a similar pattern.

R. In this plan, steps with only two treads (RR) are indicated by three fine lines. Since a riser is usually 8 inches high, the three risers (RRR), the elevated area or platform, are 24 inches high.

S. A balustrade or railing with stanchions or uprights set 3 feet apart is represented by a solid line broken at regular intervals with a dot.

T. A planter containing plants is indicated with a fine line.

U. A skylight or glazed ceiling is represented by the dotted (or broken) line, which indicates something above ground level.

V. Plants are drawn as a circle of jagged lines.

W. A closed-back display window area with a full wall is indicated as a solid line and a sliding door (I) with two lines, one for each panel.

X. An open-back window with a full view of the store beyond is represented by two fine lines. The thin line in the back (XX) indicates the end of the raised platform. If there were no line, it would mean that the display window was at ground level, not elevated at all.

Y. A shadow box display case with a glass front (solid fine line) and sliding panels in back (two lines, one for each panel).

Figure 25.8 is part of an actual fixturing floor plan of a department in a large retail store. It is drawn and reproduced to a scale of $\frac{1}{8}$ inch = 1 foot. The architectural symbols are the same as those used in any architectural floor plan. As discussed and illustrated in the previous section, the basic construction elements are:

A. The heavy line represents a constructed wall that serves as the perimeter or enclosing wall of a particular area or department.

B. The thin, straight, broken line is the boundary of the department and the delineation between the selling area and the walkway or aisle. In the store layout, that line could also indicate a change in flooring materials: hard floors (wood, ceramic, asphalt, or vinyl tiles) for the aisle, and soft floors (carpeting) in the department.

C. The shaded-in rectangles represent the columns necessary to the building's construction. As one looks at this plan, it is simple to see the pattern and spacing of the columns.

D. A platform, facing the aisle, designed to hold a display setup is represented by fine lines drawn in the shape of the setup. Directly behind are two columns enclosed within a semitriangular partition.

E. The two dotted lines indicate an archway or opening in an otherwise straight wall. This is the entrance into the fitting room area.

F. The traditional symbol for a door is a thin line plus an arc.

G. The individual fitting rooms are drawn with solid lines for the walls and a thin lines plus arcs for the doors. The arc shows the direction and extent of the door swing.

The fixtures on the floor plan are represented as follows:

H. Wall-hung merchandise: The two thin lines, perpendicular to the constructed wall, are brackets that are connected into a slotted system set in or on that wall. Many perimeter walls have slotted uprights. The broken line between the two brackets indicates the hang-rod. It is depicted by a broken or dotted line because it is above the floor level. The dotted line that is spaced about 1 foot out from the hang-rail is an overhang or valance extending out from the wall. It covers the hang-rods and is probably equipped with secondary lighting for merchandise and the back wall.

I. Binning on the perimeter wall: The dotted line in front of it is an overhead fascia or canopy with lighting.

J. A cash register and wrapping station, known as C/r or cash/wrap desk: It is often combined with a column, as shown here represented by a shaded rectangle. The column provides an electrical outlet, necessary for most new registers, as well as visibility. A shopper can see a column from across the floor, and thus, more easily find the cash/wrap station. The register and wrapping station are represented by fine lines. "X" marks the space for the register. A large shaded-in rectangle is immediately behind the cash register and wrapping station configuration.

K. A column enclosure: It is a shield or mask built around an actual column and used either decoratively or functionally. It is represented by a shaded-in rectangle for the column and fine lines in the shape of the enclosure. Sometimes, the sides are mirrored to provide ambience as well as mirrors to enable shoppers to examine the merchandise. Sometimes, they are used as a backup for a mannequin platform (see N) or to hold merchandise from attached hang-rails or waterfalls.

L. A T-stand: The small, special item or featured attraction displayer often used to line the aisle as a "come-on" is indicated with a small circle and angled fine line drawn through it. They are also used throughout the department as "reminders."

M. A round rack, in this instance, on a "Y" frame: Depicted here is a standard unit, 3 feet in diameter. The broken circle that extends out another foot from the inner ring indicates where the outer edges of the hanging garments will extend beyond the fixture itself. Thus, a 3-foot round rack will actually take up a space on the selling floor measuring 5 feet in diameter.

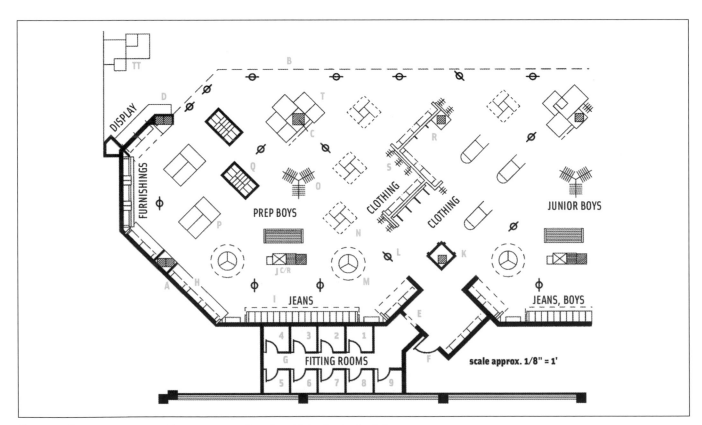

Figure 25.8 A section of an actual department store floor plan with the floor and wall fixtures.

N. A quad rack, or four-armed fixture that shows four face-out groups of merchandise: Again, the broken square encompassing this fixture indicates the outer edges of the hanging garments extending beyond the floor unit itself.

O. A "Y" rack: It takes up a large area on the floor and does not hold nearly as much merchandise as might be fitted into that same space on a different fixture. It does, however, present a different look, a different directional setup in merchandise presentation. The short bars extending from the three major arms of the unit are the "hangers," and again suggest the amount of space they will require.

P. A group of three tables in a cluster: Sometimes, these tables will have drawers or cabinet space below the table top for extra stock.

Q. A multiple binning raised up on a base or a table: This is indicated by a rectangle. Fine lines are drawn within the rectangle in the configuration of the bins.

R. A low partition, not a floor-to-ceiling, constructed wall: The short lines that are perpendicular to the "wall" suggest that they are brackets that fit into slotted uprights.

S. Waterfalls or a "face-out" arrangement for merchandise: The three arms that extend out are crossed with "hangers" to show that the merchandise will face forward.

T. An arrangement around a column of platforms, pedestals, or cubes for a mannequin presentation: This is represented by a pattern of squares surrounding a column.

TT. Another cube or pedestal buildup: This buildup is shown as large and small squares in the shape of the buildup.

Other Types of Dimensional Drawings

It is also recommended that the display person learn to make an elevation of an object or area. Whereas the plan view gives the length and width (or depth) of an area, the **elevation,** or flat, front-on view, is another two-dimensional view that shows the width and the height. The elevation is used in conjunction with the plan. It supplies the missing measurements and answers questions like these: Does the table have drawers or cabinets below? Does the unit have legs, or does it sit directly on the floor? How many bins or shelves will fit on the wall?

The display person can also attempt to master a simple **isometric perspective** or projection, which is a type of mechanical, scale drawing that gives all the measurements (height, width, and depth), thereby providing a more natural, three-dimensional representation of an object or area. It is actually a form of shop drawing, and a carpenter or builder could take the measurements directly from the drawing, and at the same time see what the unit will look like. This type of dimensional representation starts with a correct and well-drawn floor plan.

Store Planning as a Career

Store planning is a growing field that visual merchandisers can enter. There is no way that one chapter or even an entire book will create a store planner, but many of the techniques that store planners use have been discussed in this text.

A knowledge of mechanical drawing and drafting is essential. The store planner must be able to communicate in the language of plans and elevations—and all in scale. The awareness of the importance of color and texture (Chapter 2) and the impact of light and lighting (Chapter 4) on color and on the merchandise are essential to the store planner. He or she must understand also how color, light, and texture will suggest certain "clichés" of ambience (Chapter 2).

Fixtures are the "furniture" of the store (Chapters 12 and 14), and the store planner must know the various types that are available and what they will do for the merchandise and the store's image. It is a function of the store planner to use the floor space—and the air space—to their fullest. He or she must devise economical and creative methods for housing stock and highlighting displays. Sometimes, the store planner will use real furniture and antiques (Chapter 15) as fixtures or props in order to get a desired effect for a unique shop or department.

Mannequins and forms (Chapters 9 to 11) are the "handmaidens" of display and they serve the store planner well. They can be used instead of signs to designate what is being sold in an area or to add a high point in an otherwise flat merchandise presentation. Mannequins add drama as aisle liners or as centers of interest in island presentation; they are invaluable to the store planner, especially where a store has no display windows.

Any display person who wishes to become a store planner should consider studying, in depth, interior design, materials and methods of construction, perspective rendering, the history of furniture and decoration, furniture construction, and lighting techniques. There are some schools that do grant degrees in store planning. This is a relatively new field and one that has much to offer the display person who wants to advance in retailing. Individuals interested in store planning might contact the local chapter of the Institute of Store Planners (ISP) or the American Society of Interior Designers (ASID) for more information on schools with store planning curricula.

Store Planning and Design: A Recap

- Duties of a store planner include the following:
  a. To design an efficient and attractive selling environment that will promote maximum sales and savings in labor and energy.
  b. To combine the selling space with the "behind-the-scenes" service area where stock is maintained and the nonselling activities of the store are carried on.
  c. To set up traffic patterns that will promote customer movement from areas that get the greatest exposure to remote corners and back areas.
  d. To promote and sell, stock and show. The store planner selects the selling vehicle for the specific merchandise being offered.
  e. To enhance the store's image and, thereby, add stature to the merchandise being offered.
- Scale is the relative proportion of one object to another.
- Rehabilitation is the remodeling, redecorating, and refixturing of an existing structure, but does not necessarily involve gutting or rebuilding.

- Materials needed to draw up a floor plan include a drawing board, a T-square, a triangle, a compass, a french curve, a scale ruler, graph paper, tracing paper, hard pencils, a ruby eraser, and a kneaded eraser.
- A floor plan is a flat representation that gives the length and width (or depth) of an area as seen from overhead, while an elevation is a flat, front-on view that shows the width and height.
- A knowledge of mechanical drawing is essential to a store planner. He or she must also be aware of color and texture; the impact of light and lighting on merchandise; and the types and availability of fixtures, mannequins, and forms.
- A prospective store planner should study, in depth, interior design, materials and methods of construction, perspective rendering, the history of furniture and decoration, furniture construction, and lighting techniques.

Questions for Review and Discussion

1. What are the main roles and responsibilities of a store planner?

2. With what individuals will a store planner need to work closely in order to achieve the best possible results in store design and layout?

3. List the "behind-the-scenes" areas and social amenities that must be included in the floor plan.

4. Describe the preparation and communication that must take place before drawing the floor plan for a store.

5. If a store planner is going to design a plan for a 100-foot by 200-foot specialty store, how large will the plan be using ¼-inch scale?

6. What is a scaled floor plan and what are the benefits of its use?

7. How does a scale ruler work?

8. What is a template and how is it used in floor planning?

9. Describe the symbols used to illustrate the following features:
   a. steps
   b. a mullion
   c. a column
   d. a sliding curtain
   e. a door
   f. a cash/wrap station
   g. a round rack
   h. a quad rack

10. Explain the differences between a floor plan, an elevation, and an isometric perspective. What is the purpose of each?

11. In what areas must a visual merchandiser be knowledgeable in order to be a successful store planner?

CHAPTER TWENTY-SIX

Visual Merchandising and the Changing Face of Retail

AFTER YOU HAVE READ THIS CHAPTER,
YOU WILL BE ABLE TO DISCUSS:

- Three retail store formats that have been taking an increasing "slice" of the retail pie over the past two decades.

- Specific visual merchandising considerations for a big box or superstore, discount/factory outlet store, or vendor shop.

- Ways in which large, hanger-style stores can be "warmed up" through effective store planning and display.

VISUAL MERCHANDISING AND THE CHANGING FACE OF RETAIL: TRADE TALK

> big box store
> category killer
> discount store
> drive aisle
> factory outlet store
> mom-and-pop store
> shop-within-a-shop
> superstore
> vendor shop

During most of the 20th century, most people in the United States shopped in department stores, large specialty stores, and in small **mom-and-pop stores** that usually were geared to local neighborhood trade. The 1950s saw the start and eventual spread of malls and shopping centers and the small specialty chain stores that began to proliferate across the country. It was the late 1960s and early 1970s that ushered in the "boutique" phenomenon: small specialized **shops-within-a-shop** that began to show up in the major department stores, targeted at specific markets and age groups. Designer shops also appeared on the better fashion streets in the larger cities as the "prêt-a-porter" concept became a viable opportunity for designers to spread their wares about.

Americans have always been brand conscious and responded to "names" in advertising. With the growth of TV and more nationally distributed magazines, name brands featured in ads and commercials became a draw or magnet when those names appeared in department and speciality stores. People through the ages must have waited for "sale" events in order to shop "discount" though they didn't know that that was what they were doing. It wasn't until the 1970s that discount shopping, factory outlet stores, and value-oriented malls became a considered competition to the traditional retail stores.

The 1980s was a decade of expansion—and of consolidation. Speciality stores like Banana Republic, Gap, Benetton, and The Limited seemed to pop up in malls and on shopping streets across the country while department stores were disappearing, changing names and/or identities. Many mom-and-pop shops and small independent stores gave up the fight against the spread of the specialty chains.

The 1990s has witnessed the growth of a new phenomenon: the **superstore** or **big box store.** In giant, hangar-like constructions of concrete, cement, steel, and glass—covering vast areas from 20,000 to over 100,000 square feet—retailers collect a vast assortment of usually one specific kind of product and then turn these monster spaces into **category killers.** The term refers to the fact that they do "kill off" the smaller stores that carry that same category of merchandise because the giant has a greater selection and usually a better price and offers the selection in an open, easy-to-shop space.

Another recent addition to the retail format vocabulary is the vendor shop. Though the concept of brand name shops-within-a-shop is not new, the recent approach is. Today's vendor shops are miniatures of the designers' or brand names' own retail stores and though located in department and speciality stores, the brand name manufacturer controls how the shop looks and how the merchandise is presented. In this chapter, we consider how these new retail concepts rely on visual merchandising and display—on the selection of fixtures, graphics, signage, and decoratives to create the desired image for the buying public. Visual merchandising and display more than just attracts them—it keeps them in the store.

Big Box or Superstore

It is all size and selection. These giant retail boxes are often located along main highways and feature bold graphics, signage, and colors on their facades to attract the traffic and invite the shoppers into their open parking lots. Everything here is done to make the shopping experience easy and fun even though the shopper isn't actually aware of the miles of walking that is involved. Concrete floors may be tiled, there may be areas of carpeting or an occasional wood floor, but mostly the floors are painted in colors to help the shopper move around the space and to define different areas in the store. The open, exposed ceiling is almost always filled with pipes, ducts, and vents that control and carry the electricity, water, heating, and air-conditioning apparatus. Sometimes the high ceilings are pierced with skylights that allow the natural daylight to mingle with the many sources of artificial light provided to properly illuminate the space.

Today's shopper wants comfort, convenience, and value. The shopper also wants selection, service, and entertainment. He or she wants to enjoy the time spent in

Figure 26.1 Color is used to help shoppers get around in the hypermarket/superstore. Areas are marked off with strong colors for the perimeter walls, columns, and the signage: even the fixtures are finished in the area color. In this mega-store the dark blue refers to hard goods, electronics, and such, the red area is for family fashion, and the yellow area is for fresh and packaged foods. *Gran Bazaar, Toluca, Mexico.*

from the ground. The merchandise might be home appliances, computers and/or electronic equipment, home repair, or home fashion accessories. The displays will show compatible pieces of the merchandise arranged in "live-in" settings that often suggest a particular lifestyle. There can be a vignette setting of a sophisticated kitchen for a working couple, a rustic hunting lodge kitchen for a weekend house, or even a kitchen for a person who would rather paint or play an instrument than cook. These are settings with personality and the vignettes add life, vitality, and color to the warehouse setting as well as humanizing the products.

Figure 26.2 Big spaces need big statements as their focal points. At Toys'R'Us in Times Square, New York, the brightly painted and illuminated ferris wheel fills the central atrium of the multi-level store. Its movement is the center of attraction and attention. The store's color-filled departments radiate out from this central spectacular. *Toys'R'Us, Times Square, New York.*

the store so the retailer, the architect/designer, the visual merchandiser, and the display person have to "warm up" and personalize the vast space into smaller, more comfortable, life-size spaces that have a feeling of intimacy. Also, the retailer's goal is to prolong the shopper's stay in the store, so the retailer has to provide reasons to stay. Cafes and food courts, interactive displays, video monitors, music, aromas, lighting effects, and places where children can be safely left to play and be amused while the parents are free to shop are some of the best "reasons."

The big boxes are humanized by lifestyle displays on the major aisles or the **drive aisles.** Drive aisles are main aisles that lead and direct shoppers. These displays feature the merchandise that is stocked behind, often on giant industrial fixtures that may reach up 10 to 12 feet

In these wide open spaces signage is very important. From the entrance, the would-be shopper wants to know where to go to find whatever he or she is interested in finding. It is the oversized signage and sometimes the giant graphics that serve as directional guideposts. Color-keyed banners, streamers, and pennants not only add spice and color as they hang down from the exposed ceiling, they can also help to divide the space into specific areas—all coded by the color: for example, blue = home, green = office, red = travel, yellow = entertainment. The on-the-aisle displays and the computerized kiosks stop the shopper and reveal the things he or she hadn't planned to look at or consider. A centrally located and well-identified information or service desk is essential for those who are too impatient or too unwilling to read signs or follow fluttering flags.

The lighting in the store must reinforce the displays along the way: highlight them and turn them into focal points that will attract and stop the shopper on his or her way. The graphics should not only set the lifestyle concept for the product, but also help to explain how, when, and where the product will work. Some big box operations have electronic stations near the entrance where shoppers can punch in what they want and be shown, on a monitor, the quickest way to get to the product. Some computerized stations, in the departments, will provide specific answers to specific questions about the products contained in this area.

Though merchandise in the big box stores is often crated and boxed and stacked ceiling high, samples must be available to be seen, touched, tested, and tried. Simple, easy to read, and easy to understand signage should be provided near or on the sample product to make it self-explanatory. Here, too, a simple display, a prop, a background panel, a graphic, or a floor pad—whatever—can enhance the product and make it more relevant to the shopper: a wicker basket overloaded with colorful T-shirts standing next to a washing machine, a stuffed toy dog with a doggie bowl standing and staring at a refrigerator, bags of popcorn and pizza boxes piled up on the floor in front of a TV set, and so on.

The big box phenomenon is now moving into town and taking over old, no longer used movie houses, deserted supermarkets, and—quite naturally—untenanted warehouses. The major problem is providing sufficient parking spaces, especially where shoppers have to pick up and move large, clumsy, and often heavy crates or cartons. Big box stores are not only for "hard goods." The new two- and three-story Borders and Barnes & Noble bookstores may fit into this category, but are really more like superstores or category killers. They not only have a vast selection of books for all ages and for all interests, but they will also carry magazines, writing materials, reading related gifts, CDs, tapes, and computer software. They seem to have everything and anything anybody would hope to find relating to literature, how-to, hobbies, and entertainment. Here, too, the cafe/coffee shop has become the add-on "entertainment" factor along with celebrity appearances. These attractions do prolong the visits to the bookstores. In some instances, the cafe has become the primary reason for the visit and the book-related purchase is the afterthought.

Discount and Factory Outlet Stores

Discount, factory outlet, and value-oriented shopping: these are buzz words that get the shopper's instant attention and are often enough to bring on a shopping spree. These magical terms seem, more and more, to be the "open sesame" to sales. Time- and money-conscious shoppers all have the same goal in mind: they want the best for the least and preferably in the most comfortable and convenient stores.

Unfortunately, some retailers haven't learned that just offering merchandise at reduced prices is not enough. The merchandise has to look good; it has to look as though it is worth more. There is a big difference between a discounted dress and a distressed, "as is" garment. Showing the discounted merchandise in a cold, sterile warehouse setting doesn't necessarily work, either. Harsh bright lights, cold fluorescent ceiling tubes, shiny chrome fixtures, screaming signs, and garish decor do not add stature to the fashion image or the product of the store. They only say "cheap," and shoppers are not looking for "cheap." They are in search of "value."

There has been a proliferation of factory outlet malls, centers, and strips across the United States, and the concept is being introduced abroad. It is not unusual in these "value-oriented" shopping clusters to find famous fashion names like Calvin Klein, Liz Claiborne, Ralph Lauren/Polo, and Anne Klein, or respected, well-adver-

Figure 26.3 The Nike Factory store is identified by the Nike "swoosh" logo and the lifestyle graphics that appear above the merchandise on the perimeter walls. Though the garments are "discounted" and the setting is "industrial/commercial," the products are still presented with care and coordinated for ease of selection. Note how the shirts are arranged by color and sample shoes are displayed over the boxed stock. *Nike Factory Store, Guadalajara, Mexico, Ares Design.*

tized brand names like Timberland, Mikasa, Bass Shoes, Bogner, and London Fog. Shoppers arrive by the carloads: tour busses can be found filling the parking lots like a herd of lumbering elephants as they disgorge thousands of bargain hunters daily. The hunt is on! Often these factory outlet/discount malls will rival the regular malls for ambience, amenities, and for the comforts and conveniences they provide. These are attractively landscaped areas, sometimes with interesting themed buildings and a plethora of inexpensive fast-foods available in well-lit and well-cared for food courts. The only thing that is "discount" is the price of the merchandise. Since many of these individual shops or stores bear illustrious names, as much care, effort, thought, and taste go into the design and merchandise presentation inside as go

into the boutique, of the same name, in a department store or on a fashionable shopping street. The materials and detailing may be less elegant or refined, but the shopper is still aware of the fashion attitude; the image behind the name on the front of the retail space.

As important as the lighting and the overall design of the shop is the visual presentation. The shoppers who are attracted to these outposts of savings are also looking to save time and conserve energy—as well as money. While it can sometimes be fun and an adventure to go rummaging through piles of garments heaped indiscriminantly atop lopsided tables, it is certainly simpler and less of a hassle to find the desired color, size, style, and price range in neatly and intelligently organized groupings. Just as these shoppers are likely to frequent upscaled malls and better department stores, they expect to see displays showing the garments arranged, accessorized and coordinated, and given dramatic life via dimensional forms and arresting props. Shoppers will understand the absence of chic, of-the-moment mannequins, but they cannot accept the worn, weary, and wigless forms of a generation ago. Again, simple and smart mannequin alternatives will do nicely to suggest the body and form and carry off the whole ensemble.

Though more energy-efficient and economical fluorescent lamps may be used in the lighting plan, the plan should also include the atmospheric and accent lighting necessary for the store's image and for accentuating the featured merchandise. The display person must always remember to flatter the shopper as he or she tries on a new garment. Within spending or budgetary restrictions, these **discount/factory outlet stores** are still promoting the fashion images the shopper associates with the designer or the brand name as these images appear in ads in magazines and on TV.

Vendor Shops

Levi's, Coach, Calvin Klein, Liz Claiborne, Ralph Lauren/Polo, Tommy Hilfiger, and so many other well-known and

Figure 26.4 For this Timberland vendor shop, FRCH Design created a selection of tables, floor fixtures, displayers, and a modular wall system so that the pieces could be combined in a variety of ways to show off the Timberland collection. The modularity of the elements means that the fixtures and graphics can be reconfigured to fit into any size or shape space. The graphics and signage units are all part of the vendor's package to the retailer. The vendor shop is the "ultimate" in point-of-purchase design. *Timberland vendor shop, FRCH Design Worldwide.*

nationally advertized brand names and fashion designers share a unique situation in retailing today. They are not only the manufacturers and suppliers of the merchandise that carries their names, but they are also the retailers. It is not unusual to see free-standing stores—even super-stores—bearing these illustrious names on major fashion streets sometimes next to stores that also carry those brand name products. Backed up by the image created by their national campaigns on TV, in magazines, and on giant billboards, they have further enhanced their image with a store design and merchandise presentation that becomes as much a part of their design signature as the photos and graphics used in the ads.

However, these major suppliers of fashion have in the past and probably will in the future continue to sell their products in major department and speciality stores. The brand name/designer supplier has often tried in the past and not always successfully to establish its own look and identity within the department where it is located. By featuring the graphics and signage and the fashion attitude of the line, the supplier tried to promote the brand name by separating this line from the others around it. Today, we find, more and more, small distinctly different "shops" or "boutiques" within a single department: each with its own fixturing and furniture, its own graphics, signage, and lifestyle imagery, merchandise presentation, and sometimes even lighting. We are seeing more of these vendor shops taking over whole departments in stores.

The **vendor shop** will often be a "miniature" of the brand name/designer's freestanding store or will try to recreate, in the limited space, the essence of that retail image. The fixturing, the lighting, the use of graphics, and merchandising techniques will attempt to immediately establish a continuity with the brand name/designer's own, freestanding stores. It is a fully realized shop-within-a-shop, which carries a selection of the brand name/designer's products. Usually, but there are exceptions, the supplier will provide the fixtures and decor for this space, specify the lighting requirements, and also dictate how the merchandise will be visually presented. The retailer (the department or specialty store) yields up some of the precious sales floor space in exchange for the national or worldwide advertising campaigns and special promotions sponsored by the brand name/designer. The right mix of brand names in a department can add stature to the store's fashion im-

age and create a magnet for certain target markets. The brand name can be a bankable asset for the store.

The new vendor shops are being designed by store designers who are accustomed to working with retail space as a total entity. They are sensitive to the retailer's image even as they create the specific and signature look for the brand name/designer. The designers create flexible and adaptable modular components that can be integrated into most retail settings. The basic pieces are like "building blocks"; they can be added on, subtracted from, rearranged, and changed to suit spaces ranging from 100 square feet to well over 1,000 square feet. Gerald Birnbach of Retail Design & Display of Granite Falls, New York, notes, "When a retailer willingly gives up some real estate to a brand name marketer, that vendor is also able to display its full range of products in a tailored environment that helps eliminate some of the competition. In return, the vendor participates in the cost of the shop."

These up-scaled, well-designed, and beautifully fixtured shops are, in a way, demanding that retailers live up to the design standards being set by the vendor shops. There are many valid reasons for including vendor shops within larger retail stores, but there are problems as well. The biggest problem is that the retailer is inviting stiff competition into his or her sphere of retailing and opening up how the store's own lines are being presented in comparison to the slick, professional look of most vendor shops. If the retailer's lines don't look as good—or better—then the retailer's profit line can suffer.

The answer is to look to the "visual" aspects of the business: the store's design and the lighting; the visual merchandising of the stock; the displays that add interest, image, and personality; and the amenities provided for the customer's comfort and convenience.

Kiosks and Retail Merchandising Units (RMUs)

Big box stores and category killer stores are part of today's retail scene, but there is also action at the other end of the retail scale. We are seeing small and compact retail stores making an appearance and some of them are on wheels. They are moveable and can be brought to where the shopper is.

Carts have been around since the advent of wheels. All it takes to make a cart is a flat bed, a railing or fence to

Figure 26.5 The simplest cart combines a pair of large wheels with legs that will help keep the unit upright when at rest. It is readily moveable and can show merchandise on all four sides. There is even a cash drawer in the compact design. Lighting here would probably be battery operated. *Design: Custom Woodcraft, Inc.*

keep the wares from tumbling off, a pair of wheels, and a vertical post to keep the cart standing upright when not in motion. Today the cart has evolved for more specific uses and become a retail merchandising unit, or RMU. This new hybrid has not only been appearing with more and more frequency in the wide open aisles of malls and shopping centers, but also in air terminals, train stations, movie houses, ball parks, sporting arenas, museums, and a multitude of other public spaces where people can gather and indulge in browsing and shopping for fun.

The advantages of the kiosk/RMU are manifold: it is moveable, adaptable, and compact, and can go almost anywhere and show off almost anything. The unit is readily open for business and just as simply closed up at

the end of the business day. What makes it especially important is that in a relatively small space—maybe 5′ by 5′—it is possible for a startup entrepreneur to test out a concept or a new product and its possibilities for success in the market without having to rent a store and furnish and insure it. Neither does he have to stock much more merchandise than he needs on an RMU. If the RMU succeeds, the next stop can be a move into an actual retail space. In addition to being an incubator for a concept that can grow and develop, it is also a means of bringing more visibility to an existing brand name or product by having it appear in malls and traffic centers in readily identifiable and recognizable kiosks. Most ballparks and sporting arenas have souvenir stores where team-endorsed products can be purchased, but the management has found that several RMUs spread around the park or arena are even more effective in bringing the branded merchandise out to the fans.

RMUs have found great favor with mall operators. The advantages are many but the most important one is that they add to the tenant mix and the sense of excitement one feels in a mall where the small, colorful, kiosks-on-casters fill the wide spacious aisles with color, light and a new selection of arts, crafts, and small impulse items. The design of the retail merchandising unit can be individualized and specialized for a branded product, or the kiosk can be designed as an integral part of the mall's

Figure 26.6 The basic RMU or kiosk is shown here both with the stock on view as well as closed up for the night. The doors that close up the unit swing out during business hours and the grids attached to the doors are used to display product. The lighting is self-contained in the unit. *Design: Creations of Dallas.*

Figure 26.7 An RMU with lower shelves on three sides and a cash/wrap counter that fits into the rear of the unit. This kiosk was designed exclusively for the South Park Mall so that there would be a consistent look to the portable/moveable mini-shops on the main aisles of the mall. Each shop carries the vendor's name under the mall's logo sign. *Design: TL Horton Design.*

architecture—or the ball park, train station or museum. Although mall management may dictate the style of the kiosk/RMU it provides to freelance vendors, franchisees, and licensees, it will often have only limited control—mainly size—on the RMUs brought in by national brands that rent floor space in the mall. Jim Allen, Vice President of Retail Development for Simon Property Development, one of the largest mall management companies in the US, said, "The primary method of tailoring the units is through colors, materials and surfaces that are used in the mall. We also tailor the design of the top of the unit to fit in with the property." TL Horton, a

designer of RMUs, said, "With the focus on successfully presenting merchandise, the wagon wheel (of the cart) was eliminated and lower shelving was added. Fluorescent lights were replaced with low-voltage halogen fixtures. Kiosks became taller and identification became more prominent. Support columns were slotted to allow for additional merchandising." Many of these rolling kiosks feature wrap-around shelving and storage areas for additional stock within the space.

The usual RMU is 5′ by 5′ in footpad and most malls restrict the height from 7′ to 9′. Thus, the signage on top can be seen from a distance over the heads of the mall strollers. The unit's superstructure or roof is vital for purposes of identification and recognition. It is here that the designer can add decorative elements and materials to the unit that will tie in with the design of the mall—or the brand's retail image. It is also here that the all-important lighting is concentrated. The lighting can be in the form of electrified tracks that carry the adjustable lamp holders or the low-voltage halogen or incandescent lamps may be extended out on brackets to illuminate the merchandise on the unit. Goose-neck fixtures can be used and bent to target special areas. Sometimes the superstructure will contain plastic panels that carry the tenant's name or the brand name, which will be illuminated by fluorescent tubes set behind the panels. The internal illumination makes the signage, and the kiosk, even more visible in the mall aisle.

With the 5′ by 5′ floor space and the wrap-around shelves on the lower portion of the RMU, there is often a central, vertical display area that rises up from the counter height to show off merchandise at eye level. The slotted uprights make shelving and face-out hanging possible. With this format the vendor is usually stationed beside the unit and thus available to serve shoppers on all sides. Some kiosks are designed larger and may take up spaces 5′ to 7′ in width and up to 10′ in length. In these designs the attendant is often positioned inside the unit and surrounded by counters on four sides, with vertical displays at the ends.

These larger units are designed as modules with parts and pieces that can be added or subtracted as needed. There may also be auxiliary units that stand beside the RMU that can, if desired, be incorporated into the unit when needed. Some designs include corner elements that can be moved in where rounded shelves might or-

Figure 26.8 This illustration shows the several individual modular pieces that can be combined in a variety of ways. It all depends upon the size and shape of the space the kiosk/RMU will occupy on the floor and the type of merchandise to be displayed. The central core of four uprights anchor the design, carry the overhead lighting and signage, and can be capped with a "roof" or ceiling, or slotted to accept brackets for shelves, etc. *Design: Creations of Dallas*

Figure 26.9 The RMU goes out to meet the shopper. This unit is part of the out-of-door excitement that is the Fremont Street Experience in Las Vegas. The casters on the bottom make this unit easy to move and the awnings are necessary to shield the shopper and the merchandise from the strong Vegas sunlight. *Design: TL Horton Design.*

dinarily be, and used for storage or as cash/wrap surfaces. In those RMUs that have the salesperson surrounded by the modules, usually one section will roll out or slide back to allow the server to get in and out of the unit.

Although the big wheels are gone, there are casters with stoppers on them to allow the RMU to be moved from area to area. The out-of-door units may be designed with larger casters and greater mobility as they may be moved more frequently and over greater distances. Security is always a serious consideration in an RMU design. Obviously, the tenant will not be removing all the products nightly only to restock each morning. As the merchandise needs to be protected when the vendor leaves, the kiosk may feature roll-down canvas covers that can be lashed and locked, or wrap-around wire mesh guards that "disappear" into a hidden slot during the daytime hours. Some kiosks are designed with sliding doors that can be locked to close off the merchandise on the upright displayers while the shelves below fold-up against the body of the RMU, and the displayed stock are locked in cabinets built into the lower part of the RMU.

With branding becoming more and more important and the desire to take the brand name and merchandise up front to the buying public, the RMU is growing as a retail venue. All sorts of spaces are opening up and inviting kiosks/RMUs in as viable vending set-ups. Being able to merchandise where shoppers are is what it is all about. What the RMU does is show a selection of what is available, swiftly satisfying the impulse shopper. It is all about impulse; about seeing something where you ordinarily would not expect to find it, and buying it in a hassle-free situation. The RMU allows a concept to have an "out-of-town" tryout before hitting the "big time." It is also the fastest way for the brand name retailer to get exposure in many markets and in a signature vehicle that can become as recognizable as the brand name or logo.

Figure 26.10 This is a super kiosk! It not only contains several different sizes of merchandising modules, display fixtures, and illuminated towers, it is also equipped with a computer and TV monitor for its private "consultation area" and to connect to the Salon located in another area of the mall. This setup brings into prominence the beauty and hair product line of Jacques Despars and also introduces the Salon, which is in a different part of the mall. *Jacques Despars Kiosk, Design: GHA, Montreal, Canada.*

Visual Merchandising and the Changing Face of Retail: A Recap

- During the 20th century, retail store formats have evolved from department stores, large specialty stores, and small mom-and-pop shops, to malls and shopping centers, and finally to the emergence of big box stores (or superstores), discount/factory outlet stores, and vendor shops. These new formats offer new challenges to the display person/visual merchandiser.

- Big box stores are giant retail boxes that need to be "warmed up" through layout, lighting, and display techniques into smaller, more comfortable, life-size spaces. Lifestyle vignettes are an effective way to personalize a display and lead the shopper into a selection of nearby merchandise.

- Large, legible signage or graphics are needed to help shoppers navigate within the big box stores. Some stores include electronic or computerized stations that provide directions to merchandise within the store or answers to specific questions about products.

- Discount or factory outlet stores are oriented to time- and money-conscious shoppers who want the best for the least, but in a store that is still comfortable and convenient. The store layout, lighting, and merchandise displays here should emphasize "value," not "cheap."

- Though the emphasis in a discount/factory store is on energy-efficiency and economy, atmospheric and accent lighting can be used to supplement fluorescents to create an image for the store, to accentuate featured merchandise, and/or to flatter the shopper as he or she tries on a garment.

- Vendor shops are shops-within-a-shop—retail formats that offer brand name or designer merchandise in a boutique setting within a larger retail or department store setting. Often these shops are "miniatures" of freestanding designer stores.

- New vendor shops are designed to provide a signature look that can be accommodated to various dimensions and settings. Modular components provide the store designer with flexibility, allowing very small or very large spaces to present merchandise in a visually consistent way.

Questions for Review and Discussion

1 Name a specific big box store or superstore with which you are familiar. How does this store use lighting, graphics, signage, or lifestyle displays to enhance the merchandising of its products?

2. Why would a discount or factory outlet store want to consider ambience, amenities, and the comfort and convenience of shoppers in its design and merchandise displays when people who shop in these stores are looking for a less-expensive alternative to mall and department stores?

3. List the advantages and disadvantages to a brand name supplier/designer of presenting its merchandise in a vendor shop within a larger department or retail store.

PART SIX
RELATED AREAS OF VISUAL MERCHANDISING AND DISPLAY

THE FINAL SEGMENT OF THIS BOOK is devoted to miscellaneous areas that are a part of, or closely related to, visual merchandising. With the growth of self-service retailing and the increased competition for consumer dollars, point-of-purchase (or POP) displays have proliferated. Chapter 27 addresses the booming POP industry, focusing on the presentation of merchandise to the customer at the crucial point of purchase.

The ins and outs of trade show and exhibit design are explored in Chapter 28. This is a wide-open field for those with a background in display, commercial or graphic arts, or interior design.

Next, the world of fashion is examined, specifically with regard to setting the scene for fashion shows. This job often falls on the visual merchandising staff of the retail store, often with little or no budget or staff. A successful fashion show requires a great deal of resourcefulness on the part of display personnel, as Chapter 29 makes clear.

Trade organizations related to the visuals merchandising field are identified in Chapter 30. Most visual merchandising professionals find that involvement with industry trade organizations provides them with the support, resources, and inspiration necessary in their occupations.

Chapter 31 identifies career opportunities in visual merchandising and related areas. The importance of a résumé and portfolio are also discussed.

CHAPTER TWENTY-SEVEN

Point-of-Purchase Display

AFTER YOU HAVE READ THIS CHAPTER,
YOU WILL BE ABLE TO DISCUSS:

- Displays that are considered POP.

- Reasons for the use of POP by retailers.

- Functions of a POP display unit.

- The product categories utilizing POP fixtures
  and materials.

- Materials used in the design of a POP unit.

POINT-OF-PURCHASE: TRADE TALK

appliqué
blind embossing
die cutting process
embossing
hot stamping
injection molding techniques
injection molding tool
lamination
layering
papier-mâché
paper sculpture
permanent unit
point-of-purchase (POP)

point-of-purchase advertising
   institution (POPAI)
rubber mâché
semipermanent unit
silk-screen printing
sonic seal
temporary or promotional
   unit
thermoplastics
thermosetting plastics
tie-ins
vacuum forming process

Point-of-purchase (**POP**) has been around since long before the cigar store Indian sculpted out of wood, clutching a handful of tobacco leaves, and garishly painted in green, red, and gold. It stood outside cigar stores and tobacco shops announcing to one and all on the street that tobacco products were sold just inside. Point-of-purchase signage probably goes back even further than the Middle Ages when red cylinders bandaged in white announced to one and all the presence of the barber and blood-letter in the community. A walk down the crooked, cobblestoned streets of Salzburg, Austria, is a walk through two or three centuries of POP signage: three-dimensional objects that proclaim a product or service and even suggest its quality. Thus, there are giant keys hanging out over the locksmith's shop; gilded pretzels call to those seeking a bakery, just as the giant violin would entice a musician in search of a violin maker. For those who never learned to read—or those who could not make out the words from a distance—these giant replicas provided the information.

Point-of-purchase has become in recent times a complete and convoluted industry. It is display, fixturing, store design, and advertising all in one. It is the total image fabrication of a product; the attraction to the product as well as the provider of the product on the selling floor. It is the "shill" that stands out front and invites the shopper to come inside where the product is on view. It is the silent or not-so-silent salesperson who points out where the product is once the shopper is inside, and it also explains what the product is all about. Point-of-purchase also stacks, stocks, holds, and coordinates the product or products in a manner that both enhances the unit(s) and is convenient to the shopper. This full range of service to the shopper and the promotion of the product has made the POP industry the biggest and fastest growing extension of the display/fixture and advertising industries. In 1996, the total expenditure for POP advertising, signage materials, and in-store media provided to retailers by the vendors was in excess of $12.7 billion dollars.

What Is POP?

Point-of-purchase used to be synonymous with "impulse shopping." It used to be associated with things sold at the checkout counter or the cash/wrap desk; the prepackaged, boxed, and shrink-wrapped items the

Figure 27.1 To promote the new Blossom line of toiletries in the Victoria's Secret Beauty stores, the company went all out with printed banners on translucent fabric, cardboard counter cards, and special tie-in shopping bags. They all carried the cherry blossom graphic art that appeared on the packages of the new line. The pink table covers and sprays of artificial cherry blossoms helped carry through the pink to red color scheme. *Victoria's Secret, Watertower, Chicago.*

shoppers didn't really need but were intrigued enough to pick up and buy. Today's POP is much more than the neon-outlined clock, the guzzling beer running from bottle to glass and back forever captured in a bas-relief of plastic, or the cardboard box that opens into a "dump truck" carrying a load of candy bars.

Point-of-purchase units can be displays, displayers, fixtures, and auxiliary items provided by the vendors or manufacturers to the retailers who stock and sell their products. The displays, fixtures, and assorted signage can appear outside the store—in the windows—and inside the retail setting on ledges, counters, shelves, on the selling floor, or suspended from the ceiling. The POP displays and fixtures can be made of cardboard, paper, wood, plastic, and metal, or any combinations of these materials.[1]

More often than not, a POP unit is not designed to exist by itself but is part of an overall promotion or scheme that can involve dozens of coordinated elements—each located and doing its work in another area of the retail setting. The coordinated units are designed to promote the product or brand name, the image of the product, the customer's self image, the advantages of this product over others similar to it, and the eventual stocking of the product being offered. The campaign or promotion can run the gamut from posters, cards, and banners to counter or ledge displays to mass merchandising fixtures on the floor.

Figure 27.2 Timberland ordered these fully-dimensional counter display units to emphasize the comfort value of their shoes. These were shown in-store on counters or on display tables as well as in windows where they were surrounded by the shoes. The use of wood and authentic reproductions of an antique shoe form and clamp along with the recognizable Timberland signature yellow color made an immediate appeal to the mostly male target market. The displays also furthered the Timberland brand image. *Design: Fitch, Powell, Ohio.*

Why POP?

Some of the reasons for POP promotions and the use of POP materials are:

1. The appearance of the sign or display in the retail setting where the product is available, can and does often encourage the consumer to make an on-the-spot decision to purchase.
2. The sign or display flags the shopper—gains attention—and brings the consumer to the product.
3. Point-of-purchase not only enhances the product's image or its timeliness when part of a special promotion like Halloween/Easter/Fourth of July, it can also serve to explain the product and thus inform the shopper.
4. Coordinated promotions can stimulate the consumer not only to buy the product, but to buy other products that are being promoted along with it, such as combining a soft drink or beer promotion with snacks like nuts, pretzels, or potato chips.
5. The POP display or sign can reinforce a price message—or stimulate an immediate action response from the consumer because "now" is the time to take advantage of a special promotion, a giveaway, a contest, and so on.

---

[1] See Glossary of Point-of-Purchase Display Terms.

Therefore, POP displays and designs:

- Attract attention to the product.
- Promote or reinforce brand name recognition.
- Show and explain the product. Educate the consumer.
- Answer relevant questions: price, size, applications, and so forth.
- Hold stock or arrange stock for the shopper's convenience.
- Increase sales by coordinating items—or by "impulse sales."

Who Uses POP and Where?

There are several major markets and manufacturers in those markets who are the most frequent purchasers of POP. They, in turn, give the material to the vendors to promote and sell their products. We have grouped these markets and a brief list of their products below. These groups are recognized by the Point of Purchase Advertising Institute (**POPAI**—pronounced "popeye"), an important industry organization of manufacturers and producers of POP material and the purchasers of POP products. A brief list of products within each market follows:

Food and Paper Goods
Frozen and fresh foods, foods packed in cans, cases, cartons, tins, bottles, and bags. Anything from deli to salad dressings, from cake mixes to dog treats and snacks. Paper towels, napkins, picnic plates, soaps, cleaners, and detergents also come under this category.

Transportation Industry
Automobile showroom displays, gas and petroleum products, work stations, car accessories, tires, batteries, hubcaps, cellular phones, and so on.

Personal Products
Shoes and shoe care, sportswear, active sports clothing, sneakers, sports equipment, bodybuilding equipment, eye fashions, costume jewelry, watches, pens, and related items.

Figure 27.3 The on-the-floor display stands also appeared as vertical highlights in shoe windows to point up Timberland's Shoes for Children. The smaller scale and the softening element, such as the rounded shelves, complemented the children's shoes being shown. The Timberland logo (the oak tree) and the signature color (yellow) tied this product display in with the Timberland brand image. *Design: Fitch, Powell, Ohio.*

Beverages
Beer, soda, soft drinks, liquors, wines, and other such beverages.

Health and Beauty Aids
Shampoos, hair products, skin care, vitamins, over-the-counter drugs, cosmetics, toiletries, perfumes.

Hardware/Building Materials
Lumber, roofing, insulation, paints, lighting fixtures and lamps, wood flooring, carpeting, doors, cabinets, and related items.

Services and Unclassified

Fast-food operations, lotteries, educational products, books, paperback books, vending machines, games and toys, airlines, cruise lines, hotels, travel, lawn care, and so on.

Household Goods

Garden supplies, dishes, pots and pans, coffee brewers, baking equipment, tools, TV, radios, VCRs, home entertainment, lawn and patio furniture, kitchen fixtures, and similar products.

Tobacco

Cigarettes, chewing tobacco, and related products.

Considering the above breakdown, it is apparent that POP signs, displays, and fixtures appear most frequently in the following retail outlets:

- Markets/supermarkets and hypermarkets
- Convenience operations
- Mass merchandisers, such as Kmart and Wal-Mart
- Home improvement centers
- Drugstore chains and pharmacies
- Department and specialty stores
- Wine and liquor stores/packaged goods stores
- Sporting goods operations
- Office supply outlets
- Bars, taverns, cafes
- Automotive after-markets: service centers combined with auto showrooms

POP Longevity

Point of purchase units can be **permanent, semipermanent, temporary** or **promotional.** Depending on the product's quality, styling, and end use, a POP counter display or store fixture can be constructed out of wood, wire, or plastic and be expected to last for a year or more in a drugstore or mass-merchandiser operation. A permanent fixture displayer may be considered where the product is not likely to change in design or in packaging very rapidly and usually is a more costly item than an "impulse" item. A permanent display may show off products like watches, fountain pens, samples of wood flooring, tires, or vacuum cleaners. If a new product is added or a design is changed, often the displayer/fixture design of a permanent unit is generic enough to accommodate the new product, or it is designed to be adaptable to possible changes of stock. The displayer/fixture will be more costly to produce, there may be less units produced but what is made to stand up to wear and tear for a year or so will be considered "permanent" for that expected period of time. Included in this category are items also like neon signs, and acrylic etched signs, electrified clocks, and illuminated menu boards.

The semipermanent fixture or counter unit is usually expected to be in use for about six months to a year, and though it is constructed to be rigid and "tough," the materials may not be as "fine" or "refined" as the materials used in a permanent fixture/displayer.

The temporary or promotional unit has the shortest life expectancy. It is designed to serve on the counter, on the floor or on the shelf for a few weeks, a month or two at the most. Usually it is a timely or seasonal piece that ties in with other media—such as ads or TV commercials. Promotional displays could be created for Halloween, the Super Bowl game, New Year's Eve celebrations, Easter, a new color palette of cosmetics for fall, the introduction of a "new and improved" product in a new and unfamiliar package. There may be life-size cutouts, dump bins, banners, dangles, shelf talkers, buttons, brochure holders, take-one pads, sampling-in-store—all tied in with the single promotional theme. Once the action or event is over, so is the life expectancy of the promotional POP unit that is often produced of cardboard, corrugated materials, or lightweight vacuum forming.

Designing the POP Unit

Before the designer can start the process of creating the desired unit, he or she must have the following information.

Product

What is it? Who can and will use it? What is the target market or the customer base? Is this a new product—or a "new and improved" product? Is there a new formula—a new shape or size—a new package? How is the product packaged? If this is not a new product, how has it been displayed before?

Unit

What is this unit to do? Is it a display, a displayer, a stocking unit, a dispensing unit, a demonstration piece, a sign? If it is a display, will it be used on the counter, in a window, or on the floor? How many products will it show? Does the unit need to incorporate a take-one pad, a brochure or leaflet holder, a mock-up of the product?

If it is meant to contain and show stock on the selling floor, how many pieces of product will be supported? Will the unit have only one product or does it have to show off a line of products; that is, a line of hair conditioners and shampoos designed for different types of hair, or a selection of vitamins?

Where will this unit be used and in what kind of setting: a supermarket, a drug store, a department store, cafe, or convenience store?

Timing

A very important element, not only in the designing of the unit but in determining how the unit will be constructed or executed, is how long the unit is expected to function. Is the unit to be part of a special promotion event, something that will come and go quickly—something with a limited period of usage—or is it expected to serve for several weeks or a selling season?

Should this be a permanent unit that will be constructed of sturdy, durable materials that will stand up

Figure 27.5 Interactive kiosks or fixtures or stations are becoming more and more popular. They attract and involve the nimble-fingered, digitally adept Generations X and Y. This unit appeared in malls and served as a source of information as well as entertainment. It also featured visual images of merchandise featured in participating stores in the mall. These appeared on the flat plasma screen set atop the kiosk. *Centerline Kiosk by Pioneer Plasma Display.*

Figure 27.4 For use in the Hush Puppy outlet stores, this free standing displayer was designed in wood and metal. The vertical panel, in the back, carried a graphic message panel that could be changed seasonally or for special promotions. The giant wheel, up front, made the fixture moveable, but it stood solidly once it was in place. *Design: Fitch, Powell, Ohio.*

to the handling and traffic on a busy floor for an extended period of time?

Is the unit to be part of an advertising campaign and therefore relate to messages that will appear in TV commercials, in magazine and newspaper ads—and also include the same images that will be appearing in the other media? Is it a promotional piece for Halloween, a Rose Bowl game tie-in, a golf tournament, a Fourth of July celebration?

The amount of time the unit will be used will, to a large degree, affect how the piece is constructed: cardboard versus plastic, paper versus fabric, and so forth.

Tie-Ins

We have just mentioned above, the possible **tie-in** with an overall promotion. If the unit is to be part of an overall, all-inclusive promotion, like the launching of a new perfume or a Christmas campaign for a sparkling wine, what is the basic concept of the promotion? What images will be used? What copy or tag lines? What promotional elements should be included in this POP unit? Who else is working on the promotion? What other POP units are being designed for the promotion? Are there magazine and newspaper ads being produced—TV commercials, radio spots, a celebrity tie-in, a new pack-

age being introduced, a color scheme, a graphic image? Just how much are you expected to conform to the other elements in the promotion? Very likely, you may be bidding on several related parts of the promotion such as banners, streamers, counter and/or window displays, table covers, and so on.

End Usage

What kind of store will the unit appear in? High fashion? Popular priced? A department store or specialty store or a mass merchandiser? Again, referring to the target market, is this a specialty targeted market such as Asian, His-

Figure 27.6 The US West kiosk was part of the POP promotion designed for that company by The Retail Group. In addition to the interactive stations and the display of new products in this modular on-the-floor construction, brochures explaining and showing the products were available in the brochure holders situated between the screens. *Design: The Retail Group.*

panic, African-American, Irish (for St. Patrick's Day when everybody seems to be Irish)? Knowing the specific market, if there is one, can provide the designer with guidelines and parameters; certain colors may be more effective for one ethnic group than another and some designs or elements may be taboo (some Asians consider the number 4 as "death," and in some societies white is a color associated with funerals).

Production Run

Of course, it is very important to know how many pieces will be produced. How large will the run be? What techniques will be best and most economical for that production number? Should it be vacuum formed or injection molded, lithograph offset printed or silk-screened? The size and number will affect the cost of the dies, tools, plates, and/or screens. If it will be a large run, then the dies and molds must be constructed of materials that may be more costly but will hold up for the projected run and the large number of "shots."

Shipping

How are the units to be shipped? Where are they to be shipped and in what stage of assembly? Will all the pieces be packed in several giant crates and shipped directly to the manufacturer/vendor and then distributed to several strategic locations before being sent to the retailers? Will the pieces be shipped unassembled, partially assembled, or fully assembled in individual cartons and sent directly to the retailer, timed to get there for the specific promotion or will it go to another POP producer where the units may be prepacked or have additional coordinated POP units added to these before being shipped? What kind of cartons or crates will be required? How big? How strong?

Light and Motion

Is this unit to be enhanced with light, motion, or computer chips so that the shopper will be able to interact with the product or the display or get special information? These elements add to the cost of the unit. How much can the unit be enhanced with decoratives, appliqués, and so on, before over-costing the unit?

Cost

And now—down to the basics: How much? You may not get a direct answer, but as a designer it does help to have an idea of the target market's price range while working in the design process and in selecting construction and finishing techniques. If no answer is forthcoming, look at the pieces that have been used in the past by this vendor for this product, "guess-timate" what it might have cost, and use that as a starting point. The designer does not have to be the estimator. The estimator is the person who puts all the probable costs and probable expenses together to determine a price per unit. It does help if the designer is knowledgeable about how much materials cost and what is involved in the various processes. In POP, thousands of units and nickels and dimes per unit can make the difference in getting or losing the job. If any field calls for care and efficiency in estimating and production, this is it!

Specialists in POP Design

The POP industry, like many other fields where there are technical processes and a complexity of materials, has its specialists. These are the authorities—the people who spend all of their time sharpening their talents and learning ever more and more about their specialties. These are the suppliers. These are the people who run the silk-screen operations, do vacuum forming and injection molding, the die cutters and the die tool designers, the casters, the molders, the printers, the stampers, the suppliers of papers and plastics. A good POP designer is not expected to be a specialist in every technique. However, the designer should understand what the particular technique or process will do and how it will do it—when it will be most effective and efficient; when it will be the best solution for the design—and the cost. *But*—the details, the little variations and adaptations of the actual process should be worked out in conjunction with one of these specialists or technicians who really knows how to make a mold or die, how to get the most out of the material, and how to make whatever process is used cost-efficient. These are the "tricks of the trade" and these specialists know it. In the end, the designer is only as good as the specialists he or she works with.

Materials Used in the Construction of POP Displays

Depending on the products, the intended use, the time it is expected to be on view, and the budget, the displayer

Figure 27.7 The ultimate in brand promotion! The Coca-Cola shop on Las Vegas Boulevard in Las Vegas features myriad Coca-Cola red products emblazoned with the comapany's logo. Shown here is a display of some of those branded products offered for sale as well as an oversized Coca-Cola bottle that anchors the set-up and serves to recall the traditional Coke bottle. Hanging around the square column are die-cut cardboard cut outs of the Coke bottle and some of the other bottled drinks prepared by the company. This store is the ultimate vendor's shop and does a terrific job in projecting the brand's image. *Coca-Cola, Las Vegas.*

or fixture can be made of a wide variety of materials: paper, cardboard, foamcore, various thicknesses of wood, pressed board, plastic, or metal.

Paper and Cardboard

Probably the most popular medium for POP units is paper. Paper can be used for signs and banners, especially when permanence is not of the utmost importance but cost is. Paper is available in many different surface finishes and textures, thicknesses, and in a brilliant spectrum of colors. Paper can be applied, cemented, or laminated onto cardboard. Cardboard is also a form of paper and is available from thin pliable sheets to fairly rigid sheets with a tremendous range in between. The thickness or density of the board—the ply—will determine how it is used in the POP program. Is it for a sign? Is it for a display? A brochure holder? Will it be a container and support several pounds of products on top of it? And if so, how much weight? Is the POP unit expected to be in use for just a week or two for a special promotion? Or is it expected to be in service for a month or a season? The time the unit is to be used may also affect the ply of the paper or board.

There are also corrugated materials that are available in rolls and in sheets, in different surface finishes and thicknesses. Though lightweight, they do provide strength and support for units constructed out of them or reinforced with them.

Foam boards, though not paper, but rather a sandwich of two pieces of paper with a filler of styrofoam or some other foam material between them appear on the market under a variety of trade names. Foam boards are produced in thicknesses that range from about 1/4 inch up to one inch or even more. They are extremely versatile and dependable players on the POP production team since they can be die cut, scored, laminated onto, printed on, or used to construct small fixtures and displayers.

Paper is often flat—as printed sheets—but paper can be dimensionalized: folded; scored; cut into contoured shapes; cut and creased and folded into boxes, containers, pop-up or pop-out displays; or appliquéd or layered for a dimensional effect. Paper products can also be embossed or treated to create three-dimensional textured surfaces. Some of the processes usually associated with paper, cardboard, and corrugated board will be discussed below.

Paper Printing Techniques

Most large runs of cardboard and paper POP displays are printed by a process known as four-color lithography or offset printing. It is a fast and economical technique to use where a large quantity of the same design is to be reproduced in full color. In color lithography, the artwork is reduced to four separate plates—one for each of the four standard colors—yellow, cyan (a blue-green), magenta (a blue-red), and black. Other colors are produced by printing one color over another, for example, to reproduce green, yellow is laid down (printed) and the cyan is printed over it. The usual technique is to start with the lightest color—the yellow—and end up with the black color that tends to define and provide depth of the colors. The color separation, the individual plates for the four colors, and the four separate runs through the press—one for each color—are basically expensive, but become extremely practical and economical when the cost is amortized over a large number of units, usually numbered in the thousands.

The offset process is limited in that it can only handle certain substrata—the papers or boards—it can print on. The offset process requires plates and a printing "bed," and so the size of the stock to be printed will be determined by that plate and the bed of the printing press. The bed is the surface in which the paper is laid during the printing process. The usual "bed" size is about 30 inches by 4 inches, though some special presses may have larger "beds" and thus accommodate larger pieces of stock.

When the printing is on paper, it may sometimes require that the print be applied to a stronger, firmer, or sturdier backup piece like cardboard or corrugated board. In this case, the printed piece has to be cemented onto the stronger back piece, and this is usually accomplished by the lamination process, which is described later in this section.

Silk-Screen Printing or Screen Printing Process

Another very effective technique for reproducing copy or artwork for displays and displayers is the **silk-screen** technique that was fully described in Chapter 21. The emphasis in that chapter was on short runs and mostly for use in-store for cards and posters. Therefore, the screens would probably be cut by hand on film positive, which is either amber or ruby-red clear. However, in the POP industry, where the runs are much larger, the artwork that is reproduced can be more complex, or more sophisticated results are expected, the screens are usually prepared photographically. Some handcutting may be combined with the photographic process especially where there are simple bands or forms of solid color.

What makes the screen printing process so very special in the POP industry is that it is so adaptable and it can be used on almost any material available. Where the lithograph offset printing techniques and the other variations are mainly adapted to paper or very lightweight board, silk-screening can be done not only on paper or board of any thickness, but it will also work on hardboard, corrugated, outdoorboard, foamcore, gater board, and parchment; on fabrics such as silk, satin, nylon, bengaline, felt, or canvas; and on plastic materials such as Lexan, Plexiglass, styrene, rigid or limp vinyls, acetate, nylon, mylar, pressure sensitives, and static clings. It is also possible to screen on wood, glass, and metal.

The size of the litho/offset print can only be as large as the printing bed. In the screen printing process, it depends on the screen, which can be as large as 8 feet by 4 feet or even larger if necessary. Screens used to be made of fine silk but today most commercial printing houses prefer to cover their wood stencil frames with manufactured fabrics. Another plus for this technique is that one can print with a vast variety of paints, inks, and dyes depending on the materials to be printed upon. If lacquer (nitrocellulose lacquer) is to be used, then the screen will have a water-based stencil. Water-based paints require a water-resistant, direct emulsion screen; a direct emulsion over the frame. Oil-based paints can be used either with water-based or lacquer stencils. The paints, dyes, or inks can be shiny or matte finishes, produce fairly flat or raised surfaces, be enhanced with glitter or flock, be opaque or transparent, metallic or Day-Glo. It is possible to print an opaque white over a black base or a real metallic gold or silver over any color. Glossy and flat colors can be combined on the same design just as transparent dyes and opaque paints can be mixed to create the desired effects.

As previously mentioned, the screen or stencil will be prepared by hand cutting or by photographic means, depending on how involved or complex the artwork is, what the artwork is (a photograph, a painting, a line design, a cartoon sketch, and so on), how fine the finished piece has to be, what the substrate material will be, and the finish required.

Photographic silk-screens start with the finished art that is to be reproduced. Just as artwork is separated into four basic colors for lithography or offset printing, so is this artwork first separated into a positive form; right-reading, film positives with the emulsion side up. One film is made for each basic color plus one for black. Unlike the offset process, which works with negatives, the positive film is now attached to the screen by being put into a vacuum blanket. This ensures a bonding without distortion, air bubbles, and so forth. The screen with the film attached is then exposed to a high-density direct light. The light will not pass through the areas where the emulsion now adheres to the screen and the emulsion hardens and sets, bonding with the fabric of the screen—when hit with the light. After this occurs, the positive film can be removed from the screen, washed down with warm water and some light pressure, and stored away for future reference or for reuse if anything happens to the screen.

Where the light did not penetrate, the emulsion will wash off of the screen. This is the area where the paint will eventually pass through. No paint will pass through where the emulsion has bonded to the fabric of the screen. The same process is repeated for each screen needed for the job. A four-screen job will require that this procedure be done four times—one for each color screen. On each screen, the emulsion will be washed away only in those areas where the color will be desired so that the printing media can pass through.

Another very important advantage in the screen printing process is that colors can be changed without making new plates or, in this technique, new stencils. If the manufacturer or vendor has a graphic design that will be used several times but wants to change the color scheme to suit the various seasons of the year, the screens are thoroughly washed after the first use to remove all traces of paint from the screens; not to clog up the openings. The screens are stored until they are needed for the next season and new and different colors are run on the same screens. For example, an Easter background may be yellow overprinted with pink and lavender while a Christmas background may be white overprinted with red and metallic gold. The screens remain—the artwork is the same—only the colors change and, of course, the substrate can vary.

The silk-screening or screen printing process is especially effective in printing the pressure sensitive and electrostatic clings and decals that are applied on glass and on complex or convoluted shapes that cannot easily be printed on or hot stamped.

Dimensionalizing Paper and Cardboard Displays

Die cutting is the most often used method for adding a dimensional quality to a display, displayer, card, or poster. Die cutting can create interesting outlines and silhouettes and cut-out openings from paper or board. It can be used to score the board so that it can be bent or folded in a variety of ways. It can create locks and tabs so that pieces can be folded along the score or crease lines and then assembled by locking the die cut tabs through the cut-out slots to make boxes, trays, or easeled stands for cards, posters, or displays. Die cutting adds the third dimension to the unit, which adds interest to the total design. A well-designed cutting die can score and cut a piece of cardboard so that it can be folded or locked into a back panel with a pair of side panels and even a raised platform or tray or brochure holder in the middle—all out of the single piece of cardboard and without glueing. The silhouette of the side wings and the back panel can be decorated with curves or jagged lines or even die cut to look like latticework.

Dies are expensive and should be designed in conjunction with a die maker; a specialist who knows how to get the most out of each blade used in the die. Some dies are "basic" and they can be used over and over again on many different jobs such as an easel die or a box die, while others may serve only for one special display unit. In smaller runs and where the cuts or silhouettes are not too complicated, the display producer may use a cut awl machine, or bandsaw with a template as a guide. It is possible to get a fairly accurate cut, but there will be slight differences from stack to stack due to the human element involved. The cut awl operator can only cut a few boards at a time or a stack of paper about one inch thick. The result can be fairly crisp and clean, but when precision matching between slots and tabs is essential or where intricate interior cuts may be required, this method is decidedly limited in its effectiveness.

Die Cutting Process   The die cutting process requires a die—a cutting tool designed to suit the material being cut. The technique is similar to cutting out cookies from rolled dough. The shape of the cookie will respond to the contour or outline design of the cookie cutter. Pressure will need to be exerted to allow the cutting edge of the cookie cutter to go through the layer of dough. The die in the die cutting process is placed on the stationery, back plate of the machine. The paper or board to be cut is placed on the movable bed of the press machine and carefully lined up to correspond with the die. The bed is then raised to meet the die on the rear panel. Many tons of pressure is exerted causing the machine to open and to cut the paper or board.

The die is actually a steel rule set in wood. To make the die, a piece of thick plywood is used for the base and the die designer draws the cutting and scoring lines on the board. Using a jigsaw machine, the lines that have been drawn are cut out of the wood leaving a groove or channel into which the steel cutting blades can then be inserted. The curved and arced lines will be made by the steel blade being forced, in the channel, to conform with the desired curves and arcs. There are "bridges" left in the channels during the routing process of making the mold. These "bridges" are small stops in the channels so that the wood block doesn't fall apart. The cutting blades that go over these bridges are called notches. Where a score line is desired instead of a cut-through line, the blade that is inserted in the wood base is slightly lower than the cutting blade and the scoring blade's edge is rounded rather than knife-sharp. This blade can then make a "cut score" which actually cuts through part of the board for a sharp right-angle crease or a "crease score," which is softer, and a rounded bend in the board.

Rubber pads are set around the cutting blades so that the sheet can more readily be ejected after the pressure has been applied. It also makes handling the cutting dies somewhat safer. In the "make ready" die, the blade is dulled, purposefully, in several spots to leave "nicks," usually in the corners. The size of the nick will depend on the thickness of the paper or board being used. Nicks are made where the cutting blade has not penetrated completely. They hold the die cut pieces in place in the full sheet from which they were cut. "Stripping" is the step that follows, in which the die cut pieces are separated from the excess, surrounding stock. If the unit or units (the die cut pieces) will not be stripped until they arrive at the place where they will be used, such as at the retail setting, the nicks hold the pieces in place during shipping. When the die cut sheets arrive at their destination, the excess paper or board can be removed by pushing or tearing around the notches or perforated

outline. A single die cut sheet may hold several dozen individual tags or cards or just one single unit or display.

The die cutting machine used for smaller runs is often the platen press or clam-shell press that has been described above. Basically it opens and closes like a clam shell. For larger runs and high-speed die cutting, there are more sophisticated presses that require a more complicated "get ready" die. These units work like printing presses where one sheet is automatically fed into the press at a time, pressure is applied on the die from above, and the machine then pushes out the die cut sheet of paper or board at the other end. At present the largest die possible is a 50-inch by 74-inch finished sheet since the largest bed on a press can only accommodate a sheet of 52-inch by 76-inch stock.

Lamination   Lamination is a process whereby two or more materials are joined together into a single piece, using glue or cement. The process refers to the bonding of a printed sheet of paper or a decorative finishing paper onto a sturdy undesigned cardboard. The supporting board provides weight, strength, substance, and body, while the printed— usually lithographed—paper on top contains the graphics and/or message.

In the process, glue is distributed evenly on the back of the sheet that is then bonded to the supporting board. Pressure is exerted on the sandwich as well as some heat and then the piece is allowed to dry overnight. The moisture evaporates and the two pieces are now one and inseparable.

Decorative foils are often bonded onto coarse chip boards and then they may be embossed in another dimensional process. Fine veneers of wood—fractions of an inch thick, almost paper-thin—are also laminated onto heavy, serviceable, and nonglamorous plywood backing.

Other Dimensional Effects

Appliqué   A flat POP display can be given greater depth and interest with the addition of some three-dimensional appliqué or attachment. Some examples of appliqué include: paper lace glued on the edge of a fan, a paper flower placed behind the ear of a photograph of a Polynesian beauty, or a piece of fabric tucked into the pocket of a silk-screened pinstripe jacket. Since this is usually a manual process, it can add quite a bit to the cost of manufacturing the unit, but because it is so effective, it can be worth the added cost.

The appliqué serves to break the flat design, making it more of a dimensional display and less of a poster. Sometimes, these softening elements are sent along with the unit, and the retailer is requested to add a boutonniere or to pin on a piece of bridal net. In this case, the producer does not need to handle each unit separately. The packing is simplified and the appliqué looks fresher for the viewer. The retailer, however, must be agreeable to adding these final touches.

Layering   Dimension also can be achieved by superimposing different shapes, one on top of the other, to add a sense of depth to the POP display. These layers can be set one directly on another, or they may be separated from each other by blocks and tabs. Using a tab or a fold-back flap to attach a layer will give the effect of greater depth, but the POP unit will still pack fairly flat.

Embossing   A raised, embossed, or relief impression can be made on a piece of artwork when, during the printing process, specific lines etched into a die appear on the printed surface. Or sometimes, a die is placed underneath a piece of artwork and pressure is applied from below, creating a raised pattern on the surface of the artwork. The embossing, in either case, creates a raised or textured surface.

Blind Embossing   A method of adding dimension to a surface and creating a raised design without the use of inks or paints.

Paper Sculpture   A technique for creating full round or bas-relief decorative designs and objects by means of scoring, folding, cutting, curling, and applying papers of assorted colors, textures, and weights such as the Japanese art form of origami.

Papier Mâché   A technique for producing three-dimensional objects, such as mannequins, by means of molding pulped paper. The pulped paper is mixed with glue and, sometimes, with a whitening substance. This "mushy" material can then be shaped, filled into molds, or formed around shapes or forms. As the mâché dries, it becomes harder, stronger, and more durable. Strips of paper can also be moistened with paste and layered over and over in a mold or around a form to make a papier mâché reproduction of the unit. There is some shrinkage as the unit dries. It is also called "paper stucco" when used to create architectural details such as moldings or frames. This is a "hand process" and is not recommended where there are long runs or many products to be reproduced.

Rubber Mâché   A rubber, latex-like compound is poured into a specially made hollow mold and allowed to dry or set or is force dried by being heated in an oven. The excess material, which did not set or harden, is poured off and the "rubber" unit is allowed to cure and become fully rigid. It usually requires a minimum of smoothing, rasping, or sanding to finish the surface that was formed by the inner surface of the mold. When finished, the piece should be fairly firm and resistant to breakage. The piece can then be painted, gilded, textured, and made to resemble natural materials such as wood or stone. This too is basically a "hand" operation that is not suited to big, commercial runs.

Plastics

Plastics are very important in the manufacturing processes used in making POP displays, displayers, fixtures, and signage. They afford a great variety of materials used in POP production: from sheets that can be cut out and used to construct complete units; to shelves on wire or wooden units; to backgrounds for displays; to platforms or risers; to materials that can be bent, formed, and shaped; to materials that can be molded or extruded from molds or dies. Some plastics are available in sheets of different thicknesses and colors. They have certain unique properties such as being resistant to water, breakage, or shattering; strong to support great weights; or soft and pliable. Some plastics are available in granule or powder form and need chemical catalysts or heat to expand and fill in hollow mold cavities. Some plastics respond to heat, others resist heat.

There are two very important categories of plastics: thermoplastics and thermosetting plastics.

Thermoplastics

Thermoplastics are resins or plastics that can be repeatedly softened by the increase of temperature, that is, the application of heat. When the thermoplastic material is in a gel-like or softened state it can be formed, shaped, or even reshaped. To harden or set the material in its new form/shape, the material has to be cooled. Once cooled and "cured," the thermoplastic retains the shape until it is once again subjected to great heat. This material is very important in the vacuum forming processes. Some thermoplastics are: polythylene, polypropylene, PVC, polystyrene, acrylic, and ABS.

Thermosetting Plastics

In contrast, **thermosetting plastics** once cured and set become infusible and insoluble. In some stages of the production, the thermosetting material may be liquid in form. The curing process—where the softened material hardens in the desired shape or form—can be accomplished by the application of heat or the addition of chemicals. Once that shape is assumed, the material cannot be reshaped or reformed like the thermoplastics. Some thermoplastics can be converted into thermosetting plastics by being crosslinked with other plastics or chemical additives. Some thermosets are: polyesters, ackyds, melamines, epoxies, and phenol formaldehyde. In selecting a plastic material for POP production, the designer must know what the desired end product will be. What is it expected to do and for how long it is expected to be in use? Cost is also a major factor to be considered. Plastics are usually more expensive than paper products but they can do things that paper cannot—and they can last longer. Plastics are used for: outdoor signs, indoor signage of a semipermanent nature, fixtures with bases, and shelves that will be exposed to wear and tear on the selling floor. Fixtures that need to be theft-proof with a "look but don't touch or take" attitude may require plastic envelopes or enclosures.

Processes for Producing Plastic POP Units

Semidimensional units can be vacuum formed or made by an injection molding technique, sonic seal, or hot stamping.

Vacuum Forming Process   Vacuum forming is an "extreme" form of embossing. In this technique a lightweight, thermoplastic material is used. The plastic sheet is capable of being shaped and formed when heated and when cooled will retain the new shape or form. The plastic sheet is heated and softened and then forced over a mold or die usually placed beneath it. Pressure is exerted from above that causes the now pliable plastic to take on the contour and shape of the mold below. Suction, also applied from below, ensures the skin-like fit of the plastic to the mold; it also helps to cool off the plastic so that it will keep the new shape. When the plastic is "set"—returned to room temperature—it maintains the shape of the mold. The process is then repeated with another sheet of plastic.

There are four types of plastics used in the vacuum forming process and they are all thermoformable materials; when heated they leave the solid state and become malleable, pliable, or formable. Most popular and most inexpensive are the styrenes or polystyrenes. The sheets are available in a variety of thicknesses and in many colors, both shiny and matte. The main problem with this group of plastics is that they can shatter and the clear sheet is not truly clear. The other classifications used in this process are the acetates, the vinyls, and the polychlorides which are really clear, and available in a range of colors and thicknesses. They are basically stronger and more durable than the styrenes. Where the vacuum formed unit is required to support weight such as a cantilevered shelf or the base of a fixture, the latter three materials are probably better to use in the vacuum forming process.

The all important element in the vacuum forming process is the mold. The mold can be constructed originally of wood, putty, clay, or any combination of materials and then hardened. Since the pressure exerted by the vacuum forming press is anywhere from six to eight tons of pressure, the original mold or construction can only be used to make several sample units. One of them will be turned into a production mold by being reinforced with a wood frame and filled with cement or epoxy.

In preparing the production mold, the plastic shape —one of the sample pieces—is placed in a box lined with plaster of paris. The epoxy (or cement) is then poured into the hollow shell or form. Pins are inserted into the epoxy-filled mold to create the air holes that are necessary for the vacuum and suction to work during the shaping process. The new epoxy mold is then sanded, smoothed, and polished and made ready for use in production.

Each time a sheet of plastic is brought down under heat and pressure to conform with the mold it is called a "shot." Depending on the number of "shots" or pieces required to be made from the mold, the mold has to be corrected. For shorter runs—a few thousand—the epoxy mold is effective, efficient, and relatively inexpensive to make. For more "shots" poured or liquid, aluminum molds may be preferable, but they are more expensive to generate. The most durable mold is one made of cast aluminum. It is also very important in designing a mold that there be no undercuts or indentations that will hinder or even make it impossible to lift the molded piece of plastic off of the mold.

After the sheet has taken on the form of the mold, it must be trimmed and the excess material removed. This is often done with a die or powerful "cookie cutter" (see "Die Cutting Process" earlier). The die may be placed in with the mold so that the pressure exerted from above to soften and shape the plastic will also cut off the excess material of the sheet. If there are any internal cuts or openings needed in the mold such as a slot or a shape, another die may be used to affect those cuts.

Usually the molded piece is half or partially rounded. It may be anything from a low relief to a half ball. When a full round or totally three-dimensional piece is required, two halves or two separate molded pieces that will then be glued or notched or stapled together are used. For example, if a giant Christmas ornament is desired, then two half rounds would be formed and then joined together. This is a separate process. The die that is designed to trim off the excess material may be made with a lip or extension that can be used in the joining process.

Injection Molding Techniques   All the processes used in the injection molding and vacuum forming of three-dimensional pieces for POP require heat plus pressure. The amount of heat and pressure will vary with the specific technique or machinery used. In most instances, the plastic material is heated in a barrel or chamber in the machine and then it is pushed through, in measured quantities, to fill in the hollow cavity of the mold. Heat may be applied when the material is inserted into the hopper—the opening that feeds the machine—when the material is in the mold. In order for the plastic piece to be formed, the mold has to be cooler than the material injected into it.

Pressure may be exerted by pushing or ramming the heated or softened material into the mold or while the plastic material is in the mold to guarantee that the plastic material fills in all parts of the cavity of the mold. Some pressure may be exerted in the removal of the finished molded piece from the mold.

Injection Molding Tool   The usual injection molding tool is made of aluminum since it is easier to tool, costs less, and takes less time to make. However, where very large runs are anticipated, the tool can be made of steel. The typical mold is made in two parts: the cavity side, which is the "face" of the desired product, and the ejector side, which is the "back." The "shot" of melted plastic passes through a nozzle in the injection molding machine into the sprue or opening in the cavity part of the mold. The "gates" control how much material goes through the "runners." Pressure is maintained on the mold till the gates "freeze." The plastic material is, therefore, trapped in the hollow space between the cavity half and the ejector half of the mold and it takes on the shape of that hollow form. The material is cooled in the mold and when it has set sufficiently to hold the desired shape or form, the ejector pins in the ejector part of the mold push the finished piece out.

Sonic Seal   Very often a product that is made by injection molding may require two or more separate molds to make up the finished piece; for example, a shaped box with removable top. The box, the cover, and the bottom of the box are each molded separately and then "hand" assembled. The cover will be set on top of the box but the base may have to be welded on. Instead of cement or chemical bonding agents, this process is accomplished with a sonic sealer. This machine electronically fuses and melds the pieces together so that it is not only secure but, if necessary, it can be waterproof.

Hot Stamping   A process for applying the product's name or logo, decorative designs, or copy onto dimensional plastic pieces such as shelves, platforms, or back panels is called hot stamping. This is accomplished by placing the plastic surface to be decorated underneath a sheet of colored plastic film of the desired color. The "artwork" is raised on a rubber plate that is set in the heat and pressure machine above the coloring film. When pressure and heat are combined, the rubber plate is pressed down on the color film, which in turn leaves the desired colored imprint on the plastic piece that is held in place below. It is not unlike a rubber stamp leaving its imprint on paper, but instead of ink, colored film is the medium.

Sometimes the logo or design is raised and is part of the molded plastic piece. In that case the rubber plate is flat and has no design. The heat and pressure force the colored film to yield the color to the raised design on the piece of plastic and, at the same time, bonds the color.

When two or more colors are used, the process is repeated with another rubber plate and the other desired colors of film.

Wood and Metal

Along with some plastics, metal and wood are used for more permanent POP displayers and fixtures. They are stronger and more durable than paper and cardboard or extruded plastic shapes. However, they are more expensive to use.

Wood has a "natural" look and provides a sense of warmth to the product as well as a "residential" quality to the design of the fixture. Shoppers associate it with furniture and with the shop furnishings or fixturing of better shops and boutiques. Home fashions and home products look more intimate on wooden fixtures. Very often wood or a wood-finished piece (covered with a wood veneer or laminate) are used in vendor shops—especially when the manufacturer wants to achieve an upscale look or wants to appeal to the rugged, masculine lifestyle. Since wood suggests a better or finer product, watches, pens and pencils, jewelry, and other expensive items may be housed in wood on the floor or on the counter. Outdoor products are given a more rustic look from a wood-finished displayer.

However, since some solid woods are too expensive to use in mass-merchandised POP items, it is likely that the fixtures and displayers will usually be made of some of the wood "look-alike" materials and possibly finished with a veneer or very fine sheet of fine wood. The inexpensive solid woods such as pine may be weakened by the knots or the finished pieces may end up looking too provincial or "country-style." Also, soft woods will scratch or dent when kicked or mistreated by the shoppers. In working with wood, the designer also has to consider the backs of the units: Will it be visible? Do they have to be finished? Sometimes the back of a single-faced piece can be finished with a lesser wood or a more utilitarian substitute rather than the same wood used on the face of the unit. Not only is this economical, it may also strengthen the finished piece.

It is not unusual to see wood combined with metal in permanent fixtures and displays. Welded metal pieces may be used for the framework and then combined with wood shelves or panels and/or signs. A wood fixture may be equipped with metal grills, grids, or expanded metal shelves that look lighter and are lighter than wood. Also, grids or grills will permit the ambient or targeted light to pass through the floor fixture or wall unit so that the products on the lower shelves are illuminated.

Wood dowels or metal rods can be used to carry or support vacuum formed or injection molded shelves, bins, or trays, thus making the units more permanent on the selling floor.

POP Design Checklist

The designer has now accumulated the necessary data and is ready to proceed. It is advisable to consider every POP unit as part of an overall promotion and as the ultimate message of the advertisement. The POP unit can support a shrinking sales force by answering customers' questions; supplying the necessary information; giving prices and construction details; and showing the available selection and range. It can offer a sample, supply a taste, or be tested. It can be, if well designed, an asset to the merchandise retailer with limited sales help or fixtures—the customer is where the sale is made!

When designing, the following checklist may be helpful since it asks all the questions that the unit will be expected to answer:

1. When is the unit to appear? What is the timing?
2. Toward whom is the product or service directed? What is the target market?
3. What is the purpose of this unit? Is it to introduce a new product? An improvement? A new style?
4. Is there an ad or TV campaign planned in conjunction with this unit? Will the POP design carry the same ad message?

5. Does the unit have anything to do but carry the message? Is it a sampler? A tester? A stocking or restockable unit?

6. What POP units have been done in the past for this product or manufacturer?

7. What are the competitors doing with their POP programs?

8. In what types of retail operations will these units be used? Where will they be located in these stores? Will other POP units be used in coordination with this piece?

9. What quantities will be required?

10. What is the budget?

11. How long will this unit be used? Is it to be reusable?

12. Will the finished unit be bulk shipped or individually packed and shipped? Will they be sent by public conveyance or personally delivered by a company representative?

13. Should the unit include samples? Dummy boxes or bottles?

14. If the unit is to be stocked and prepacked, how many items should the POP piece carry?

15. Would the client like light or motion? Is there room in the budget for special effects: appliqué, vacuum forming, embossing, complicated die cutting, and so on?

16. What materials and/or techniques would the client prefer?

17. Who installs the unit? The customer? A sales representative?

18. Would the client like to see rough sketches? A comprehensive ("comp")? A model?

19. How is the client to be charged for the designs or comps?

20. Would the client like to see some auxiliary design concepts that would reinforce the message being presented in the POP unit; for example, table-tents, shelf readers, overhead banners or streamers, decals, buttons, T-shirts, and so on?

Point-of-Purchase: A Recap

-   Point-of-purchase (POP) is the total image fabrication of a product.

-   Point-of-purchase units can be displays, displayers, fixtures, or auxiliary items provided by vendors or manufacturers to retailers.

-   Some reasons for using the POP display are as follows: It encourages the consumer to make an on-the-spot decision to purchase; it gains attention and brings the consumer to the product; it explains the product and informs the shopper; it can coordinate with other promotions and induce sales of related products; and it can reinforce a price message.

-   Product categories utilizing POP include: food and paper goods, personal products, beverages, health and beauty aids, hardware and building materials, household goods, tobacco, fast-food operation, lotteries, hotels, and vending machines.

-   Point of purchase units can be permanent, semipermanent, or temporary or promotional.

-   When designing a POP unit, the display person must consider the type of product; the target audience; where the unit will be used; whether the unit will be permanent or expendable; the life expectancy of the unit; promotional tie-ins; the type of store in which the unit will appear; the amount of units to be produced; the method of shipment; whether light, motion, or computer chips will be involved; and how much the unit will cost to produce.

-   The POP unit can be made of a wide variety of materials: paper, cardboard, foamcore, various thicknesses of wood, pressed board, plastic, or metal.

Questions for Review and Discussion

1. What is the function of POP display in retailing today?

2. List five items that could be considered POP units.

3. Why has POP become such a growing and important business in the past decade?

4. What can POP do that "regular" display cannot?

5. What industries are heavy users of POP? In what types of retail outlets do POP units commonly appear?

6. Explain the three categories of life expectancies for POP units.

7. In designing a POP unit, what factors would be taken into consideration?

8. What is a POP specialist?

Chapter Twenty-Eight

Exhibit and Trade Show Design— Industrial Display

AFTER YOU HAVE READ THIS CHAPTER,
YOU WILL BE ABLE TO DISCUSS:

- The differences between exhibits and trade shows.
- The unique characteristics of the various types of exhibits.
- Common traffic patterns created in exhibits.
- The considerations involved in planning and selecting an exhibit system.
- The use of graphics, types of light, special effects, and amenities in attracting attention and enhancing an exhibit.
- The importance of tie-ins for successful trade shows and exhibits.

EXHIBIT AND TRADE SHOW DESIGN: TRADE TALK

amenities of design	permanent exhibit
animation	photomurals
audio-visuals	special effects
ambient lighting	supergraphics
blowups	task lighting
exhibit	temporary exhibit
exhibit systems	theme
lettering	tie-ins
live action	trademarks
logos	trade show
movement	traveling exhibit
outdoor exhibit	

Exhibits are the display and showing of special materials that have been collected and then edited for presentation. The major purpose of an **exhibit** is to stimulate and create interest for a particular product, idea, or organization. The exhibit itself is organized and orchestrated for the enjoyment and enlightenment of a special audience or market, and may be used to educate, advertise, or propagandize.

A trade show is a commercial display of new products or concepts presented to a select group of prospective buyers or consumers. The "sale" may be direct (with purchases being made at the site of the exhibit) or indirect (may lead to eventual purchases). Please keep in mind that many of the principles of exhibit and trade show design, described below, apply equally to merchandise display and visual presentation.

Types of Exhibits

Permanent Exhibits

The concept of a **permanent exhibit** should be abolished from the world of merchandise display and visual presentation, an area in which nothing should ever be considered unchanging and immutable. The idea of setting up an educational or promotional exhibit and of allowing it to remain frozen in time and space—for an unlimited period of time—is against everything for which merchandise presentation stands.

Many museums have permanent exhibits in which paintings, sculpture, and other artwork are lastingly framed, hung, and encased. There is no surprise, novelty, or excitement in an unchanging, permanent display. The dioramas in museums of natural history are permanent too; polar bears frozen forever on graying icebergs; Indians gathering dust and cobwebs in crumbling adobe huts. Though the preparation and installation of these extravaganzas are costly and time-consuming, they can become too familiar and even boring for the faithful museum visitor.

If the installation cannot be changed or relocated after a particular interval, it would probably be best for the viewer and the object being viewed, if it were curtained off or blocked off with another exhibit for "a pause that refreshes." Even a permanent exhibit should be a limited showing of something from the permanent collection which can then be replaced with another display. If the object is world-famous and many persons come especially to see it (e.g., the "Mona Lisa," a Michelangelo sculpture, and so on), then the presentation and the area around the exhibit should be refreshed with a new attitude or look by adding changing floral arrangements, trying period furniture settings, experimenting with different lighting techniques, or using new background colors or textures.

Temporary Exhibits

A **temporary exhibit** is usually the presentation of an item or items that are on loan for a limited time. The showing schedule is announced and the duration of the showing is advertised and publicized. The arrival and showing of the treasures of King Tut at a local museum

Figure 28.1 An exhibit or a tradeshow stand must—like a display window—attract the attention of the show-goer, and bring him or her closer to the confined space. Muzak created quite a stir with their giant silver sphere surrounded by dozens of truncated plastic cones that served as seating for the weary show attendees. Inside the specially constructed and sound enhancing sphere guests could be enveloped in the sounds of Muzak. *Muzak, Globalshop, Chicago. Design: Karim Rashid.*

for a one-month showing is an excellent example of a temporary exhibit. The arrival and opening date is publicized and anticipated by the public. The limited stay creates the necessary impetus to have the public come and see the exhibit while the artwork is on loan.

A community room in a library, town hall, or department store might house temporary exhibits sponsored by local clubs, artists, or artisans of the community. A public service area in a large corporate building or a shopping center may also hold temporary exhibits which could be either educational or promotional (e.g., a Red Cross life-saving exhibit or an automobile show).

Trade Shows

Trade shows are commercial ventures wherein a manufacturer or distributor will show a line of merchandise, introduce a new product or an improvement on an existing one, or exhibit for the sake of "goodwill" or company image.

The company seeking goodwill (instead of showing its merchandise) may provide, in a setting of plants and seats, an arrangement of a very few choice objects; perhaps, the earliest prototypes of their product or "antique" versions of the products the company is producing today. This is the "soft sell" approach, and such an

Figure 28.2 It is all about standing out in a crowd, making a memorable statement, being seen—and found in the color-infused exhibit floor. This view of the show floor shows how ALU's space, wrapped in red and orange translucent fabric, manages to step out from its surroundings. *ALU, Globalshopo, Chicago. Photo: Charlie Mayer for ALU.*

exhibit would be designed to show the historical perspective of the company and the product rather than to place the emphasis on the current product or line.

Often, trade shows are produced in large exhibition halls in which several hundred exhibitors battle for attention in rather open and exposed areas. The management of the exhibit hall or the organization sponsoring the show may set restrictions concerning the height of a booth or exhibit, the use of opaque walls, fireproofed materials, lighting equipment, overhead signs, and sound equipment. The union regulations that govern the setting up, lighting, trimming, and the eventual dismantling of the show can be a serious problem for the trade show designer. Following these regulations can become costly and time-consuming. The storage of shipping cases and crating material may also present problems. This rather specialized subject of trade shows will be considered more fully throughout this chapter.

Traveling Exhibits

A **traveling exhibit** is a broad, all-inclusive term for movable or portable displays. A traveling exhibit is conceived and designed to be moved from one location to another and to be assembled quickly, with few changes and a minimum of professional assistance. Some traveling shows are actually large buses or vans that have been converted into "galleries on wheels." The viewer enters at one end of the vehicle and exits from the other, after having seen the complete showing. Often, the government will produce a traveling show that will visit schools and libraries. The van or bus may be parked in the parking lot, or out in front of the institution, and the students will be invited in to see the special collection.

Other traveling shows are not designed to move "as is" in their own vehicles. These shows use collapsible panels, frames, or stands that can be reassembled and will adapt to a preestablished plan or pattern in an area of a specific size. Sometimes, the designer may have to supply several alternate arrangements for the panels or frames in order to accommodate variations in floor layouts or space allocations.

This basic concept of traveling shows capable of being reassembled is often the principle upon which many trade show exhibits are based. Since the manufacturer or exhibitor may have to show in several different markets (different trade shows in different cities) within the same

Figure 28.3 A traveling or temporary show or exhibit has been prepared for Toyota with graphic panels, signage, and special platforms for the autos with interactive stations attached. Visitors can step up to a monitor and keyboard and get information about the displayed auto. This exhibit stands in an aisle in the Arundel Mall for a limited time. When the time is up, the platforms, graphic panels, and signage will be removed and trucked to another mall or public place where it will reassembled. Since it is all modular—the new arrangement will be made to suit the space. *Toyota, Arundel Mill Mall. Design. George P. Johnson Co. Photo: Bill FitzPatrick.*

short selling season, the exhibit may have to be assembled and used for a week or less, then be broken down, crated and shipped off to the next exhibit hall, where the following week it has to be reassembled and ready for the new trade show. The exhibit designer may have to add or subtract panels or frames from the exhibit depending, again, on the allotted space and restrictions set by the new exhibit management.

Outdoor Exhibits

An **outdoor exhibit** may take place in a garden, a park, a parking lot, or in the middle of a shopping mall. Depending on the material to be shown, this can be the most challenging type of exhibit. The garden or park setting is ideal for sculpture and other dimensional objects that are not affected by heat, cold, rain, or snow. The natural light and setting can be glorious "props" for these natural but "hard" materials. Other exhibits (art shows, craft shows, and such) may suffer from the uncertainty of the weather. Strong winds and strong sunlight (to say nothing of sudden rain) can be discomforting to the viewing public and play havoc with the show itself. Where the exhibit can be contained under a roof—a pavilion or a tent—the exhibit is more manageable. With an overhead enclosure, the designer can make plans despite the sun, gusts of wind, or unexpected showers.

Planning the Exhibit

Audience

As in all displays, the market is a prime consideration. What is the age and intelligence level of the viewing audience that will come to see this show? Are they children, teenagers, adults, or all of the above? Are they knowledgeable on the subject or must they be directed and oriented to the material to be presented? Are they coming with a preestablished interest or curiosity about the subject (which is usually the case with trade shows), or must they be stimulated to rouse their interest in the show? What is their average interest span? How much material will they be able to absorb in one visit through the show?

Armed with the answers to these questions and other information supplied by the exhibitor, the designer can then plot the exhibit within the anticipated length of the visit to the show and arrange the material for its best acceptance and viewer stimulation. Depending on the material and the floor plan or the traffic pattern of the show, which will be discussed shortly, the designer can help set the pace for the viewer at the exhibit. This should permit the viewer to spend as much time as desired where he or she pleases. Again, this is ideal in a trade show exhibit where the viewer is usually a potential customer, and the viewing is done with an eye toward buying.

Subject

The better organized the exhibit, the more readily it will be understood and accepted. If the exhibit is based on a single, unifying theme and all the material is related (e.g., fashions of Coco Chanel), the background needs to be explained or illustrated only once, at the beginning. That one explanation then serves as a guide for everything that follows.

At a trade show, it is simpler and more effective to show one product or a related line of items rather than present a complete spectrum of unrelated and sometimes conflicting merchandise. Where many diverse

Figure 28.4 Visona produces fixtures and systems that can be used by retailers to show a variety of clothing classifications. To create interest and show their diversity in the large exhibit space, Visona created a series of "rooms" or mini-departments with colors and garments targeted at a specific age group or lifestyle. The shopper interested in children's wear is attracted to the yellow and black themed space. *Visona, Euroshop, Dusseldorf, Germany.*

items must be presented, the good designer will use some device or gimmick (color, line, dividers, graphics, and so on) to unify the dissimilar and individual pieces into a harmonious and controlled flow. At a recent trade show, the manufacturer of a diverse line of mannequins (from a very realistic to very abstract, from child to adult) had all the mannequins dressed in black and gold. Though the fashions and styles were varied, in keeping with the type of mannequin used, the black-and-gold color scheme made a strong, unifying impact.

Whatever the subject matter of the exhibit, the exhibitor and the designer must supply an avenue of interest for the audience to follow, in which the theme, product, or premise is presented in an appealing, coherent, and compelling manner. There should be a point of view expressed, and that point should be presented up front, at the beginning, so that all that follows is an explanation and an elaboration on the basic theme. A good exhibit presents, stimulates, and leaves an impression, but never confuses. Even if it is a goodwill, prestige, or institutional type of exhibit, the exhibitor still has the opportunity to publicize, either directly or indirectly, his or her product and to stimulate a demand for his or her services.

Size of the Exhibit

The size of an exhibit is commonly a great variable. When dealing with a particular gallery, museum, library, or exhibit area, where the space devoted to showings is relatively constant, the exhibit designer "knows the territory," what can be done and how much can be shown effectively. On the other hand, the designer of a traveling exhibit supplies panels, frames, and stands that will require a certain amount of space in which to set up the show correctly. The persons who receive the exhibit (the staff decorators) must then make the design work within their actual space.

A well-designed traveling exhibit will have a degree of flexibility drawn into the plan. The design will either expand or contract as space permits. Sometimes, that means adding some purely decorative filler panels, plants, or additional material. It might require omitting some secondary material in order to make the best presentation of the major items. A display that will travel and be set up in any number of different spaces should have auxiliary floor plans, alternative arrangements, and sketched recommendations accompanying the exhibit. The show that is "mobile" (i.e., set on a train, bus, or

van), is already limited in size by the unit that houses and carries it.

The design of the individual trade show exhibit will vary with the particular exhibit hall and its space allocation. The exhibit floor is divided into booths that may be 8 feet by 8 feet, 10 feet by 10 feet, or 12 feet by 12 feet, depending on the module of space that is most economical for the hall's management. The exhibitor reserves a booth or a combination of booths, so that the exhibit area (based on a 10-foot module as an example) may be anything from a 10-foot by 10-foot space (one booth); to a long, narrow rectangle measuring 10 feet by 40 feet (four adjacent booths); to a square block, 20 feet by 20 feet (two booths wide by two booths long). The size and shape of the total space will determine the layout and traffic pattern of the total booth area, the location of the entrance and exit from the display area, and the amount of material that can be shown.

Ideally, the space should be related to the subject matter. Statues and large architectural pieces need open spaces so that they can be viewed from all sides as well as from a distance. Coins, jewelry, manuscripts, and small collector's items are more effective in smaller, more intimate surroundings.

When space is "unlimited," the exhibit may show too much, in too diversified a manner. A very long exhibit is more likely to weary and confuse the viewer, and eventually lose his or her interest. Also, the intended impact can be lost.

When the amount of material (like a retrospective showing of Picasso's works or the full line of General Foods' products) is staggering and requires lots of space and material, it is advisable to have a catalog or guidebook available for the visitor. As the viewer threads his or her way through the maze of myriad objects, the booklet will supply the basic information and the necessary background material that would have only cluttered the exhibit if additional signs had to be included. It also provides a route for the viewer to follow. The guidebook provides the viewer with a means to locate what he or she actually wants to see and to spend time where the viewer feels it will be most beneficial and instructive.

The size of the exhibit is especially important when the exhibit must be crated to be shipped to the next show place. The cost of crating and shipping is a very big part of the exhibit budget, and the designer must consider

Figure 28.5 Space on the trade show floor is limited so if the trade show management and the actual exhibit hall permits it, the exhibit designer can go up instead of out. Working with modules and structural systems, the designer has capped the ground level exhibit with a mezzanine and a connecting staircase that leads to a café/conference area. It is away from the noise and action of the floor but still open to partake of the excitement generated below. Interactive fixtures are shown on a series of platforms at ground level to play up the diversified capabilities of the exhibitor. *Winntech, Globalshop, Chicago.*

this in the original plan. It will affect the framework used for the show and the manner in which the show is set up and taken down.

Design and Layout: The Traffic Plan

Once the size of the exhibit is specified and the material to be shown is selected, the designer starts by plotting the traffic patterns within the booth. This is most important and may determine which structural materials are used.

The traffic plan is the basic consideration in moving people through an area. The layout may be in long lines following the perimeter walls. The latter creates a gallery effect with series of straight lines, panels, or "walls." The gallery effect may be accomplished with freestanding panels displaying exhibit material on both sides.

The path may follow a zigzag of screens folded into a series of V-shaped bays. These bays or alcoves may be used to separate or highlight certain material, contain a case or riser, or to create a setting for a dimensional object. Or, the floor plan can be a pattern that combines straight panels with an occasional "V" for emphasis or as a change of pace.

The maze is another option in exhibit design. In this case, the traffic flow is directed by "pointing arrows" and the viewer is swept along by a series of angles and turns.

Figure 28.6 Looking for privacy in a very public space, South Beach Visuals has created a "wall" around its space with a limited entrance into the actual exhibit. The kind of merchandise shown inside is sampled in the displays and graphics on the perimeter wall and on the plasma screen at the entrance. Once inside the attendee can see all of the new items and be attended by the sales-staff. *South Beach Visuals, Globalshop, Chicago.*

He or she has no alternative but to follow along the prescribed route. The maze allows more material to be shown because the aisles are usually narrower, the material is shown on two sides of the frame or panel, and the convoluted floor pattern permits the use of more panels in the allotted space. Although the viewer is shepherded through the presentation, there can be bunching or tie-ups with people getting "stuck" in funnel-like openings. A viewer who decides to go back to look at something previously passed can cause a problem in the traffic flow. Rarely does the maze layout allow the viewer the freedom of selecting a course through the show at his or her own tempo. Some viewers may resent the "herding" quality and the "closeness" of this type of exhibit layout.

Whatever type of traffic plan or floor plan is used, a change of pace should be built in. Long gallery runs, although exceptionally well-suited to certain material, can be enhanced when balanced with a few bays or aisles for added interest or emphasis. An occasional maze might supply just the right ambience for other materials, or work to separate groups of products. However, if the visitor feels restricted, inhibited, or confused, the purpose of the exhibit may be lost.

Theme

A good exhibit has a **theme** or unifying element, for example, "The History of Product X," "The Development of a New Product," "100 Years of Men's Fashions," and so on. The exhibit should start with the main idea and then elaborate and illustrate the premise behind the show. Something should get the visitor's attention or pique the curiosity, enough to make the viewer want to go on and see more.

If graphics are used, they should start out with an effective statement, up front. If the area lends itself to it, a dramatic and enticing entrance is always effective. It is like the overture to a musical; stimulating and exciting, with just a bar or two of what is to come, and enough to set the feet tapping and the senses moving in the right direction. The opening statement can be heightened by means of light, lighting effects, a dynamic color, or animation. If there is copy, a headline, a quote that sets the theme, it should be easy to read and provocative. As mentioned previously, brochures or guidebooks should be available at the entrance or start of the exhibit.

Color and Texture

Color is always vital to a presentation, whether it be by its presence or its absence. If an exhibit is mainly black and white (i.e., printed materials, photographs, and so on) then the designer may have to use colored backgrounds to add pace and pizzazz to the show. A change of color may serve as a "punctuation mark" to indicate the end of one idea or phase and the introduction to the next one.

Colored or neutral backgrounds may be necessary to overcome the existing background color of the exhibition area. If the exhibit hall is white and airy, and the presentation requires deep, dark colors and dramatic shadows, the designer may accomplish this by means of colored panels, dropped ceilings, or special lighting effects. Optically, color can stretch walls, bring them closer together, open or close areas and, thus, seemingly affect the architecture of the show area. (See Chapter 2.)

Texture is also a tool that can be used by the designer. Color and texture can be used on the walls, panels, ceilings, and floor to set the traffic pattern of the show. The designer can lay a path of carpet or tiles that contrasts with the existing floor of the display space. Imagine a red velvet runner leading around a painting or sculpture exhibition, or a green "grass" matting used to set a crafts show inside an enclosed brick or stone space.

Graphics

Logos and Trademarks

A successful exhibit often will carry through its theme by means of an identifying and well-publicized **logo** or **trademark.** The logo or decorative motif appears on posters, in mailings, and in the ads for the show. It may be part of the catalog cover design or on the brochures or giveaways. Souvenirs like T-shirts, pennants, posters, scarves, and so on, will often be identified by the same logo. A dramatic, dimensional representation of the logo can be the entrance to the exhibit.

Lettering

Any copy used, whether for headlines, captions, or for general information, should be in a style that is consistent and in character with the material being exhibited. Various fonts are available for sign printing machines, which the designer can use to facilitate the makings of signs. (See Chapter 21.)

Instead of being printed, the signs can also be made with three-dimensional letters. There is a great variety of these letters from which to choose. They may be made of plastic or stamped out of cardboard or foamcore. These "3D" letters are available in sizes ranging from about $1/2$-inch to 6 or more inches in height, and in a wide variety of styles and colors. Though, initially, they are more expensive to purchase, they are reusable if handled with care. Dimensional letters add quality and character to a display. The shadows created by their thickness improve the overall look of the show, especially when the material on display is flat and nondimensional.

The style of **lettering** can suggest what the exhibit is all about. Elongated, elegant sans-serif lettering speaks of refinement, classic qualities, and uniqueness. P.T. Barnum, a "Gay Nineties" type of compressed lettering, is right to evoke the "old-fashioned," with warm, pleasant feelings for "the good old days." Heavy, expanded letters are more contemporary, hard-hitting, and emphatic. Italics can be exciting and stimulating. Obviously, what the words themselves say is very important, but what they look like can have more impact.

Supergraphics and Line

A long, straight, unbroken gallery wall can become an exciting, moving, and dazzling background by means of a **supergraphic** pattern superimposed on it. The designer may plan a dynamic line design full of sharp angles, crisp turns, and abrupt movements to become the background for what might otherwise be a rather staid and pedestrian showing. Visually, the supergraphic, done in a bold, contrasting color scheme, becomes the actual eye-arresting background, while the neutral gallery wall seems to fade away. The dynamic movement suggests the "path" for the presentation, and the viewer is "led" along by it. The supergraphic technique also works on self-standing screens, frames, or modular construction.

Photomurals and Blowups

Oversized photographs and enlargements of detailed drawings and printed material can be used effectively in promoting the theme of an exhibit. A greatly enlarged

Figure 28.7 Graphics play an important role in exhibit design. They can be used as beacons or attention-getters, signage to explain what is going on, or to show lifestyle settings for products. In this stand, semi-sheer fabric drapes hanging from curved rods create areas-within-the-area as well as a maze-like traffic pattern. Guests move through these curtains to find graphic billboards that explain the product and also show how the company's systems can be used. *ALU, Euroshop, Dusseldorf, Germany.*

graphic, over life-size, adds impact to an idea and turns a minute phrase into a mighty statement.

In a showing where crowds are anticipated, the photographic enlargement makes it possible for the viewers in back to see what is going on up front. The surprise of seeing a 6- or 8-foot closeup of a face or pattern, as one turns from one aisle into another, can be just the thing to add impetus and tempo to the next group of objects to be viewed. A grainy or grayed photomural may be the

right tone and texture for appliquéd cutout letters with a message.

In a crowded exhibit hall, where many exhibitors are striving for attention, **photomurals** or **blowups** can be very effective. Murals or long continuous pictorial illustrations can serve as a bridge between groups of ideas, explain the passage of time or a change of locale, or supply a historical setting. The mural can supply the atmosphere or background that will make what follows more readily understood. A giant map can set the scene for what comes next. A regatta of ancient sailing vessels entering a port can explain the change from the "old world" to the "new." A greatly enlarged etching or line drawing of a street fair in 18th-century London can set the mood for an exhibit of the everyday utensils and handicrafts of that time and place.

Where words may be difficult to read or where too many words would be required to explain the "why," "what," "where," and "when," a pictorial representation may do it best. The exhibit designer will find thousands of picture books and line illustrations that can be blown up photographically or printed as ozalids or blueprints (or as black or brown prints).

Heights and Elevations

Eye level is a very important consideration in planning an exhibit. It is not enough to simply place material to be viewed at 5 to $5\frac{1}{2}$ feet off the ground. Where it is anticipated there may be crowds or several layers of viewers lined up for a glimpse of the material, the designer should hang the work above regular eye level. This is an accommodation to the people in the back who may have to look over the heads and shoulders of those in front. It also adds a change of pace to what otherwise might be a routinely hung show.

There is no hard-and-fast rule for the height or level of presentation at a showing. Basically, it should be determined by the individual object being presented. Some things look better when viewed from above; that is, the viewer looks down on them (e.g., coins, jewelry, manuscripts, miniatures); other objects are best displayed when the viewer can look up to them; while still others need a straight-on view. Thus, the presentation will depend on the material, the type of exhibit, the construction of the exhibit, and the main object or thrust of the show. If a dramatic story is being presented, or the development of a product or theme, then a straight-on showing may be best. If it is a showing of artwork of various materials and techniques, the exhibit can be made more interesting when a variety of heights is used in displaying or setting up.

In any long presentation, whether it be a gallery run or an unbroken lineup of screens or panels, a "change of pace" is necessary. The viewer's eye needs a rest, a pause. It is quite monotonous to see object after object on the same background color, lit with the same intensity. In such a case, after a while, all the objects on view tend to blend together. Varying sizes can break this routine pattern. One large unit might be balanced by several smaller ones that fill the same amount of space. (See Chapter 3 for a discussion of balance and symmetry.) A break in the imaginary top or bottom line will cause the piece that extends above or below the others to receive more attention. Interspersing an occasional panel of a contrasting color will also relieve the overall sameness of the presentation and focus in on the uniqueness of the one that has been treated with special emphasis. Using plants and flowers will also help reduce the potential for monotony.

The use of museum cases and pedestals can add momentum to the pace and rhythm of a show. If photos and manuscripts have been carefully mounted on a vertical surface (a wall, panel, and so forth), then placing a book, manuscript, or photo on a pedestal, at a different eye level, will emphasize the importance of that particular object. The viewer is "forced" to look at this part of the show in a different way, switching eye level, the angle of the head, in fact, his or her whole concentration. Subsequently, it registers on the viewer that this is something special, different, more important.

Clusters of platforms of assorted heights are effective for exhibiting three-dimensional objects. A riser can bring an otherwise unimpressive object to new "heights" of importance in the viewer's eye. For example, a vase on a pedestal is special and unique. A vase along with several others, at the same level in a display case, is just another vase. Separate and apart, it becomes extraordinary.

A dimensional cube or riser can also become an island in an aisle and serve as a separation in a traffic pattern. The riser can also be used to direct traffic around a run of panels or frames. The platform serves to break away from a flat gallery presentation, or to fill in the bay or "V" formed by a folded screen. For a traveling exhibit,

cubes can be designed with open bottoms and made to fit one inside the other so that they will stack and ship more easily.

Exhibit Systems

Exhibit systems used for store planning and display have been discussed in Chapter 14. Although they were introduced as a fixturing concept, many were brought on the market specifically to serve the exhibit industry.

Figure 28.8 Many of the exhibits shown are constructed of systems especially designed to create the single and multiple storied exhibits. In this ALU exhibit not only are the various systems and fittings being shown but the entire structure is also composed on ALU fittings. The bold red entry and the red and white striped floor along with the bright white lighting make this exhibit a real draw. *ALU, Globalshop, Chicago.*

As previously mentioned, systems are available in steel, aluminum, wood, and heavy-duty, but brightly colored, plastic. Most systems seem to be designed with an infinite collection of joiners, end caps, and accessories. Some even come with built-in lighting. The systems may be super-sleek, ultra chic, high tech, or look like a warehouse construction. Some are designed to "disappear," be all but invisible, while others are meant to make a decorative statement. Systems go from simple ladder constructions to very complex webs and grids.

Some systems are preset regarding their use, and there is little the designer can do to alter the physical setup. Other systems offer a varied collection of modular, multi-sized, notched panels that can be creatively built into an intricate "house of cards" that stands, or into folding screens, cubes, and such. In selecting a system, especially one that will be used for temporary setups and for traveling or trade shows, the following criteria should be considered:

- Is it compact?
- Is it light?
- Is it easy to assemble and dismantle?
- Is it easy to maintain?
- Is it flexible and adaptable?
- Is it modular?
- Are replacement parts and accessories readily available?

Exhibit designers would do well to check with organizations such as the Point of Purchase Advertising Institute (POPAI) in New York City, as well as larger trade show buildings for lists of current manufacturers of portable trade show booths.

Theft and Vandalism Control

Unfortunately, theft and vandalism are problems that the display designer must help to control. The designer has to plan for the safety and protection of any irreplaceable materials on view. Sometimes, it does not require more than clear plastic shields hung down in front of the flat exhibit, or the setting of objects into glass- or plastic-enclosed museum-type cases. If the objects are especially precious, the shield or case may have to be wired into an alarm system.

Security guards may become part of the exhibit landscape, not only as symbols of authority and guardians of the material, but also to admonish viewers who touch and stroke. In some cases, the appearance of security in the form of television cameras, sensor equipment, and locks on cases may be enough to protect the exhibit. Ropes and stanchions can also be used to keep the exhibited material out of arm's reach. The rope and stanchion combination can also be used to control and direct traffic.

An electric eye may be necessary in some extreme cases, but they are usually not activated until after show hours. Good lighting, which is discussed below, can also be a means of security. Things are much more likely to disappear from dimly lit rooms or heavily shadowed areas. Nooks, crannies, and culs-de-sac may make wonderful display areas, but they can provide the mischief-maker with an out-of-sight spot to work some potential maleficence.

Trade show exhibits are often conceived as vehicles for testing and sampling products, and it is difficult for the visitor to realize that the material on view may not always be taken as a sample. The designer, therefore must arrange to protect what is only for show and make clear by the location and the container used what legitimately may be taken as a sample or a souvenir. A collection of brochures and pamphlets for distribution can be set up, in front, with a sign to the effect that the visitor is welcome to take one. If the printed material is not for the taking, it could be matted and framed and set under glass.

Lighting

Lighting is such a crucial element that it often makes or breaks an exhibit. The kind of lighting used is determined by the type of material to be displayed. Too much light, as well as too little, too many spotlights, not enough shadow—can destroy some presentations, especially where a mood has to be created or where dimensional objects are displayed and shadows are necessary to give them form. A dark, dark show can be great for ambience and mood, but a serious drawback for seeing what is being shown. The exhibit designer, just like the retail merchandise presenter, must balance the primary or general lighting with the secondary lighting. It might be useful, at this point, to review the lighting techniques and materials described in Chapter 4, Light and Lighting.

Daylight

Daylight, or natural light, can wreak havoc with the overall lighting scheme of an exhibit. It is never the same. It changes during the same day. It changes with the lo-

Figure 28.9 Lighting on the trade show floor can be an effective beacon or come-on. Light attracts, especially when used in bold sweeps as shown here to create a surround to encase the actual exhibit. The swirl of translucent fabric on an aluminum frame rises up in the middle and is illuminated from within. Spotlights on tracks are used under the illuminated superstructure to accentuate the actual elements being presented. *Grupo Huitzil, Globalshop, Chicago.*

cale and the time of the year. It may be too blue or too yellow. It may be gray and dull or filled with bright sunshine.

It is difficult for the designer to plan for and counteract the pervasive flood of natural light in an area that has many windows or a giant skylight. Vast, cavernous exhibit halls make it difficult for the designer to achieve a special atmosphere or mood. If budget and installation time permit, and if regulations allow, the designer may opt for screening off or blocking out windows. It is an added expense and there can be construction problems, but a "ceiling" might be lowered over the exhibit area to screen out overhead daylight where it exists. This "ceiling" does not have to be more than a dark, opaque fabric pulled taut across the exhibit space, or a series of paneled frames dropped from above or bridging the perimeter walls of the display.

Not all exhibits suffer from the use of daylight. For some, it is a plus. Flower shows, sculpture exhibits, craft shows—virtually anything that is appropriate for an out-of-doors setting—will be enhanced by daylight.

The designer should find out, in advance, if the general lighting is mainly fluorescent, incandescent, or HID, and what can or cannot be done with the lighting plan. It may be possible to turn off the overhead lighting in the particular exhibit area or change some of the lamps from cool to warm, or from warm to cool. A forewarned and prepared designer is never at a loss. "Magic" is still possible. The design may make use of ambient lighting.

Ambient Lighting

Ambient lighting is the mood-producing light used in an area or exhibit. Colored filters can be used, adding warmth and depth where needed, or strong, sharp accents of color to excite or stimulate the viewer. Ambient lighting is part of secondary lighting and makes use of floodlights, filters, and wall washers. It can include indirect lighting devices: lights hidden behind foliage, a riser, or behind a baffle or valance dropped from overhead.

Ambient lighting can also include the use of chase or flashing lights, mirrored balls to reflect pinpricks of light, and revolving color wheels. It can consist of an outlined entrance in Tivoli lights (small, clear, decorative globe-shaped lights of low wattage), or neon tubes twisted into graphic shapes or signs.

Figure 28.10 Bold sweeps, curves, and twists of white translucent fabric shaped over bent aluminum frames create eye-filling and visitor-attracting exhibits. These metal rod and fabric exhibits are lightweight, easy to assemble, easy to break-down and inexpensive to transport to the next show where they can be assembled—possibly in a different configuration. They also serve as backgrounds for changing color spectaculars, or as projection surfaces for logos, exhibit names, product visuals, etc. *Transformit, Euroshop, Dusseldorf, Germany.*

Task Lighting

Task lighting is the all-important spotlighting and highlighting of an exhibit. This puts the light where it really counts and makes the items stand out and show up at their very best. Some exhibit areas or rooms are equipped with ceiling track lighting, which can facilitate the spotlighting and floodlighting of a show. In this setup, the designer may be in control of both the general lighting and the special lighting.

Small objects in cases can be lit with miniature pinspots of bright incandescent light, tubular lights, or even pencil-like fluorescent lamps. Some objects are especially attractive when lit from behind or below. Frosted glass panels and shelves are good to use in these instances. Wherever and whenever possible, the designer should try to hide the source of light. No matter how attractive the lamp or the lamp holder, it might compete for the viewer's attention. Not only might it detract from the subject view, it could prove to be an irritant to the viewer.

Special Lighting

Backlighting objects or photographic transparencies can be especially effective when the area in which they are to be used has low-level lighting. Illuminated cases appear more brilliant when the surroundings are darkened. Rear projection and slide shows need controlled, general lighting to work. The use of "dissolves," where one object seems to fade away and another object takes its place, requires a timer device.

Thus, lighting can help tell the story, set the scene, and emphasize or enhance an object. It can isolate one item or unify a group of unrelated pieces. It can create the mood or ambience, add drama and excitement. Lighting can create a sense of direction, a path for traffic to follow, and set a pace and tempo. On a trade show floor, with dozens or hundreds of exhibits vying for attention, good lighting can be the beacon that brings in the crowds.

Special Effects

In addition to lighting, color, line, texture, and graphics, the designer can add touches of unique excitement to an exhibit through the use of **special effects** that will increase the viewer's enjoyment of the show and his or her comprehension of what is being presented.

Movement and/or Animation

Motors

Just as flashing lights are more emphatic and attention-getting than a constant glow from a lamp, so is **animation** more eye-catching and startling than a stationary display. The **movement** can be smooth and subtle, such as a turntable slowly rotating and showing an array of items or a complete front-to-back display of a single item. The turntable may be a heavy-duty floor unit made to sustain a great deal of weight, a tabletop unit for smaller and lighter pieces, or one that is suspended from above to put a graphic mobile into a spin or to activate a flutter of ribbons. Ceiling motors can be used for a variety of motion effects.

Conveyer belts bring an exhibit to a stationary audience. The conveyer belt works like a track that goes around the exhibit area and brings a continuous display of material before the viewer who remains in one place. This is easier on the viewer, but much more complicated for the display designer and the construction of the exhibit. Crowds will always collect around a display of miniature trains that circle around and around the tracks, winding their way through a set but convoluted pattern. In its simplest form, the "train and tracks" can be a relatively easy yet eye-catching device—if it goes with the theme and tone of the exhibit.

Models and Miniatures

Every Christmas there are long lines stretching around department stores featuring animated windows. The stuffed animals jerk right and left and the pixies move up and down. The simplest actions and movements please millions. Even without the animation, miniatures attract and fascinate audiences. Scale models are informative as well as intriguing and might do a better job of instructing than a full-size replica. For the exhibit designer faced with space restrictions and traveling and shipping schedules, the model setup and the use of miniatures can be extremely useful.

Lighting

As discussed earlier in this chapter, flashing and chasing lights can also supply "motion" to an exhibit. A light going on and off behind a transparency set into a light box will get attention. A motion message, as the name implies, is an electrified billboard on which the message runs across the board and can be changed by a keyboard programmer. This is a rather new entrant into the exhibit and display field, and is actually a miniature version of the famous, outdoor, multibulb signs used in New York's Times Square.

Audio-Visuals

Television screens and monitors or **audio-visuals** are always noticed and watched. People will stand outside a display window to watch flickering figures on a silent screen, or line up in a store to see five or six screens showing the same program.

When the designer and the exhibitor decide on a slide, tape, or film presentation which may take several minutes to view, they might want to consider setting it up somewhere beyond the main flow of the show. A piece of film or tape, or a slide show played and viewed on a screen, may cause a tie-up in the traffic flow, unless space is provided for the group as it gathers to watch.

TV monitors can also be used as directories to tell what is going on and where the action is taking place.

Live Action

Live action must be carefully planned. A live demonstration can quickly draw an audience, but just as quickly lose one. People will stand around, intrigued and delighted, watching a mime, a magician, a puppeteer, or performing animals, but will lose interest completely by a poorly delivered sales pitch.

Some exhibitors still feel strongly that a scantily clad young woman will draw an audience, and they will depend on her charms to get attention. She may draw an audience, but does she necessarily sell the product or deliver the message? Is the audience she draws the right audience for the product being shown? A person in an animal suit can be fun, but is this in keeping with the image of the exhibitor?

Greater anticipation and excitement is generated when the live performer is not always "on," but makes scheduled appearances. In this way, the exhibitor can gain an audience in the exhibit area and "sell" the product or idea to those who are waiting to be entertained or to those who have just been amused. It can also be used as a means of controlling traffic.

Audience Involvement

More and more exhibit designers are finding that an exhibit or display that involves the viewer physically is very effective and leaves a long-lasting impression on the participant. When a person makes contact with the materi-

Figure 28.11 The long space has been divided with a series of "bars" where guests can sample the liquors, get information, recipes, etc. Each bar unit also carries a hidden supply of additional bottles on the floor. The funnel shaped roofs of fabric and aluminum rod are internally lit for attention value. The unit in the center of the space is an enclosed "conference" room and the outside is covered with giant graphic blowups of the products, which are illuminated for additional attention-getting value. *Future Trends, Night Club & Bar Show, Las Vegas. Design: Chicago Exhibit Products.*

als on view, turns a crank, pushes a button, switches on a sound recording, changes the location of an object, tastes, smells, touches, or in any way makes actual contact with the material—he or she becomes personally involved with the display, and the displayed items become part of his or her experience.

Children's museums are presenting more "hands-on" exhibits than ever before. The hands-on experience allows the observer to pace the show according to his or her own level of interest. The participant will spend more time at some displays and less at others.

Computerized material, involving keyboards and video terminals, is also becoming increasingly popular. People enjoy testing themselves or challenging the "unknown brain" within the machine.

The problems inherent in the "hands-on" approach are many. A particular display may be such fun that people will gang up to "play" with it. The net result can be a traffic jam. Some viewers play roughly and can break or foul up a machine or keyboard. Other viewers may pass up pertinent material in favor of the "fun and games," not getting the full value of the total exhibit.

Also, special lighting requirements may be necessary. It is not unusual for displays with screens to require darkened areas.

Today's display designer has to be aware of the many miracles of modern technology in order to produce exhibits that not only attract but impress.

Making the Exhibit Special

Throughout this book, the word "image" has appeared over and over again because it is an essential part of the personality of an organization. It is what makes one group or store different from another, even though the product or idea offered may be almost the same. It is the "packaging" or "gift wrap" of an organization that makes the consumer reach out for its product. In being special or getting attention, the image must always be considered. A person hanging from the edge of a roof will gain attention, as will wearing bright red satin to a graduation ceremony. Filling an exhibit with lively piglets will draw crowds, but what does it say about the sponsor of the space?

In keeping with the tone, style, tradition, and position of the exhibit sponsor in the business community, the designer has to plan carefully for "special attention." Many of these attractions are the **amenities of design,** the gracious, nonselling aspects of the setup and the surroundings, those features that satisfy the aesthetics or personal comfort of the viewers.

The Amenities

Plants and Flowers

These are obvious "audience pleasers," and yet, often omitted. The greenery adds life and sparkle to an inanimate presentation, and, in its naturalness of form, can break up a stiff, regimental presentation of straight lines, angles, and rectangles. Plants will do well for a limited showing under what can become adverse conditions: no sunlight, too much heat from strong lights, lack of air, too much smoke, and friction from passersby. Artificial plants will also work, but many people do not find them satisfactory substitutes.

Designers may also use branches and twigs to introduce a sense of freedom and movement to an exhibit that is all straight lines and sharp angles. In water-filled

Figure 28.12 Hundreds of oranges on strings hang in a series of concentric circles over a giant white circular floor mat on which the company's many attributes and talents are printed in a graphic pattern. The sales staff was dressed with white coveralls trimmed in orange and wore orange athletic shoes. Seating was provided around the perimeter of the 30′ circle. The unexpected effect of suspended oranges floating in space and visible throughout the exhibit floor was a great draw for the company. *Winntech, Globalshop, Chicago.*

containers or set into moistened florist foam, the leafy branches will do quite well for a short time. Flowering plants can add a lovely touch of color to a showing. The cost may be negligible in comparison to other expenditures, and worth it for the effect they produce. Cut floral arrangements can be luxurious and eye-filling, but require more tending and will need replacing if the show lasts more than a few days. Though in the long run, it may be more expensive than an outright pur-

chase, plants can be rented. Some florists will come in and "care" for their charges while the plants remain on view.

Seating

Unless this is an exhibit that will draw large crowds and must be scheduled to get people in and out within a particular time frame, it is a nice and friendly amenity to provide some form of seating. At a trade show, where space is at a premium, some exhibitors, nevertheless, will arrange for seating within the exhibit area. It is easier to sell someone who is seated than a "person-on-the-run." The longer the exhibitor can keep a potential customer within the confines of a booth, the greater the potential for making a sale. (Where order writing is anticipated, tables may be necessary.)

In other exhibits, benches set along the way can provide happy rest stops. The designer can plan these islands of seating in relation to the presentation and the general traffic flow. Some pieces or items need to be studied more than others, and a conveniently located seating arrangement allows those who would like to sit and observe the piece, to do so. In a large exhibition hall where a single exhibit is on view or where the exhibit may cover several salons or floors, the designer may break up the showing with rest areas. Some persons may find it too exhausting or strenuous to cover a big show without an occasional rest. A large corporation sponsoring an institutional type of display may provide the seating as its contribution to goodwill. By doing so, it may not be selling a particular product, but it will be selling its name, its reputation, and its image.

Refreshments

A coffee cart or wine bar is a deluxe addition to an exhibit and will pay off in its ability to "hold" a viewer in an exhibit area. This is especially true at trade shows. Refreshments relax the viewer and offer an essential change of pace. They can be as varied as a sampling of an exhibited food product, canapés, cheese and crackers, cookies, jars of hard candies, and assorted hard or soft drinks.

At some trade shows, there are regulations about what may or may not be served in display booths. The show management may opt for setting up its own hospitality booths which will supply or sell food to the show visitor. To the viewer who plans to spend several hours in the exhibit hall, this is important.

Tie-ins

To make an exhibit especially memorable or special, one must go beyond the confines of the actual showing. It has already been mentioned that an exhibit has to be produced, packaged, and sold. Sometimes, it is the packaging and salesmanship, more than what is being shown, that makes a show successful. Many shows succeed, in large measure, because of their **tie-ins.**

The production and promotion of an exhibit often requires posters, mailings, catalogs, publications, and a long list of souvenirs. Today, the poster is not simply a card to include in a display window; it has become a piece of graphic art, to frame and hang. The effectiveness of the show's logo or design and the poster can sometimes "make" the show. A good display designer should be aware of the advertising requirements for promoting a show and be ready to assist with concepts and tangible product ideas.

Community involvement is very important, too. It is advantageous to be able to tie in with other groups or products. If it is an artistic or cultural promotion, department and specialty stores may become involved in promoting the show. They may devote valuable window space to the exhibit and even use posters and the show logo as part of their presentation. Local "talk shows," both on radio and TV, are always looking for interesting and timely subjects to discuss and show. An exhibit can get free advance publicity more easily if there is a gimmick or handle to work with.

T-shirts, banners, bumper stickers, and shopping bags are only a few of the identifiable objects that can be used to promote a show once it has begun. The materials the viewers take away with them will proclaim the show to others who have not yet been there. These are the most effective "ads." They are "testimonials" from satisfied customers. A shopping bag or tote with a logo imprint can start a kind of self-interrogation: "What kind of show is it? Why is everybody going to see it? What am I missing?" Many people want to be where "everybody" is and doing what "everybody" is doing. These tie-in concepts reinforce the poster, the fliers, and the mailings.

The trade show exhibitor can also gain from tie-ins and giveaways. The silk-screened plastic bag is always a show favorite. It is lightweight, reusable, and great for carrying the brochures and samples the visitor accumulated during a tour through the show building. The logo or trade name emblazoned across the bag advertises the sponsor and his or her product, and suggests a visit has been made to the sponsor's booth, even if it was only to pick up a bag.

Americans are button collectors. Pin a button on trade show visitors, and they will very likely remain wearing it all the time they are on the show floor. In this way, the show visitor becomes a walking signboard. Flowers, live or artificial, are always popular. Tags and balloons are eye-catchers and not expensive to have produced in volume. Imprinted ballpoint pens and pencils will be picked up and carried away. They will keep selling weeks later, far away from the show.

The ideal giveaway should be lightweight, compact, practical, reusable, and long-lasting. From the exhibitor's point of view, it should be inexpensive and imprinted with his or her logo, name and, possibly, the address. The more discrete the imprint, the more likely it is that the giveaway will be kept and used. There are many manufacturers of such souvenirs, but since the exhibitor's name will appear on it, it is up to the designer and the exhibitor to make sure that the "giveaway" is worthy of their image.

Exhibit and Trade Show Design—Industrial Display: A Recap

- An exhibit is the display and showing of special materials that have been collected and edited for presentation. The major purpose of an exhibit is to stimulate and create interest for a particular product, idea, or organization aimed at a special audience.

- A trade show is a commercial display of new products or concepts presented to a select group of prospective buyers or consumers.

- Types of exhibits include permanent, temporary, trade show, traveling, and outdoor.

- The size of an exhibit can vary greatly and the designer must determine what can be done within a space and how much can be shown effectively.

- A traveling exhibit must have flexibility so that it can expand or contract as space permits.

- Trade show exhibits will vary with each exhibit hall and its space allocation. The exhibition may require a number of modules put together to accommodate the material, or may be contained within one module.

- Common traffic patterns at exhibits include long lines following perimeter walls; a zigzag of screens folded into a series of V-shaped bays; and a maze layout where the viewer is swept along by a series of angles and turns.

- When planning an exhibit, the following must be considered: size of the exhibit; design and layout of traffic patterns; theme or story of the exhibit; and color and texture of the presentation.

- Graphics can identify an exhibit, call attention to it, promote the theme, supply atmosphere and background, and add a change of pace to a routinely mounted show.

- In selecting a system, the following criteria should be considered: compactness, lightness, ease in assembling and dismantling, maintenance, flexibility and adaptability, whether the system is modular, and whether replacement parts and accessories are readily available.

- Theft and vandalism may be controlled in a number of ways: clear plastic shields hung down in front of the flat exhibit; setting of objects in museum-type cases; wiring cases to an alarm system; hiring of security guards; security cameras and sensor equipment; ropes and stanchions; electric eyes; and good lighting.

- Types of lights used in exhibit design include daylight or natural light, fluorescent light, incandescent light, ambient light, spotlights, and track lights.

- Movement, animation, lighting, models and miniatures, audio-visual effects, TV monitors, and live action are special effects that can enliven and enhance an exhibit.

- Special amenities can bring attention to an exhibit as well as satisfy the aesthetics or personal comfort of the viewer.

- Tie-ins can make an exhibit especially memorable and can be produced in a number of different ways.

Questions for Review and Discussion

1. Identify exhibits that you may have visited or that have been hosted in your community.

2. Give an example of a trade show that you may have attended or that has been held in your community.

3. Distinguish among permanent exhibits, temporary exhibits, and traveling exhibits.

4. What problems must be overcome in the design of outdoor exhibits?

5. Explain the relationship between the size of the exhibit and the potential traffic pattern that will be created.

6. Why are height and elevation such important factors in exhibit design?

7. What is an exhibit system? What criteria should be used in the selection of an exhibit systems?

8. What is the difference between ambient lighting and task lighting? Give examples of each.

9. What special effects might be used to add excitement to an exhibit?

CHAPTER TWENTY-NINE

Fashion Shows

AFTER YOU HAVE READ THIS CHAPTER,
YOU WILL BE ABLE TO DISCUSS:

- The importance of a central theme in the creation of a fashion show.

- The various ways of creating unique backdrops for fashion shows.

- Props that can be effectively used in fashion shows.

- How lighting should be used in fashion shows.

FASHION SHOWS: TRADE TALK

theme

travelers

A fashion show[1] can be enhanced by display techniques, but it is a different kind of "theater." The major difference between a fashion show and display are the movement, the animation, and the choreography that are essential to a fashion presentation using live models. If there is no movement, why use live models? The movement of a line of models requires timing, planning, and pacing.

It is essential to provide room for the models' movements (i.e., stages, runways, walkways, aisles, and so on). Not only do the models need room in which to move, but the clothing being modeled does also. A cape may be "flung," a skirt swirled, or a jacket removed.

The fashion show should have a **theme,** a central basic idea on which the show is built. The theme will suggest the type of merchandise being shown and the audience for whom it is being prepared. The store could do a "back-to-college" show for high school and college students, a bridal show for prospective brides and the all-important mother of the bride, or a fall showing of new fabrics and trends for the store's special customers. In any and every case, there should be an idea, a "handle," gimmick, catch-line, or phrase that will not only "set" the show, but also suggest the signs to be used, the advance publicity, and the printed programs.

In some ways, a fashion show is like doing a window display as part of a promotion. The setting of the fashion show can be compared to the background of the window display. (Basically, the main difference is the length of time the shopper is involved with each. A fashion show can last for thirty minutes or more.) If the background setting makes too strong a statement, it can get in the way of the proceedings.

If a setting is used, it should be open and neutral; pleasant, suggestive, but not intrusive. It should say "something," but not too definitively. A skyline, if it is semiabstract or stylized, can suggest city clothes, career fashions,

---

[1]For more information on producing a fashion show, refer to *Guide to Producing a Fashion Show,* by Judith C. Everett and Kristen K. Swanson (Fairchild Publications, 1993).

and even after-dark styles. A balustrade with a garden beyond could suggest formal wear, a garden wedding, daytime dresses, even "Tennis, anyone?"—if done properly. Ideally, the background can be a vignetted drawing or painting that sits well back on the stage and does not try to upstage the merchandise being paraded in front of it.

A series of curtains on a track (**travelers**) can be used to set an entire show with six or seven "scenes." A variety of blinds that can be rolled up or down could also be used to set a show: bamboo blinds for beach and resort wear, Austrian blinds for formals and bridals, Roman shades for daytime and dress-up, colored venetian blinds for career fashions and even sportswear or separates. A few potted plants, center stage, rear, or masking the entrance or exit of an impromptu stage, can be effective without being distracting. The live green plants or the colors of flowering plants can create a setting, completely camouflaging an open space on the selling floor or brightening up a community room.

Certain devices will always work in a fashion show setting. They say, quickly and effectively, what has to be said. Stairs, ramps, platforms, and risers are always good, but can be dangerous if not used properly.

A well-designed staircase provides a dramatic entrance because there is sweep and movement in the model's descent. If the steps are too deep or too high, however, the model will look awkward walking up and back. A ramp with a gentle incline can also be effective, but rushing down because the incline is too steep, or trudging up a ramp can make even the most graceful model in the loveliest outfit look ludicrous. A platform or two can be used to step onto, turn about on, and step down from. This makes for good choreography, while allowing the garment to be shown to its best advantage. Turntables can be used effectively, especially as an "entrance," where the model goes from an almost back view into a front view before stepping off.

Archways, doorways, beaded curtains, the opening of curtains, and so forth, will all work when the models make their entrances. They can also be used effectively in combination with steps, ramps, and turntables.

Figure 29.1 The fashion show has moved beyond the boutique, special events center, and tent set up during Designer and Prêt-à-Porter Week. It is now an every-two-hours feature attraction in the Fashion Show Mall in Las Vegas, as well as a special events feature in many other malls and shopping centers. It gives the retailers in the mall the opportunity to show off their wares in a structured affair with an eager audience in attendance. At the Fashion Show Mall, the runway and the stage rise up from the floor to the accompaniment of a light and sound show with graphic-filled screens overhead. Music and lighting enhance the models walking the long runway and the overhead screens announce the designer or retailer whose garments are on display. At the show's end, the runway and stage descend below the floor level and "disappear." *Fashion Show Mall, Las Vegas.*

Settings or props that take up too much stage or runway space can be a problem. The designer can emulate Japanese theater techniques and have specially dressed, "invisible stagehands" dress and redress the stage with each change of merchandise. It does, however, require special props, and the movement of the stagehands can clutter and detract from the fashion showing.

Often, the best props or scene-setters are the ones the models bring in and take off with them. A model carrying a beach ball, an umbrella, a book or newspaper, a camera, an attaché case or an artist's portfolio, a hat box, a bunch of flowers or a fan, a bunch of balloons, a big stuffed animal—any of these can set the scene. The prop also adds sparkle or serves as an accessory to the costume, whatever it might be. With one of these props, the model also has some "business" to do that will play up the costume and humanize his or her actions. Also, this portable prop does not take up performing space or slow down the pace of the show.

Lighting is most important. In a window or ledge display, the display person arranges the lights for shadows as well as highlights. The object that is being lit is fixed in one place, and the lights are fixed on that location. In a fashion show, it is desirable that the light follow the model, keeping the model in the spotlight. If that is not possible, then the traffic route—the stage or runway or both—should be bathed in strong light and the audience left in the shadows. This is especially true when the "runway" is really not much more than a path on the floor and the seated audience is almost at the same level. In such a situation, unfortunately, the patrons on one side can be a distraction for the patrons on the other side and, as in an open-back window, they can conflict with the featured performers.

If the show runs longer than fifteen minutes, it is desirable to have some lighting changes. These changes may consist of filter colors, the degree of whiteness, or direction of the light. Prolonged exposure to the same degree of brightness can render the viewer insensitive to what is going on.

Different types of merchandise can be "explained" by different colored lights on the background: yellow for sports and swimwear, blues and violets for formal wear, pinks and reds for lingerie and intimate apparel, and cool blue light for outerwear. The use of colored light to bathe or wash the background can actually set a scene without a prop.

Most shows today use music, live or taped, to create the tempo for the showing. It gives the models a beat to move to, and it takes the viewer along with the sound. A change of tempo is effective in delineating "scenes" and merchandise groupings. The music and the lights are basic requirements for a fashion show, and the decor and props are extras.

As previously noted, there should be a theme, a logo, a concept, or a symbol that is carried through the whole show—from the preliminary announcements until the finale. If the store were doing something as simple as "New Directions for Spring," for example, the logo could be a weather-vane, a windmill, a street sign, or a montage of arrows. The design logo could then be used on posters, mailings, and programs (if any are printed). A giant blowup or a simple, overscaled construction of that logo could be the "setting" for the show. The scenario or commentary for the show should include words or phrases indicating direction. If the store has a storewide promotion going on and the fashion show will tie in with it, the theme, logo, and so on of that particular promotion should be elaborated on in the fashion show.

Fashion Shows: A Recap

- Every fashion show should have a theme that will suggest the type of merchandise being shown and the audience for whom the show is prepared.

- A theme will not only "set" the show, but also suggest the signs to be used, the advance publicity, and the printed program.

- A background should be pleasant and suggestive but never intrusive.

- A series of curtains on a track, called travelers, can change background scenes, as can a variety of blinds that can be rolled up and down.

- The best props for a fashion show are the ones a model can carry, such as a beach ball, an umbrella, a book or newspaper, a camera.

- In a fashion show, the light should follow the model. If this is not possible, the stage or runway should be bathed in light.

- If the show runs longer than fifteen minutes, it is desirable to have some lighting changes. These can be accomplished by use of color filters, a change in the degree of whiteness, or a change in the direction of the light.

Questions for Review and Discussion

1. What is the major difference between a fashion show and a display?

2. Explain the correlation between a fashion show setting and the background of a display window.

3. What devices can be used to create new scenes for fashion shows?

4. Determine the theme for a showing of men's fashions for Father's Day. The show is to be held in a retailer's own men's wear department, so space is limited. How would you set the scene? What types of props, lighting, and music would you use?

CHAPTER THIRTY

Trade Organizations and Sources

AFTER YOU HAVE READ THIS CHAPTER,
YOU WILL BE ABLE TO DISCUSS:

- How guilds can help to support the efforts of visual merchandisers.
- The leading visual merchandising trade organizations.
- The services and benefits available to members of the various visual merchandising trade organizations.
- Other sources of information and ideas for individuals in the field of visual merchandising.
- Why visual merchandisers should maintain research files.

TRADE ORGANIZATIONS AND SOURCES: TRADE TALK

ADA's
DD & I
guild
ISP
NADI
PAVE
POPAI
trade organizations
VM & SD

Though visual merchandisers are often artists and craftpersons involved in aesthetics and the arts, they are also essentially businesspeople. They are in the business of presentation, and their purpose is to sell the store and the merchandise within it. As businesspeople and craftspeople with specific talents, there are **guilds** available to them. The guilds are different from trade unions. While unions might have a widely diversified membership, the **trade organizations** to be discussed here were formed specifically for the creators and/or the end users of the mannequins, fixtures, props, decoratives, foliage, point-of-purchase (POP) displays and displayers, store furniture, and so on.

Most of these organizations sponsor trade shows once or twice a year. The trade show is an exhibit of basic products as well as the new products conceived by designers who are employed by the manufacturers. These products and concepts, it is hoped, will enhance the presentation of merchandise, suggest new trends in store fixturing, and/or reinforce an advertising campaign. These shows are generally scheduled for those times of the year that are convenient for the supplier and the buyer, while still allowing the end user sufficient time to order for an upcoming season, a store opening, or a new promotional year.

Very often, buying offices, resident buyers, and fashion forecasters will plan group meetings for these show times. Visual merchandisers and their staffs as well as store planners will be invited to attend these industry meetings in the same city, at the same time. These meetings add another dimension to the trade show and make attendance even more worthwhile.

Major Organizations

Described below are some of the major organizations that are essential to the craft and profession of visual merchandising. They are presented in order of their seniority—the length of time they have been effectively serving the industry and the people in that industry.

Point of Purchase Advertising Institute (POPAI)

The Point of Purchase Advertising Institute (**POPAI**, pronounced "popeye"), headquartered in Washington, DC, was formed as a nonprofit organization in 1938. It was created to serve those who make and utilize advertising and merchandising units used at the point where a sale is made. The Institute's membership includes the designers and producers of the displays and fixtures as well as the advertisers who order these pieces and the retailers who use them. Today, POPAI is an international organization and one of the most active and aggressive trade associations in the marketing field.

Among the many services offered by this organization to its membership are workshops and seminars that deal with problems and new trends that develop in the field. The organization also sponsors research studies on buying habits, customer reactions to advertising, and techniques and current practices in the marketplace.

An annual trade show is sponsored by POPAI, in which the latest and most innovative concepts in signing and display are shown, and new materials and techniques are introduced. Top marketing executives as well as display producers visit this exhibition. The organization also makes awards to the outstanding signs and displays of the year.

POPAI maintains an information center that distributes many publications of interest to advertisers and marketing people. It publishes *POPAI News* and prepares operating guidelines and bulletins to keep its membership informed on current matters of importance to them. There is also a public relations program, a speaker's bureau, and an active educator membership. The group is most cooperative with schools where advertising and display is taught and actively promotes the career openings in the POP field. It also sponsors an annual POP design competition for college students.

National Association of Display Industries (NADI)

The National Association of Display Industries (**NADI**), headquartered in Hollywood, Florida, was organized in 1942 by leading manufacturers, designers, distributors, and importers in the visual merchandising field. It was conceived as a viable source for creating new business for the industry and to arrange a showcase for all that is new and innovative.

Though its membership consists almost exclusively of the producers and distributors of visual merchandising and store planning materials, NADI does participate in research programs intended to benefit the customers of its products. An Education Advisory Board works closely with schools that offer visual merchandising curricula. There are scholarships and grants as well as a cooperative work plan designed to foster closer relations between the manufacturers and the future display persons. In addition to maintaining the most accurate and complete mailing lists in the industry (available only to its members), the group offers a free employment information exchange that can be used by store management, visual merchandisers, and manufacturers.

NADI feels that a strong industry organization will not only benefit the producers, but also strengthen and assist the visual merchandisers in their quest for stature and greater recognition in the retailing industry. It enables them to do their jobs more effectively by having better fixtures, mannequins, and props with which to work. The NADI co-sponsors the annual Globalshop trade show in March and the ShopXpo that occurs in New York City in early December. www.NADI-Global.com

Institute of Store Planners (ISP)

The Institute of Store Planners (**ISP**) was formed in 1961 to gain professional recognition for persons involved in the business of store planning and design. Professional membership is granted to persons twenty-five years of age or older who have been working a minimum of eight years as full-time store planners. They are expected to be able to assemble and analyze merchandising data and be capable of applying this information to a working store plan. The store planner should be able to create and/or supervise the execution of the interior design: prepare the necessary drawings, establish budgets, and work with architects and engineers on the structural and mechanical elements of the job.

An associate member has to be twenty-one years of age or older and have had at least three years of full-time employment and experience as a store planner. The in-

dividual has to be professional, capable of reading and interpreting plans, and seeing them through to completion. Trade membership is open to any reputable industrial concern that supplies either the materials or services necessary to the store planning profession. This would include manufacturers of fixtures, merchandisers, woodworking, store furniture, interior design materials, and so on.

The professional membership includes architects, store planners, and interior designers. Some of these professionals work for a department store, on staff, and are actively involved in the daily changes and alterations in the store as well as advance planning for new stores to be built or rehabilitated. Others are either self-employed or work as part of a design office or an architectural concern.

ISP has an active education program, sponsoring scholarships for students in store planning programs in schools across the country. There are also newsletters, publications, and many regional and joint meetings that are often combined with presentations by trade members. There are several local chapters which plan special programs for their groups. www.ISPO.org

Planning and Visual Education (PAVE)

Founded in 1992, the Planning and Visual Education partnership's objective is to encourage students to study in the field of retail design and planning and visual merchandising through its annual Student Design Competition. Additionally, PAVE seeks to encourage retail management, store planners, visual merchandisers, architects, and manufacturers to interact with and support design students. This is accomplished through seminars, workshops, and its annual fund-raising Gala with proceeds dedicated to financial aid and internships for qualified students. www.P-A-V-E.info.

National Association of Store Fixture Manufacturers (NASFM)

This is an organization of over 700 store fixture manufacturers and suppliers who together produce more than 85% of all fixtures manufactured in North America. They are a resource for locating fixtures and fixture producers, and their annual Buyer's Guide and online searchable database (www.nasfm.org) are valuable tools available to retailers, designers, and specifiers. NASFM sponsors an annual store design challenge, "Retail Design Awards," and also is a co-sponsor of Globalshop.

In-Store Marketing Institute

This membership-based "think tank" organization is dedicated to satisfying the needs of the in-store marketing professionals and point-of-purchase field in general, and provides them with a constant update of what is happening in the retail field. The Institute publishes the *P-O-P Times* and *P-O-P Design* monthly magazines and also sponsors the P-O-P Show, P-O-P Senior Executive Congress, and In-Store Marketing Summit. www.instoremarketer.org.

Sources of Information and Ideas

Trade Shows

Currently, the biggest and by far the most inclusive annual trade show for the store designer/visual merchandiser and retailer is Globalshop. Introduced only a few years ago by the editors of *Display & Design Ideas* magazine, the show has grown until it now fills over one million square feet in conference center venues ranging from Chicago to Las Vegas and Orlando. The show usually occurs late in March and a thousand exhibitors from around the United States, Europe, and Asia show their latest and most innovative materials, fixtures, lighting, techniques, and technology. The show lasts only three days and is attended by chain operators, department and specialty store personnel, consumer product manufacturers, discount and mass merchandisers, and, of course, store designers, architects, visual merchandisers, and display persons.

Globalshop, today, is actually five trade shows in one. It combines the Store Fixturing and the Visual Merchandising Shows with the POPAI Retail Expo, the Exhibit Ideas Show, and the Retail Operations and Construction Expo. With one admission, visitors can tour all the exhibit spaces and find ideas, materials, or products in unexpected places.

The centerpiece of each show is an exciting presentation of new vendor shops especially created for some of the country's best known brand marketers. Another feature is the seminar program sponsored and developed by Professionals for the Advancement of Visual Education (**PAVE**). Leaders in the retail industry, famous architects and designers, outstanding visual merchandisers, or "people in the news" make presentations at these seminars. For anybody interested or involved with retail presentation, this is a show not to be missed.

The display person in search of mannequins, fixtures, or props would do well to visit New York City in early December when the ShopXpo is co-sponsored by the NADI organization in conjunction with another related show at the Javitz Center. At this time and throughout the year there are numerous showrooms open for viewing in New York featuring noted mannequin, fixture, and decorative manufacturers. Even if store planning is the activity that the visual merchandiser intends doing, these are still the trade shows to see. Also, the trade show booklets are invaluable listings of who's who in the field, what is available, and where it can be obtained.

Trade Magazines

Display & Design Ideas (**DD&I**) is a monthly tabloid-size magazine published by VNU Business Publications, USA that contains "product news and design solutions for store planning and visual merchandising." *DD&I* is also the major sponsor of the aforementioned Globalshop trade show. The publication is free to subscribers, and it contains stories on new retail operations, current trends in retail store formatting, fixturing, and lighting concepts. The editors will often poll their readership on questions relevant to their work. These surveys may focus on budgets, personnel, education, what products readers use, what products they would like to have, and so on. In addition, the magazine is filled with colored ads for all types of products and materials related to store design, visual merchandising, and display. An inquiry card is included in each issue for the convenience of the reader. By circling the number corresponding to the number on the ad, the reader will, for the price of a single stamp, receive brochures, booklets, and samples from numerous manufacturers and suppliers.

The visual merchandiser should subscribe to **VM&SD** magazine, published in Cincinnati, Ohio. In this monthly magazine, in addition to articles relevant to merchandise presentation and store planning, there are dozens of advertisements for the many elements necessary for the successful installation of windows and interiors. By filling in the numbers on the request card that is inserted at the back of the magazine, the display person is assured a steady flow of brochures, booklets, and illustrative material on new products and designs.

Visual Reference Publications of New York publishes a monthly magazine, *Retail Design & Visual Presentation,* which presents new retail stores, store promotions, and window displays, as well as articles of interest to store planners/designers and visual merchandisers. The material is international and shows what is being done in various parts of the world. In addition, Visual Reference Publications is the foremost publisher of hardcover, fully illustrated, color books on display ("Store Windows" series), store planning and design ("The Stores of the Year" series), and other design areas such as cafes and restaurants, supermarkets, specialty food stores, etc. It is advisable to get on their mailing list for current brochures listing their newest books. www.visualreference.com. Also, for over fifteen years the company has become the foremost publisher of hard cover, full-color, illustrated books on store design, restaurant design, display, graphics, and POP design. Many of their past books are now "collector's items" as designers try to find copies of earlier books to fill in sets like Stores of the Year, Store Windows, and Store Fronts & Facades.

Other Publications

Creative Magazine: Point of Purchase, Exhibit Design, Sales Promotions.
www.creativemagazine.com.

Chain Store Age: www.chainstoreage.com.

Brandweek: Point of Purchase and sales promotions. Published along with Adweek by VNU Business Publications, USA.

Research

The visual merchandiser should keep an active research file of booklets, brochures, photographs, ads, swatches, and any other bits and pieces that will someday make the designing or installation of a display better and simpler to execute. It is never too soon to start amassing this type of material.

Since this is an ongoing sort of collection, it should be reexamined often, updated, and kept viable. With outdated material weeded out, an "idea" that was filed away might stimulate a whole new set of promotional concepts. Photographs from fashion magazines can often suggest new arrangements for mannequin groupings, color schemes, or even fashion accessorizing. A postcard from some exotic, faraway place in the tropics may become the starting point for a display—as a background for a swimwear presentation, for example.

Keeping a reference file is an absolute "must." It gives the visual merchandiser/display person a place from which to start. Ideas evolve from other ideas.

Trade Organizations and Sources: A Recap

- Guilds support the efforts of visual merchandising by sponsoring trade shows during the year. Such shows will feature concepts and products that will enhance merchandise, suggest new trends in store fixturing, and/or refine an ad campaign.

- Trade shows often give visual merchandisers and their staffs the opportunity to attend industry meetings being held in the same city.

- The leading visual merchandising trade organizations are:

  Point of Purchase Advertising Institute (POPAI)
  National Association of Display Industries (NADI)
  Institute of Store Planners (ISP)

- Visual merchandising trade organizations offer various benefits, as follows:
  a. POPAI offers seminars and workshops dealing with problems and new trends; makes awards; maintains an information center; publishes guidelines and bulletins; maintains a public relations program.
  b. NADI presents various awards at trade shows sponsored twice a year in New York; participates in research programs; works closely with schools that offer visual merchandising curricula; offers scholarships, grants, and cooperative work plans; maintains an accurate and complete mailing list, available to members only; offers free employment information.
  c. ISP has an active education program sponsoring scholarships for students in store planning programs across the country; offers newsletters, publications, and many regional and joint meetings that are often combined with presentations by trade members.

- Other sources that may be used by individuals in the field of visual merchandising are trade shows and trade magazines. The biggest and most inclusive trade show is Globalshop, held each year in Chicago. It attracts exhibitors from around the United States, Europe, and Asia.

- The visual merchandiser should keep an active research file of booklets, brochures, photos, ads, swatches, and any material involving design and display. Subscriptions to magazines and trade journals can also provide useful information and help stimulate ideas.

- Research files can help the display person keep up with new ideas in the field and might stimulate a whole new promotional concept, suggest new arrangements for displays, or lead to the evolution of new ideas.

Questions for Review and Discussion

1. Why are visual merchandisers considered businesspeople, as well as craftspersons?

2. State the meaning of the acronym and the main purpose for each of the following trade organizations. What activities are conducted in order to achieve each organization's goals?
  a. POPAI
  b. NADI
  c. ISP

3. Name three trade publications directly related to the field of visual merchandising. In what ways might trade publications be used by visual merchandising professionals?

CHAPTER THIRTY-ONE

Career Opportunities in Visual Merchandising

AFTER YOU HAVE READ THIS CHAPTER,
YOU WILL BE ABLE TO DISCUSS:

- Other areas of opportunity for individuals with a background in visual merchandising.

- The basic areas that a résumé should cover.

- The purpose of the portfolio.

- The attributes of a good visual merchandiser.

CAREER OPPORTUNITIES IN VISUAL MERCHANDISING:
TRADE TALK

portfolio

résumé

To a person considering visual merchandising as a career, the term too often implies merely doing displays in a department or specialty store. Visual merchandising or display is much more than that. The career possibilities and the fields in which one can practice the techniques of "showing" and presentation are myriad. Though trends in fashion have great influence on what the visual merchandiser/display person is showing, be it books, luggage, or even auto tires, visual merchandising is more than fashion and fashion accessories.

Visual merchandisers can find careers in the field of commercial exhibiting, museum and graphic art exhibiting, the staging of fashion shows, point-of-purchase design, store planning, and packaging. Display persons may work as trimmers, decorators, or designers in a department or specialty store, or for a manufacturer of display fixtures or props. They may work as freelance trimmers for individual stores or manufacturer showrooms. With trade shows becoming more and more important and appearing with greater frequency in more cities, visual merchandising has become a lucrative field for the adaptable and capable display person.

Trade Show and Exhibit Design

In addition to trade show designing, there is a need for exhibit designers for museums, graphic arts areas, and for commerce and industry. The trade show or exhibit designer works with limited space to visually showcase a particular product (or products), a name or company image, or paintings, sculpture, photographs, or graphics. In some ways trade show and exhibit design is closely allied to showroom display and merchandising, which is another excellent field for display persons and visual merchandisers. Very often the showroom is tied in with trade shows and as each season is introduced or as new products are revealed as part of a market week, the showroom is reorganized, rearranged, refixtured, and retrimmed to enhance the look of the products and suggest to the buyers in the showroom that something new is happening here and now. It is a combination of display, stage setting, and visual merchandising.

Home Fashions and Food Presentation

With the increased interest in home fashions and changing attitudes toward how to present furniture and home furnishings, this vast field has become another area for career opportunities for the visual merchandiser. Furniture is now sold in lifestyle displays or vignettes, not as chairs and sofas, but like coordinated pieces of an outfit. Pieces are shown with all the accessories and decoratives in a setting that suggests a particular look—or lifestyle: the casual, pastel Southwest look; the relaxed New England cottage style; the contemporary, sophisticated urban scene; high tech; eclectic; and so forth. It takes a visual merchandiser to design these abstracted or vignetted stage sets that create an ambience for the furniture and accessories. There are jobs available in wholesale furniture showrooms, in department stores, and in furniture and home fashion retail stores.

As mentioned in Chapter 21, the presentation of food —fresh or prepared—has expanded the opportunity horizon for display persons. Supermarkets as well as specialty food shops, gourmet take-outs, and "traiteurs" are all in the business of showing food stuff at its very best. It is more than the final touches added by the chefs and bakers, it is now what the visual merchandiser can add to the look with lights, color, textures, and imaginative decoratives. TV commercials, cooking and food magazines, and the ever growing number of cookbooks need "stylists" or "presenters" who really know how to make the foods come alive.

Styling

Individuals with visual merchandising skills and training often get involved in styling as a career. There are different kinds of stylists, including those for films, commercials, magazines, or catalogs. There are also fashion show stylists, manufacturers' stylists, advertising stylists, and photographers' stylists. A stylist "styles" the shoot, the event, or the line according to the image that is to be projected. Designing is usually not part of the job of a stylist. Rather, a stylist will put together the fashion and apparel looks to be presented. Working with a theme specified by the director, the stylist will coordinate the separate pieces, accessories, models, and props to be presented. Most stylists work on a freelance basis and have a specific specialty (i.e., film, advertising, food, and so on). These jobs require a high level of creativity and flexibility in scheduling.

Party Design

Party design is another relatively new and very big market with job openings for visual merchandisers. It includes conceiving a theme for a party, designing or selecting the invitations, the table linens and service, the centerpieces, the decorations in the room, the favors and sometimes even planning the menu and food service. Whether it is a birthday, confirmation, engagement, wedding, anniversary, charity affair, or testimonial dinner—this is big business. Everybody who hosts a party wants that party to be unique, different, and memorable. The party designer can turn an ordinary event into an affair to remember. This type of design can extend into the commercial field with planning and executing receptions at trade shows, gallery openings, and any place where "taste" is important and a lasting "image" is to be produced.

Special Events

Have you ever thought of how many parades there are each year, how many beauty pageants, how many special baseball games or football games, Special Olympics, and so forth, that call for spectacular, overscaled presentations and settings? It takes visual merchandising talent to design and make up the floats that are so much a part of every parade—that make each new moving "display" something to "ooh" and "aah" over. What about the runways and the "Ziegfield Follies" settings that distinguish the beauty contests, pageants, or fashion shows? Actually, staging fashion shows, whether for designers, de-

partment stores, or even charities, is a business that might be an attractive calling for some. Theme parks are opening all over the country and they need visual merchandising talent, just as many malls do.

Malls

Mall management hires visual merchandisers to mount the spectaculars that are usually staged in the rotundas, the central atriums, or on stages set up around the mall. Here the designers are dealing with two, three, and sometimes four stories of vertical space and, to be effective, these "production numbers" have to be BIG. We are dealing with oversized, overscaled, and overwhelming. Visual merchandisers will combine and coordinate merchandise from many retailers into one theatrical extravaganza—in a setting to match.

There are also opportunities with the producers of the overscaled displays and props that are designed especially for areas like malls and large public spaces—particularly at Christmas and Easter. All those Santa houses, Santa's thrones, gumdrop forests, 8-foot ornaments and 20-or-more-foot trees have to be designed, constructed, decorated, and then installed—and that all takes people with taste, talent, flair, and a background in display.

Store Planning and Fixture Design

Store planning and design can be rewarding careers. However, the display person really needs more background, more education, training, and experience in the commercial interior design field. There are also openings for people who can design the fixtures and furnishings used for the visual presentation of merchandise. This is an extremely good field though it may lack the "theater" and "razzle-dazzle" of what we think of as "display." It is the design and construction of decorative drapers, of unique hangers, racks, and even the wall and floor modular systems.

Display Decorative Manufacturing

Most people on the street don't realize that the decorative props, the unusual elements in a display, the fun figures or painted background panels are often designed and produced by display manufacturers and then purchased by visual merchandisers for use in windows and store interiors. This is a very big business as anyone who has ever attended a National Association of Display Industries (NADI) trade show will admit. This is a different challenge for the display person; to be a prop designer, a prop maker, or even a salesperson "on the road" or a showroom "rep" for a display manufacturer.

Mannequins

That, of course, leads us to the whole mannequin and mannequin alternative industry—which is part of the display manufacturing industry. Here the skills of sculptors, stylists, makeup artists, wig makers, finishers, and refinishers are required.

Point-of-Purchase (POP)

Point-of-purchase design is indeed a vast and attractive field for visual merchandisers. This field needs designers, graphic artists, modelers, and model makers. It needs people with flair, imagination, and yet with a down-to-earth attitude on how to get the job done effectively and efficiently. Staple guns, invisible wire, and some Scotch tape can work in a fashion window display—but POP units must stand up to the real world where they are usually located. This is a very challenging field, with myriad opportunities.

Tools for Getting the Job

Résumé

A thoughtfully planned and well-written **résumé** may not get you a job, but it may certainly succeed in getting you the all-important interview. The résumé is "you on paper." It acquaints the reader with your goals, qualifications, education, and experiences. For positions in visual merchandising or related areas, the résumé might be written in a very standard manner or in an individualized, more imaginative style. However, don't underestimate the power of a neatly organized and perfectly typed résumé.

Depending on experience and accomplishments, a résumé will vary in length. However, your résumé should cover these basic areas:

- Name, address, and telephone number
- Occupational goal
- Education
- Work experience
- Special skills and interests

Portfolio

Aside from the standard résumé for most jobs in the field of visual merchandising, the candidate is requested to present a **portfolio** to the prospective employer. A portfolio should represent a collection of an individual's best and most creative work, including photographs of previous displays, sample sketches, copy design, floor plans, fixture designs, and so forth. Once on the job, smart individuals will continue to build their portfolio in preparation for new job opportunities or possible promotions within the company. For freelance visual merchandisers, a quality portfolio is essential. It becomes a "calling card" and a "reference" showing prospective customers what you are capable of doing for their store, showroom, or exhibit.

A balanced representation of abilities is recommended for inclusion in the portfolio. Of course, employers expect to see only the candidates' very best work. Neatness is critical! Messy, smudged sketches or poorly matted photographs are a sure sign of lack of attention to detail—fatal for most job seekers.

It is not important that the work be shown in an expensive leather portfolio. Any folder or binder that will protect your work and help make a neat presentation is acceptable. Each item in the portfolio should be clearly labeled (careful with spelling!) for easy identification.

An Effective Visual Merchandiser

One should select the direction or field that seems to offer the greatest potential for personal development and financial gain. This decision should take the following into consideration: the individual's temperament and talent, his or her degree of creativity, willingness to interact with people, and ultimate goals and ambitions.

Some people want to lead or direct. They are organizers and administrators. The visual merchandising field needs people who can organize, arrange, plot, and plan in an orderly manner with one eye on the budget and the other on the calendar and the time schedule. These talents are necessary to the creative process of display.

Some display persons, on the other hand, have "star" personalities. They need to razzle-dazzle, to sparkle, and erupt in creative outpourings. They are filled with imagination, touched with flair, and tingling with excitement. For them, the planning, scheduling, bookkeeping, and nitty-gritty of following the "book" can be utter torment. It would be a waste to misuse or misdirect their unique talents.

Other display persons may find the mechanical aspects of drafting and the specifics of space and layout more to their liking. They could be in tune with interior design and all it entails. For them, a career in store planning or the designing of commercial interiors might provide the greatest satisfaction.

Personal gratification is most important in the development of a career. Since so much of our time is spent on the job, it is imperative that we like what we do, that we are happy and enthusiastic doing it. With so many diversified and fascinating areas from which to choose, no display person should ever be bored or unhappy.

No matter in which direction he or she goes, first and foremost, a visual merchandiser is a merchandiser, a person whose business it is to sell or promote by means of presentation. Whether presenting a garment, an organization, or an idea, we expect a display person to be an artist and/or a designer. Creativity and imagination are his or her major attributes. Most people not involved in the industry tend to take window and interior displays for granted. They do not realize the time, thought, planning, and preparation that go into creating a display. It takes talent to dress a mannequin or rig a form, to create the semblance of life, or to create animation in nonanimated objects.

The display person is a fashion coordinator—should be *au courant*, knowing the trends, the looks, the newest styles. He or she needs to know from where, in the long history of fashion design, these "new" designs evolved. He or she must find the settings, props, and accessories that will enhance these new trends.

The visual merchandiser should be a connoisseur, a collector, and an avid reader, a student of the world, past and present. In trash heaps, in secondhand stores, and at house razings, he or she may find tomorrow's display setting or a prop or a fixture that was not originally designed to be a fixture. The visual merchandiser should be able to see beauty where others may not, and then be able to make that beauty visible to all.

A good display person should be an interior designer, a space planner, a lighting expert, a landscape gardener. The display person may even be called upon to brighten up and lighten up an architectural colossus perpetrated by an architect with an "edifice complex."

Some builders have been known to construct monuments rather than marketplaces. They build in and leave little room for change, and change is the life force of fashion.

The store planning and display departments are called upon to do seasonal shops and special selling environments. They are expected to come up with clever, bright, and inexpensive ideas that change a "blah" department into a stimulating selling ambience. The ebb and flow of the traffic within the store, and the direction of that traffic past the eye-stopping displays and into sales areas, are part of the store planner's art form.

The visual merchandiser must be involved in a store's advertising, copywriting, signage, and graphics. He or she must be able to communicate with co-workers, management, and potential customers. This communication is written as well as oral. The display person should be able to write simple, direct, understandable sentences. Often, the visual merchandiser is called upon to write the copy line and card heading that adds meaning, and sometimes humor, to the merchandise presentation.

And always, the good visual merchandiser is learning. He or she is always studying the world around, past the display window, outside the store, and beyond the parking lot. It requires constant preparation to do a good and thorough job.

Let us assume now that you already are a display person. You have selected a particular field in which you feel comfortable, happy, and fulfilled. What are you going to do to maintain that feeling? Are you still growing, learning, and stretching your talents? Here is a checklist for you to consider every once in a while, especially when you feel your job is not quite what you think it should be.

1. When is the last time you read a book that really stimulated you to think? When did you last feel that you learned something and expanded your horizons?

2. How long has it been since you have been to a museum, a gallery, an art show? Have you been keeping up with what is new in the world of art, or what was very old but is suddenly new and fashionable? Are you keeping up with the new media, new techniques, new approaches to presentation?

3. When did you last involve yourself with the new directions in the field of graphics, with posters, layouts, signage techniques and devices, and with new typography and methods of graphic reproduction? Are you keeping up with the advances in photography, holography, and calligraphy?

4. Do you remember the last experimental play or movie you saw? Even if you hated it or were totally confused by it, did you try to get something out of it?

5. If you have traveled, what have you seen and absorbed that you cannot get from a picture, postcard or a guidebook? Did you wander through foreign streets picking up sounds, smells, and sights that someday may serve as inspirations for displays? Are you really looking, or are you just sight-seeing without really absorbing the sights?

6. Have you taken any courses lately? Not simply for credit, but just because you wanted to know more about something—anything? Are you still growing intellectually? Are you learning more about your profession and the world?

7. What does your reference library look like? Are there cobwebs spread over dusty and neglected books, or is it continually growing, constantly in use, a viable shelf of wonders? Do you allow yourself to get "lost" in these books? Do you use your dictionaries and learn to delight in language so that you may communicate better with those around you?

8. Look in the mirror—the full-length one! Take a real, long look. Do you look like a person who is involved with fashion and with the presentation and promotion of new looks and ideas? Do you look, feel, smell, act, and react like a person who is a trendsetter? Are you sending off "sparks"? Are you sending out messages? Are you communicating?

9. And, in a quiet moment, think about this: Are you growing as a person? Are you honest, ethical, and sincere in what you do?

Check your score and see how you rate. You may find some of the "problems" with your job are really problems within yourself. You are in the "showing business." You are supposed to be an "image maker," but your own personal image must also be created, fostered, and developed.

Career Opportunities in Visual Merchandising: A Recap

- Visual merchandisers can pursue careers in the fields of commercial exhibiting, museum and graphic arts exhibits, staging of fashion shows, point-of-purchase (POP) design, store planning, and packaging.

- Visual merchandisers may also work as trimmers, decorators, or designers in a department or specialty store; for a manufacturer of display fixtures or props; as freelancers in individual stores; for a manufacturer's showroom; or for trade shows.

- Further career options for the person with visual merchandising training lie in the fields of home fashions and styling for films, commercials, magazines, catalogs, and photographers.

- Party design is a fairly new field open to the trained visual merchandiser; as is the area of special events such as parades, beauty pageants, fashion shows, and theme parks.

- Basic areas covered by a resumé should include name, address, telephone, occupational goal, education, work experience, and special skills and interests.

- A quality portfolio is essential because it becomes a person's calling card and reference. It should represent a collection of an individual's best and most creative work, including photos of previous displays, sample sketches, copy design, floor plans, fixture designs, and such.

- In selecting a career within the field of visual merchandising, one should select the direction or field that seems to offer the greatest potential for personal development, job satisfaction, and/or financial gain.

- The decision to enter a particular field should take into consideration the individual's temperament and personality, his or her degree of creativity, willingness to interact with people, and ultimate goals and ambitions.

- Creativity and imagination are the major attributes of a visual merchandiser.

Questions for Review and Discussion

1. For each of the following career areas, explain how visual merchandising skills could prove to be beneficial.
   a. trade show and exhibit design
   b. home fashion field
   c. styling
   d. party design
   e. special events
   f. fixture design
   g. POP

2. What are the two basic tools needed to get a job in the visual merchandising field? Describe each thoroughly.

3. What items should be included in a visual merchandising portfolio?

Glossary of Point-of-Purchase Display Terms

The following terms are relevant to the construction and setting up of POP units. They include general terminology used in the industry to describe display units seen both outside the store and inside on the selling floor, on the counters and ledges; overhead; on shelves, wall units, and gondolas; and on the walls and back bars.

A

A-board/A-frame A pair of A-shaped frames, like sawhorses, joined together with a cross member at their tops, used to carry signboards. The frames are often made of metal tubing or PVC tubing and the units are designed so that the signboards or plaques can be easily changed. Mostly used outside stores like convenience stores and gas stations.

aisle jumper A wire that is stretched over the aisles in a supermarket, drugstore, or warehouse-type retail operation. Flags, banners, or special promotional signs can be attached to or folded over the wire to provide information and/or decoration above eye level.

aisle talkers Signs, cards, or informative plaques that extend out at right angles from the shelves or fixtures. They reach out to greet the shopper walking in the aisle.

arch A frame, usually made of metal, that extends up from one gondola or floor unit, bows up and over an aisle, and then comes down to rest on another gondola or floor unit. Visually, arches turn an aisle into an arcade of half circles upon which double-sided banners, signs, or messages can be attached.

assortment display A display unit that presents a variety of products or of sizes, shapes, and colors of a particular product—like a cookie display that may contain several different types of cookies all manufactured by the same company.

B

audio-visual displays Displays designed with custom video or audio computerized electronic devices to provide shoppers with messages they can "see" and/or hear. These are relatively expensive and are used where the information is rather specific or complicated.

autolock style A tray or box that snaps open, complete with the bottom in place and does not require any special locking of tabs, flaps, or slots, or any gluing or stapling. A collapsible unit that unfolds into a piece with sides and a bottom all in one.

B

back bar unit A sign, plaque, or decorative piece that is designed to be applied to the wall behind a serving bar. It can be a clock, a decorative dimensional piece like a high-relief bottle of beer in ice, or product logo executed in neon, or edge-lit plastics.

back card A sign, card, or message plaque applied to the back of a floor unit, a dump bin, a pile-up of merchandise, and so forth. It brings the message up above the products—closer to the shopper's eye level.

backlit shadow boxes/displays Shadow boxes or frames with deep sides and a back that are equipped with interior lighting (strips of fluorescents) that illuminate the photo-transparencies that are over the front of the frame or shadow box.

baked enamel signs Permanent signs that are screened on metal panels. Synthetic resins are used in the screening process and then the metal panel is baked at high temperatures. This speeds up the drying process and also bonds the paint to the metal surface.

ballot boxes A box with a slit or slot on top into which forms, coupons, and so forth can be deposited to be removed later by the proper authorities. The box will usually carry a message and provide some interaction with the shopper at the counter. They are used for lotteries, "give-away contests," drawings, requests for more information, and so on.

band wrapping Strips of printed paper or plastic that are used to hold two or more products together as in a special "buy-one, get-one" offer. It can also combine the product with a "gift with purchase" or combine two different but related packages into a single "deal" like disposable razor with shaving cream.

banners Colorful pieces of fabric, plastic, or treated paper—usually with grommets or holes punched on top, used as attention-getting decorative devices outside and inside the retail setting. They are often triangular in shape but can be rectangular or square as well. They may sometimes carry the imprint of a name or logo—or individual letters that when strung together spell out a message.

bin A container or box to hold products or merchandise. It can vary in size, shape, and proportion and can be constructed of cardboard, plastic, metal stampings, wood, and so forth. Bins can be grouped together to hold a variety of products in an assortment display. See *assortment display.*

blank dummy A full-size model of a proposed display, fixture, or container, which is not colored—has no artwork or actual copy or decor. A sample piece that will show the construction, size, dimensions, and the usability of the finished unit.

blister packaging A method of prepacking small merchandise on cards over which a plastic, see-through bubble has been heat sealed in place. The product is visible and protected in shipping and ready to be set out on the selling floor.

bottle glorifier A special display unit to show off a single bottle—usually perfume or toiletries. The actual bottle may be recessed into a special niche in the display or elevated on a pedestal or base. The bottle glorifier can also be a simple background for the bottle that separates it from all the color and activity going on around it or a display card attached to the bottle.

bottle necker/topper A die cut cardboard or plastic ring plus sign that fits around the neck of the bottle. The bottle necker or topper brings attention to the product and also provides relevant information.

broker A "middle man" who buys and then sells a product without making any changes in the design or packaging of the product. In the POP field, it may also refer to firms that design and sell POP designs but do not actually manufacture the finished pieces themselves.

bubble pack See *blister packaging.*

bubble up A display technique that uses a glass tube with a ball at one end in which a liquid and a gas are contained. When the unit is warmed (plugged in to an electric outlet or connected to a battery, the gas is activated and the liquid in the tube begins to bubble. This causes an unending flow of bubbles through the tube. The technique is used in the POP field to suggest the sparkling effervescence of wines and champagnes in vacuum formed glasses and bottles—or in mugs and bottles of simulated beer.

bulk shipments Products that are shipped in bulk rather than in individual boxes or containers, for example, raisins shipped in a drum or barrel as compared to a dozen one-pound boxes shipped in a carton.

bump-ons Small "cushions" or raised tacks of metal, plastic, or rubber that are used on the bottom of counter units as "feet" or levelers.

C

cantilever A shelf, bracket, or arm that projects out from a flat surface, like a wall, and is not supported or reinforced by any structural member at the far end. Also the arm or bracket that projects out from the wall and is used to support a shelf, sign, and so on.

card holders A frame or container used to display a message or a price-bearing card. The holder is often designed with a device to make it self-standing, or to attach to racks, shelves, uprights, and so forth.

carton A box or container usually made of bendable board (cardboard or corrugated board) that may contain a product like a carton of cigarettes. It also refers to larger containers that may contain numerous individual boxes or cartons.

carts Mobile floor stands. A floor unit/fixture on wheels that can be rolled around and easily moved from one location to another on the floor.

case cards Message cards or signs that can be slipped into an open case of goods on the floor or on a counter.

The elevated sign or header brings the message up above the assembled products contained in the case or carton below.

case wraparounds A decorative or promotional sheet of printed material—usually corrugated—that wraps around a carton or case that will eventually stand out on the floor. The wraparound "decorates" the case and/or provides special promotional information.

cash register display A presentation of impulse-type items on or near the cash register or an illuminated sign that is applied to a cash register on a bar or the back bar. See *back bar units*.

ceiling mobiles Paper or plastic cutouts that are organized or clipped together to become a single dangling display piece hung from the ceiling or from a ceiling grid. The assorted pieces may be notched together or assembled on a shaped wire frame and this mobile will turn and spin—stimulated by the air currents in the store. These mobiles are usually promotional pieces that tie in with other POP units on the floor and counter.

chalk boards Blackboards usually with the name or logo of the product line on them, which are provided by the manufacturer to the vendor. Daily specials and price changes can be quickly and easily altered since the chalk markings are easy to erase.

changeable letter sign A signboard with removable letters. The background panel is usually ridged or rippled —like corrugated material—and the individual plastic cutout letters are slipped into the ridges and will hold until the message has to be changed. The manufacturer's name or logo appears on the frame that contains the background panel.

change tray/holder The scooped out dish of glass or plastic or the textured rubber or vinyl pad with the manufacturer's name or logo engraved or raised on it. The change tray/holder or pad sits next to the cash register and the customer's change is delivered into the receptacle.

checkout counter pieces An advertising unit at the checkout counter that not only promotes a product, but also provides a useful service; a clock, a weather barometer, a pen or pencil holder for the shopper's check writing convenience, a change tray, and so on.

checkwriters A checkout counter unit that serves as an image or name projection for a product or brand name at the cash register. It also serves as a minidesk since it provides a smooth writing surface and often has a pen attached to the unit for the convenience of the shopper who pays by check.

chip A small, compact electronic circuit unit that can be added to a displayer unit to provide prepared audio-visual information. See *audio-visual displays*. Also called integrated circuit or silicon chip.

clocks One of the many useful and desirable POP units provided by the manufacturer that can have a long life in a retail environment. The clock—which may have the brand name, logo, or representation of the product on the clock's face—is usually battery operated. Clocks may be vacuum formed, made of plastics, enhanced with running lights, "bubble-ups," or moving elements.

coffin case A refrigerator case in a supermarket or convenience store that opens from the top and unfortunately does resemble a rather squarish coffin.

cold cathode lighting An instant-starting type of fluorescent lamp that uses cylindrically formed electrodes. Like neon tubing, cold cathode lighting can be bent to conform with special desired shapes or outlines. It has a useful life of up to 25,000 hours which approaches "permanent lighting," and no wiring troughs or ballasts are needed for installation.

combination features A sales technique of presenting two or more products at a single, special, "unit" price. See *band wrapping*.

combo display A unit that is designed to function either as a floor unit or a counter unit if sufficient floor space is not available. The unit may come with a base element that can be used if the piece will stand on the floor or be omitted if the display piece or fixture will sit on a counter or ledge.

combo-pack A sales promotion technique that calls for two or more different but related items to be packaged and promoted together; for example, a hair shampoo and conditioner, a cologne and deodorant, or a jar of peanut butter and a jar of jam.

co-packing Combining two or more products into a promotional prepack displayer or merchandising unit. Also see *combo-pack*.

counter cards Small cards with the name of the product and possibly specific information about the product, located on the counter or at the point of sale near the assembled stock of product. An easeled card, on the counter, that provides information.

counter mats Messages printed on paper, cardboard, vinyl, or fabric and used as flat mats or runners on counters or bars.

counter units Any one of many specialized merchandisers or displayers set on a counter, ledge, or table and used to display and/or hold small merchandise. By the nature of its location and use, it is usually small (under 3 feet), narrow, and portable. Ideally it should not obstruct the salesperson's view of the customer and the store. Counter units should facilitate the handling and sampling of merchandise and, if possible, prevent pilfering. The units may be constructed of cardboard, wood, metal, plastics, or any combination of materials.

coupon pad A pad of coupons or promotional offers, usually attached to a counter card or to the face or side of a counter or floor unit. The shopper is invited to "take one." A form of interaction with the display unit. Also called *take-one pad*.

cross-merchandising Several different products that are related in use but may be produced by different manufacturers are shown together in a single display or fixture, such as beer and snack foods or peanut butter and jelly. By showing the products together, the consumer is likely to buy both products at the same time. See *related display*.

customer involvement Displays and fixtures that get the shopper to interact with them; for example, by pressing buttons, turning dials, physically touching or moving something, pulling off a coupon, or lifting out a brochure.

cut-case A shipping case or carton, usually of corrugated board or solid fiberboard, that is designed to open up and convert into a series of shelves or bins to hold the product and the promotional signage. A well-designed cut-case is usually preperforated, die cut and/or scored to make the conversion simple, fast, and efficient.

D

dangles/danglers See *ceiling mobiles*. A graphic sign or panel that is suspended from the ceiling and will move in the air circulating through the store.

DC motors Motors that are designed to use only direct current where the current flows only in one direction. The AC or alternating current, however, reverses its direction of flow, usually at 60 cycles per minute.

dealer incentive Some useful or durable and "desirable" part of a POP display or promotional unit that the retailer can keep or take home after the promotion is over, such as a battery-operated clock, an ice chest or cooler, barbecue tools or mitts, and so forth.

dealer's privilege A dual-sided sign that carries the vendor or manufacturer's name or logo on one side and a "goodwill" message from the retailer on the other side; for example, "Thank you for shopping here" or "Please beware of pickpockets."

debossed sign As opposed to an embossed sign, which has some copy or artwork raised up from the surface of the sign, the debossed sign has a "carved out" or "depressed" look, with copy or artwork cut into the surface of the sign.

decals/decalcomania A transfer piece of artwork or copy. The artwork or message is printed on thin, special paper or vinyl material, and when the paper is moistened or pressure is exerted on the piece of vinyl, the design is transferred to the new surface and the now-blank piece of the decal is disposed of. See *electrostatic vinyl decals, pressure-sensitive adhesives and decals*.

demonstration display An educational display whose main purpose is to show how the product works, what it does, and the advantages of the product. This can be an audio-visual display, a mechanized display, or one requiring the shopper to interact with it.

demonstration stand A platform, cube, or table surface where a product can be shown in use and the consumer can be instructed in how the product works; for example, a corn popper popping, cooking utensils, a stain remover, a new food product.

dioramas Three-dimensional scenic displays that may be enriched with light and motion.

direct shipment POP units that are sent directly to the retailer or dealer, sometimes with the merchandise order. The POP producer does not first send the material to the manufacturer or vendor, but straight to the end displayer of the material.

dispensers A POP card, sign, or unit that includes a coupon pad or booklet or brochure holder or a displayer/fixture that holds some merchandise that the shopper can remove from the unit, such as boxes of Tic-Tacs, lipsticks, mechanical pencils, eyeglass wipes, and so on.

display card A card with copy that is attached to or elevated near the stock of product on the floor, on the shelf, or on the counter. See *counter cards, header.*

display carton A carton made of corrugated board or solid fiberboard that is printed on both sides before being assembled. It is designed to be opened and folded in such a manner that the interior printing carries the message, illustration, or decorative elements that will enhance the promotion—and the products contained within the carton. See *shipper's display.*

dissolve units Mechanized or illuminated signs or displays where the message or artwork "dissolves" or melts away and another message or image takes its place.

double face display A display unit where the copy, message, or identifying logo appears on both sides of the display, or a unit that can be seen and understood from front or back.

drop shipment Units shipped directly to the dealer or retailer in time for the breaking promotion—or to a number of warehouses maintained by the vendor/manufacturer from which they will be distributed.

dummy A term in graphics to describe a rough layout done in scale and in proportion to the finished artwork and/or copy. It shows the piece "roughly" as it will eventually appear. A mock-up. See *blank dummy.*

dummy merchandise Empty cartons, boxes, packages, or bottles filled with colored water, used to simulate the more expensive actual products in a unit that people can touch. Not only are these dummies lighter, they are also inexpensive, expendable, and cut down on pilfering.

dump bin/dump table A box or enclosure into which small products are loosely "tossed" or dumped. A POP open box or barrel with signage that carries promotional merchandise. The dump table has also a "helter-skelter" look of merchandise tossed onto a table and almost always is used for sale merchandise.

duplex See *shipper's display.*

E

easels/easel cards A die cut and scored cardboard flap that is attached to a cardboard sign or display to keep it straight and erect—like a "third leg." An easel is also an adjustable tripod stand or frame used to display or hold a poster or design.

electronic interactive units Displays or displayers equipped with electronic chips that respond to the shopper's interaction with the unit. It can be a response to a button being pushed, a surface being touched, or some element being moved.

electrostatic vinyl decals Transfer artwork or messages printed on electrostatic vinyl film that is charged so that it clings or adheres to any smooth or slick surface like plastic, glass, or metal. A form of decal. This kind of decal is easy to remove and may be reusable.

electrostatic window clings See *electrostatic vinyl decals.*

end caps/end aisle displays An additional table or container, an extension surface or bin at the end of a stocking fixture, such as a dump bin at the end of a gondola facing the traffic aisle.

end displays A mass presentation of merchandise at the end of a gondola or fixture. The display is located on the aisle and thus gets lots of traffic and attention. See *end caps/end aisle displays.*

F

facings The number of boxes, cartons, or packages that appear up front on a shelf in a fixture or gondola.

floor pyramid A four-sided buildup of product boxes, cartons, or containers on the selling floor that diminishes in width on each side as the pile rises up to resemble a pyramid.

floor stands/merchandisers Freestanding, self-supporting fixtures, racks, stands, merchandisers, and displayers on the selling floor as opposed to those specifically designed for counter or window use.

free light A transparency or translucent sign viewed with light picked up from other illumination sources near the unit that looks as though it were actually lit up. This technique makes the most of the existing light surrounding the POP unit.

front end merchandisers Single-faced or -sided merchandising units that can only be accessed from the front. The sides and back are usually enclosed. This type of unit is often used against a wall or partition, or backed up with another front-end merchandiser facing in the opposite direction.

G

gazebo Merchandising in the round. A merchandised and stocked structure, which is often the high point or focal point in a department or on the selling floor. The structure may be round, hexagonal, or octagonal and provided with several openings so that shoppers have access to the merchandise from many directions. It is based on the 19th-century summerhouse or garden house, which was usually constructed of latticework and jigsaw work. It can be used as a boutique, a shop-within-a-shop, or a highlighter.

gift with purchase A sales incentive device whereby the vendor/manufacturer offers a free item or "gift" with the purchase of the promotional product, such as a sample size of cologne with each purchase of X dollars of a toiletry. It can be a *combo-pack* (see entry) or a prepackaged "gift" that is put into the shopping bag along with the purchase. This technique is especially popular in the perfume industry.

glorifier A display unit that presents and enhances a single product. See *bottle glorifier*. The glorifier may also be an overscaled reproduction of the product standing on a base with or without a background card.

glow panel A luminescent illuminated plastic panel that has been enriched with a name, logo, or product representation. When lit, the panel glows.

gondola A long, flat-bottomed merchandiser with straight upright sides. Usually designed to hold adjustable shelves and may be combined with cabinets or storage areas below. There can be a center divider panel (perpendicular and equidistant to the ends), which then makes the gondola double-sided with shelves on either side. Gondolas are commonly used in groups on the selling floor and oriented toward aisles or walkways. They are frequently found in markets, supermarkets, drugstores, and mass-market operations.

gravity feed A dispenser displayer or fixture that is designed so that when a product is removed another slides down into the vacated space by means of the pull of gravity. The products may be housed in vertical or diagonal chutes or channels and new products can often be fed in from the top, as in cigarette machines.

H

header A sign or copy panel raised over a display of products, which provides the pertinent promotional information. A header is usually more informative than a "riser." See *pole sign*.

I

impulse items/merchandise An item or piece of merchandise that gets attention and is purchased on impulse—the spur of the moment—rather than by plan. A spontaneous appeal created by seeing the merchandise, sometimes in relation to another piece of merchandise.

inflatables Especially contoured and constructed vinyl or plastic "balloons" that can be dimensionalized when inflated with air or helium. They can be great big reproductions of products (bananas, cans of soda or beer, and so on) logos, symbols, comic strip characters, or everyday objects blown up out of proportion to float over a floor unit or hang down from a ceiling. The inflatable may also be used as a premium or give-away with or without purchase.

inner supports Structural reinforcements, by use of egg-crate construction or additional pieces of corrugated material, to cardboard floor stands, dump bins, or merchandisers that carry the accumulated weight of many products displayed on it.

in-store demonstration Specialized selling, often enhanced by display, whereby a manufacturer's representative will show or explain the product; the application of a new cosmetic, sampling newly prepared foods, the use and special attributes of new equipment, and so forth.

interactive computer displays See *electronic interactive units.*

interactive display A unit that responds to the shopper's questions by providing the answer. To "ask," the shopper has to press a button or touch a panel. See *customer involvement.*

interactive manually operated units Displays or displayers that the shopper has to "animate"; for example, by pushing or pulling levers, turning sheets, or applying pressure.

island display A merchandise presentation or fixture that can be approached from all sides and gives the shopper access to the merchandise from any side. See *floor pyramid, gazebo.*

island floor stand A fixture or unit that can be approached from any direction and will provide product to any side of the unit.

J

jumble basket See *dump bin.*

K

KD display A display that is shipped in parts—unassembled—and that requires some time and effort to put together before the unit can be shown or used. The display or displayer may be shipped flat or in parts for the economy of shipping costs, and then be opened, tabbed, locked, or even screwed into a finished shape.

kick plate/band A horizontal panel, usually 3 inches or 4 inches wide at the base of counters and floor units. It is often slightly recessed from the face of the unit and it takes the scuffs and kicks of people standing in front of the unit.

kiosk A self-standing booth or structure on the selling floor that may accommodate a salesperson as well as merchandise. A miniboutique, outpost, or an enclosed information desk.

L

lazy Susan displayer A displayer that can be rotated either manually or by means of a motorized turntable. It affords the shopper the ability to see all of the products displayed on the round fixture without having to walk around the piece. See also *spinner racks.*

leaflet dispenser A brochure holder. A counter unit that usually consists of an easeled card sign and a pocket in which leaflets or brochures are contained. It can be made of cardboard or of a more permanent material, such as wood, metal, metal stampings, or plastics. Some leaflet or brochure dispensers are floor units and consist of a number of pockets, bins, or compartments to hold an assortment of printed material.

lenticular A plastic panel with specific light properties that has been grooved so that when printed and viewed from different angles, the printed image looks different and assumes a three-dimensional quality. Also called *three-D displays.*

leveler A fixture attachment consisting of an adjustable screw and a pad. Used on the foot or base of a floor unit/counter/table to accommodate any irregularities of the floor surface. By adjusting the levelers, one can raise or lower one side or the other.

life-size cutouts Lithographs, blown up to "life size" or an exaggerated size of persons, celebrities, brand spokespersons, or "characters" associated with a particular product. The figures are laminated onto a rigid board and easel to be self-standing on the selling floor, in the window, or on a ledge. A dynamic tie-in with other print media, advertising, or TV commercials that also use that celebrity or "character" to promote the product.

light boxes A box with a light source attached to the back wall and a transparency on the front of the box. The inner illumination makes the transparency light up, usually in color. See *backlit shadow boxes/displays.*

light thief See *free light.*

literature holder See *leaflet dispenser.*

literature racks Floor or counter units with pockets or receptacles in which brochures, booklets, or leaflets are stocked. It may be single- or double-faced or full round with a lazy Susan turntable base. Also used for selling "pocket" books.

logo/logotype A trademark, emblem, or insignia that represents the individual manufacturer, vendor, product, and so forth. It may be a decorative grouping of letters that are part of the name of the company or product or an ideograph or stylized symbol or character that represents the company or item; for example, Tony the Tiger, the Pillsbury Dough Boy, the Dutch Boy for Dutch Boy paints, and an assortment of cartoon characters like Fred Flintstone in "The Flintstones."

M

mass displays A volume display of product. A floor pyramid would be an example of this type of presentation. Also see *pallet displays*.

mechanical book A motion display that simulates the turning pages of a book. A small AC motor provides the power that turns the horizontal, cardboard cylinder to which the pages are attached. As the cylinder turns, the pages flip over from front to back.

menuboard A board with an imprint of the vendor's name or product that can be hung on a wall over a counter and upon which the retailer can list specials or prices. Can be a changeable letter sign or a chalkboard.

mobile See *ceiling mobiles, dangles/danglers*.

mobile floorstand See *carts*.

model/mock-up See *blank dummy, dummy, prototype*.

modular systems/displayers A system of design based on using modules or pieces of the same size or multiples of the same size. A module is a basic, interchangeable, same-size unit that can be added to or subtracted from the total design. In floor units and especially in vendor shops, this system makes for greater flexibility and mobility. It is possible to make adjustments or changes depending upon the amount of floor space available (or wall space if the unit will be set against a wall). Most important in a modular system is the strict adherence to the dimensions, the detailing of the connectors and connections, and the ability to rearrange parts visually and simply. Sometimes filler pieces are provided when the modules do not exactly fill up a space.

motion displays Displays, dangles, or even fixtures that are equipped with motors and thus have moving parts. The motion can be an "arm" and "hand" holding a product which moves to and fro—a product that rises and descends into an icy cold brook, a unit with a turntable that slowly rotates or provides changing images. The motors are often battery operated.

movable merchandisers Similar to carts. Metal floor units that are designed with wheels so that the fixture when loaded with product display can be moved from one location to another on the selling floor.

moving letter sign An electrified sign. The panel is usually horizontal and the surface is covered with myriad small lights. A computer chip sets up a pattern and that pattern, in turn, lights up the lights on the panel in a succession of images that are the letters that spell out the message. The illusion is of a continuous horizontal band of copy that passes through the framed area. Also frequently used in windows.

moving message sign See *moving letter sign*.

multideck A floor or counter unit that consists of several shelves or platforms arranged vertically one over the other like tiers in a wedding cake.

multisided unit A floor displayer/fixture that can be approached from several directions and can service shoppers from many different sides like an island display.

music modules/chips Computer chips that can be installed in a fixture or display to play a tune or jingle. The chip usually has to be activated by a button, a switch, or by body heat. Music chips can even be installed in magazine ads.

O

off pack A display or displayer that has coupons or a coupon pad attached to the unit along with the products but the two are not combined. A coupon can be taken without taking or buying the product. See *coupon pad*.

on pack/out pack A coupon or premium that is tied in with or packaged with the product to make it an even more desirable purchase.

overlays A cloth or panel that can be laid over a floor-length tablecloth on a display table. It is usually colored and imprinted with a product or brand name and used as part of an overall promotion. This unit is especially popular in cosmetics and toiletries where square or small round cloths are draped over floor-length tables that blend with the store's decor. See *tablecloth*.

over-the-wire banner A printed sign or banner that is usually long and narrow and has the message or artwork printed in two sections. One message reads right side up—the other is upside down. When the streamer or banner is folded over a wire stretched above eye level (see *aisle jumper*), the message can be read right side up from either direction. It can also be used over an *arch* (see entry).

p

pallet displays A mass display of products that is packed and delivered to the retail store on a pallet or a flat wood base. The total collection of products and the supporting pallet are wrapped in corrugated, heavy board or thick vinyl that is removed when the product is set out on the floor.

pilfer-proof displays Displays or fixtures that are designed to cut down on theft on the selling floor. More costly products are usually housed in plastic towers or enclosures that only a salesperson can open or the products are tied into the fixture to make removing the product difficult. At most, the pilfer-proof techniques can only hope to deter the shoplifter or thief.

polecat A trademarked name for a telescoping pole unit that can be extended as it is opened up. It can be used to support signs above eye level, carry special lighting, and so on.

pole sign A sign on a pole or tall extender rod that rises up from a mass display of products on the selling floor. The sign support is usually hidden by the clustered merchandise, which also hides the pole. Could be used with a *pallet display* or *floor pyramid*.

pop-up displays As this name implies, these displays are die cut and scored, assembled, and then folded and shipped flat. When opened up on the counter or window, such as in a children's book, the display stands up and may have several layers or depths to create a truly dimensional effect not unlike the old Victorian greeting cards.

porcelain signs A technique for making permanent signs. The porcelain finish or design is applied to the metal panel usually by means of the silk-screening process, and after each color is applied, the sign is baked to fuse the color onto the metal. See *baked enamel signs*.

portable reefer A refrigerator case that can be easily moved on the selling floor. It is equipped with wheels to facilitate movement.

posters/poster frames Signs or messages printed on paper, cardboard, fabric, vinyl, plastic, and so forth that are used for promotional events and special announcements. The poster frames may be standard 22-inch by 28-inch frames into which new signs can be inserted or special sizes especially created for the vendor to provide to the retailer, which will only fit the signs supplied by the vendor.

prepack display A display that has already been stocked by the manufacturer and is delivered to the retailer ready for immediate use on the floor or counter. It only requires that the retailer open up the display to reveal the products in place. See *shipper's display*.

prepacking Merchandise that is packed and sealed at the manufacturer and sold to the shopper in the retail setting in the sealed package. See *blister packaging*.

pressure-sensitive adhesives and decals An adhesive material like Scotch tape or masking tape that will stick to another surface when pressure is applied. Pressure-sensitive decals are printed on the adhesive-backed materials and will also adhere when pressure is applied.

product glorifier See *bottle glorifier, glorifier*.

product-in-use display A demonstration-type display that shows how the product can be used or permits the shopper to "try" the unit.

promotional display A special event that has a limited "run" or time of exposure. It is usually in and out of the stores in 2 or 3 weeks. It could be a holiday theme, such as Halloween, a Rose Bowl game, the Olympics, or a Mother's Day or Father's Day promotion. Usually the promotion will include displays, signs and/or banners, counter or window units, and maybe even floor units.

prototype A standard for comparison or measurement. A correct or accurate example that is the standard for all future reproductions. A first unit against which all other pieces will be fashioned.

public service display   A "goodwill" display. Not unlike a dealer's privilege. A unit like a clock, a barometer, or other useful or informative item that is not necessarily related to the product, but which is provided by the manufacturer/vendor and carries the name of the product or the logo.

purchase with purchase   A sales promotion device often combined with the introduction of a new product, especially in the perfume and cosmetics areas. The shopper can purchase a bag, a towel, or some useful product at a special price when he or she also buys the new product; for example, a small travel bag for $15 with the purchase of over $30 of the product line.

pylon   A tall, vertical element that carries a message, sign or display. See *pole sign.*

R

rack   A floor fixture usually constructed of metal, mesh, wood, plastic, or any combination of the above. It can be equipped with shelves, bins, pockets, hooks, or a combination of displaying and stocking elements. It is usually used stacked with related items and with products manufactured by the same firm. It could be a complete shop-within-the-shop—like a mini-vendor's shop.

related display   A presentation on a counter or on the floor where several different but related products are shown on the same fixture/displayer. It could be beer, pretzels, potato chips, and napkins in one setup or shampoos, conditioners, combs, and brushes in another. The products may be used in a promotional manner (buy-one, get-one) or to encourage related sales. See *cross-merchandising.*

revolving display   See *lazy Susan displayer, shipper's display.*

riser   The card, sign, or panel that rises over the product presentation whether the merchandise is stacked on a counter or arranged on the floor. A *back card* (see entry) or a *pole stand* (see entry).

rotating display   See *lazy Susan displayer, shipper's display.*

S

self-selector   A fixture or displayer set up so that the shopper can pick out the color, size and/or shape of the individually packaged items on the unit without difficulty. It could be a thread displayer where the different size spools, different deniers, and colors are all organized and labeled to help the shopper find what he or she wants quickly.

shadow boxes   See *backlit shadow boxes/displays.* Small display windows outside a store or located inside the store. They are often no more than 3 or 4 feet tall by 2 or 3 feet wide and completely enclosed. Used for the presentation of small and expensive pieces.

shelf extender   A special addition to an existing shelf like a clip-on or screw-on tray or bin that, in effect, makes the shelf deeper and also allows related items or special new items to be displayed up front in the added-on space.

shelf management system   An organizer, bins, channels, depressions, or pockets—usually vacuum formed or injection molded—that keeps an assortment of related items in an orderly and space-efficient manner.

shelf miser   A specially designed fixture or displayer that makes maximum use of the allotted shelf space by getting more products available in the same *facings* (see entry). It could be a variation on a *gravity feed* dispenser (see entry) where the products are held vertically and more front shelf space is available for display of product.

shelf organizer   See *shelf management system.*

shelf strips   An attachment that fits under the price railings on a gondola or shelf into which the vendor can apply attention-getting messages.

shelf talkers   A die cut and/or scored cardboard sign or message that extends out from a shelf but is actually attached to the shelf by a strip of pressure-sensitive tape.

shipper's display   A prepack in which all the parts to be used and sold are included in the single shipper or shipping carton. More complex than a carton display, to which it is related. The shipper display may be a floor unit or a counter unit.

shrink wrap/pack   A form of packing or wrapping in which a vinyl material is used around the product and the vinyl is then heated. The heat causes the plastic to "shrink" and it becomes a "skin" around the product. It is like a blister pack but more contoured to the shape of the product encased in the treated plastic.

SKU/stockkeeping units The term applied to each individual variation of a brand or product or item that includes but is not limited to size, count, style, flavor, and so on, for which a different UPC (bar code) is required.

slip sheet Sheets of paper or lightweight board that are slipped between freshly printed or surface treated materials to keep them from rubbing against each other. Also the dividers between displays and/or products in the same carton or container.

spectaculars Outdoor displays or signs that are designed with lights, motion, and/or special effects, such as puffs of smoke, revolving and dissolving elements, strobe flashes, and so on. The same term can be applied to floor or counter units that combine light, motion, and maybe even sound effects.

spinner racks Racks, displayers, or fixtures on the floor or on the counter, that are designed to rotate a full 360 degrees. The unit may have a ball-bearing base like a lazy Susan or it may have a mechanized turntable powered by batteries or electric current.

spring-fed trays A variation of *gravity feed* units (see entry).

spring poles Spring-loaded poles. Vertical members with retractable spring-like caps and/or foot pieces that make it possible to wedge the upright unit between the floor and another surface (such as a ceiling above). The tension of the spring against the unyielding top and bottom surfaces makes the pole rigid, secure, and capable of bearing or supporting other elements. Also called vertical tension rods.

standees See *life-size cutouts*. Outdoor displays that have been enhanced with color, lighting effects, animation, and/or dimensional appliqués.

static stickers See *electrostatic vinyl decals*.

stringing Signs, pennants, or banners hung in an orderly pattern over a wire stretched across the floor or between gondolas.

SU display A display that is shipped "set up" and ready for use in the store. A prepack could be considered a type of set-up display. An SU display is in contrast to the KD or knocked-down, unassembled or partially assembled display. See *carton, shipper's display*.

T

tab An add-on to a display or sign that is applied for extra emphasis. It is also the shaped ear-like piece that fits into a slit or slot to lock together a die cut or scored box, easel, or display.

tablecloth Printed or appliquéd cloths designed to enhance a promotion. They are usually popular in department and specialty stores, where they are draped over round tables set out on the floor and then stacked with perfumes or toiletries. A display, a displayer or glorifier and can be backed up with banners or streamers of the same color and fabrics to enhance the total promotion of the product. See *overlays*.

take-one pad See *coupon pad*.

T-bar A frame shaped like a letter "T" onto which two signs or panels can be attached so the design can be read from two directions.

tent cards/tents Small cards, folded in half and set on a table, counter, or bar like an inverted "V." It usually carries a message on both sides like a miniature *over-the-wire banner* (see entry) but without a wire and selfstanding.

three-D displays See *lenticular*.

timber topper Trademark name for tension spring mechanisms and made to fit on the tops and bottoms of 2-foot by 3-foot lumber. The lumber is then wedged into an upright (or vertical) position between the floor and ceiling (or between two walls) and held rigid by the tension of the springs at either end.

tooling The process of getting ready for point-of-purchase production; the making of tools, dies, jigs, screens, plates, and so forth.

touch activated screens/touch sensitive screens Screen panels in counter or floor units that respond to the touch of the customer's hand to change the message, answer questions, or provide information. A form of interactive display.

trademark According to the U.S. Trademark Association (USTA), ... a word or design or a device or a combination of these used to designate the product of a particular company, organization, or trade association. Used to identify a single product or a line of products made by one manufacturer or sold by one company. Never the generic term for the product. Used on goods, packaging, business documents, advertising, promotion, and display."

traveling display Reusable displays that are designed to withstand the rigors of being moved from one retail outlet to another. It is often fitted with a special packing crate that can be easily stored or can be incorporated into the display like a base that can be covered or draped with fabric. The display is usually expensive, animated, and enhanced with lighting effects.

tray A small extension or a shaped "dish." It may be a shaped compartment that can be added to a shelf or floor unit to separate and hold different items apart but still together on the same unit.

turntable A mechanically rotated horizontal plane or disk, sometimes set into a platform or used as a platform. To get the turntable to rotate continuously, the motor must be activated either by electric power or battery power.

V

valance A horizontal band that finishes off the area above the wall fixtures, or a horizontal sign panel that may be shown at just above eye level.

vendor shop A shop within the retail establishment that is a showplace for a particular vendor/manufacturer or brand name. Within the space allocated by the retailer, the vendor creates a distinctive selling environment that complements the product line and projects the product's image. The vendor provides the fixtures, the furnishings, and the signage for this "shop."

W

wall-mounted signs Single-face signs or panels that are attached directly to the wall.

wobblers Like danglers, these lightweight, cardboard displays hang over freezer cases and react to the blasts of air that come from the opening and closing of the case doors.

Indexes

Retailers Index

Subject Index